Lecture Notes in Computer Science 1941
Edited by G. Goos, J. Hartmanis and J. van Leeuwen

Springer
Berlin
Heidelberg
New York
Barcelona
Hong Kong
London
Milan
Paris
Singapore
Tokyo

Atul K. Chhabra   Dov Dori (Eds.)

Graphics Recognition

Recent Advances

Third International Workshop, GREC'99
Jaipur, India, September 26-27, 1999
Selected Papers

 Springer

Series Editors

Gerhard Goos, Karlsruhe University, Germany
Juris Hartmanis, Cornell University, NY, USA
Jan van Leeuwen, Utrecht University, The Netherlands

Volume Editors

Atul K. Chhabra
Verizon Communications
500 Westchester Avenue, White Plains, NY 10604, USA
E-mail: atul.k.chhabra@verizon.com or atul.k.chhabra@ieee.org
Dov Dori
Massachusetts Institute of Technology
School of Engineering, Engineering Systems Division
77 Massachusetts Avenue, Cambridge, MA 02139-4307, USA
E-mail: dori@mit.edu

Cataloging-in-Publication Data applied for

Die Deutsche Bibliothek - CIP-Einheitsaufnahme

Graphics recognition : recent advances ; third international workshop ;
selected papers / GREC '99, Jaipur, India, September 26 - 27, 1999.
Atul K. Chhabra ; Dov Dori (ed.). - Berlin ; Heidelberg ; New York ;
Barcelona ; Hong Kong ; London ; Milan ; Paris ; Singapore ; Tokyo :
Springer, 2000
    (Lecture notes in computer science ; Vol. 1941)
    ISBN 3-540-41222-0

CR Subject Classification (1998): I.5, I.4, I.3.5, I.2.8, G.2.2, F.2.2

ISSN 0302-9743
ISBN 3-540-41222-0 Springer-Verlag Berlin Heidelberg New York

Springer-Verlag Berlin Heidelberg New York
a member of BertelsmannSpringer Science+Business Media GmbH
© Springer-Verlag Berlin Heidelberg 2000
Printed in Germany

Typesetting: Camera-ready by author, data conversion by DA-TeX Gerd Blumenstein
Printed on acid-free paper   SPIN: 10781331   06/3142   5 4 3 2 1 0

Preface

This edited volume contains refereed and improved versions of select papers that were presented at the third IAPR[1] Workshop on Graphics Recognition (GREC'99), held at Rambagh Palace in Jaipur, India, 26–27, September 1999. The workshop was organized by the TC10 (Technical Committee on Graphics Recognition) of the IAPR. Edited volumes from the previous two workshops in this series are also available as *Lecture Notes in Computer Science* (volumes 1072 and 1389).

Graphics recognition is the study of techniques for computer interpretation of images of line drawings and symbols. This includes methods such as vectorization, symbol recognition, and table and chart recognition for applications such as engineering drawings, schematics, logic drawings, maps, diagrams, and musical scores. Some recently developed techniques include graphics-based information or drawing retrieval and recognition of online graphical strokes. With the recent advances in the field, there is now a need to develop benchmarks for evaluating and comparing algorithms and systems. Graphics recognition is a growing field of interest in the broader document image recognition community.

The GREC'99 workshop was attended by fifty-five people from fifteen countries. The workshop program consisted of six technical sessions. Each session began with a half-hour invited talk which was followed by several short talks. Each session closed with a half-hour panel discussion where the authors fielded questions from the other participants. Several interesting new research directions were discussed at the workshop.

After the workshop, all the authors were invited to submit enhanced versions of their papers for this edited volume. The authors were encouraged to include ideas that came up during question–answer sessions or at other occasions during the workshop. Each paper was reviewed by two researchers in the field. At least one of the two reviewers was physically present at the workshop. And, at least one of the reviewers was on the program committee of the workshop. A subset of the revised papers was accepted for publication in this post-workshop proceedings volume.

The book is organized into six main topics reflecting the six sessions in the workshop. The part on *vectorization* begins with Tombre et al.'s thorough exposition on how to select a vectorization method, or a sub-step of a method, based on the stability and robustness criteria, while minimizing the number of parameters. Elliman describes a vectorization algorithm that he contrasts with Dori's sparse pixel vectorization (SPV) method. Both methods operate by finding the medial axis of a line and both try to identify junction regions that are problematic to vectorize. SPV finds the medial axis using sub-sampling; Elliman proposes using contours of a stroke (which he calls "crack following") to find the medial axis. Adam et al. present a sequence of document recognition tech-

---

[1] The International Association for Pattern Recognition, http://www.iapr.org

niques applied to complex French telephonic network documents with the goal of separating the documents into information layers.

The part on *maps and geographic documents* begins with Watanabe's overview of the field. Den Hartog et al. describe a knowledge-based system for polygon classification in geographic vector data. Compared with a human operator, the system drastically cuts down on processing time while maintaining the same level of accuracy as a human. Interestingly, the types of errors made by the system differ from the types of errors a human operator makes. Adam and Dinstein propose compound-regulated morphological operations to better capture the geometrical structure in signals with application to maps and line drawings. The next two papers (by Kwon, Shimasaki and Watanabe) deal with the detection of houses and house blocks. The first attempts to find point houses in topographic maps. The next finds connective relationships among house blocks in house maps.

The third section focuses on *graphic document analysis*. It begins with Lopresti and Nagy's very interesting (tabular) discourse on tabular document recognition. Stückelberg and Doermann propose overcoming the limitations of sequential recognition and processing by using a model-based approach. Their probabilistic framework is motivated by the shortcomings of Kopec and Chou's document image decoding (DID) approach. Chhabra et al. present a client-server methodology for implementing graphics recognition systems in large organizations. This approach has several advantages over installation of stand-alone graphics recognition software and over X-windows-based LAN access to graphics recognition engines. Lahoti et al. propose a new and compact representation for block layouts in document images. Yamada and Watanabe present an application of graphics recognition to identify people in Japanese comic strips.

The topic of greatest interest at the workshop was *graphic symbol and shape recognition*. The overview by Cordella and Vento categorizes the techniques according to representation, description, and classification. Jiang et al. propose generalized median graphs for learning the representation of graphical symbols from examples. Velveny and Martí present a Bayesian framework for deformable matching of template representation of hand-drawn graphic symbols. Anquetil et al. propose a combination of radial basis function networks, fuzzy clustering, and genetic algorithms for a classifier with a built-in notion of rejection. Cordella et al. present a skeleton-based shape decomposition technique. Ramel et al. use a structural graph as the image representation for recognizing hand-drawn chemical formulas. Adam et al. use a combination of Fourier–Mellin transform and other invariants for recognition of text in technical drawings. The remaining papers in this part cover emerging areas in graphics recognition. Two papers by Müller and Rigoll focus on graphics-based retrieval of drawings and images from image databases. Both of these problems are addressed using hidden Markov models. Jorge and Fonseca attempt to recognize geometric shapes interactively. They use temporal adjacency and global geometric properties of a multi-stroke hand-drawn geometric shape. The method has been illustrated well for a small vocabulary of geomtric shapes. The technique is suitable for personal digital assistants.

Interpretation of *engineering drawings and schematics* has long motivated the field of graphics recognition. Dov Dori used the object process methodology (OPM), a graphics-based visual formalism, for designing the machine drawing understanding system (MDUS). Here he describes the OPM formalism in detail. The other papers in this part (by Mukerjee et al., Cao et al., and Ritchings et al.) focus on drawing interpretation in different domains – 3-D reconstruction from 2-D mechanical drawings, interpretation of construction structure drawings, and analysis of scanned cable and associated diagrams.

And finally, Bob Haralick introduces the section on *performance evaluation* listing the key ingredient of evaluation for document recognition applications; performance must be measured as a function of predefined categories of documents, noise perturbation parameters, internal algorithm tuning parameters, sampling variations, and the specification of the algorithm. Chhabra and Phillips briefly present the edit cost index as a goal-directed way to evaluate the performance of vectorization systems. Wenyin et al. evaluate the MDUS system to empirically determine the edit cost in terms of time taken to correct the mistakes in vectorization. In the last paper, Wenyin et al. study the impact of the algorithm parameters on the performance of line segmentation using their SPV method.

As at the past workshops, a graphics recognition contest was planned for GREC'99. However, the contest could not be completed at the workshop. It was held after the workshop. The results will be reported in the proceedings of ICPR 2000[2].

We owe special thanks to the contributing authors and the reviewers. Thanks are also due to the session chairs who helped stimulate useful discussions at the workshop. Most of the post-workshop refinements that you see in the papers here are due to ideas that were generated during these discussions and due to the suggestions of the reviewers. We are grateful to Eugenia Smith of CEDAR, State University of New York (SUNY) at Buffalo, for handling the payment processing work related to the workshop. Thanks to Prof. Sargur Srihari of SUNY Buffalo for providing the services of Eugenia Smith and for allowing us to use an account at the University at Buffalo Foundation.

The next Graphics Recognition Workshop, GREC 2001[3], will be held in Kingston, Ontario, Canada, in September 2001.

July 2000   Atul K. Chhabra
                                                                        Dov Dori

---

[2] The IAPR International Conference on Pattern Recognition, Barcelona, Spain, September 2000
[3] http://www.cs.queensu.ca/grec2001/

Organization

Workshop Chairs

Atul K. Chhabra
Verizon Communications
500 Westchester Avenue
White Plains, NY 10604, USA
atul.k.chhabra@verizon.com

Dov Dori
Faculty of Ind. Eng. and Management
Technion-Israel Institute of Technology
Haifa 32000, Israel
dori@ie.technion.ac.il

Program Committee

Keiichi Abe, Japan
Dorothea Blostein, Canada
Santanu Chaudhury, India
Marc-Pierrot Deseilligny, France
David Doermann, USA
Robert Haralick, USA
Rangachar Kasturi, USA
Noshir Langrana, USA
Lawrence O'Gorman, USA
Ihsin Phillips, USA
Karl Tombre, France

Adnan Amin, Australia
Horst Bunke, Switzerland
Luigi Cordella, Italy
Its'hak Dinstein, Israel
Georgy Gimelfarb, New Zealand
Osamu Hori, Japan
Young-Bin Kwon, Korea
Gerd Maderlechner, Germany
Theo Pavlidis, USA
Arnold Smeulders, The Netherlands

Additional Referees

Bertrand Coüasnon
Dave Elliman
Marlies de Gunst
George Nagy
Jean-Marc Ogier
Toyohide Watanabe
and other anonymous reviewers ...

Philippe Dosch
Marco Gori
Jurgen den Hartog
Daisuke Nishiwaki
M. Vuilleumier Stückelberg
Tomoyuki Yatabe

Table of Contents

IV Graphic Symbol and Shape Recognition

V Engineering Drawings and Schematics

VI Performance Evaluation

Part I

Vectorization

Stable and Robust Vectorization: How to Make the Right Choices*

Karl Tombre, Christian Ah-Soon**, Philippe Dosch, Gérald Masini, and
Salvatore Tabbone

LORIA,
B.P. 239, 54506 Vandœuvre-lès-Nancy CEDEX, France `Karl.Tombre@loria.fr`

Abstract. As a complement to quantitative evaluation methods for
raster–to–graphics conversion, we discuss in this paper some qualitative elements which should be taken into account when choosing the
different steps of one's vectorization method. We stress the importance
of having robust methods and stable implementations, and we base ourselves extensively on our own implementations and tests, concentrating
on methods designed to have few, if any, parameters.

1 Introduction

Vectorization, i.e. raster–to–vector conversion, has been at the center of graphics
recognition problems since the beginning. Despite a lot of efforts, and many
proposed solutions—including a lot of commercial software—, we have not yet
reached methods which can be considered as sufficiently stable and robust to
work as standalone "black boxes". The commercial software packages solve this
problem by providing their vectorization method with a number of parameters,
adapted to the various categories of drawings to be processed. The user is then
in control of the whole process, although families of drawings can be associated
with standard sets of parameters.

We believe in another way: one important factor for robustness it to minimize
the number of parameters and thresholds needed in the vectorization process [27].
Thus, we have been working on an approach combining several methods, each
of which having no or very few parameters, instead of implementing a single
method with many parameters. In this paper, we discuss the elements to be
taken into account when choosing one's vectorization method. We have no aim
at being exhaustive in our coverage of the numerous existing methods, but we
concentrate on the main paradigms used, and in many cases on methods we have
implemented and tested ourselves; we believe they are representative of the field.

2 The Quality of a Vectorization Method

For the sake of simplicity and conciseness, we will not discuss the phases which
come prior to vectorization, such as binarization, even though there is a clear

---

* This work was partly funded by France Telecom CNET.
** Now with Business Objects, Paris.

Atul K. Chhabra and D. Dori (Eds.): GREC'99, LNCS 1941, pp. 3–18, 2000.
© Springer-Verlag Berlin Heidelberg 2000

relationship between the quality of the latter's output and the quality of the vectors obtained. Nor will we consider the recognition and interpretation processes which may run after vectorization, although they often put requirements on the properties of the vectors yielded by the process.

As implied by the name, raster–to–vector conversion consists in analyzing a raster image to convert its pixel representation to a vector representation. The basic assumption is that such a vector representation is more suitable for further interpretation of the image; this typically holds for a scanned graphical document, but may be completely wrong for other kinds of documents.

Thus, the main quality requirement for a vectorization method is that the resulting vectors are well suited to the purpose for which they have been computed. For instance, if the main purpose is to store huge amounts of data in vector format, the total number of vectors often becomes an important quality factor. On the other hand, if high-level symbol recognition is to be performed on the vectors, we may prefer having more vectors, i.e. a lower data compression factor, but higher accuracy for some model-based recognition process to work well. If the application is to convert city maps with individual property limits, the precision with which vectors and junctions are positioned becomes crucial.

This variety of quality factors explains the difficulty in evaluating the performances of vectorization methods. The ideal would be to do some kind of goal-directed evaluation, as has been done for topics such as binarization [28] or thinning [20]. But in graphics recognition, there tends to be as many different goals as there are different projects! Therefore, the recent efforts on performance evaluation for vectorization have taken a different path: providing synthetic images rendered from selected CAD drawings, for which ground truth is available as a set of vectors. Even with this simple and uniform approach, different metrics can still be chosen for measuring the quality of a given vectorization, and as the contest at GREC'97 showed [8,23], it is not always easy to come out with a clear winner: for instance, is it more important to have well-positioned vectors—even if this means that some ground-truth vectors are split into several vectors in the vectorization result—or to have the same number of vectors as in the ground truth?

In the following discussion, we try to take into account several of these possible criteria, giving the pros and cons of various approaches.

3   Which Steps Are Involved in Vectorization?

Whereas a user would tend to look at vectorization as a whole, engineers and researchers involved in designing good raster–to–vector methods know that there are several steps in this process, each with specific quality requirements:

- The first step is to find the lines in the original raster image. Whereas the most common approach for this is to compute the skeleton of the image, a number of other methods have been proposed.

– The next step is to approximate the lines found into a set of vectors. This is performed by some polygonal approximation method, and there are many around, with different approximation criteria.

– After approximation, it is often necessary to perform some post-processing, to find better positions for the junction points, to merge some vectors and remove some others, etc.

– A last step sometimes performed is to find the circular arcs. We will not elaborate on this step in the present paper; our choices for arc detection are described in another paper [13].

Of course, we are aware that it is too simplistic to present vectorization as being these four steps applied successively. Many vectorization systems actually perform them in a different order, or merge several of them into a single step—such as finding the lines and approximating them simultaneously, for instance. But we feel it is nevertheless important to discuss separately the criteria for choice of each of these steps.

4   Finding the Lines

The first step in vectorization is to process a raster image, supposed to contain graphics[1], in order to extract a set of lines, i.e. of chains of pixels. The most intuitive definition for these lines is probably that they represent the set of significant medial axes of the original image, considered as a shape.

There are three main families of approaches for this step:

1. The first method which comes to mind is to compute the medial axis, i.e. the skeleton of the raster image. This is the most common approach, and skeletons are known to yield good precision with respect to the positioning of the line. But they also tend to give lots of barbs when the image is somewhat irregular, so they need some clever heuristics or post-processing steps, that weaken their generality and robustness. Another weakness of skeleton-based methods is that they displace the junction points, compared to the position wanted by the draftsman.

2. A second family of methods is based on matching the opposite sides of the line. These methods are better at positioning the junction points, but tend to rely too much on heuristics and thresholds when the drawings become complex.

3. A number of sparse-pixel approaches have also been proposed. The general idea is to avoid having to examine all the pixels in the image, by using appropriate sub-sampling methods which give a broader view of the line. One limitation of these methods is that they are prone to "double detections" in some cases.

---

[1] We suppose in this paper that some text/graphics segmentation method, such as [15], has already been applied to the original image and that we work on the graphics part.

4.1 Skeleton-Based Methods

The main family of methods for finding the lines is that of computing the skeleton. There are two well-known paradigms for skeletonization methods:

- The first is that of "peeling an onion", i.e. iterative thinning of the original image until no pixel can be removed without altering the topological and morphological properties of the shape [19]. These methods require only a small number of lines in an image buffer at any time, which can be an advantage when dealing with large images. But on the other hand, multiple passes are necessary before reaching the final result, so that computation times may become quite high.
- The second definition used for a skeleton is that of the ridge lines formed by the centers of all maximal disks included in the original shape, connected to preserve connectivity. This leads directly to the use of distance transforms [4,22], which can be computed in only two passes on the image. However, it is difficult to compute the distance transform without storing the whole image in memory.

In our group, we have been testing both approaches. For thinning, we applied the well-known algorithm illustrated by Fig. 1. This must be followed by a barb removal procedure, which takes as parameter the maximum number of pixels to remove from free-end chains. The algorithm is straightforward and gives good results, but is very sensitive to noise.

0 0 0	1 x 0	1 1 1	0 x 1
x 1 x	1 1 0	x 1 x	0 1 1
1 1 1	1 x 0	0 0 0	0 x 1

x 0 0	x 1 x	x 1 x	0 0 x
1 1 0	1 1 0	0 1 1	0 1 1
x 1 x	x 0 0	0 0 x	x 1 x

Fig. 1. Usual structuring elements used for thinning. In each case, the central pixel is set to 0 when the configuration is found (x means don't care). The algorithm consists of successively applying each of these structuring elements on the whole image, and to iterate as long as some pixels are deleted. The 8 elements can be applied in a single pass on the image through pipelining techniques

We have also successfully tested the use of skeletons computed from distance transforms. To guarantee the precision of the skeleton, we advocate the use of chamfer distances, which come closer to approximating the Euclidean distance. A good compromise between precision and simplicity seems to be the 3–4 chamfer distance transform (see Fig. 2), for which a good skeletonization algorithm has been proposed by Sanniti di Baja [10]. A single threshold on the significance of a branch enables correct removal of the smallest barbs.

V_2	V_3	V_4
V_1	X	V_5
V_8	V_7	V_6

First pass : $Y = \min(V_1 + 3, V_2 + 4, V_3 + 3, V_4 + 4)$

Second pass : $Z = \min(Y, V_5 + 3, V_6 + 4, V_7 + 3, V_8 + 4)$

Fig. 2. Computing the 3–4 chamfer distance transform in two passes over the image, the first from left to right and from top to bottom, the second from right to left and from bottom to top. Sanniti di Baja's algorithm performs some post-processing on this distance transform, such as changing labels 6 to 5 and 3 to 1; see reference [10] for details

After extracting the skeleton, the result of the process is a set of pixels considered as being the medial axes of the lines in the drawing. This set must be linked, to extract the chains making up the lines. Although many applications require some kind of chaining, there are surprisingly few papers or even textbooks giving explanations on the way it is to be done. In algorithm 1, we give some details about a chaining algorithm we have designed, which takes advantage of the topological properties of the skeleton.

4.2   Matching Opposite Contours

Another family of vectorization methods is based on matching the opposite contours of the lines, working either directly on the contours of the binary image, or on a polygonal approximation of it. We experimented this approach ourselves some years ago, in the REDRAW system [2], and we still use it for thick lines. The basic principle of our algorithm is to work on the contours of the image, and not on the skeleton. The contours can be directly extracted during connected component labeling, and are oriented so that we know on which side the shape is. Polygonal approximation is performed on these contours, and opposite segments are matched; junction points are detected as being located at the intersection of matches involving adjacent segments (see Fig. 3). This method works nicely on straight lines; it gives good junction locations and is much less sensitive to noise than skeleton-based methods. However, as illustrated by Fig. 4, it often involves one–to–many or many–to–many matches, and this again leads to hard-to-master thresholds and heuristics in the case of complex drawings, with many curved lines, hatching, etc.

4.3   Sparse-Pixel Approaches

The paradigm of the third vectorization family is to take a "broader view" of the drawing to be analyzed, by avoiding systematic processing of all the pixels. The best representative of this family is the series of algorithms developed by Dov Dori's team [11,12]. We designed ourselves a method in this family [29], based on previous work by Lin et al. for a diagram understanding system [21]. The principle, illustrated by Fig. 5, is to split up the image into *meshes* and to

---

Algorithm 1 Building chains by linking the pixels of a skeleton image

---

Mark all skeleton pixels of degree $\neq 2$, or of degree $= 2$ when 4 pixels make up a square
Delete isolated pixels
while there are marked points left **do**
　Choose a marked point p
　Create list l_p of all non-null neighbors of p
　while $l_p \neq \emptyset$ **do**
　　Choose a point q from l_p
　　Set p temporarily to 0 to prevent premature looping
　　Create a new chain c as $[p, q]$
　　if q is marked **then**
　　　continueChain $\leftarrow$ false
　　else
　　　continueChain $\leftarrow$ true
　　　Set q to 0
　　end if
　　while continueChain $=$ true **do**
　　　$q \leftarrow$ getNonMarked4Neighbor(q)
　　　if none is found **then**
　　　　$q \leftarrow$ getMarked4Neighbor(q)
　　　　if none is found **then**
　　　　　$q \leftarrow$ getNonMarked8Neighbor(q)
　　　　　if none is found **then**
　　　　　　$q \leftarrow$ getMarked8Neighbor(q)
　　　　　　if none is found **then**
　　　　　　　$q \leftarrow$ getAnyNeighbor(q)
　　　　　　end if
　　　　　　continueChain $\leftarrow$ false
　　　　　end if
　　　　else
　　　　　continueChain $\leftarrow$ false
　　　　end if
　　　end if
　　　Append q to c
　　　if continueChain $=$ true **then**
　　　　Set q to 0
　　　else if we are on a loop **then**
　　　　Add p to c again to finish the loop
　　　end if
　　end while
　　Add c to the list of chains
　　Restore mark on p
　end while
　Set p to 0 (it is completely processed)
end while
while there are pixels still unprocessed (they belong to perfect loops) **do**
　Start over again by marking a non-null pixel
end while

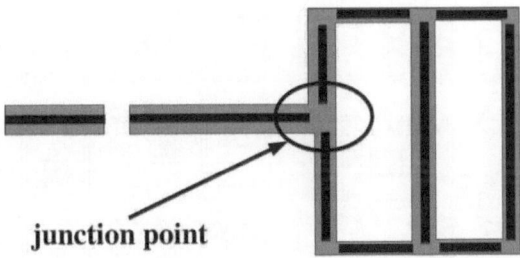

junction point

Fig. 3. The basic principle of the REDRAW vectorization method

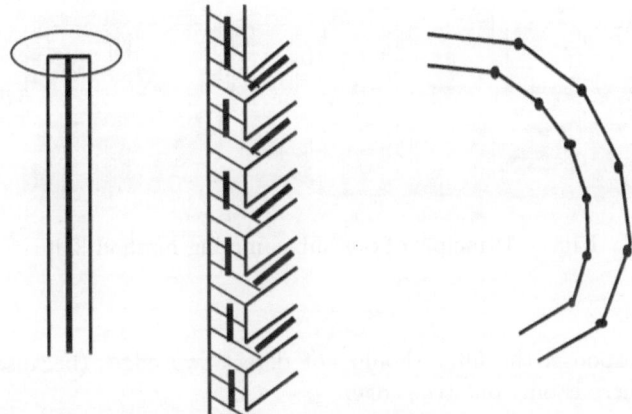

Fig. 4. Some of the difficulties with the matching approach: extremity segments must not be matched (this involves a threshold); one–to–many matches lead to complex matching methods; many–to–many matching strategies become necessary for curved lines, which leads to the use of thresholds and/or heuristics

extract lines by only analyzing the borders of the meshes. The results yielded by the method are good, but the choice of the sub-sampling rate (size of the mesh) is not always straightforward.

4.4 Elements of Choice

In his ground-breaking work on edge detection, Canny [5] shows how three sometimes conflicting criteria must be taken into account to design a good edge detection filter. Let us paraphrase these criteria with simple words:

- detection: the filter must detect the true edges and not noise edges;
- localization: the filter must position the edges correctly, with minimal displacement;

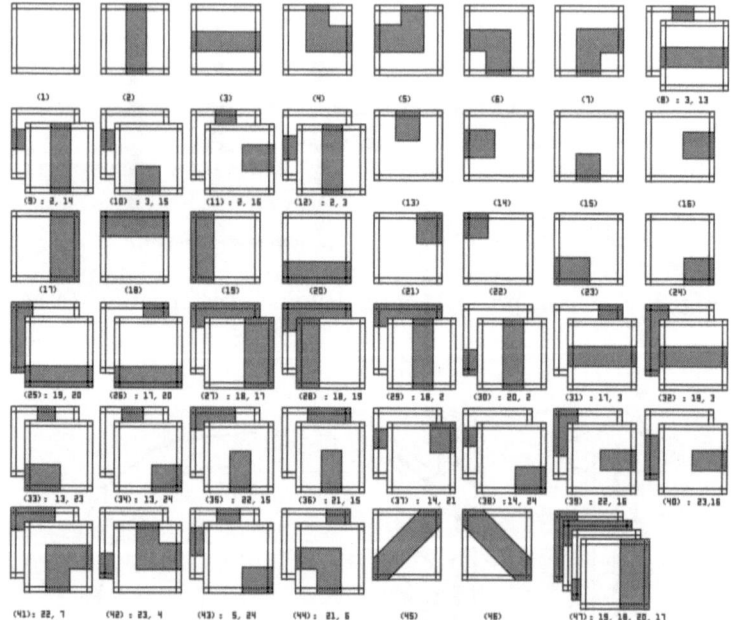

Fig. 5. Principle of our sub-sampling method [29]

- single response: the filter should not detect two edges (because of noise) where there is only one true edge.

Our impression is that, while lacking the same kind of fundamental work on the vectorization problem, our community has designed a number of methods which take these different criteria more or less into account:

- skeleton-based methods have a good localization rate, but tend to be very sensitive to noise, has we have seen;
- contour matching methods have a better detection rate, a relatively good localization factor, but rely on heuristics and complex matching schemes (when the drawing is not simple) which do not guarantee a single response in all cases;
- sparse-pixel approaches work surprisingly well with respect to localization, but some of them (our sub-sampling method, for instance) may miss too small details, and our experiments show that they are also prone to double responses in some cases.

In addition, the correct positioning of junctions is often very important in our applications. All skeleton-based methods are weak with respect to the correct restitution of the junction at the location the draftsman wanted it to be. This is a direct consequence of the fact that the skeleton follows the medial axis of the shape, whereas the position of the junction as envisioned by the draftsman is *not* on the medial axis of the shape (see Fig. 6). Contour matching methods are much better in positioning the junctions; this explains why some authors propose combined methods, such as using the skeleton for positioning of the lines and contour matching to reduce noise and to have better junctions [16]. In sparse-pixel approaches, the junctions are also relatively well detected, but as all pixels are not explored, some methods tend to find junctions where there were none, as we experienced in our mesh-based method (see Fig. 7).

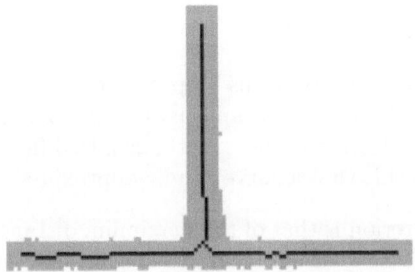

Fig. 6. Position of the junction point with a skeleton-based method

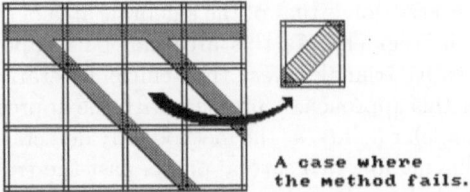

A case where
the method fails.

Fig. 7. False detection of a junction in the mesh-based method [29] : as only the borders of the meshes are explored, the method falsely assumes that there is a junction between the two hatching lines

Table 1 summarizes our elements of choice, comparing the different families of methods. We are aware that our ratings may be subjective, especially as we try to factorize the behavior of large families of methods, which is not always possible without being unfair to some specific algorithm. In the present situation, our team tends to prefer distance transform-based skeletons in our graphics recognition systems. However, this is not an absolute position; especially for the thick-line layer, contour matching seems to yield better results, as thick lines in the architectural drawings we work on are usually horizontal or vertical.

Table 1. Elements of choice

	Skeleton	Contour matching	Sparse-pixel
Localization	++	+	+
Detection	−	+	+/−
Single response	++	+/−	−
Junctions	−	+	+/−

5   From Lines to Segments

The lines extracted from the previous step are to be represented by a set of segments. This is done by polygonal approximation. Here also, many methods exist. The first level for classifying these methods into different families is that of the criterion used to decide that a curve can be approximated by a line segment.

- The most usual criterion is that of the maximum distance between the curve and the segment. This leads to recursive splitting of the curve at the maximum deviation points, until all segments are valid approximations. As the positions of the extrema points of the segments tend to be constrained by the initial pixel positions, it may make sense for the method to be followed by a fitting phase, where each segment is displaced to best fit the original curve. However, in the case of vectorization, this leads to the additional problem of keeping correct junctions while fitting each segment to the curve.
- A second possible criterion is that of the algebraic area of the surface between the curve and the segment. As this area can be computed iteratively, as the sum of successive triangles, very time-efficient iterative methods can be implemented for this approach. A problem with the approach is that it tends to displace the angular points, as the method only detects a change of general direction after having followed several points past the true angle.
- Other criteria include various angular measures [14] and curvature computations [3].

In our experiments, we have used two methods, representing the two first families mentioned above. For the recursive splitting approach, we have implemented Rosin and West's recursive split-and-merge method [26], which has the advantage that it does not require any user-given threshold or parameter. The principle is to recursively split the curve into smaller and smaller segments, until the maximum deviation is 0 or there are only 3 or less points left. Then, the "tree" of possible segments is traversed and the method keeps those segments maximizing a measure of significance, which is defined as a ratio between the maximum deviation and the length of the segment. Recently, Rosin has proposed other possible measures of significance [25], and we plan to explore this further.

We have also used for many years an iterative method, that of Wall and Danielsson [30], enhanced in our team with a direction-change marking procedure to preserve the angular points. The method only needs a single threshold, on the ratio between the algebraic surface and the length of the segments. It is fast and efficient, but not as precise as the former. On the other hand, Rosin and West's method tends to split up the lines around a junction into too many small segments (see Fig. 8). This is a direct consequence of its preciseness and of the previously mentioned displacement of junction points by skeleton-based methods.

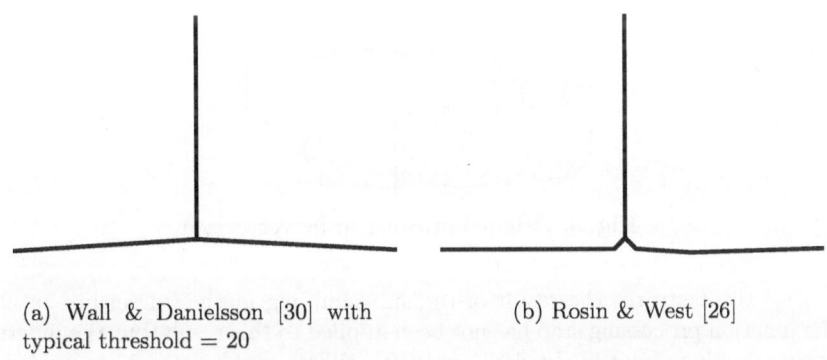

(a) Wall & Danielsson [30] with typical threshold = 20

(b) Rosin & West [26]

Fig. 8. Comparison of two polygonal approximation methods applied to Fig. 6

Based on these experiments, and depending on the ultimate goals for the graphics recognition process, we would recommend the following choice for the polygonal approximation method to be used:

- If the simplicity of the resulting set of vectors is important, the best choice is probably an iterative method like Wall & Danielsson's. It will give a number of segments closest to the number in the original drawing. However, it is not optimal with respect to positioning of these segments.

  A possible improvement of the method would be to perform several approximations with varying thresholds, to have some kind of "multi-scale" approximation, and to merge the results in order to optimize a $\frac{precision}{number}$ ratio.

- If the precision is the most important criterion, Rosin & West's method seems to us to be a good choice. An additional advantage of the method is that it does not require any explicit threshold or parameter. However, our experience is that symbol recognition processes tend to be disturbed by the symbol being split up into too many segments [1]. Also, as already said, the approximation will be precise *with respect to the original curve*, which does not necessarily correspond to the expected line, as we have seen with the displacement of junctions in a skeleton.

  Possible improvements include better significance criteria [25] and the use of post-processing steps, as will be explained in Sect. 7.

6   Visual Comparison

We are perfectly aware that it is difficult to visually assess the quality of a vectorization process. However, we will try to illustrate some of the features of the various methods discussed in the previous sections. For this, we chose a simple engineering drawing (Fig. 9).

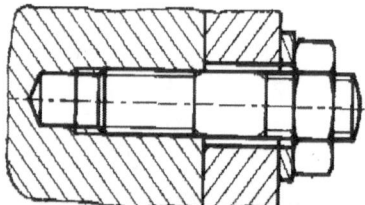

Fig. 9. Original drawing to be vectorized

Fig. 10 illustrates the result of the sub-sampling method described in [29]. The junction processing step has not been applied to this result, but the junction information is present in the data structure. What can be noticed is that due to the sub-sampling effect, some parts of the hatching lines are incorrectly oriented, as the mesh intersects with the line in such a way that the rewriting rules see a vertical or horizontal segment, instead of an oblique segment. This is illustrated by Fig. 10.b.

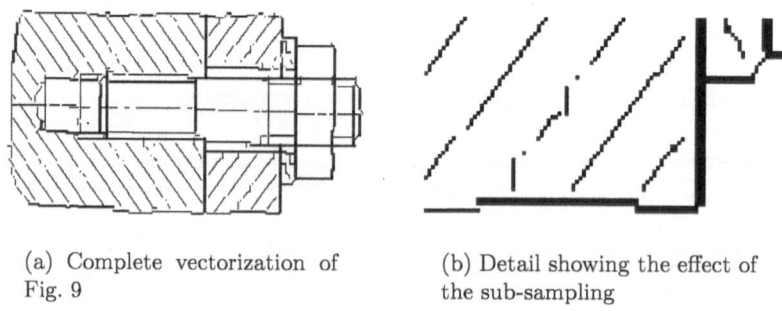

(a) Complete vectorization of Fig. 9

(b) Detail showing the effect of the sub-sampling

Fig. 10. Result of vectorization through sub-sampling [29]

Figure 11 compares the results obtained by approximating a 3–4 chamfer distance skeleton (Sect. 4.1) of Fig. 9 with the two polygonal approximation methods previously mentioned (Sect. 5). It is of course difficult to see the differences on a global view; we therefore have chosen a typical zone and zoomed in on it, to illustrate the difference in behavior between the two approximations.

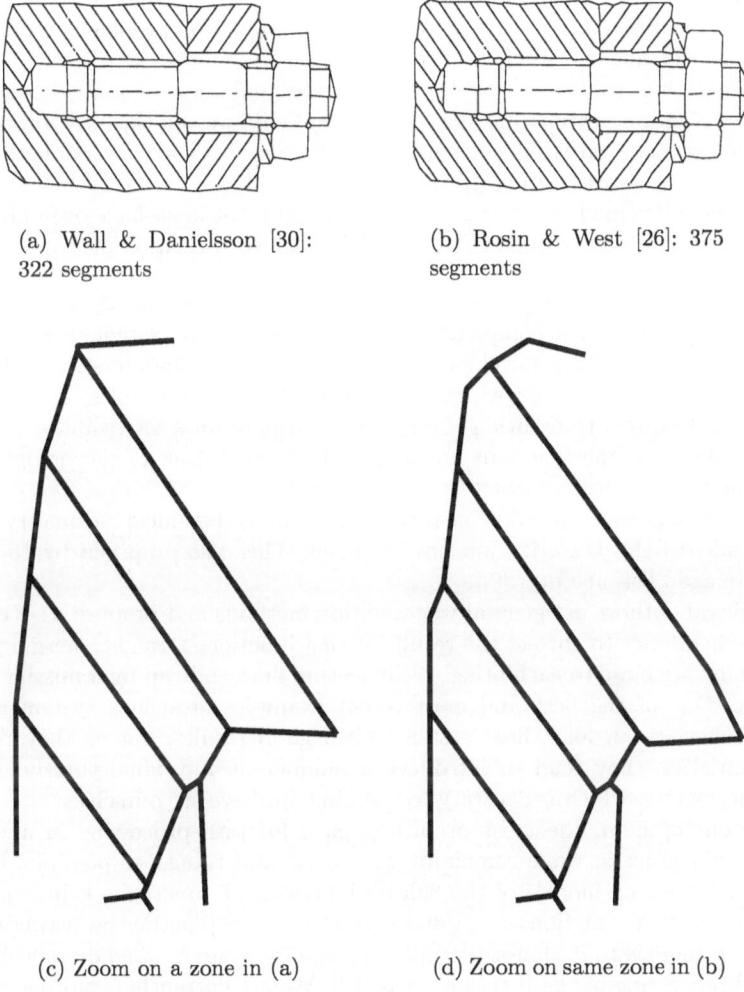

(a) Wall & Danielsson [30]: 322 segments

(b) Rosin & West [26]: 375 segments

(c) Zoom on a zone in (a)

(d) Zoom on same zone in (b)

Fig. 11. Comparison of two polygonal approximations

7   Post-processing

In the two steps described until now, we have never used any explicit knowledge about what vectors are supposed to be in a graphical document. The line finding methods working on the binary image only use simple topological, geometric and photometric rules to somehow find the medial axes in the image. As we have seen with skeletons, this can lead to results which are contrary to what the drafts-man expects. The same can be said of the approximation algorithms we have described, which only use some deviation criteria to compute an approximation of the original curve, without making any assumption about what this curve is supposed to represent. Actually, the same approximation algorithms are also used in very different contexts, such as object recognition problems in computer vision, for instance.

Therefore, it is often necessary to add contextual knowledge at some stage of the vectorization process. For the sake of simplicity, we call this post-processing, although we are aware that some authors include contextual constraints throughout their vectorization process.

As the following brief survey shows, many different ideas have been proposed for adding this kind of domain knowledge to the vectorization process:

- When processing large number of very specific documents, it may make sense to develop a completely *ad hoc* vectorization system. For instance, Chhabra et al. have developed efficient methods for finding straight lines in telephone company drawings containing a lot of large tables [7]. In such a case, the direct recognition of the longest straight lines solves all the junction problems, as the junctions are simply the intersections of the straight lines found.
- It is also possible to add constraints, describing the "ideal" geometry of the result, to the vectorization process itself. This was proposed by Röösli & Monagan [24] at GREC'95.
- Several authors use general vectorization methods and propose a set of simple heuristics to correct the result, setting junctions straight, merging those which are close to each other, reconnecting lines split up by a missing pixel, etc. One of the best and most recent examples of such a system is that of Chen et al. [6]. These systems yield good results, but as they rely on heuristics, they tend to introduce a number of additional thresholds and parameters, which is contrary to the aims we have set ourselves.
- In our opinion, the most promising path for post-processing in a vectorization process, while remaining as generic and robust as possible, is that of introducing models of the "ideal" junctions (T junctions, L junctions, X junctions, Y junctions ...) and correcting each junction by fitting one of these models to it. Janssen proposed a similar system based on morphological processing of the junction areas [17]. We are currently exploring various fitting methods, hoping to report soon on promising results in that area.

In addition to these "post-processing" methods, we need to follow the evolution in neighboring fields, where new methods may emerge. Even if they must still be considered to be too experimental or too computationally expensive to be applicable for real-size graphics recognition problems, they may mature in the coming years to propose alternatives to the current techniques used for computing a "skeleton" or for approximating a line. This includes ideas like the use of energy minimization techniques to compute the medial axis of shapes; for instance, a recent paper proposes a statistical framework based on Markov random fields, which yields surprisingly good results on simple shapes [31]. Another idea, in the area of approximation, is to decompose the curve to be approximated into a series of orthogonal basis functions [9].

8   Conclusion

Without aiming at presenting a complete state of the art of vectorization methods, we have tried in this paper to explore the main criteria for choosing a robust vectorization method, and the most common paradigms used in the different steps involved. As it seems difficult to provide a universal measure for assessing the performances of vectorization, we believe that the elements of choice given can be complementary to statistical performance evaluation processes.

References

1. C. Ah-Soon and K. Tombre. Network-Based Recognition of Architectural Symbols. In A. Amin, D. Dori, P. Pudil, and H. Freeman, editors, *Advances in Pattern Recognition (Proceedings of Joint IAPR Workshops SSPR'98 and SPR'98, Sydney, Australia)*, volume 1451 of *Lecture Notes in Computer Science*, pages 252–261, August 1998. 13
2. D. Antoine, S. Collin, and K. Tombre. Analysis of Technical Documents: The RE-DRAW System. In H. S. Baird, H. Bunke, and K. Yamamoto, editors, *Structured Document Image Analysis*, pages 385–402. Springer-Verlag, Berlin/Heidelberg, 1992. 7
3. H. Asada and M. Brady. The Curvature Primal Sketch. *IEEE Transactions on PAMI*, 8(1):2–14, 1986. 12
4. G. Borgefors. Distance Transforms in Digital Images. *Computer Vision, Graphics and Image Processing*, 34:344–371, 1986. 6
5. J. Canny. A Computational Approach to Edge Detection. *IEEE Transactions on PAMI*, 8(6):679–698, 1986. 9
6. Y. Chen, N. A. Langrana, and A. K. Das. Perfecting Vectorized Mechanical Drawings. *Computer Vision and Image Understanding*, 63(2):273–286, March 1996. 16
7. A. K. Chhabra, V. Misra, and J. Arias. Detection of Horizontal Lines in Noisy Run Length Encoded Images: The FAST Method. In Kasturi and Tombre [18], pages 35–48. 16
8. A. K. Chhabra and I. T. Phillips. The Second International Graphics Recognition Contest—Raster to Vector Conversion: A Report. In K. Tombre and A. K. Chhabra, editors, *Graphics Recognition—Algorithms and Systems*, volume 1389 of *Lecture Notes in Computer Science*, pages 390–410. Springer-Verlag, April 1998. 4
9. T. J. Davis. Fast Decomposition of Digital Curves into Polygons Using the Haar Transform. *IEEE Transactions on PAMI*, 21(8):786–790, August 1999. 16
10. G. Sanniti di Baja. Well-Shaped, Stable, and Reversible Skeletons from the (3,4)-Distance Transform. *Journal of Visual Communication and Image Representation*, 5(1):107–115, 1994. 6, 7
11. D. Dori. Orthogonal Zig-Zag: an Algorithm for Vectorizing Engineering Drawings Compared with Hough Transform. *Advances in Engineering Software*, 28(1):11–24, 1997. 7
12. D. Dori and W. Liu. Sparse Pixel Vectorization: An Algorithm and Its Performance Evaluation. *IEEE Transactions on PAMI*, 21(3):202–215, March 1999. 7
13. Ph. Dosch, G. Masini, and K. Tombre. Improving Arc Detection in Graphics Recognition. In *Proceedings of the 15th International Conference on Pattern Recognition, Barcelona (Spain)*, September 2000. To appear. 5

14. J. G. Dunham. Optimum Uniform Piecewise Linear Approximation of Planar Curves. *IEEE Transactions on PAMI*, 8(1):67–75, 1986. 12
15. L. A. Fletcher and R. Kasturi. A Robust Algorithm for Text String Separation from Mixed Text/Graphics Images. *IEEE Transactions on PAMI*, 10(6):910–918, 1988. 5
16. O. Hori and A. Okazaki. High Quality Vectorization Based on a Generic Object Model. In H. S. Baird, H. Bunke, and K. Yamamoto, editors, *Structured Document Image Analysis*, pages 325–339. Springer-Verlag, Heidelberg, 1992. 11
17. R. D. T. Janssen and A. M. Vossepoel. Adaptive Vectorization of Line Drawing Images. *Computer Vision and Image Understanding*, 65(1):38–56, January 1997. 16
18. R. Kasturi and K. Tombre, editors. *Graphics Recognition—Methods and Applications*, volume 1072 of *Lecture Notes in Computer Science*. Springer-Verlag, May 1996. 17, 18
19. L. Lam, S.-W. Lee, and C. Y. Suen. Thinning Methodologies — A Comprehensive Survey. *IEEE Transactions on PAMI*, 14(9):869–885, September 1992. 6
20. L. Lam and C. Y. Suen. An Evaluation of Parallel Thinning Algorithms for Character Recognition. *IEEE Transactions on PAMI*, 17(9):914–919, September 1995. 4
21. X. Lin, S. Shimotsuji, M. Minoh, and T. Sakai. Efficient Diagram Understanding with Characteristic Pattern Detection. *Computer Vision, Graphics and Image Processing*, 30:84–106, 1985. 7
22. C. W. Niblack, P. B. Gibbons, and D. W. Capson. Generating Skeletons and Centerlines from the Distance Transform. *CVGIP: Graphical Models and Image Processing*, 54(5):420–437, September 1992. 6
23. I. T. Phillips and A. K. Chhabra. Empirical Performance Evaluation of Graphics Recognition Systems. *IEEE Transactions on PAMI*, 21(9):849–870, September 1999. 4
24. M. Röösli and G. Monagan. Adding Geometric Constraints to the Vectorization of Line Drawings. In Kasturi and Tombre [18], pages 49–56. 16
25. P. L. Rosin. Techniques for Assessing Polygonal Approximation of Curves. *IEEE Transactions on PAMI*, 19(6):659–666, June 1997. 12, 13
26. P. L. Rosin and G. A. West. Segmentation of Edges into Lines and Arcs. *Image and Vision Computing*, 7(2):109–114, May 1989. 12, 13, 15
27. K. Tombre, C. Ah-Soon, Ph. Dosch, A. Habed, and G. Masini. Stable, Robust and Off-the-Shelf Methods for Graphics Recognition. In *Proceedings of the 14th International Conference on Pattern Recognition, Brisbane (Australia)*, pages 406–408, August 1998. 3
28. Ø. Due Trier and A. K. Jain. Goal-Directed Evaluation of Binarization Methods. *IEEE Transactions on PAMI*, 17(12):1191–1201, December 1995. 4
29. P. Vaxivière and K. Tombre. Subsampling: A Structural Approach to Technical Document Vectorization. In D. Dori and A. Bruckstein, editors, *Shape, Structure and Pattern Recognition (Post-proceedings of IAPR Workshop on Syntactic and Structural Pattern Recognition, Nahariya, Israel)*, pages 323–332. World Scientific, 1995. 7, 10, 11, 14
30. K. Wall and P. Danielsson. A Fast Sequential Method for Polygonal Approximation of Digitized Curves. *Computer Vision, Graphics and Image Processing*, 28:220–227, 1984. 12, 13, 15
31. S.-C. Zhu. Stochastic Jump-Diffusion Process for Computing Medial Axes in Markov Random Fields. *IEEE Transactions on PAMI*, 21(11):1158–1169, November 1999. 16

A Really Useful Vectorization Algorithm

Dave Elliman

School of Computer Science, University of Nottingham, UK
dge@cs.nott.ac.uk

Abstract. A novel algorithm for the vectorization of binary images is described. It is based on a data structure formed by crack following the outlines of the dark region of the image and applying a heuristic to decide which edges lie along the direction of the vector at any position. The regions are divided into classes, described as strokes and junctions respectively. The idea of a junction as a region containing more than one stroke is introduced, and this is used to inform the process of vectorization in these areas. The quality of the vectors produced compares favourably with those produced by other algorithms known to the author, and the implementation is reasonably efficient, a typical A4 drawing is processed in under ten seconds on my 300 MHz Pentium lap-top.

1 Introduction

More than a hundred papers have been published on the topic of Vectorization in the in the last ten years. It might be expected that the seemingly simple task of converting a binary image to a vector representation had been exhaustively studied and that robust universal algorithms would be available to the research community. In fact this is not yet the case and even the most sophisticated algorithms produce results in certain circumstances that would be considered erroneous when evaluated by a person was familiar with the application domain from which the image was taken. The most recently published algorithm at the time of preparing this paper was Sparse Pixel Vectorization (SPV)[1]. This is a sophisticated algorithm that follows horizontal and vertical estimates of the medial axis position. This sub-sampling of the image makes the algorithm particularly fast and for much of the image high quality line-work is produced as evidenced by the examples shown in the paper. A closer examination reveals some loss of detail in regions where there are zigzags in the lines. There is a tendency for circles to become octagons with small breaks in the lines along the 45 and 135 axes of the image, there are places where arcs become straight lines, and small features can be lost altogether. SPV would be a strong contender in any competition to establish the best performing vectorization algorithm available today, yet it has serious shortcomings that would be unacceptable in many commercial applications, and which would limit the effectiveness of further post-processing. The algorithm described here is almost certainly somewhat slower, but likely to be more accurate. There is a family likeness to SPV in that both algorithms operate by finding the medial axis using the mean point of horizontal and vertical run lengths, and both try to identify junction regions that are

Atul K. Chhabra and D. Dori (Eds.): GREC'99, LNCS 1941, pp. 19–27, 2000.

particularly problematic to vectorize. The way such regions are handled is very different, and no effort is made to gain speed by sub-sampling the pixel image as this is not used at all in the really useful algorithm. Instead crack following is used to generate an outline of the dark regions in the image as a rapid first stage in the processing [3]. The edges of binary pixels are all that need be considered from this point on, and that constitutes a substantial reduction in the volume of data to be processed. There is no loss of information in this process and it was preferred to sub-sampling for this reason. The algorithms were developed entirely independently, and this likeness is perhaps indicative of a growing consensus on the most effective approach to practical vectorization.

2 Approaches to Vectorization

These are effectively and comprehensively summarized by Dori [1][2] and by Lam [7]. The original approach of thinning applied pixel erosion to the boundaries of dark regions until a single width skeleton remained. A simple line following procedure is then used to generate the appropriate. Thinning tends to be a computationally expensive process as it involves sampling the entire image in an iterative manner until no further changes are made. Various strategies can be used to increase the efficiency of the process, but simply maintaining a list of current edge pixels results in a much faster algorithm, as these are the only candidates for erosion. One a pixel has become skeletal it can be removed from further consideration, further streamlining the algorithm. The main drawback to thinning is not its speed, but rather the poor quality of the resulting skeleton. Thinning uses a local mask, often merely 3 by 3 pixels in size to decide if a pixel should be removed. This means that some patterns close to the edge of a dark region will be seen as skeletal and this will result in either a small spur or whisker, or cause the vector to be displaced towards the boundary. If a T-junction between two lines is thinned, a cusp is usually formed at the junction between the lines. The effect is remarkably similar to the effect observed if one is impolite enough to make lines of sugar on the table with a sugar dispenser in the shape of a T, the crest of the sugar exhibits a similar cusp. Curves of any kind will become much more like the contour of a UK fifty pence coin, and in general the skeleton will weave drunkenly from one side of the dark region to another, generating a plethora of whiskers in the process. The method does have the advantage of maintaining continuity, and that the skeleton is constrained to remain entirely within the dark region. The small spurs can be removed by post processing, and some kind of line fitting can be used to make cosmetic improvements to the result, but the result rarely seems acceptable. The root of the problem is the extremely restricted region that is used to make the thinning decisions. This is too small for a meaningful local averaging to take place. An alternative approach used by some workers has been to imagine a small tracking point that moves along dark regions in a given direction, correcting its trajectory each time it encounters the boundary. Joseph [5] used this approach in his Anon drawing recognition system. It was reasonably fast, but suffered from poor quality skeletons as the tracking point bounced from one edge of a line to another in a manner reminiscent of an out of control bobsleigh. The intention was to remove the line as it was tracked, but this was only partially successful, and in some area two (or more) vectors would be generated from the same line. The approach is believed to have been inspired by a commercial product that is used to digitize maps. Interestingly this impressive machine often requires manual intervention at junctions. SPV is similar to Anon in some respects, but includes a powerful improvement in that the midpoints of scan lines are recorded in order to generate the vectors, and this results in a major improvement to the quality of the skeleton produced. The third category of algorithms considers the shape of the contour of the dark region, and uses this to generate the medial axis. This has the advantage that a more global averaging may be used to gain a smoother result. However the approach tends to break down at junctions resulting in discontinuities in the skeleton. The algorithm described here is best included with this class, but the problem at junctions is to a large extent overcome. Before describing how this is achieved, it is important to consider the nature of the skeleton that such an algorithm intends to achieve.

3   A Formal Definition of the Medial Axis?

Vectorization algorithms have also been skeletonization algorithms and medial axis transforms. The latter term in particular implies that there is a particular medial axis that could be defined for any arbitrary shaped region. It would be of enormous value if such a property could be defined and agreed upon. At last algorithms could be developed and compared with one another in a full objective way. The search for such a definition has been illusive and more or less abandoned in favour of using manual digitization to establish ground-truthed documents as measure of algorithm performance. Perhaps this state of affairs is partly a result of failing to understand the nature of the problem. Vectorization is appropriate for artifacts that were produced using some kind of writing instrument that leaves a visible trail, usually a pencil or pen whether propelled by a human hand, or mechanical means. Of course this trail or stroke may have been produced in an entirely different process using a laser printer or a printing press, but the idea of a two dimensional path in space remains the key idea. There may be strokes of differing thickness produced by different instruments, for example the outline of a view in an engineering drawing is usually twice as wide as the line-work in the dimensioning information. A calligraphic pen will produce a stroke on continuously varying width. Perhaps this is stating the obvious, but the output from a Vectorization process should be a set of (perhaps closed) paths with associated thickness information. The description should contain sufficient information to re-create the original drawing process within some arbitrary bound of precision. If the problem is seen from this perspective the reason for a failure to define a medial axis becomes immediately apparent. Where a stroke crosses a path that has already been made a junction is formed, and this point may be crossed yet again by the writing instrument thus producing ever more complex junctions. In practice the most complex case the author has seen was one where twenty-two lines interested in an engineering drawing of a boat. A junction thus has two medial axis paths if two strokes cross at this point. In fact it has as many axes as strokes that pass through the region. The really useful algorithm divides a dark region into two classes, strokes and junctions, and it attempts to find a single medial axis for the former case, and to interpolate the correct number of medial axes for the second. The algorithm will now be described in detail as a series of stages.

3.1   Stage 1: Crack Following

In this stage the binary image is converted into a data structure formed by following the cracks between the dark and light pixels. A highly efficient algorithm has been developed to carry out this process [3] which works direct from a compressed run-length version of the image, such as is used within TIFF Group III and Group IV files. This new representation is generated in a single pass of the compressed file using minimal memory, and without ever expanding the image into a pixel representation. The processing time is indistinguishable from that needed to read the highly (using Group IV) compressed file. The result is a tree of outlines with alternate levels representing white to black and black to white transitions. The outlines themselves are represented using an efficient chain code. The result of this process for a fragment of cursive script is shown in fig. 1 below:

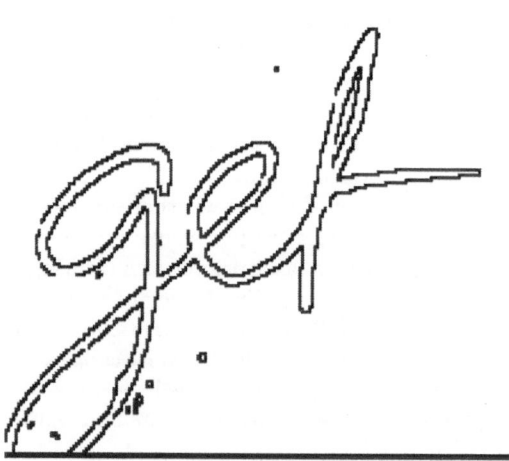

Fig. 1. The Result of Crack-Following

3.2   Stage 2: Form Links that Are Part of Strokes

The outline representation may be seen as a set of directed vertical single pixel high crack, and a set of directed horizontal single pixel wide cracks. Arbitrarily the left side of a directed crack will be black, and the right side white. This means that outlines of holes are ordered clockwise, while main outlines go anticlockwise. Each such crack has one and only one matching mate that will be the closest one of the same orientation but opposite sense when measured across the dark region. Each of these matching pairs of edge is linked, forming a criss-cross grid over the entire area enclosed within the outline. The aim now is to eliminate many of these links, leaving only those that are believed to be perpendicular to the local stroke direction. A simple heuristic might be applied here. Short links are intuitively to be preferred to long ones. The links might be sorted in order of length, shortest first. Each shortest link could be taken in turn and all those that cross it removed from consideration. This process would continue down the sorted list until no links remained to be removed. Indeed the first implementation of the algorithm did exactly that. It was immediately realised that this led to small spurs and spurious vectors. For example, where a single dark pixel occurred on the side of an otherwise straight edge it would be guaranteed that the single pixel width link across this would be made in the early stages of the process. A more complex heuristic was devised which combine the length of a link with its distance from a closed or bifurcating path around the adjacent outline. More work is needed to achieve an optimum heuristic, but the results are not strongly sensitive to this. The links are sorted on the basis of the heuristic and taken in turn as described above.

The outline representation may be seen as a set of directed vertical single pixel high crack, and a set of directed horizontal single pixel wide cracks. Arbitrarily the left side of a directed crack will be black, and the right side white. This means that outlines of holes are ordered clockwise, while main outlines go anticlockwise. Each such crack has one and only one matching mate that will be the closest one of the same orientation but opposite sense when measured across the dark region. Each of these matching pairs of edge is linked, forming a criss-cross grid over the entire area enclosed within the outline. The aim now is to eliminate many of these links, leaving only those that are believed to be perpendicular to the local stroke direction. A simple heuristic might be applied here. Short links are intuitively to be preferred to long ones. The links might be sorted in order of length, shortest first. Each shortest link could be taken in turn and all those that cross it removed from consideration. This process would continue down the sorted list until no links remained to be removed. Indeed the first implementation of the algorithm did exactly that. It was immediately realised that this led to small spurs and spurious vectors. For example, where a single dark pixel occurred on the side of an otherwise straight edge it would be guaranteed that the single pixel width link across this would be made in the early stages of the process. A more complex heuristic was devised which combine the length of a link with its distance from a closed or bifurcating path around the adjacent outline. More work is needed to achieve an optimum heuristic, but the results are not strongly sensitive to this. The links are sorted on the basis of the heuristic and taken in turn as described above. The result is shown in the figure below: The result is shown in the fig. 2 below:

Fig. 2. Special Node Points On the Outline

3.3   Stage 3: Generate Vectors for the Strokes and the Junctions

If the link at a node is traversed, and the outline followed backwards, crossing any other links with nodes at either end until the original point is reached, then the number of links crossed is termed the arity of the node. This is one for end points, two for the change in matching direction transitions, and four where two strokes cross. It is now straightforward to extract strokes from regions that are not junctions. The mid-points of links are followed, and nodes of arity two result in a simple interpolation between the two regions. These strokes are extrapolated to the true end of the stroke from a not of arity one. At junctions the appropriate links are matched together and multiple strokes pulled out to complete the vectorization. An unexpected benefit of the approach that proves extremely powerful is that it becomes possible to extract a stroke, but to repair the area where it crosses a junction. This allows text to be extracted despite it crossing bounding boxes or lines, leaving the other features intact. In editing an engineering drawing, a line can be extracted and all the features it crosses can be repaired, which offers a huge saving in time and effort in raster editing and greatly facilitates segmentation of the image. An example of the algorithm's results is shown below with the original raster image on the left, and the vectorized result on the right.

The relationship between the various classes is shown in the diagram below, which uses the UML notation of Grady et al [4]. A binary image can be represented without loss of information as a set of Outlines. Each Outline that represents a white to black transition is then transformed to a set of Strokes and Junctions, once more without loss of information. Vectors are polylines with thickness, and these are derived directly from the Strokes which represent a single pass of the stylus. The junction regions are interpolated, and may thus contain

Fig. 3. The Result of Making Links

from two to any number of strokes. In order to be able to rapidly derive vectors as they run along the Strokes, and then traverse Junctions, an index structure is used to enable this to be carried out without searching. This structure also incorporates a spatial index using a quadtree so that searching in a given neighborhood can be carried out rapidly. This is important in post-processing where it is necessary to identify line-types and the faces referred to by leader lines and so forth.

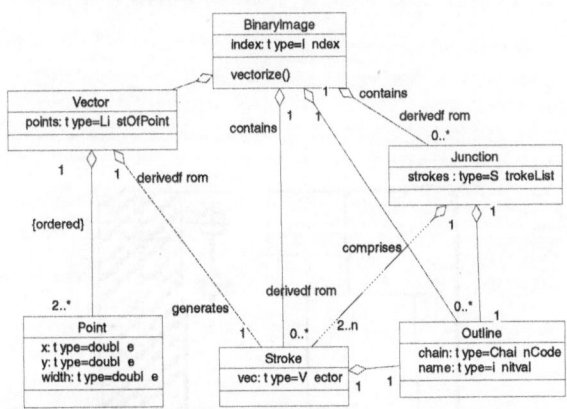

Fig. 4. UML Diagram Showing the Class Structure Used

The quality of the line-work produced from this algorithm has encouraged further processing. A constraint-based correction algorithm has been used to produce three accurate views (within a threshold) from a scanned orthographic projection. This has then been passed through out three-dimensional reconstruction algorithm to produce a surface model that can be displayed either as a wire frame or shaded perspective view. Either of these can be observed from any angle. The Algorithm has been used a the first stage of an automatic process from scanning of a paper image through vectorization, correction to 3D reconstruction is now viable at least for reasonably simple objects.

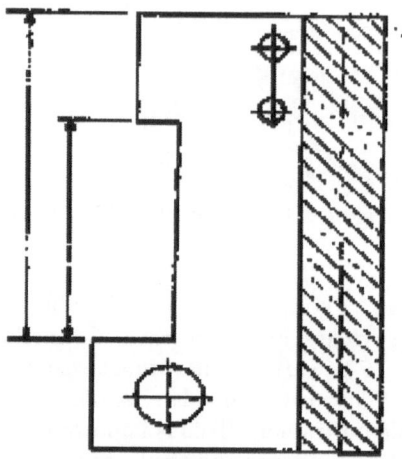

Fig. 5. The Original Image

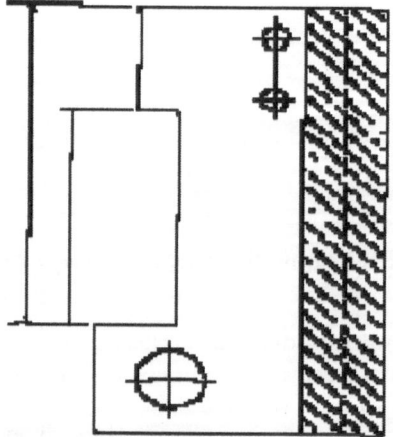

Fig. 6. The Vectorized Result

4   Conclusions

An really useful vectorization algorithm has been developed that supports many higher level processes in document processing from raster editing, to document understanding, cursive script recognition, and drawing recognition and reconstruction.

References

1. Dori, D., Liu, W.: Sparse Pixel Vectorization, An Algorithm and its Performance Evaluation. IEEE Transactions on Pattern Analysis and Machine Intelligence, Vol. 21 No **3** (1999) 202–215   19, 20
2. Dori, D.: Orthogonal Zig-Zag: An Algorithm for Vectorizing Engineering Drawings Compared with Hough Transform. Advances in Software Engineering, Vol. 28 No **1** (1997) 11–24   20
3. Elliman, D. G.: Document Recognition for Facsimile Data. Document Image Processing and Multimedia (DIPM'99), IEE Press London, March (1999)   20, 22
4. Booch, G., Jacobson, I., Rumbaugh, J.: The Unified Modelling Language Users Guide. Addison-Wesley Press, (1998)   24
5. Joseph, S. H., Pridmore, T. P.: Knowledge Directed Interpretation of Engineering Drawings. IEEE Transactions on Pattern Analysis and Machine Intelligence, Vol. 14 No **9** (1992) 202–215   20
6. Kasturi, R., Bow, S. T., El-Masri, W., Shah, J., Gattiker, J. R., Mokate, U. B.: A System for Interpretation of Line Drawings. IEEE Transactions on Pattern Analysis and Machine Intelligence, Vol. 12 No **10** (1990) 978-992
7. Lam, L., Lee, S., Suen, C. Y.: Thinning Methodologies - A Comprehensive Survey. IEEE Transactions on Pattern Analysis and Machine Intelligence, Vol. 14 No **9** (1992) 869–885   20

Processing of the Connected Shapes in Raster-to-Vector Conversion Process

Sébastien Adam[1,2] , Rémy Mullot[1], Jean-Marc Ogier[1], Claude Cariou[1],
Joël Gardes[2], and Yves Lecourtier[1]

[1] Laboratory PSI, University of Rouen
76 821 Mt St Aignan Cedex
Tél: (+33) 2 35 14 65 88   Fax: (+33) 2 35 14 66 18
{Sebastien.Adam,Remy.Mullot}@univ-rouen.fr
[2] CNET (BEL/OLI)
6 Avenue des Usines, BP 382, 90 000 Belfort
Tél: (+33) 3 84 54 42 54   Fax: (+33) 3 84 54 43
joel.gardes@cnet.francetelecom.fr

Abstract. We present in this paper a methodology dealing with raster to vector conversion for technical documents interpretation. The adopted approach considers the problem of information layer separation. The retained strategy consists in applying a sequence of different specialists the aim of which is to process a particular problem. Even if many commercial systems exist, this kind of problem constitutes a real difficulty which is not completely solved. The obtained results are evaluated and discussed in the context of French Telephonic Network Documents Interpretation.

1   Introduction

Since the two last decades, processing of engineering documents have been extensively investigated. This is essentially due to the fact that, in order to optimize companies memory management, industrial sector would be very interested by a tool allowing to convert paper documents into a digital format.

In this kind of context, the French telephonic operator France Telecom has launched a project called N.A.T.A.L.I, whose investigations aim at converting its paper documentation in an electronic format. More precisely, this study deal with its 2.475.000 telephone itinerary maps (see Fig. 1). This paper proposes a methodology that consists in converting the graphic parts of map's images from a Raster to a Vector format. In the field of engineering documents vectorisation, an analysis of the bibliography shows that algorithms whose aim is to convert a connected component to vectors seem to be mature[1]. One can thus cite Hough Transform [2], Radon Transform [3], skeletonisation [4] followed by a polygonal approximation[5], line following [6] ...All these existing methods do not work perfectly, but many of them work correctly and are sufficient if their results are well used by higher level interpretation. Nevertheless, in the literature, we also observe that only a few methods

Atul K. Chhabra and D. Dori (Eds.): GREC'99, LNCS 1941, pp. 28-35, 2000.

are able to process correctly the problem of detection/recognition of characters and symbols overlapping graphics. These « trouble maker » entities are problematic for two main reasons.

Fig. 1. A portion of a map including different layers

At first, they are considered as graphic parts of the document, what provides inconsistencies in the network interpretation. Moreover, strings reconstruction, which constitutes an important step in the document analysis device since network and symbols are always semantically associated to a string, will be disturbed by a missing character. Fig. 3 shows an example of a vectorisation result which illustrates this problem : the pointed "L" will be considered as a part of a linear object and will miss in the string "L2T"). Consequently, we considered this problem by taking into account different "points of view" of our interpretation device through the use of four « specialists ». In this communication, we present the methodology and the results of each of these specialists

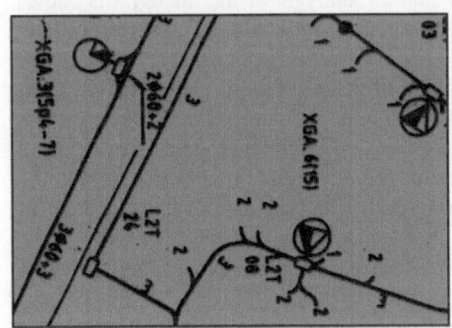

Fig. 2. Itinerary image example   **Fig. 3.** Converted Image

2   Segmentation Specialist

As one can see on the Fig. 1, France Telecom itinerary documents are composed of three overlaying layers, respectively corresponding to the cadaster, the network and the background. In this context, the first specialist that we use to separate characters and symbols from other layers is a segmentation tool that takes place at the beginning of the interpretation device. The goal of this operator is to segment, from the original acquired Grey-Scale image, the information of telephone network infrastructure in different layers : cadastral layer, background, network layer

Each of these layers is quite well identifiable on the global histogram of the image. Indeed, one can distinguish three main modes that have to be threshold, in order to separate the different layers (mode 0 : central mode, which corresponds to the cadastral layer – mode 1 : mode corresponding to the network layer, and mode 2 corresponding to the background layer, see Fig. 4).

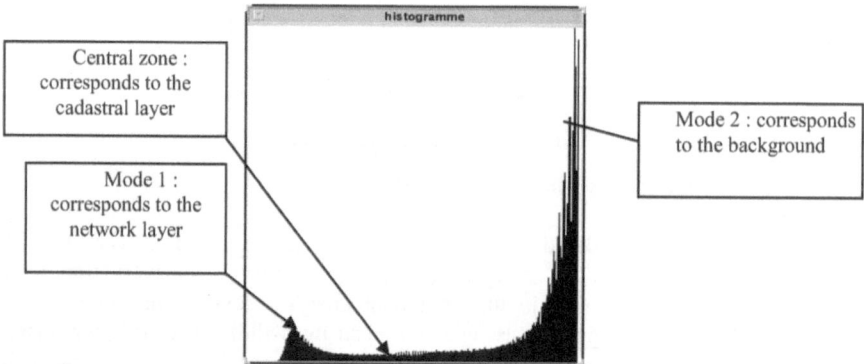

Fig. 4. Global histogram illustrating the different layers

In order to perform this operation, classical operators are placed within a segmentation strategy allowing to extract this information by refining progressively the thresholds proposed by different methods such as Otsu's [7] and Kittler's methods [8]. Indeed, a synthesis of the bibliography and an analysis of the histograms shows that these methods are the most adapted, notably in terms of integration and processing time.

Nevertheless, the results of the implementation of these methods show that a global thresholding technique does not allow to discriminate efficiently the different layers without noising them. In order to optimize the thresholding technique as a function of the context, our proposal consists in implementing a strategy allowing to compute the optimal threshold within successive and progressive stages, and as consequence to find the best resulting layers.

The strategy we applied for the extraction of the network is performed through three stages :

Phase 1 : this phase consists in classifying each pixel of the image by using the thresholds computed by the OTSU's technique. At the issue of this processing, pixels are labeled as a function of their class (network, cadaster or background) which is considered as hypothetical. Some overlapping exist between the central zone class of and the ones associated with the network and the background.

Phase 2 : The second phase integrates topologic criteria to refine the classification obtained at the end of the preceding stage. Indeed, the mode 2 can also contain elements belonging to the network. These elements represent mainly transitions between the network components and the cadaster or background ones. As a consequence, an association of the pixels of this central mode class is performed by using a proximity criterion. The whole of these processing provides a class corresponding to the network, for which some components are connected.

Phase 3 : Then, the class issuing from the previous stage is considered as a mask on which an analysis of the gray levels is going to be performed. This analysis allows to refine values of thresholds, by using Kittler thresholding technique.

As a conclusion, one could say that this segmentation specialist relies on an optimized combination of different thresholding techniques (Otsu's and Kittler's one), in order to adapt the thresholds as a function of the information that is to be extracted.

This specialist permits to obtain a good separation rate between network and entities such as characters and symbols since less than 2 % of them stand on a bad layer. On table 1, one can see a comparison between our technique and classical operators directly applied on the Grey-Scale image

Table 1. Results obtained by the segmentation specialist

Characters	KITTLER	OTSU	OUR STRATEGY
Correctly extracted	75 %	93,6 %	98,6 %
Network connected	19,6 %	6,4 %	1,4 %
Background associated	5,4 %	0 %	0 %

Nevertheless, these forgotten characters, as well as some intentionally connected symbols, constitute a major problem for the following interpretation process.

3   Symbol Specialist

In order to make easier the vectorisation step and, as a consequence, the semantic reconstruction of the document, we use a second specialist the aim of which is to extract France Telecom symbols (see Fig. 2). By observing itinerary plans, one can note that the symbols are always characterized by the presence of occlusions (loops).

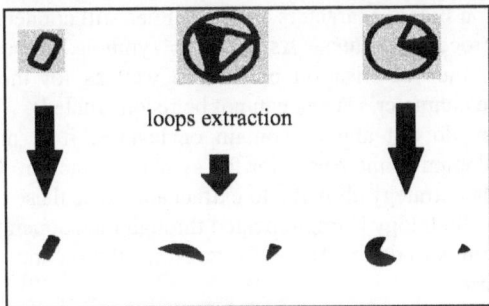

Fig. 5. Extraction of loops for the recognition of symbols

Consequently, we used this particularity to detect and recognize symbols. Our methodology is based on a hypotheses « emission / validation » principle. Indeed, since our document model is very hierarchical, definitive decisions can not be taken until the whole document has not been entirely semantically reconstructed.

Concerning these symbols, hypotheses are emitted through the detection of occlusions (Fig. 5). Then, by calculating some features on theses outlines (such as area, length of the perimeter, number of segments obtained by a polygonal approximation of the contours ...), a decision tree using Min/Max. learned values permits to validate or reject the emitted hypotheses.

On the just higher abstraction level, symbols including several occlusions are reconstructed through an analysis of proximity. Nevertheless, it is important to note that hypotheses are not definitively validated since they have not been semantically linked to a string.

Obtained results are very encouraging since more than 99 % of the symbols (corresponding to the France Telecom equipment called "Concentration Point (PC)") are detected and well recognized. This good detection rate permits to erase the majority of the connected symbols as one can see on Fig. 6 and Fig 7.

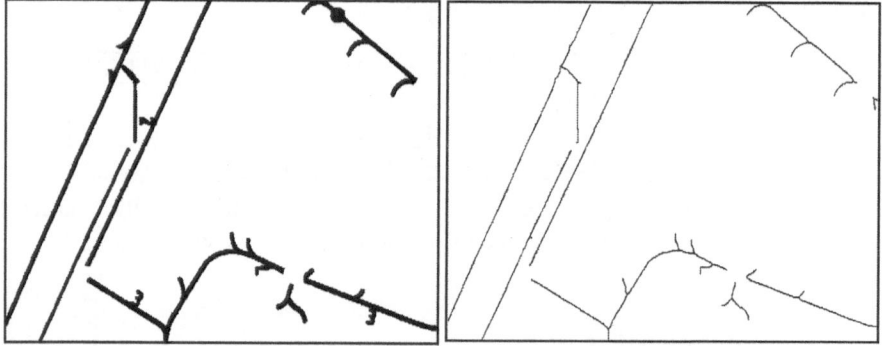

Fig. 6. Results of the symbols detection   **Fig. 7.** Vectorisation after symbols deleting

4   Connected Characters Specialists

As one can see on Fig. 6, characters are sometimes still connected to the network after the previous processing steps. As well as symbols, these characters are really problematic for the vectorisation process as well as for the reconstruction of the document (since character's string can not be reconstructed).

Since characters do not always contain occlusions, it is not possible to use the methodology adopted in the part 3 for the symbol extraction. Consequently, we have developed another strategy allowing to extract and erase these entities.

This original methodology is implemented through the cooperation of two specialists ; the first one permits to detect Area Of Interest for the second one which validates the emitted hypotheses.

4.1   «Area Of Interest» Specialist

As well as the Symbol Specialist, this first tool is based on a hypotheses « emission / validation » strategy. The emission is perfomed through a pre-vectorisation step based on a skeletonisation algorithm [9] followed by a polygonal approximation [5]. Then, a decision tree, based on primitives such as thickness mean, thickness homogeneity and length are used to validate these hypotheses. Thereby, for example, segments whose length and thickness are out from a learned interval, are rejected from the network layer and become hypotheses for the connected characters or symbols layer.

This methodology permits to detect more than 90 % of the overlapping characters but also creates an important false detection rate. That's why a second specialist is used to detect good hypotheses in this large list.

4.2   OCR Specialist

This last specialist has to detect and recognize characters in A.O.I. in order to validate hypotheses emitted by the "AOI specialist". This operation is performed thanks to the use the Fourier Mellin Transform [10] in a filtering mode [11]. It consists in sliding 33 prototype filters $h_{p,q}(.,.)$ within the A.O.I. and in observing if the filter provides a pre-specified response (a decision method taking into account confidence and spatial criterions is used). As it is impossible to develop here the whole methodology adopted (including theoretical considerations about the FMT) , we suggest the readers to refer to [11] in order to have a precise point of view about it. Nevertheless, we give on fig. 8 a synoptic of the used algorithm, the filter bank being calculated following Eq. 1. ('l' and 'k' are the coordinates of the filter, 'p' and 'q' the parameters of the FMT.

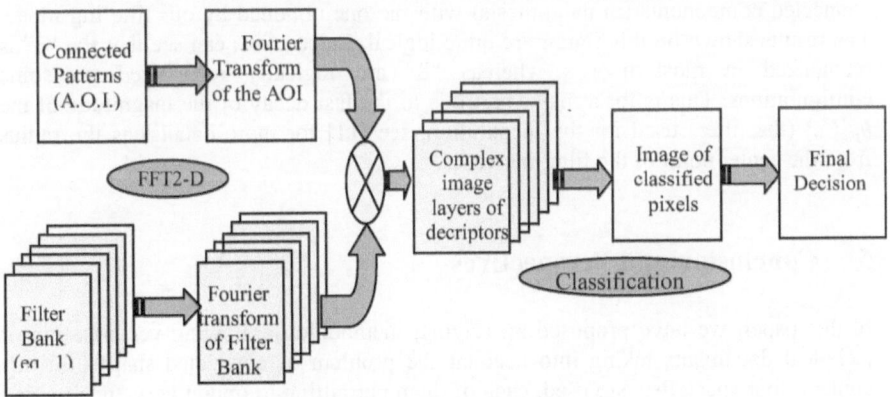

Fig. 8. Synoptic of the filtering mode

$$h_{p,q}(k,l) = \frac{\exp\left\{-i\left[\frac{p}{2}\ln(k^2+l^2)+q\tan^{-1}\left(\frac{l}{k}\right)\right]\right\}}{(k^2+l^2)^{1-\sigma_0/2}} \tag{1}$$

Results obtained with this tool are satisfying in regard with recognition rate which reaches 90 % (on a small but representative France Telecom database). An objective comparison with others approaches is difficult because, as far as we know, only a few techniques presented in the literature are able to detect / classify connected components. The Figure. 9 illustrates the results obtained by this specialist on synthetic images.

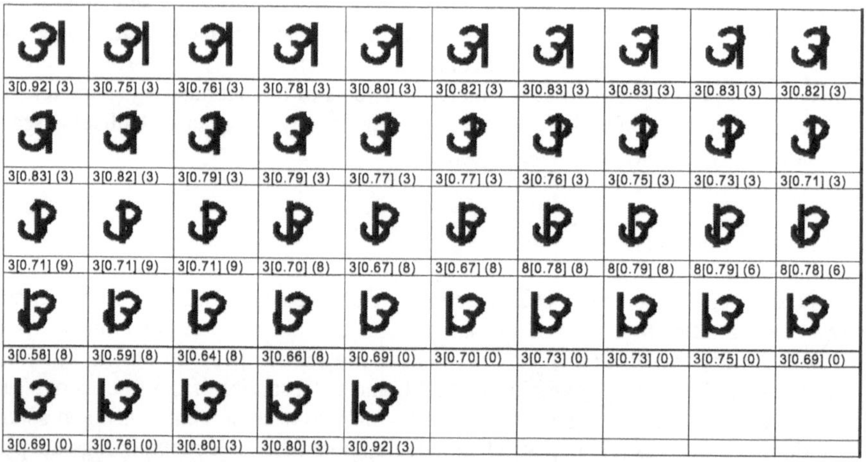

3[0.92] (3)	3[0.75] (3)	3[0.76] (3)	3[0.78] (3)	3[0.80] (3)	3[0.82] (3)	3[0.83] (3)	3[0.83] (3)	3[0.83] (3)	3[0.82] (3)
3[0.83] (3)	3[0.82] (3)	3[0.79] (3)	3[0.79] (3)	3[0.77] (3)	3[0.77] (3)	3[0.76] (3)	3[0.75] (3)	3[0.73] (3)	3[0.71] (3)
3[0.71] (9)	3[0.71] (9)	3[0.71] (9)	3[0.70] (8)	3[0.67] (8)	3[0.67] (8)	8[0.78] (8)	8[0.79] (8)	8[0.79] (6)	8[0.78] (6)
3[0.58] (8)	3[0.59] (8)	3[0.64] (8)	3[0.66] (8)	3[0.69] (0)	3[0.70] (0)	3[0.73] (0)	3[0.73] (0)	3[0.75] (0)	3[0.69] (0)
3[0.69] (0)	3[0.76] (0)	3[0.80] (0)	3[0.80] (3)	3[0.92] (3)					

Fig. 10. Illustration of OCR specialist results

In this table we compare the result given by a classical approach which consists in extracting a set of Fourier Mellin descriptors from the center of gravity of the connected components (in parenthesis) with the one obtained by our filtering mode. The results shown on this figure are quite logical. Indeed, one can see that the "3" is recognized in most images whereas "8" are logically recognized on some configurations. This is for a major part due to the fast decay of the magnitude of the $h_{p,q}(.,.)$ (the filters used for the recognition, see [11] for more details) as the radius from the center point of the filter increases.

5   Conclusion and Perspectives

In this paper, we have proposed an original methodology allowing vectorisation of technical documents taking into account the problem of connected shapes. In this context, four specialists are used, each of them permitting to obtain very encouraging results in terms of overlapping entities suppression. Indeed, on a small but representative France Telecom Database, the adopted approach permits to detect more than 90 % of connected symbols and characters.

The perspectives of this work are numerous and concern different points such as the integration of contextual information in order to obtain a robust interpretation device. For example, the use of a grammar of strings seems to be promising in order to have a new mechanisms to detect "AOI" for the OCR specialist. Another promising perspective for the final OCR validation is the use of the orientation estimation.

References

1.   K. Tombre, Analysis of Engineering Drawings : State of the Art and Challenges. Proceedings of GREC'1997.
2.   H. Maitre, Un panorama de la transformation de Hough, Traitement du Signal (TS), Vol.2, N°4, 1975.
3.   S. R. Deans, Hough Transform from the Radon transform, IEEE Transaction on Pattern Analysis and Machine Intelligence (PAMI), Vol. 3, N°2, 1981.
4.   L. Lam, S.-W. Lee et C. Y. Suen. Thinning Methodologies - A Comprehensive Survey, IEEE Transaction on PAMI, 14(9) :869-885, 1992.
5.   T .Pavlidis, Algorithm for graphics and Image Processing, Computer Science Press, 1982.
6.   C. C. Han and K. C. Fan, Skeleton generation of engineering drawings via contour matching, Pattern Recognition, vol. 27, 261-275, 1994.
7.   N. Otsu, A threshold selection method from grey level histogram, SMC, 1, 62-66, 1979.
8.   J. Kittler, J. Illingworth, Minimum error thresholding, Pattern Recognition, 19, 41-47, 1986.
9.   G. Sanniti di Baja, Well_shape, Stable and Reversible Skeletons from the (3-4)-Distance Transform, Journal of visual communication and image representation, Vol. 5, 107-115, 1994.
10.   G. Ravichandran, M. Trivedi, Circular-Mellin Features for Texture Segmentation, IEEE Trans. on Image Processing, 1995.
11.   S. Adam , J. M. Ogier , C. Cariou, R. Mullot, J. Gardes, Y. Lecourtier, Multi-Scaled and Multi Oriented Character Recognition : An Original Strategy, in Proc. IAPR-ICDAR'99, International Conference on Document Analysis and Recognition, Bangalore, India, September 1999.

Part II

Maps and Geographic Documents

Recognition in Maps and Geographic Documents: Features and Approach

Toyohide Watanabe

Department of Information Engineering,
Graduate School of Engineering, Nagoya University
Furo-cho, Chikusa-ku, Nagoya 464-8603, Japan
watanabe@nuie.nagoya-u.ac.jp

Abstract. The objective in the recognition of maps and geographic documents is to extract the topological configuration among composite elements (or objects) or to distinguish the constructive relationships among related composite elements as well as to recognize composite elements individually. Of course, the maps and geographic documents reflect the structural features mapped deformedly from the corresponding geographic configuration in the real world. Some composite elements are often overlayed and intersected mutually. This drawing feature makes it difficult to accomplish the recognition objective smartly.

In this paper, we discuss the application-dependent features, approaches and paradigms in the recognition of maps and geographic documents. In particular, we intend to make the recognition framework of maps and geographic documents clear so as to be distinguished characteristically for graphics recognition or drawings interpretation with respect to the above discussion viewpoints.

1 Introduction

The recognition of maps and geographic documents is one of graphics recognition or drawings interpretation [1,2,3,4] and has been attacked as one of interesting and difficult subjects with a view to extracting map composite elements automatically with respect to the composition of resource data for the construction of GIS (Geographic Information System)[5,6]. Although many trial researches or developments have been done over 20 years, the current techniques are not sufficiently applied to the generally usable products as powerful tools. The difficulty is dependent on the fact that individual composite elements and their relationships are not well defined so that computers could analyze them effectually because some composite elements are overlayed and intersected mutually. In the recognition of maps and geographic documents, the main subject focused on the extraction of topological configuration of roads[7,8], the extraction of character strings which are attached with individual map composite elements and regional relationships among them[9,10,11], and the distinguishment of symbolized landmarks such as buildings, characteristic places, etc. In these subjects, the general-purpose methods/approaches, which are successfully applicable to all existing maps or

Atul K. Chhabra and D. Dori (Eds.): GREC'99, LNCS 1941, pp. 39–49, 2000.
© Springer-Verlag Berlin Heidelberg 2000

geographic documents, have never been developed/proposed. This is because the drawing rules, specification means of notations, objectives of map composition and so on are different in accordance with individual kinds of maps and geographic documents. At least, the traditionally proposed methods/approaches are dependent on the features of recognition objects, and were in many cases developed under the recognition-object-dependent framework. Of course, in developing the recognition-object-dependent system, the heuristic knowledge is very useful to make the interpretation process flexible/adaptable.

In this paper, we address the recognition subjects in maps and geographic documents, concerning the recognition views, the recognition objectives, the approaches and the related topics[12]. First, we discuss the recognition complexity in the graphics recognition or drawings interpretation: our motivation is to make the difficulty for recognition of maps and geographic documents clear with respect to some criterion. In this case, we introduce the individuality of composite elements and correspondence among composite elements as the coordinate axes. Second, we address the recognition contents for accomplishing application-specific goals successfully. Namely, in case of extracting some information from drawings the accuracy for objects or interrelated relationships to be analytically recognized is not always required exactly according to the application-dependent objectives. This is because maps and geographic documents do not inherently keep consistent correspondence for everything in the real world by 1-to-1 relation or through well spatial/geometric representation. Additionally, the maps and geographic documents are tremendously deformed in comparison with our geographic configuration. Third, we describe the recognition means to extract map composite elements: top-down, bottom-up and so on. Although these two different means are commonly well known, the frameworks are discussed as the recognition approaches. Finally, we arrange interesting paradigms which are currently expanded: agent-based recognition, parallel recognition and so on.

2   Recognition View

Generally, in case of object recognition it is important to extract the geometric features of individual composite elements correctly and distinguish the constructive relationships among related composite elements interpretatively, using some heuristic knowledge about representation means, composition rules, characteristics of drawings, etc. In order to make the recognition complexity clear, it is effective to classify various kinds of drawings into some classes in accordance with the constructive or observable features.

1) Drawings in which individual composite elements are strictly predefined. The constructive relationships among composite elements may be specified by the description rules. These main composite elements are line segments, symbols (which are composed of several line segments) and character strings, and the configuration is very simple because composite elements are individually drawn.
   ex.) flow charts, block diagrams, etc.

2) Drawings in which composite elements and their logical relationships are almost defined under the basic composition means. The physical neighboring relationships among composite elements are almost systematically structured, though the composite elements are usually overlayed or intersected.

    2-1) The composite elements are overlayed.

        ex.) musics, etc.

    2-2) The composite elements are intersected.

        ex.) business graphs, etc.

3) Drawings in which composite elements are not always distinguished explicitly because some fragments of composite elements may be shared mutually. The objects are hierarchically or stepwisely organized as complex objects.

    3-1) The total drawings are stepwisely organized as a collection of symbolized objects.

        ex.) logic/electronic/electric-circuits diagrams, etc.

    3-2) The total drawings are constructively organized as representations integrated with composite elements.

        ex.) floor plans, etc.

    3-3) The total drawings are hierarchically organized as complex objects.

        ex.) mechanical-parts diagrams, etc.

4) Drawings in which physical shapes of composite elements are not only deformed under spatial relationships but also the directions and sizes are different individually even if symbolized representations were the same. The composite elements are overlayed and intersected mutually.

    ex.) maps, etc.

5) Drawings in which composite elements are not clearly illustrated because of hand-writing. The objects are strongly deformed and the illustrations of individual composite elements are meaningfully interpreted by not direct/local shapes but indirect/global features.

    ex.) comics, etc.

Figure 1 categorizes various kinds of drawings with respect to the relationships for both individuality of composite elements and correspondence among related composite elements. Also, depending on whether each drawing is mapped from three dimensional objects or originated in three dimensional space, these drawings are distributed. If the drawings are logical representation means, the notational features of composite elements and the composition rules among composite elements are regulated explicitly, as drawings of 2D objects. Otherwise, the notational drawing means are dependent on inherently associated features of composite elements and their relationships. Generally, the higher two-axes values for drawings are, the easier it is to specify the models for drawings.

In Figure 1, maps are located into the right-upper side, in which the individuality and correspondence are relatively lower than those in the other drawings. The lower the individuality and correspondence are, the more difficult the recognition of individual composite elements (or objects as single recognition entities) becomes. Of course, several classes of drawings illustrated in Figure 1 may be

correspondence among
composite elements

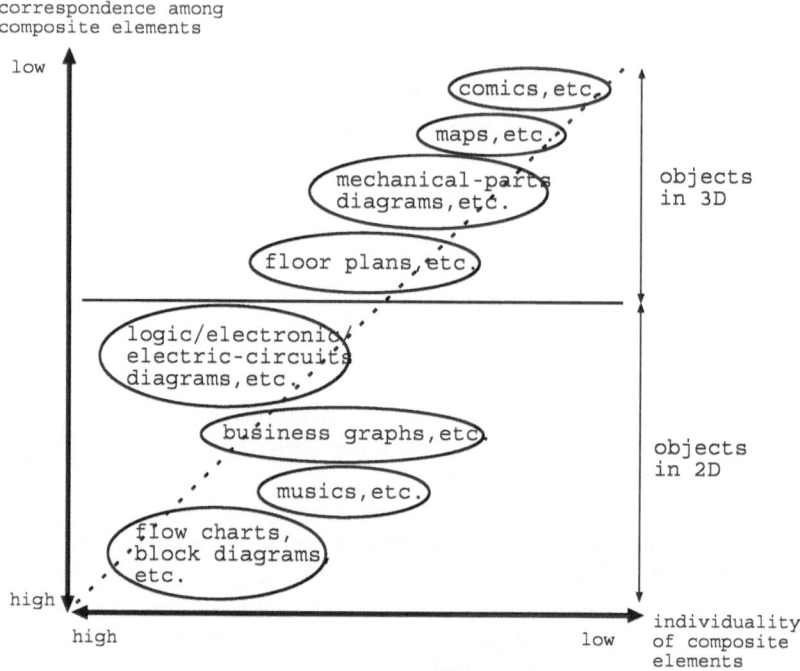

Fig. 1. Feature of drawings

not always classified clearly, as shown in Figure 1. The difficulty of recognition depends on whether the drawings are correspondingly mapped from three dimensional constructs or originated inherently at three dimensional objects. Additionally, it makes the recognition difficult because individual composite elements in case of maps and geographic documents are not well defined and also are overlayed/intersected mutually.

3 Recognition Objective

The objective for recognition may be variously determined, depending on what the final goals of applications are. For example, it is important to extract the topological structures of main roads from the original map images in case that the objective is to find/depict the route map as a path from current position to the goal position for strangers. In this case, it is not always necessary to extract all information exactly and it is sufficient to follow up only information which can guide strangers correctly. Thus, the recognition subject is very strongly dependent on the applications. Here, we classify the application-dependent recognition objectives into four types: extraction (identification), re-generation (representation), interpretation (filtering) and retrieval (filing). Figure 2 shows the recognition objectives on the categorized domains.

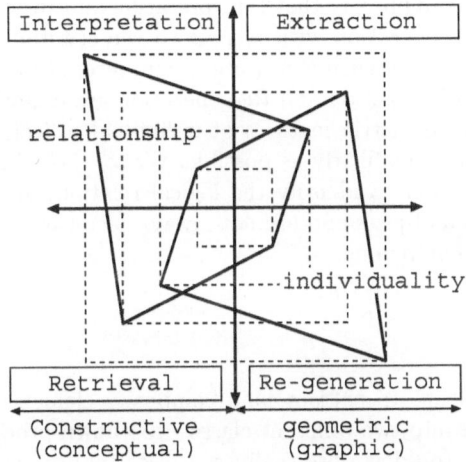

Fig. 2. Recognition objectives on categorized domains

1) Extraction: In many pattern recognition subjects the final goal is to distinguish individual objects completely. In particular, the extraction of characters or map composite elements (map symbols) in map images is typical. Generally, it is very difficult to extract all meaningful objects completely.

2) Re-generation: In case that objects or composite elements are re-organized from the original drawings, the geometric data of composite elements is important. For example, in the application for computer graphics, the original and geometric structures of objects to be manipulated independently are important recognition targets. The conversion of well-illustrations from hand-writings and hand-drawings or generation of CAD resource data from plans/diagrams is typical.

3) Interpretation: The information extraction from drawings aims to explain the content by other modal means or convert the characteristics of depicted images as another representation. For example, the understanding of comics is typical. In map recognition subject, this objective is not always applicable. This recognition objective is not to identify all objects or relationships among all objects exactly, but to distinguish the difference among particular objects or characteristic illustrations explicitly.

4) Retrieval: This objective depends on the requirements of map image database construction, and the recognition subject must distinguish individual characteristics under the attributes/objects. In many current techniques for construction of image databases, the recognition viewpoint focuses on the differences among individual images, but does not concentrate to identify objects or interpret the contents. In such a viewpoint, the recognition objective may be not dependent on the distinguishment of objects or relationships.

In Figure 2, we can observe that Interpretation and Retrieval are taken from Extraction and Re-generation with respect to the criterion of constructive (or conceptual) recognition or geometric (or graphic) recognition. Namely, the recognition objectives in Extraction and Re-generation are important to identify the physical shapes or geometric features of individual objects and are necessary to distinguish them as explicitly as possible. While, those in Interpretation and Retrieval are important to identify the logical relationships or conceptual features among focused objects and are not always necessary to distinguish clearly individual objects one by one.

4 Approach

The recognition means to extract map composite elements automatically are mainly categorized into two different classes: top-down processing and bottom-up processing. The top-down processing is successful in case that the objects or composite elements to be recognized can be well organized. In many cases, the objects or composite elements in the map recognition are not clearly specified with respect to the positions, sizes, shapes, directions, etc. Namely, though in the top-down processing the most important viewpoint is to define the target model or specify the knowledge information about features of targets declaratively, this requirement is not easy in map recognition subject. Thus, many methods which have been developed until today are based on the bottom-up processing. In the bottom-up processing various kinds of image/pattern processing routines are applied stepwise under constraint information or threshold values, attended with individual processings. Therefore, the more correctly the threshold values or constraint information are reflected from the experiments or heuristics the higher the recognition ratio becomes. Namely, the application range in the bottom-up processing is generally narrow if the constraint information or threshold values are assigned rigidly in accordance with the particular application-dependent samples in order to make the recognition ratio high.

In the map recognition, it is not easy to define the map model because various map composite elements are mutually overlayed or intersected[13]. For example, the character strings such as building names, street names, place names and so on are always overlayed on map picture elements or map symbols. This is because maps are originated inherently in three dimensional representation world and the symbols or character strings are attached to the projected illustration additionally.

In [14], the hybrid processing was proposed to extract road information from urban map images. In this case, the road information, which was firstly extracted in the bottom-up processing, is looked upon as a kind of road model in the next phase. Namely, the recognition process is divided into the road-network composition phase, based on the bottom-up processing, and the road-network refinement phase, based on the top-down processing. Of course, the road-network, which is initially constructed in the road-network composition phase and manipulated as the road model, is incomplete representation for the corresponding road configuration. When this incomplete representation should be regarded as the model, it is important how to construct: one is that the representation contains much information as possible even if it had erroneous information; and another is that the representation includes only correct information as possible. In [14], the viewpoint that the incomplete representation should not contain errors as possible was selected. Of course, even the road model which was constructed under such a strategy may contain erroneous information or mis-captured information. In the road-network refinement phase, the task is to resolve such erroneous structure or remedy inferior structure by interpreting the road-network with heuristic knowledge about road configuration.

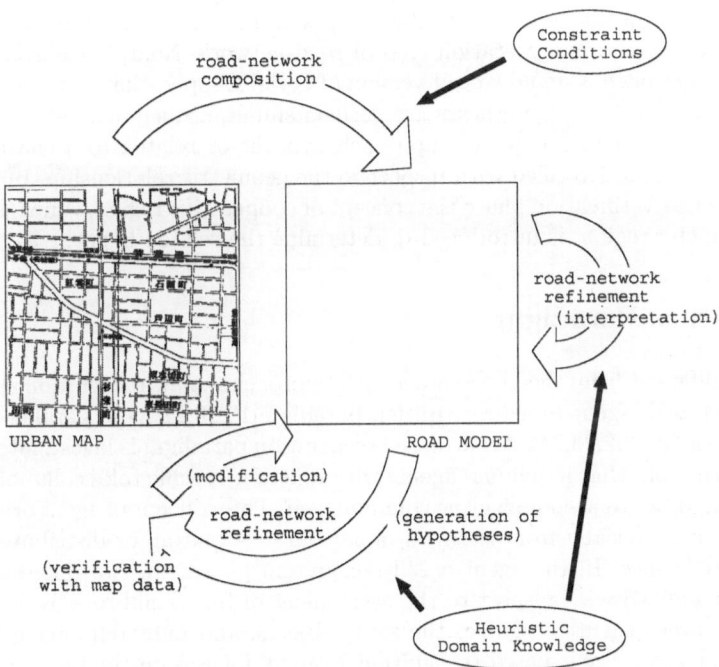

Fig. 3. Conceptual framework of road recognition

Moreover, the advanced approaches are proposed. When the above approach is called Combination approach, Serial Cooperation approach[15], Integration approach[16,17], Concurrent Cooperation approach[18] and so on were developed. In Serial Cooperation approach, the road-network refinement phase is composed of top-down processing and bottom-up processing, in which is different from Combination approach. Namely, the road-network refinement phase is furthermore divided into four steps: interpretation of road-network, generation of hypotheses, verification with map data, and modification of road-network. The interpretation of road-network and generation of hypotheses are executed in the top-down processing, while the verification with map data is done in the bottom-up processing. These four steps are repeated until the inferable facts or contradictory facts cannot newly be found out in the stepwisely refined road-network. This road-network refinement strategy is based on the generation/verification mechanism of hypotheses. Here, the hypotheses are defined as inferable or contradictory facts. Figure 3 shows such a frame work conceptually.

Integration approach makes use of information about other map composite elements in the road-network refinement phase, in addition to the framework of Serial Cooperation approach. For example, the information about character regions is useful because characters are usually overlayed on roads. In this case, the extraction procedure of character regions identifies character regions or similar candidate areas in advance. After then, the information about extracted character regions is usable in the verification step with map data under the hypotheses, generated by the interpretation step of road-network. Next, Concurrent Cooperation approach is an advanced version of Serial Cooperation approach. In this case, several related hypotheses are verified simultaneously among interrelated candidates as if in Integration approach hypotheses related to a character region were at once verified with respect to the geometric relationship. In order to achieve this verification phase the concept of cooperative region, which is similar to character region, is introduced to determine the related hypotheses.

5   Other Paradigm

Being different from the above processing approaches, new recognition strategies are proposed: agent-based recognition paradigm[19,20,21], and parallel recognition paradigm[22,23,24]. Agent-based recognition paradigm is investigated under the framework that individual agents with function-specific roles collaborate mutually in order to accomplish the common goal. This concept of agent orientation was derived initially from the field of software computing or distributed artificial intelligence. In the agent-based recognition paradigm, two different methods are applied with respect to the assignment of functional roles to individual agents: every agent recognizes the same objects, and individual agents do different objects. Agent-based recognition strategy focuses on the improvement of recognition ratio because autonomous agents can exchange mutually the intermediate or final processing results step by step if necessary, and can proceed their processing tasks incrementally by using the exchanged information.

On the other hand, the parallel recognition is useful to make the processing performance high on parallel computers or PC-cluster/WS-cluster environments. Although two parallelization methods such as data parallelization and function parallelization are applicable in general, in many cases the data parallelization method was used. This is because in image-processing/pattern-recognition procedure the same processings or processing modules to be inherently repeated are applicable to individual local image areas partially.

These paradigms are currently in experimental stage, and are not always applied sufficiently to the practical usages. These paradigms suggest effectively the new directions for architectural system configuration, as illustrated in Figure 4 [25].

6 Conclusion

In this paper, we addressed some topics, attended with the recognition of maps and geographic documents, from the viewpoints of recognition view, recognition objective, approach and so on. In particular, we discussed instinctively the recognition complexity in maps and geographic documents in comparison with other graphics or drawings, and proposed that the complexity may be defined by means of two features: individuality of composite elements (or objects), and correspondence among composite elements. Also, we discussed that the recognition objectives are dependent on the application ranges, and the high recognition ratio of targets to be distinguished is not always required as it is so sufficient that particular objects/relationships or their characteristic elements can be found. In such a discussion, we arrange the recognition objective in terms of extraction (identification), re-generation (representation), interpretation (filtering) and retrieval (filing). Moreover, we described the approaches and paradigms with a view to addressing the practical investigation.

References

1. L.O'Gorman, R.Kasturi: Document Image Analysis Systems. IEEE Computer. **7-25** (1992) 5-8   39
2. L.O'Gorman, R.Kasturi: Document Image Analysis. IEEE Computer Society Press (1995)   39
3. R.Kasturi, K.Tombre(eds.): Graphics Recognition : Methods and Applications. Lecture Notes in Computer Science. **1072** (1996)   39
4. K.Tombre, A. K.Chhabra(eds.): Graphics Recognition : Algorithm and Systems. Lecture Notes in Computer Science. **1389** (1998)   39
5. K.Tombre: Technical Drawing Recognition and Understanding: From Pixels to Semantics. Proc. of MVA'92. (1992) 393-402   39
6. G.Maderlechner, H.Mayer: Conversion of High Level Information Scanned Maps into Geographic Information Systems. Proc. of ICDAR'95. **1** (1995) 253-256   39
7. M.Ilg, R.Dgniewicq: Knowledge-based Interpretation of Road Maps, Based on Symmetrical Skeltons. Proc. of MVA'90. (1990) 161-164   39
8. W.Kim, T.Furukawa, Y.Hirai, R.Tokunaga: Extraction and Recognition of Road Segments by Spatial Filters. Proc. of MVA'92.(1992) 515-518   39
9. C.Nakajima, T.Yazawa: Automatic Recognition of Facility Drawings and Street Maps Utilizing the Facility Management Database. Proc. of ICDAR'95. **2** (1995) 617-622   39
10. A.Nakamura, O.Shiku, M.Anegawa, C.Nakamura, H.Kuroda: A Method for Recognizing Character Strings from Maps Using Linguistic Knowledge. Proc. of ICDAR'95. **2** (1995) 561-564   39
11. M. P.Deseilligny, H. L.Men, G.Stamon: Characters String Recognition on Maps, a Method for High Level Recognition. Proc. of ICDAR'95. **1** (1995) 249-252   39

12. T.Watanabe: Model-driven Recognition in Drawing Interpretation. Proc. of SCI/ISAS'99. **6** (1999) 280-287   40

13. T.Watanabe: Model-based Approaches for Extracting Road Information from Urban Maps. Proc. of CISST'97. (1997) 450-454   44

14. T.Hayakawa, T.Watanabe, Y.Yoshida, K.Kawaguchi: Recognition of Roads in an Urban Map by Using the Topological Road-network. Proc. of MVA'90. (1990) 280-287   44, 45

15. T.Watanabe, T.Hayakawa, N.Sugie: A Cooperative Integration Approach of Bottom-up and Top-down Methods for Road Extraction of Urban Maps. Proc. of ICARCV'92. (1992) 61-65   45

16. M.Nishijima, T.Watanabe: An Automatic Extraction Approach of Road Information on the Basis of Recognition of Character Regions. Proc. of ICSC'95. (1995) 173-180   45

17. M.Nishijima, T.Watanabe: An Automatic Extraction of Road Information on the Basis of Cooperative Hypotheses Interpretation. Proc. of MVA'9.6 (1996) 147-150   45

18. M.Nishijima, T.Watanabe: A Cooperative Inference Mechanism for Extracting Road Information Automatically. Proc. of ACCV'98. **2** (1998) 217-224   45

19. K.Gyohten, T.Sumiya, N.Babaguchi, K.Kakusho, T.Kitahashi: Extracting Characters and Character Lines in Multi-agent Scheme. Proc. of ICDAR'95. **1** (1995) 305-308   46

20. S.Shimada, Y.Takahara, H.Suenaga, K.Tomita: Paralleled Automatic Recognition of Maps and Drawings for Constructing Electric Power Distribution Databases. Proc. of ICDAR'93. (1993) 688-691   46

21. S.Shimada, K.Maruyama, A.Matsumoto, K.Hiraki: Agent-based Parallel Recognition Method of Contour Lines. Proc. of ICDAR'95. **1** (1995) 154-157   46

22. T.Oshitani, T.Watanabe: Parallel Map Recognition Based on Multi-layer Partitioned Blackboard Model. Proc. of ICPR'98. **2** (1998) 1604-1606   46

23. T.Oshitani, T.Watanabe: Parallel map Recognition by Pipeline Control. Proc. of ISHPC'99. (1999) 336-343   46

24. T.Oshitani, T.Watanabe: Parallel Map Recognition with Information Propagation Mechanism. Proc. of ICDAR'99. (1999) 717-720   46

25. T.Watanabe, T.Fukumura: Towards an Architectural Framework of Map Recognition. Proc. of ACCV'95. **3** (1995) 617-622   47

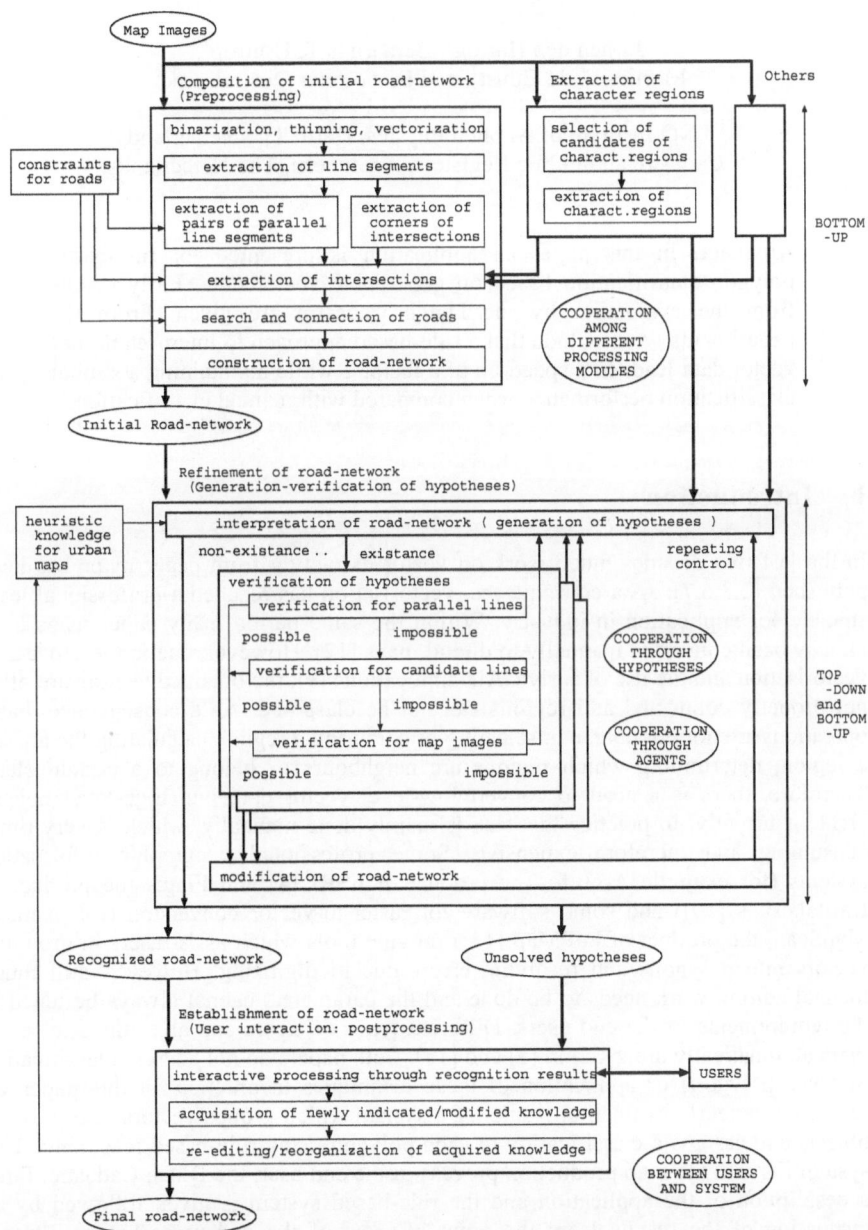

Fig. 4. Framework of map recognition

Interpretation of Geographic Vector-Data in Practice

Jurgen den Hartog[1], Bernardus T. Holtrop[1],
Marlies E. de Gunst[2], and Ernst-Peter Oosterbroek[2]

[1] TNO Institute of Applied Physics, Delft, The Netherlands
[2] Cadastre and Public Registers, Apeldoorn, The Netherlands

Abstract. In this paper an application is presented for rule-based polygon classification based on geographic vector data. Early results from the evaluation by the Dutch Cadastre are given. From the experiments we conclude that a rule-based approach to interpretation of vector data leads to a speed-up of a factor 2 while maintaining a similar classification performance when compared with manual classification.

1 Introduction

In the last two decades much work on vector extraction from paper maps has been published [2,3,6,7]. As a consequence, vectorisation has reached a professional level suitable for application in industry. Within the same period many paper maps have already been converted manually to digital maps [12]. However, due to the process of vectorisation and the use of early CAD-applications [9], the obtained vectors are often not properly connected and regions can not be classified. As a consequence, basic operations are not possible, e.g. selecting or colouring a region, calculating the area of a region, determining which regions are neighbours or belong to a certain class. Therefore, there is a need to convert low-level vector data into high-level objects [1,11]. Currently, in practice this task is mainly done manually, which is very time-consuming and therefore expensive. Some professional geographic information systems (for example ArcInfo, the product of ESRI [4] and Fingis the product of Karttakeskus [10]) and some software for raster-to-vector conversion (for example MapScan, the product of PoPMap [14]) provide tools which assist users in grouping vectors into polygons and resolving errors due to digitizing. However, still much manual editing work needs to be done and the parameters cannot always be tuned to the requirements of the end users. Different types of errors and algorithms to repair them automatically are given in [8] and [15]. Both papers do not address classification of these polygons or application of these techniques in practice. In this paper we report on the early evaluation results of a system which groups vectors into polygon objects and assigns a classification to each polygon using rule-based reasoning. This system fits into the map production process of the end user, the Dutch Cadastre. First, a description of the application and the rule-based system is given followed by an evaluation of the results from the point of view of the end user. The results are discussed and compared with manual classification, which is the only possible alternative. Finally, some conclusions are given.

Atul K. Chhabra and D. Dori (Eds.): GREC'99, LNCS 1941, pp. 50–57, 2000.
© Springer-Verlag Berlin Heidelberg 2000

2   The Application

The Dutch Cadastre is one of the users of the GBKN, a large-scale topographic base map of the Netherlands. It contains the contours of the most important topographic elements such as roads, buildings and water. Almost all of the Netherlands is mapped digitally at the scale of 1:500, 1:1000 or 1:2000.

In the digital database, every vector is part of the contour of two objects (one to the left, one to the right) and has one label corresponding to the type of one of the two objects, e.g. waterside or roadside (cf. Fig. 1). As a vector has only one label assigned while it can be part of the contour of two objects, a strict hierarchy is applied in the labels assigned to a vector, e.g. building over road. Although vector labels refer to objects, object information cannot be extracted from the database as there is no topological relation between vectors. Further, vectors are often not properly connected and they do not always intersect correctly.

In early CAD-applications, when these maps were used for reference purposes only, it did not matter that they were composed of unrelated vectors. However, current GIS applications offer possibilities for data modelling or relating administrative data to geographical data provided that the data is composed of high-level objects. This is important for the Cadastre because it allows access to its registered real estate information by means of the GBKN. In order to make this possible, the labelled vectors need to be converted to closed non-overlapping polygons with a topologically correct data structure where each polygon corresponds to the contour of an object. To enable high-level analysis and presentation of the data, each polygon has to be assigned one of seven classifications, e.g. building, (part of the) road, water or terrain (cf. Fig. 2). The remainder of this paper focuses on the polygon classification.

3   Problem Definition

To obtain a digital database with classified polygons three tasks can be distinguished:

1. Formation of polygons. In this task topological relations have to be established between the vectors, vectors have to be connected and contours have to be closed to be able to extract polygons;
2. Classification. To each polygon a classification has to be assigned;
3. Verification. After classification, the results have to be verified by the operator.

Because the GBKN-data is often incomplete, the formation of polygons can be solved partly automatically. On average 3 hours of operator time remain to add missing vectors to the database for an area of 1 km^2. Manual polygon classification is the most tedious and time consuming process. On average, 6 hours are needed for classification while verification requires another 3 hours resulting in 12 hours of manual conversion time per square kilometre.

The aim is to develop a cost effective and flexible solution for the conversion of labelled vectors into classified polygons. In the following paragraphs we will focus on our solution to the first two tasks.

Fig. 1. Example input vector data

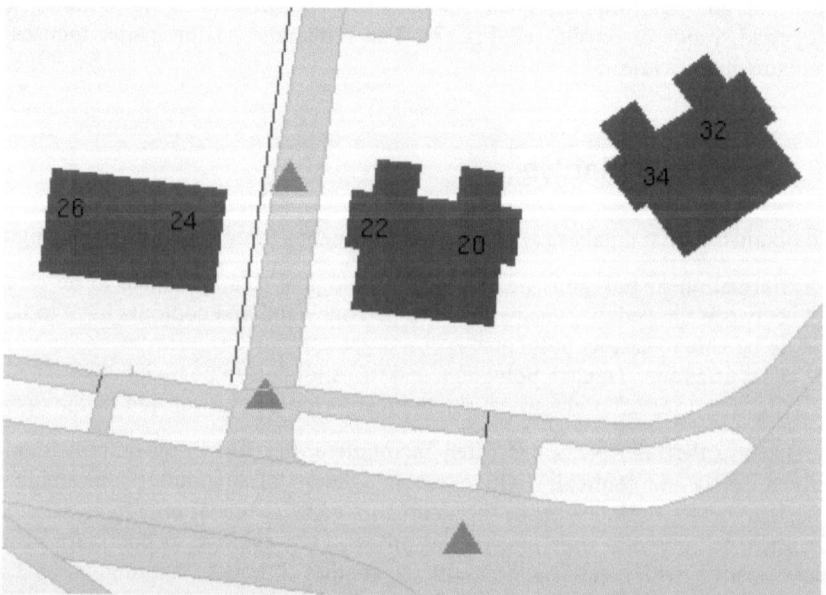

Fig. 2. Classified polygons

4   Polygon Formation

The first part of the system provides tools for the task 1. As a first step the nodes at positions were vectors (almost) intersect are computed automatically. An algorithm for node computation is designed which is driven by tunable tolerance circles and weighting based on quality attributes related to all input vectors. The weighting discriminates our approach from work by other authors [8, 15]. Spatial data organisation (clustering and indexing) is important to perform this step efficiently [13]. This step also includes cleaning of the vector data and building correct topological relations between the vectors. For example: removing overlapping vectors, correction of undershoots and overshoots at nodes and changing topologically wrong directions of vectors into their opposite. No implementation has been made yet and in the experiments available tools for node computation were used [9]. In the second step all of the polygons are closed at positions with large gaps in the contour. Because complex interpretation knowledge is needed for this step, manual editing tools are provided.

5   Rule-Based Polygon Classification

It was decided to use a knowledge-based system for polygon classification for the following reasons:

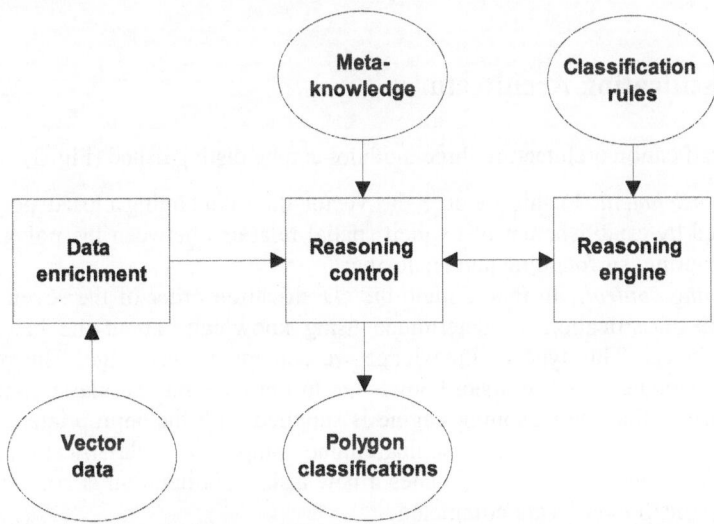

Fig. 3. Polygon classification architecture

- Easier maintenance of the classification rules;
- Flexibility for modelling differences between regions;
- Possibilities to adapt to future requirements.

Since the classification system had to be developed for an organisation with little experience with knowledge based systems, the main requirement was that the knowledge representation used by the system had to be intuitive and easily maintainable by a domain expert. Domain knowledge was partly available in documents, but resided mainly in the heads of the experts. Therefore, several interviews were conducted to make classification knowledge explicit and to obtain a uniform classification scheme.

The main types of knowledge for polygon classification are:

- Vector labels;
- Spatial relations between polygons;
- Possible symbols and texts within the polygon;
- Shape of the polygon;
- Implicit contextual knowledge. The expert recognizes a certain pattern of polygons such as parking lots alongside a road;
- Real world knowledge. For example, the expert lives in the represented area and can identify certain polygons.

The last two types are hard to model, therefore it was decided to use the first four types of knowledge to build the application.

From the analysis of expert reasoning it appeared that they usually formulated their classification decisions in terms of causal reasoning based on facts. This, together with the easy maintainability by domain experts that are relatively inexperienced with knowledge based systems, lead to the choice for a rule based classification system.

6   Classification Architecture

In the classification architecture three modules can be distinguished (Fig. 3):

1. *Data enrichment*. In this module the vector data containing closed polygons is enriched by establishment of explicit spatial relations between the polygons, e.g. neighbouring, surrounding and enclosing;
2. *Reasoning control*. In this module the classification order of the seven possible polygon classifications is determined using knowledge about the hierarchy of vector labels. This type of knowledge we call meta knowledge. The reasoning control module uses this meta knowledge to define a limited classification task, and ensures that the reasoning engine is supplied with the appropriate input data (facts) and rules. When the reasoning engine completes its classification task, the reasoning control module formulates a new task. This iteration is continued until all classification tasks are completed;
3. *Reasoning engine*. This module has been implemented by means of the rule based system Clips [5]. Clips already proved its reliability in other environments while it is a completely open system that enabled us to encapsulate it in a reasoning module. The thus resulting reasoning engine takes rules and facts about vectors (e.g. labels) and polygons (e.g. related polygons, symbols, shape) as its input, and alters the classification of polygons if needed. The rules used are tailored to a

specific task and independent of rule bases for other tasks. This greatly improves the maintainability of the rule bases.

7   Experiments and Results

In this paragraph the classification performance and the consequences for speed-up of the manual process are discussed. The classification system has been trained on a set of 14 areas, each with an area of about 1 km^2. The performance of the described system has been tested on an independent test set of 5 areas which were manually classified by an expert. In the test set a distinction between rural and suburban regions can be made. Table 1 gives an overview of the classification results on the test set based on the manual classifications. Classification results are not consistent over the two region types. In general, performance is best on rural areas and becomes less in more densely built-up areas.

From the analysis of the results three causes of classification errors were identified:
1. A situation was not covered by the rule-base (40-50%);
2. The situation was not covered by the rule-base (40-50%);
3. An erroneous identification was assigned to a vector (5-10%).

From the analysis of the errors made by the manual operator (40-50%) it appears that a human operator performs badly on small polygons in densely built regions and that an operator is often not consistent in the application of the classification specifications.

Table 1. Classification results on a test set of 5 regions

Region type	Number of	Percentage
Rural	148	97%
Rural	524	93%
Rural	548	96%
Rural	281	96%
Rural	524	93%
Suburban	472	87%
Rural	281	96%
Suburban	472	87%

With respect to speed-up of the process time needed for polygon formation and verification of the automatic classification results remains unchanged at 6 hours. Manual polygon classification of a an 1 km^2 area requires also 6 hours on average. Automatic classification of an area of 1 km^2 takes about 6 minutes on a SUN UltraSparc. Therefore automatic classification reduces the manual effort by half to approximately 6 hours.

8   Discussion and Conclusions

From the experiments we conclude that the proposed rule-based approach is a reliable and a much cheaper alternative to manual classification. With automatic classification of the polygons the operator time is reduced from 12 hours to 6 hours. Although automatic classification leads to a varying error rate, the amount of errors made by a human operator is roughly equal. The errors made by the automatic process differ from the errors made by an operator. Therefore, a combination of automatic classification followed by a visual inspection and correction by the operator will lead to a more reliable and consistent result than manual classification alone. Further, automatic classification allows for automatic detection of errors in the input data, i.e. erroneous vector labels.

From the analysis of the experimental results it appeared that about half of the errors are caused by insufficiencies in the rule-base. However, adaptation of rules or extension of the rule-base are not necessarily the solution to increase classification performance. Some situations cannot be modelled easily in a rule-based representation. Furthermore, adding extra rules to cover the erroneously classified polygons may have serious consequences for the maintainability of the rule-base. Future research will therefore concentrate on modelling new types of knowledge.

References

1.   K.-H. Anders, D. Fritsch, "Automatic interpretation of digital maps for data revision", ISPRS, Int. Archiv. of Photogr, and Remote Sensing, Vol. 31/4, Vienna, 1996, pp. 90-94
2.   J. Alemany et al. "Interpretation of paper-based maps", SPIE Appl. of Digital Image Processing X, volume 829, pp. 125-137, 1987
3.   D. Antoine. "CIPLAN, a model-based system with original features for understanding French plats", First int. Conf. On Document Analysis and Recognition (Saint Malo), volume 2, pp. 647-655, 1991
4.   ESRI, Data Conversion and Regions, ARC/INFO Version 7 User Manual, Environmental Systems Research Institute, Redlands, USA, pp. 92-96, 1994
5.   Joseph C. Giarratano, The CLIPS User's guide, CLIPS Version 6.0, NASA Lyndon B. Johnson Space Center, Software Technology Branch, May 28, 1993
6.   K. J. Goodson and P.H. Lewis, "A knowledge-based line recognition system", Pattern Recognition Letters, 11(4), pp. 295-304, 1990
7.   J. E. den Hartog, "A framework for knowledge-based map interpretation", PhD-thesis, Delft University of Technology, Fac. of Electrical Engineering, 88 p., 1995
8.   R. Laurini, F. Milleret-Raffort, "Topological reorganization of inconsistent geographical databases: a step towards their certification", Computer and Graphics, Vol. 18, No. 6, pp. 803-813, 1994
9.   R. Laurini and D. Thompson, "Fundamentals of spatial information systems, The A.P.I.C. Series, No. 37, Academic Press, 1992

10. Karttakeskus., Fingis User Manual, version 3.85, Technical report Karttakeskus, Helsinki, Finland, 1994
11. M. Molenaar, "An introduction to the theory of spatial object modelling for GIS", Taylor & Francis, London, 1998
12. P. van der Molen, "Inside the dutch cadastre", GIS Europe, (10), pp. 28-30, 1996
13. P. van Oosterom and T. Vijlbrief, "The spatial location code", Proceedings of the 7th International Symposium on Spatial Data Handling, Delft, The Netherlands, 1996
14. S. Suharto and D.M. Vu, "Computerized cartographic work for censuses and surveys", UNFPA TSS/CST workshop on Data Collection, Processing, Dissemination and Utilization, New York, 1995
15. B. Žalik, "A topology construction from line drawings using a uniform plane subdivision technique, Computer-Aided Design 31, pp. 335-348, 1999

Compound Regulated Morphological Operations and Their Application to the Analysis of Line-Drawings*

Gady Agam[1] and Its'hak Dinstein[2]

[1] Department of Electrical and Computer Engineering
Ecole Polytechnique, Montreal H3C 3A7, Canada
agam@ai.polymtl.ca
[2] Department of Electrical and Computer Engineering
Ben-Gurion University of the Negev, Beer-Sheva 84105, Israel
dinstein@ee.bgu.ac.il

Abstract. Regulated morphological operations, which are defined by extending the fitting interpretation of the ordinary morphological operations, have been shown to be less sensitive to noise and small intrusions or protrusions on the boundary of shapes. The compound regulated morphological operations, as defined in this paper, extend the fitting interpretation of the ordinary compound morphological operations. Consequently, these regulated morphological operations enhance the ability of the ordinary morphological operations to quantify geometrical structure in signals in a way that agrees with human perception. The properties of the compound regulated morphological operations are described, and they are shown to be idempotent, thus manifesting their ability to filter basic characteristics of the input signal. The paper concludes with some examples of applications of compound regulated morphological operations for the analysis of line-drawings.

Keywords: mathematical morphology, regulated morphology, compound operations, graphics recognition, document analysis, line-drawing analysis.

1 Introduction

Morphological operations can quantify geometrical structure in signals in a way that agrees with human perception. Particularly, the algebraic system of operators of mathematical morphology and their compositions are capable of decomposing a complex shape into its meaningful parts and therefore simplify image data processing to its essential characteristics. Traditional linear systems such as convolution and its frequency domain representation, on the other hand, do not

---

* This work was partially supported by The Paul Ivanier Center for Robotics and Production Automation, Ben-Gurion University of the Negev, Beer-Sheva 84105, Israel.

address directly the fundamental issues of how to quantify shape or geometrical structures in signals [1].

Considering the fitting interpretation of the binary morphological erosion and dilation operations, it is possible to observe that they are based on opposing strict approaches. The binary dilation collects shifts for which the kernel set intersects the object set without taking into account what is the size of the intersection, whereas the binary erosion collects shifts for which the kernel set is completely contained within the object set without considering shifts for which some kernel elements are not contained within the object set. As a result of these strict approaches, the ordinary morphological operations are sensitive to noise and small intrusions or protrusions on the boundary of shapes. In order to solve this problem, various extensions to the ordinary morphological operations have been proposed. These extensions could be classified into three major groups: fuzzy morphological operations [2,3], soft morphological operations [4,5], and regulated morphological operations [6,7]. A thorough discussion of these operations and the relations between them is provided in [8]. Particularly, ordinary and regulated morphological operations have been shown to be useful for map and line-drawing analysis [9,10].

This paper defines compound regulated morphological operations, and shows how the fitting property of the ordinary compound morphological operations is controlled in these operations. The properties of the compound regulated morphological operations are discussed and it is shown that they possess many of the properties of the ordinary compound morphological operations. In particular, it is shown that the regulated open and close are idempotent for an arbitrary kernel and strictness parameter, thus showing their ability to filter fundamental characteristics of the input image. Since the regulated morphological operations possess many of the properties of the ordinary morphological operations, it is possible to use the regulated morphological operations in existing algorithms that are based on morphological operations in order to improve their performance, where the strictness parameter of the regulated morphological operations may be optimized according to some criteria.

The following sections discuss the proposed approach in greater detail. Section 2 reviews the basic regulated morphological operations. Section 3 defines and studies the properties of compound regulated morphological operations. The fitting interpretation of the compound regulated morphological operations and their idempotency is discussed in Section 4. Section 5 addresses implementation considerations. Section 6 concludes the paper and provides some examples of the application of compound regulated morphological operations to map analysis. It should be noted that the propositions in this paper are provided without proofs. Proofs of some propositions may be found in [6,8].

2   Regulated Morphological Operations

The regulated morphological operations introduce a strictness parameter, which when set to its minimal value results in ordinary morphological operations. The regulated morphological operations are shown to possess many of the properties of the ordinary morphological operations. Hence, it is possible to use the regulated morphological operations in existing algorithms that are based on morphological operations in order to improve their performance, where the strictness parameter of the regulated morphological operations may be optimized according to some criteria.

Given two sets $A, B \subset \mathcal{Z}^N$, the morphological dilation of A by B is defined [11] by:

$$A \oplus B \equiv \{x \mid \exists a \in A, \, b \in B : x = a + b\} = \bigcup_{a \in A} (B)_a \qquad (1)$$

where $(B)_a$ is a shift of B by a defined by: $(B)_a \equiv \{x \mid \exists b \in B : x = a + b\}$. When A is a set of binary image pixels, and B is a set of binary kernel pixels, the dilation of A by B results in a dilation of the shapes in A (provided that the origin pixel belongs to the kernel B). The dilation operation may be interpreted in various ways. In particular, the dilation of A by B may be obtained as the union of all the possible shifts for which the reflected and shifted B intersects A. That is:

$$A \oplus B = \{x \mid (A \cap (\check{B})_x) \neq \emptyset\} \qquad (2)$$

where $\check{B}$ is the reflection of B given by: $\check{B} \equiv \{x \mid \exists b \in B : x = -b\}$. By using the fitting interpretation of dilation (2), the morphological dilation of A by B can be extended by combining the size of the intersection into the dilation process. In that sense, a given shift is included in the dilation of A only if the intersection between A and the reflected and shifted B is big enough. The obtained advantage of the regulated dilation is the prevention of excessive dilation caused by small intersections with the object set. The regulated dilation of A by B with a strictness of s is defined by:

$$A \overset{s}{\oplus} B \equiv \{x \mid \#(A \cap (\check{B})_x) \geq s\} \; ; \; s \in [1, \min(\#A, \#B)] \qquad (3)$$

where the symbol $\#$ denotes the cardinality of a set. It should be noted that since $\#(A \cap (\check{B})_x) \leq \min(\#A, \#B)$ for every x, the strictness s is bounded by $\min(\#A, \#B)$. The extensive regulated dilation of A by B with a strictness of s is defined by:

$$A \overset{s}{\underline{\oplus}} B \equiv (A \overset{s}{\oplus} B) \cup A \; ; \; s \in [1, \min(\#A, \#B)] \qquad (4)$$

Since in this definition the result of the regulated dilation is unified with the original set, the defined operation is necessarily extensive (for an arbitrary kernel and strictness).

Given two sets $A, B \subset \mathcal{Z}^N$, the morphological erosion of A by B is defined [11] by:

$$A \ominus B \equiv \{x \mid \forall b \in B \; \exists a \in A : x = a - b\} = \bigcap_{b \in B} (A)_{-b} \qquad (5)$$

When A is a set of binary image pixels, and B is a set of binary kernel pixels, the erosion of A by B results in an erosion of the shapes in A (provided that the origin pixel belongs to the kernel B). The erosion operation may be interpreted in various ways. In particular, the erosion of A by B may be obtained as the union of all the possible shifts for which the shifted B is contained completely within A . That is:

$$A \ominus B = \{x \mid (A^c \cap (B)_x) = \emptyset\} \tag{6}$$

where A^c denotes the complement of A defined by: $A^c \equiv \{x \mid x \notin A\}$. By using (6) the morphological erosion of A by B can be extended by including in the erosion of A shifts for which the intersection between A^c and the shifted B is small enough. The obtained advantage of the regulated erosion is the prevention of excessive erosion caused by small intersections with the background set. The regulated erosion of A by B with a strictness of s is defined by:

$$A \overset{s}{\ominus} B \equiv \{x \mid \#(A^c \cap (B)_x) < s\} \; ; \; s \in [1, \#B] \tag{7}$$

where it is assumed that $\#A < \infty$. It should be noted that since it is assumed that $\#A < \infty$ then $\#(A^c \cap (B)_x) \leq \#B$ for every x, and so the strictness s is bounded by $\#B$. The anti-extensive regulated erosion of A by B with a strictness of s is defined by:

$$A \overset{s}{\underline{\ominus}} B \equiv (A \overset{s}{\ominus} B) \cap A \; ; \; s \in [1, \#B] \tag{8}$$

Since in this definition the result of the regulated erosion is intersected with the original set, the defined operation is necessarily anti-extensive (for an arbitrary kernel and strictness).

3   Compound Regulated Morphological Operations

The compound regulated morphological operations are defined by using the basic regulated morphological operations. As shown later, the compound regulated morphological operations extend the fitting interpretation of the ordinary compound morphological operations, and thus share many of their properties. In particular, the compound regulated morphological operations are shown to be idempotent for an arbitrary kernel and strictness parameter. As demonstrated, the ordinary compound morphological operations are obtained as a special case of the compound regulated morphological operations.

Definition 1. *The regulated close of A by B with a strictness of s is defined by:*

$$A \overset{s}{\bullet} B \equiv ((A \overset{s}{\underline{\oplus}} B) \ominus B) \cup A \tag{9}$$

where $s \in [1, \#B]$.

Since in this definition the result is unified with the original set, the defined operation is necessarily extensive (for an arbitrary kernel and strictness).

Proposition 1. *The regulated close is decreasing with respect to the strictness s and increasing with respect to the first argument. When s is minimal the regulated close results in the ordinary close. The regulated close is translation invariant.*

$$A \overset{s1}{\bullet} B \subseteq A \overset{s2}{\bullet} B \iff s1 \geq s2 \tag{10}$$

$$A \subseteq B \implies A \overset{s}{\bullet} K \subseteq B \overset{s}{\bullet} K \; ; \quad s \in [1, \min(\#A, \#K)] \tag{11}$$

$$A \bullet B = A \overset{1}{\bullet} B \tag{12}$$

$$(A)_x \overset{s}{\bullet} B = (A \overset{s}{\bullet} B)_x \tag{13}$$

Definition 2. *The regulated open of A by B with a strictness of s is defined by:*

$$A \overset{s}{\circ} B \equiv ((A \overset{s}{\ominus} B) \oplus B) \cap A \tag{14}$$

where $s \in [1, \#B]$.

Since in this definition the result is intersected with the original set, the defined operation is necessarily anti-extensive (for an arbitrary kernel and strictness).

Proposition 2. *The regulated open is increasing with respect to the strictness s and increasing with respect to the first argument. When s is minimal the regulated open results in the ordinary open. The regulated open is translation invariant.*

$$A \overset{s1}{\circ} B \subseteq A \overset{s2}{\circ} B \iff s1 \leq s2 \tag{15}$$

$$A \subseteq B \implies A \overset{s}{\circ} K \subseteq B \overset{s}{\circ} K \; ; \quad s \in [1, \#K] \tag{16}$$

$$A \circ B = A \overset{1}{\circ} B \tag{17}$$

$$(A)_x \overset{s}{\circ} B = (A \overset{s}{\circ} B)_x \tag{18}$$

Proposition 3. *The regulated open and close are dual in the same sense that exists for the ordinary open and close:*

$$A \overset{s}{\bullet} B = (A^c \overset{s}{\circ} \check{B})^c \tag{19}$$

4   Idempotency of the Regulated Open and Close

In the previous section it was stated that the compound regulated morphological operations extend the fitting interpretation of the ordinary compound morphological operations, and that they are idempotent. The following propositions formulate these statements.

Proposition 4. *The regulated open of a shape A by a kernel B with a strictness of s may be interpreted as the intersection between the shape and the union of all the possible shifts of the kernel for which the intersection with the shape is big enough and the origin of the kernel is included in the shape:*

$$A \overset{s}{\circ} B = \left(\bigcup_{\{x \in A \ \mid \ \#(A^c \cap (B)_x) < s\}} (B)_x \right) \cap A \tag{20}$$

Based on the last proposition, the fitting interpretation of the regulated open may be visualized as moving the kernel inside the shape as close as possible to its borders, where the kernel may get out of the shape up to some extent, and then eliminating border elements that were not covered by at least one shift of the kernel.

Proposition 5. *The regulated close of a shape A by a kernel B with a strictness of s may be interpreted as the union of the shape and the intersection between all the possible shifts of the reflected and complemented kernel for which the intersection of the reflected kernel with the shape is small enough and the origin of the kernel is not included in the shape:*

$$A \overset{s}{\bullet} B = \left(\bigcap_{\{x \in A^c \ \mid \ \#(A \cap (\breve{B})_x) < s\}} ((\breve{B})_x)^c \right) \cup A \tag{21}$$

Based on the last proposition, the fitting interpretation of the regulated close may be visualized as moving the reflected kernel outside the shape as close as possible to its borders, where the reflected kernel may get into the shape up to some extent, and then adding border elements that were not covered by at least one shift of the reflected kernel.

Proposition 6. *The regulated open and close operations are idempotent:*

$$(A \overset{s}{\circ} B) \overset{s}{\circ} B = A \overset{s}{\circ} B \tag{22}$$

$$(A \overset{s}{\bullet} B) \overset{s}{\bullet} B = A \overset{s}{\bullet} B \tag{23}$$

5   Implementation Considerations

The computational complexity of the proposed compound regulated morphological operations is an important aspect that should be addressed. Considering the definitions of these operations, it could be observed that the complexity of their implementation depends on the computational complexity of the regulated erosion, regulated dilation, and the union and intersection operations. A straightforward implementation of the regulated erosion and dilation of an $M \times M$ image by a $P \times P$ kernel would result in $\mathbf{O}(P^2 M^2)$ operations, whereas a straightforward implementation of the union and intersection between n images would result in $\mathbf{O}(nM^2)$ operations. As described in [12], when using interval coding this number of operations can be reduced to $\mathbf{O}(pPm \log pP)$ and $\mathbf{O}(nm \log n)$, respectively, where p is the number of intervals in kernel and m is the number of intervals in the image.

The ratio between m and M, and between p and P, depends on the contents of the respective images. When considering the processing of ordinary maps and line-drawing images, it is possible to assume that m and M have the same order of magnitude, and that p and P have the same order of magnitude. Since in most applications $P \ll M$ and $n \ll M$, in such a case we get that the computational complexity of a straightforward implementation reduces to $\mathbf{O}(M^2)$, whereas the computational complexity of the interval coding based implementation reduces to $\mathbf{O}(m)$. It should be noted that in addition to reduced computational complexity, the interval coding implementation significantly reduces the memory requirements of the application. When processing large maps/documents, which were scanned with a fine resolution, in several different color layers, a reduction in the memory requirements of the application is essential. This reduction becomes even more important when considering a directional decomposition of each image into several directional edge planes as proposed in [10]. The computational complexity of the basic morphological and logical operations in a straightforward and an interval-based implementation (as described in [12]) is summarized in Table 1.

Table 1. Summary of the computational complexity of various operations. (a) Basic operations between n images in the size of $M \times M$, where each image has m intervals. (b) The complement of an $M \times M$ image. The parameters M and M_θ have the same order of magnitude. (c)–(e) Morphological and convolution operations between an $M \times M$ image with m intervals and a $P \times P$ kernel with p intervals. The parameter pP is obtained in a worst case situation. Its minimal value is p

	(a) Intersection Union XOR	(b) Complement	(c) Dilation Erosion (Ordinary)	(d) Convolution	(e) Dilation Erosion (Regulated)
Straightforward Implementation	$\mathbf{O}(nM^2)$	$\mathbf{O}(M^2)$	$\mathbf{O}(P^2 M^2)$	$\mathbf{O}(P^2 M^2)$	$\mathbf{O}(P^2 M^2)$
Efficient Implementation	$\mathbf{O}(nm \log n)$	$\mathbf{O}(m + M_\theta)$	$\mathbf{O}(pm \log p)$	$\mathbf{O}(pPm)$	$\mathbf{O}(pPm \log pP)$

6   Conclusion

This section presents some examples of applications of the regulated open and close operations for map analysis, and demonstrates their ability to improve the results obtained by the ordinary morphological operations when using strictness parameter greater than one. It should be noted that the examples in this section are presented in order to illustrate the advantages of the proposed compound regulated morphological operations with respect to the ordinary ones. Consequently, these results are not compared to results which may be obtained by other means. An example of objects separation by a regulated open operation is presented in Figure 1. Figure 1-a presents the initial map image, containing extracted building marks, in which some of the building marks are touching each other. Figure 1-b demonstrates the result of an ordinary open of the image in Figure 1-a by a 7 × 7 kernel. Figure 1-c presents the result of a regulated open of the same image by the same kernel when using a strictness parameter of 2. As can be observed, the regulated open operation manages to separate between touching buildings without causing significant changes to their shapes, whereas the ordinary open operation causes the removal of some buildings and changes the shapes of others.

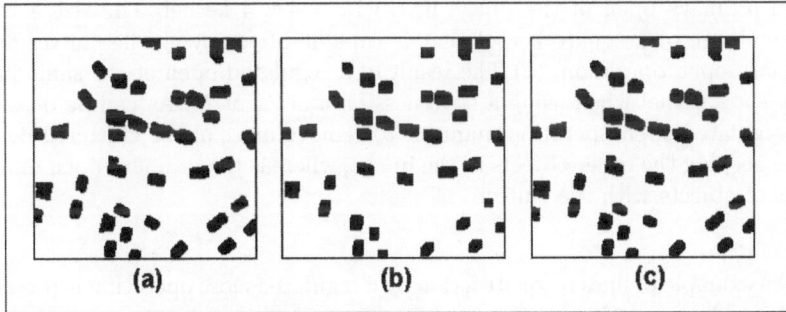

Fig. 1. Demonstration of objects separation by a regulated open operation. (a) The initial map image, containing extracted building marks, in which some of the building marks are touching each other. (b) The result of an ordinary open of the image in (a) by a 7 × 7 kernel. (c) The result of a regulated open of the same image by the same kernel when using a strictness parameter of 2. As can be observed, the regulated open operation manages to separate between touching buildings without causing significant changes to their shapes, whereas the ordinary open operation causes the removal of some buildings and changes the shapes of others

An example of cluttered overlay removal by a regulated open operation is presented in Figure 2. Figure 2-a presents the initial map image, which contains a cluttered overlay. Figure 2-b demonstrates the result of an ordinary open of the image in Figure 2-a by a 4 × 4 kernel. The size 4 is the minimal size of a square kernel that is capable of removing the clutter by an ordinary open operation. Figure 2-c shows the result of a regulated open of the same image by a 7 × 7 kernel when using a strictness parameter of 25. As can be observed, the regulated open operation manages to remove most of the cluttered overlay while keeping the other objects in the image, whereas the ordinary open removes parts of objects with the clutter.

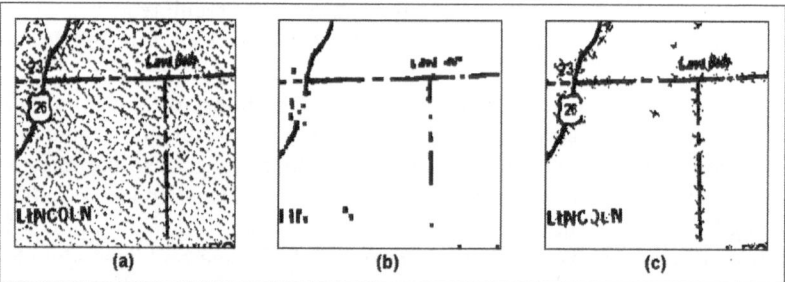

Fig. 2. Demonstration of a cluttered overlay removal by a regulated open operation. (a) The initial map image, containing a cluttered overlay. (b) The result of an ordinary open of the image in (a) by a 4 × 4 kernel. The size 4 is the minimal size of a square kernel that is capable of removing the clutter by an ordinary open operation. (c) The result of a regulated open of the same image by a 7 × 7 kernel when using a strictness parameter of 25. As can be observed, the regulated open operation manages to remove most of the cluttered overlay while keeping the other objects in the image, whereas the ordinary open removes parts of objects with the clutter

An example of lines reconstruction by a regulated close operation is presented in Figure 3. Figure 3-a presents the initial map image, containing extracted lines of roads, in which some parts of lines were erroneously removed due to the separation of touching character strings. Figure 3-b demonstrates the result of an ordinary close of the image in 3-a by a horizontal bar kernel in the size of 3 × 30. Figure 3-c presents the result of a regulated close of the same image by the same kernel when using a strictness parameter of 20. As can be observed, the regulated close operation manages to fill the gaps in the lines without causing excessive filling, whereas the ordinary close operation causes the complete filling of gaps between any pair of parallel vertical lines in the image.

The fundamental generalization of morphological operations is based on lattice notation [13]. Lattice notation provides a natural connection between union-intersection operations and supremum-infimum operations through the terminology of join-meet operations. In that sense, dilation is based on a join operation and erosion is based on a meet operation on a complete lattice. The definition of dilation as an operator which commutes with a join operation, and of erosion as

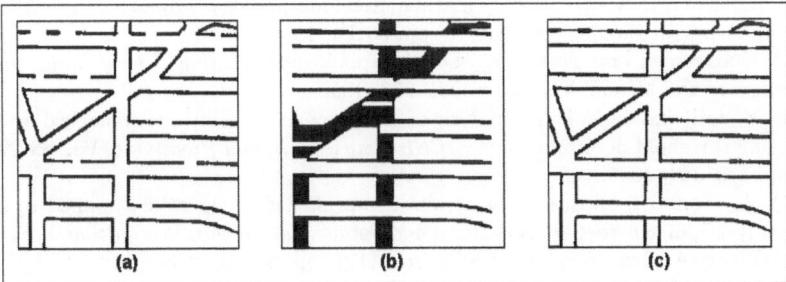

Fig. 3. Demonstration of lines reconstruction by a regulated close operation. (a) The initial map image, containing extracted lines of roads, in which some parts of lines were erroneously removed due to the separation of touching character strings. (b) The result of an ordinary close of the image in (a) by a horizontal bar kernel in the size of 3×30. (c) The result of a regulated close of the same image by the same kernel when using a strictness parameter of 20. As can be observed, the regulated close operation manages to fill the gaps in the lines without causing excessive filling, whereas the ordinary close operation causes the complete filling of gaps between any pair of parallel vertical lines in the image

an operator which commutes with a meet operation, stresses the fact that the basic ordinary morphological operations of dilation and erosion are built on the concept of two extremes such as infimum and supremum, or union and intersection. This fundamental concept explicitly propagates to derived compound operations such as open and close which consequently are also two extremes. The regulated morphological operations as defined here, are very different in that sense. Rather than relying on two basic extreme morphological operations, of which combinations derive new operations, the regulated morphological operations span a multitude of morphological operations in-between the existing ones. This methodology provides a generalization to morphological operations from which the ordinary morphological operations may be derived at two extremes. Moreover, this definition of in-between morphological operation relies on a geometric concept of kernel set fitting thus providing a conceptual support to these operations. Finally, it should be noted that while the regulated morphological operations, as defined here, are set morphological operations, these operations may be extended to gray-level images by using either threshold sets or umbra notions [14].

References

1. C. Ronse, "Fourier analysis, mathematical morphology, and vision", Technical Report WD54, Philips Research Laboratory, Brussels, Belgium, 1989. 59
2. D. Sinha and E. R. Dougherty, "Fuzzy mathematical morphology", *J. of Visual Communications and Image Representation*, Vol. 3, No. 3, pp. 286–302, 1992. 59

3. J. Bloch and H. Maitre, "Fuzzy mathematical morphology", *Annals of Mathematics and Artificial Intelligence*, Vol. 10, pp. 55–84, 1994. 59

4. P. Kuosmanen and J. Astola, "Soft morphological filtering", *J. of Mathematical imaging and Vision*, Vol. 5, pp. 231–262, 1995. 59

5. F. Y. Shih and C. C. Pu, "Analysis of the properties of soft morphological filtering using threshold decomposition", *IEEE Trans. on Signal Processing*, Vol. 43, No. 2, pp. 539–544, 1995. 59

6. G. Agam and I. Dinstein, "Generalized morphological operators applied to map-analysis", in *Advances in Structural and Syntactical Pattern Recognition*, P. Perner, P. Wang, A. Rosenfeld eds., LNCS Vol. 1121, pp. 60–69, 1996. 59

7. M. A. Zmuda and L. A. Tamburino, "Efficient algorithms for the soft morphological operators", *IEEE Trans. PAMI*, Vol. 18, No. 11, pp. 1142–1147, 1996. 59

8. G. Agam and I. Dinstein, "Regulated morphological operations", *Pattern Recognition*, Vol. 32, No. 6, pp. 947-971, May, 1999. 59

9. G. Agam, H. Luo, and I. Dinstein, "Morphological approach for dashed lines detection", in *Graphics Recognition: Methods and Applications*, R. Kasturi, K. Tombre eds., LNCS Vol. 1072, pp. 92–105, 1996. 59

10. G. Agam and I. Dinstein, "Directional decomposition of line-drawing images based on regulated morphological operations", in *Graphics Recognition: Algorithms and Systems*, K. Tombre and A. K. Chhabra eds., LNCS Vol. 1389, pp. 21–34, 1998. 59, 64

11. R. M. Haralick, S. R. Sternberg, and X. Zhuang, "Image analysis using mathematical morphology", *IEEE Trans. PAMI*, Vol. 9, No. 4, pp. 532–550, 1987. 60

12. G. Agam and I. Dinstein, "Efficient implementation of regulated morphological operations based on directional interval coding", in *Proc. SSPR'98*, Sydney, Australia, 1998. 64

13. C. Ronse, "Why mathematical morphology needs complete lattices", *Signal Processing*, Vol. 21, No. 2, pp. 129–154, 1990. 66

14. J. Serra, *Image Analysis and Mathematical Morphology*, Academic Press, 1982. 67

Detection of Black Point Houses on the Large Size Scanned Topographic Map

Young-Bin Kwon

Department of Computer Science & Engineering, Chung-Ang University Seoul,
156-756, South Korea
ybwkon@ripe.chungang.ac.kr

Abstract In this paper, an automatic method for the detection of houses which represented black points on the large size scanned topographic map is described. Various signals such as characters, lines, signs, and dashed lines may overlapped with the house symbol. After contour detection method is used for detecting isolated houses. Run-length encoding method is used for manipulating houses touching with grid lines. Character and symbol elimination and morphological operations is done for the houses touched to roads and borderlines. Various recognition results are described.

1. Introduction

Extraction of information from maps is highly necessary to establish the Geographic Information System(GIS). But, existing maps are often made by hand as a hand-printed form. There are lots of various symbols, lines, characters on the maps. Thus, it's not easy to recognize automatically existing maps. The necessity of extraction of map information and layered structure construction have been emphasized the complex organization of mixed symbol and characters makes it difficult to the automatic recognition process of maps.. Thus, in this paper, automatic recognition method of hand-made special purpose map information is implemented.

There are some methods for inputting of geographic information. One is done manually, and the other is an automatic recognition of paper-based maps. The manual process can have fewer errors because people do it. However, an inputting process is a quite routine and difficult work. It requires a quite a long time, too. But the automatic recognition is hard to be used generally because there are maps that have too various shapes of elements[1]. Thus, the automatic recognition technique is usually used for maps with constraints.

Lines on maps are represented with set of lines and points, and these elements represent one information according to a target object. Unlike general documents that have distinct target objects, there are overlapping among target objects, because lines that are parts of each target object on maps overlap one another. There are lots of cut-off of lines because symbols and characters are drawn on lines. They are about

Atul K. Chhabra and D. Dori (Eds.): GREC'99, LNCS 1941, pp. 69-80, 2000.

lines that make part of one object, gathering points and lines efficiently, and the methods for recognizing assembled target objects[2].

There are lots of researches being done in foreign countries, and it's also in Korea. Making of digital maps is on progress at the Department of National Geography, but many parts are still published by paper form. And the status of current research and development that is based on the result of map recognition is in its early stage. Thus, the special purposed maps such as military use are not digitally published. In this paper, an automatic recognition method for detection houses represented by the black points is presented

2. House Detection Process

2.1 Characteristics of Target Maps and Objects

To design an automation system on maps, map organization information is necessary. The maps used in this paper are made for military purpose, and it is 20"x20" with scale ratio of 1/50,000. Fig. 1 shows top-left corner part of the original map. The illustrated map that is dealt in this paper has tics on its corners, and longitude lines and latitude lines are drawn as lines with grid style shape. The point location where the tic located becomes the base of coordination.

Fig. 1. A part of input map

And it doesn't have symbols for crop areas, etc., which is different from general maps. Instead, there are many symbols for factories, churches, schools, buildings and houses, and English/Korean characters and numbers. The houses, which are to be extracted, are drawn as black points. This map is scanned by 400 dpi and is stored by Tiff file format.

2.2 Object Recognition Process by Classification of Touchness of the Points

As illustrated in Fig. 1, the houses which are to be extracted can exist as isolated ones in many cases. But they can touch grid lines, characters, lines which represent roads, etc., or the houses can be connected one another. Before houses are extracted, removal of lines like grids, and thick lines for characters is required. Fig. 2 shows a procedure for separation of objects from houses in order to extract jointed houses by classifying the houses on maps as non-touched and touched ones. For the non-touched houses, contour detection is simply required. However, the detection of grid lines, characters and curved line element is required for the touched houses.

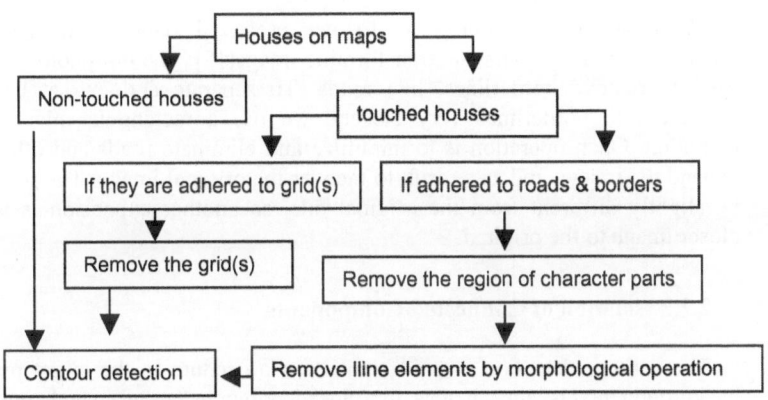

Fig. 2. Flow chart for house detection

2.2.1 Extraction of Line Elements for Grid

Line elements are important because they represent critical information on maps, documents, and images. And for dividing regions, extracting main walls of houses, analyzing documents and measuring slopes, the line elements provide very important information[2][3][4].

Houses touched by other elements are usually connected to grid lines on the map. So, it is required to remove the grid lines. The grids consist of straight line elements; thus they contain of vertical and horizontal line elements. Eliminating the line elements may separate the touched houses.

Run-Length Encoding(RLE) is originally used for image compression, and it's done by representing repetitive pixels as one code by counting the occurrence number of the specific pixels. This technique is simple and is required less computation comparing with the Hough transform in order to detect the straight line.

In this paper, a grid is composed of vertical and horizontal lines. In order to extract straight lines, black pixels may be transformed into white pixels depending on the threshold value. To be transformed, the gray value of a pixel should be greater than the threshold value. If the grid line is eliminated without any condition after transformation, it's possible that the houses which should be detected can't be extracted, because the information for the houses is lost when the houses touch the grid very closely. Thus, it's necessary to restore the lost information. As a solution, we use a method which determines whether any elements are contacted to grid lines or not, and if there are, the elements are not deleted while grid lines are being eliminated.

2.2.2 Morphological Operation

Mathematical morphology is to get preferred data by doing mathematical operations on image data and transforming images[5]. The morphological operation is used to remove borderlines, like roads. To separate and extract houses that are connected to borderlines very closely, we use a rectangular plate and do open operation. Open operation is to minimize and eliminate roads and other borderlines, expand the image, and as a result to recover the original image. The result image may be slightly different from the original one, so another expansion is applied to get closer image to the original.

2.2.3 Isolation of Connected Components

The contour detection is a differentiation procedure to the target pixels from the background pixels, thus it gets the closed polygons/curves which represent border points. The closed polygons and curves are pixels of 8-connection or 4-connection. The border lines which are got by outline extraction give information, for example, the size of area, the circumference, the shape, and the inclusion relation of connected components.
When contours are extracted, we should check 8-neighbors of a center pixel, and the 8-neighbors are stored in sequence as codes are called chain codes.

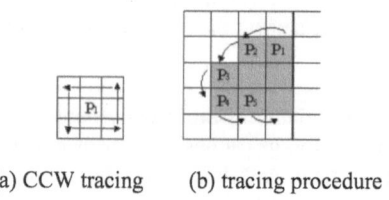

(a) CCW tracing   (b) tracing procedure

Fig. 3. Tracing the 8-connected contour tracing

In this paper, contour detection method is based on 8-neighbors. The image files are scanned from top to bottom, and if a black pixel is extracted, pixels are checked in

8-neighbors in counter clockwise(CCW) order. The border pixels among white pixels and black pixels are changed to have other predefined color, and as a result, the borderlines are detected[6][7]. The directions of border pixels and x, y coordinates are stored in the linked list, and in the upper linked list we store the minimum and maximum x, y coordinates in the set, and the number of pixels on the outline.

2.2.4 Elimination of Character Parts

In this paper, the morphological operations are used which based on erosion and dilation. But, before the operations are applied, the thick and large region of characters which has a different characteristic from grid lines should be erased, because they can be recognized as houses when they are not removed completely. Usually the thick characters are the names of regions that represented by various sizes. The sizes of characters are similar if they have same size property of font. It's often with English characters that one character has one connected component set, but with Korean characters, it's not. Korean characters which represent the names of regions tend to have two, three or four connected component sets.

As we mentioned before, it is difficult to decide that the connected component set is a part of Korean characters when we have only the sizes of connected components and the numbers of pixels which consist of contours. Thus, we choose a technique that eliminates Korean characters using the relations among the connected components. The Korean characters on maps can be classified 6 different types as Fig. 4[7].

Using the maps, it is possible to assume that more than one Korean characters are usually in the near place. So, we can first determine whether the elements we are trying to remove are one character or a part of character.

It can be known that the sizes, the distances, and the angles of the connected component sets are different from those of others, by studying the characters among sets that are thought as a part of a character.

In this paper, to eliminate the region of Korean characters, we first choose the components set which is assumed as a part of character, and search for 3 connected components which are the closest to the chosen component. The reason we search 3 components is that we should determine the fourth type of Korean character that can be shown in Fig. 4. For the 4th type of Korean characters, an inverse triangle can be formed when the center point of each connected components are linked. The other types of Korean characters may found horizontal, vertical and diagonal links or point as shown in Fig. 4. But we cannot decide the Korean character itself because the touching of symbols may produce the same component types. Thus, if we find out first 4th type of Korean character, the size information can be fitted. Then the similar size component may become a Korean character on the map. After doing that we eliminate the character string by examining the closest distance among element sets and the size of them.

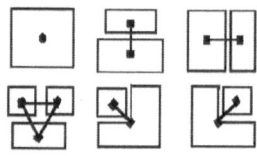

Fig. 4. Various type of Korean characters and relations between/among elements

2.2.5 Region Filling

To extract houses from maps, the character strings should be changed to have other color values, which prevent them from being included in the extraction operation. Filling regions means that changing neighboring pixels to a same predefined value. Briefly speaking, the operation fills a region with a predefined value when the 4 neighbors are examined and a pixel that has the same value as that of the center pixel is found.

2.3 Coordinate Transformation

In the result data, the direction and the center value of latitude and longitude coordinates of extracted houses should be stored. But when jobs were done manually after automatic operation was done, absolute value of x, y were added to the data, because data are not indexed with real latitude and longitude values on the image data.

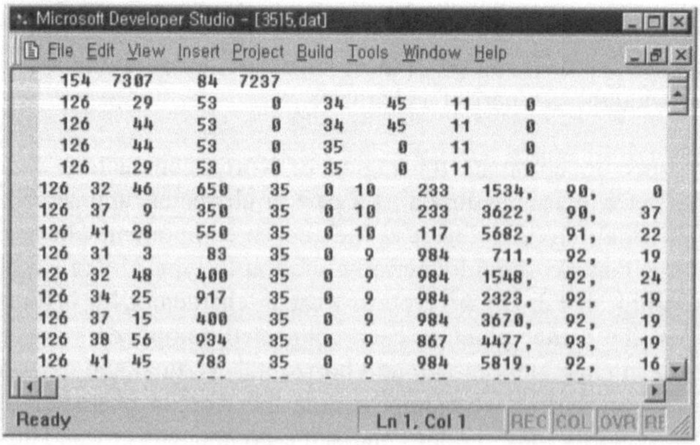

```
 ×. Microsoft Developer Studio - [3515.dat]                    _ □ ×
  ⎕ File  Edit  View  Insert  Project  Build  Tools  Window  Help        _ ⋴ ×
      154  7307    84   7237
      126    29    53     0    34    45    11     0
      126    44    53     0    34    45    11     0
      126    44    53     0    35     0    11     0
      126    29    53     0    35     0    11     0
  126   32   46   650    35     0    10   233   1534,   90,      0
  126   37    9   350    35     0    10   233   3622,   90,     37
  126   41   28   550    35     0    10   117   5682,   91,     22
  126   31    3    83    35     0     9   984    711,   92,     19
  126   32   48   400    35     0     9   984   1548,   92,     24
  126   34   25   917    35     0     9   984   2323,   92,     19
  126   37   15   400    35     0     9   984   3670,   92,     19
  126   38   56   934    35     0     9   867   4477,   93,     19
  126   41   45   783    35     0     9   984   5819,   92,     16
 Ready                              Ln 1, Col 1    REC COL OVR RE
```

Fig. 5. An example of house detection result

So, the result data are composed of 3 parts as shown in Fig. 5. First two values are the real x, y values for the tic. Second, there are 4 sets of real latitude and longitude values that were given. From the fifth column, the center position of houses as degree, minute, 1/1000 second, the x, y coordinate in the image data, and the direction of houses per 1 degree are produced.

The calculation is done by comparing the latitude and longitude of tic with the absolute coordinate on an image, and the error was maximum 0.13 seconds after the first extraction of contour, but after second trial, it was 0.26. The reason is because the value of pixel is integer, and the value of second is real number, thus the truncation error was came from the procedure of transforming integers to real numbers and real numbers to integers. The direction of houses is got by calculating average value after getting the vector value of bottom/up sides of houses. Because the house is very small, error propagation is somewhat occurred.

Fig. 6. House zoom-in and its direction

Fig. 6 shows the scanned 400-dpi image that was magnified and means a house. The direction of houses is in-between 0°~ 90°, the base point which is required to calculate vector values are got using chain code. After getting 4 corner positions, we get two angles like Fig. 6, and the average of the two angles is used as the direction of the given house.

3. Experimental Results and Discussions

The program was written on a Pentium 166Mhz PC, MS-Windows 95 and the Visual C++ was used. The data for the experiment is 1/50,000 scale map for military purpose by the Department of National Geography. The data is a 400-dpi TIFF image. The amount of data for the map is about 8 Mbytes, and 64MByets of memory space is required to manipulate the raw data, because transforming bit to byte is required.

The experiments are made in three different cases based on the touchness of the houses : slightly touched. Moderately touched and heavily touched.

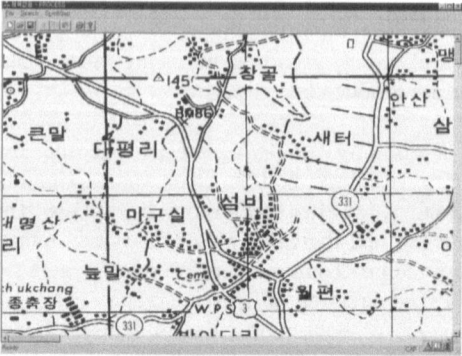

Fig. 7. Original image

Fig. 8 shows a detection result on the isolate house based on contour detection. In the figure, grey color illustrate the detected house. The houses which are touched with the grid lines and the roads are still remained.

Fig. 8. Isolated house detect

Fig. 9 shows the result of the elimination of grid and the result of house detection. The restoration procedure on the houses touched with the grid line is accomplished. In this figure, the characters, the load, and the symbols are still remained.

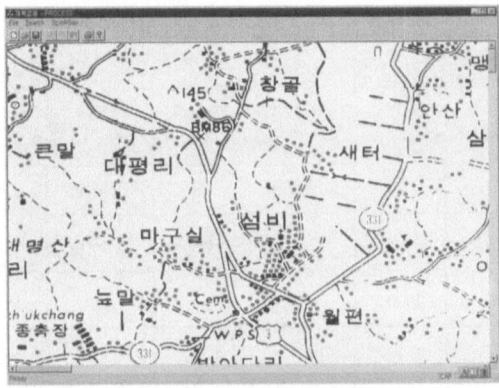

Fig. 9. House detection result after grid elimination

Fig. 10 shows the result of character elimination and morphological operation. The detected houses are indicated as black pixels. The character parts are well detected and the detection of houses which are close to road are accomplished.

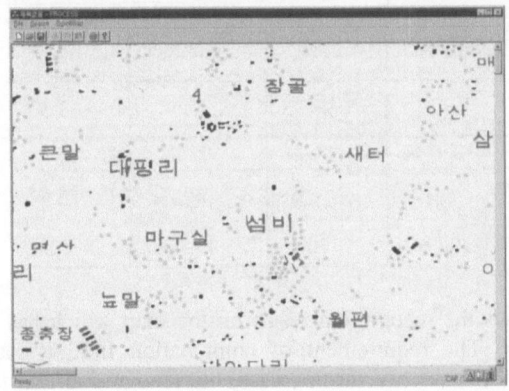

Fig. 10. Detected houses after morphological operation

The recognition result, shown in Table 1 is about a map that has grids and moderately touched houses. It shows that the recognition ratio is flat or slightly increased while the operation is going on. The purpose of this research is not for full automation, but for reducing the manual jobs. The extraction of houses by hand needs more complicated procedure than elimination of un-recognized result. Thus, in this research, we have in mind how to minimize the number of un-recognized houses. So, although the result shows that the recognition ratio is not getting better after some stage, it can give better efficiency than when it is fully done by hand.

Table 1. Recognition Result of Case II

	House detection of isolated houses only		House detection after removing of grid		House detection after character removal operation		House detection after morphological operation	
	number	%	Number	%	Number	%	Number	%
Correct recognition	1,148	74.93	1,271	81.74	1,370	84.99	1,384	85.43
Un-recogni zed	377	24.61	254	16.33	155	9.62	141	8.70
False recognition	7	0.46	30	1.93	87	5.39	95	5.87
Total	1,532	100	1,555	100	1,612	100	1,620	100

Table 2. Recognition Result of Case II

	House detection of isolated houses only		House detection after character removal operation		House detection after morphological operation	
	Number	%	Number	%	Number	%
Correct Recognition	6,931	68.72	8,114	73.30	8,435	73.60
Un-recognized	2,924	28.99	1,741	15.73	1,420	12.39
False eecognition	261	2.29	1,215	10.97	1,606	14.01
Total	10,086	100	11,070	100	11,461	100

Table 2 shows the recognition result on the map which has no grid and heavily touched houses. The requirement of computation time is less because the grid elimination is not necessary. In this case, the recognition rate is not well increased after the morphological operation. The reason why it is not performed well is that the houses are severely touched. The distinction between the lines and the houses are not operate well although the morphological operation is carried out. From the table, we can find out that the false recognition is augmented as the number of operation is increased.

Table 3. Recognition Result of Case III

	House detection of isolated houses only		House detection after character removal operation		House detection after morphological operation	
	Number	%	Number	%	Number	%
Correct Recognition	13,840	92.71	14,378	94.12	14,390	91.37
Un-recognized	779	5.22	241	1.58	229	1.46
False Recognition	309	2.07	657	4.30	1,130	7.17
Total	14,928	100	15,276	100	15,749	100

Table 3 shows the recognition result on the map which has no grid and slightly touched houses. In this case, we find out that the best recognition is obtained when the character elimination is accomplished.

After the morphological operation, the number of correct recognition is slightly increased and the number of false recognition is largely increased. The total recognition rate is decreased using the morphological operation.

From the recognition tables, the morphological operation has slight increase or even decrease of recognition ratio. Thus house detection after character removal procedure is recommended, because the manual verification procedure will follow. The minimization of false recognition is more important than slight incrementation of correct recognition for the verification process.

Because the quality of image affects the size of houses very much, with images which have enough quality, it gives good result. But with ones which have low quality, the result can get even worse.

4. Conclusion

This paper is dealt with the house detection on maps to automate the inputting process. Contour detection method using 8-direction chain code is used, and to extract information about components that are connected to others. The run-length encoding is implemented in order to eliminate the straight lines such as grid. In addition to them, by combining the closest neighbors, the regions of Korean characters are extracted, and the thin lines are removed by the morphological operation.

As you see in the result, the success of recognition is akin to the quality of images, thus it is required to add an algorithm that changes the threshold value automatically by calculating the sizes of houses whenever new maps are scanned. By doing so, it can be more robust.

The main interest of this paper is detection of houses, so others are not differentiated. The recognition results show the feasibility of reducing time and effort of inputting data by hand. From the result, the recommended way of recognition is the character elimination process which indicates the good recognition ratio and the less false recognition ratio comparing with morphological operation. For the verification process, less number of false recognition is important. But houses, characters, roads, borderlines of administrative district, and islands, etc. are required to be saved as layered vector data. And with that data, the map should be reconstructed. It is also necessary to build DB of characters on maps using character recognition method.

Acknowledgement This work is supported by 2000 Chung-Ang University's equipment support research grant.

References

1. R. Kasturi et al., "Map data processing in Geographic Information System", IEEE Computer, pp.13-21, Dec. 1989.
2. G. K. Myers, et al., "Verification-Based Approach for Automated Text and Feature Extraction from Raster-Scanned Maps", 1st GREC, pp.190-203, 1995.
3. G. Maderlechner and H. Mayer, "Conversion of High Level Information from Scanned Maps into Geographic Information Systems", 3rd ICDAR, pp.253-256, 1995.
4. M.P. Deseilligny and R. Mariani, "A Three Year Project on Topographic Maps Interpretation", 2nd GREC, pp160-167. 1997
5. I. Pitas, Digital Image Processing Algorithm, Prentice Hall, 1993.
6. H. Bassmann and P. W. Besslich, Ad Oculus: Digital Image Processing, International Thomson Publishing, 1995.
7. Min-Ki Kim, et al., "Automatic Region Labeling of the Layered Map", 1st GREC, pp.179-189, 1995.

Recognition of Connective Relationship among House Blocks from House Maps

Takamasa Shimasaki and Toyohide Watanabe

Department of Information Engineering,
Graduate School of Engineering, Nagoya University
Furo-cho, Chikusa-ku, Nagoya 464-8603, Japan
simasaki@watanabe.nuie.nagoya-u.ac.jp
watanabe@nuie.nagoya-u.ac.jp

Abstract. In this paper, we propose an experimental method to recognize connective relationships among house blocks in house maps. In house maps, some geometric constraints are imposed on the configuration among neighboring house blocks, but the connective structures are varied. Thus, it is very difficult to distinguish the constructive relationships among individual house blocks. To cope with this difficulty, we use not only block lines but also block areas, which are composed of connective background pixels in house map images. This paper describes our recognition method and evaluates the effectiveness through experiments.

1 Introduction

It is one of important subjects to extract useful and meaningful information from paper-base documents or drawings automatically in order to compose eletronic-form data libraries [1,2,3,4,5,6,7]. However, the recognition procedures have been developed individually to deal with the specific images: the general algorithm or approach to be applicable for all kinds of documents/drawings images is not usable until today. In interpreting images of area-based drawings such as tables, house maps and floor plans, which are composed of area objects partitioned by lines, connective relationships among area objects are very valuable information and often used in the recognition process [4,5,6].

Many traditional recognition procedures analyze foreground line pixels around area objects in order to extract connective relationships among area objects from these drawings: individual area objects and connective relationships among them are extracted by analyzing only foreground line pixels. This approach is effective for images in which all area objects have strong restrictions with shapes and a constructive feature of the corresponding area object appears in foreground pixels which are a part of lines: for example, in table images all item fields are rectangular and the pattern "Γ", which specifies the item field, appears on foreground line pixels [4,5]. However, it is difficult to apply this approach to the drawings in which shapes of area objects are relatively changeable because the features of area objects do not appear explicitly in surrounding lines. Moreover, noises on foreground pixels prevent precise extraction of connective

Atul K. Chhabra and D. Dori (Eds.): GREC'99, LNCS 1941, pp. 81–89, 2000.

relationships. To cope with this difficulty, we make use of not only foreground pixels of lines but also background pixels of area objects. Our method to extract connective relationships among area objects is applicable to area-based drawing images, in which area objects are completely surrounded by solid line segments.

In this paper, we deal with house map images. House maps have many house blocks, which are corresponded to houses or buildings. Since in house maps house blocks have various shapes, it is difficult to extract the connective relationships among house blocks by analyzing only foreground block line pixels. Our method can extract the connective relationships effectively by using background pixels of house block areas besides foreground pixels. We compose *block network* in order to represent the connective relationships among house blocks. This paper explains how to compose the block network and evaluates the effectiveness of our method through some experiments.

2 Block Network

Before the explanation of our method, we mention simply what interpretation the block network makes possible. According to our observation of house maps, the block network are convenient to deal with order of address numbers. Therefore we can use the block network in estimating orders of address numbers and calculating address information for individual house blocks. In our consideration, the block network provides the address estimation procedure (Figure 1) with some clues for estimating orders of address numbers.

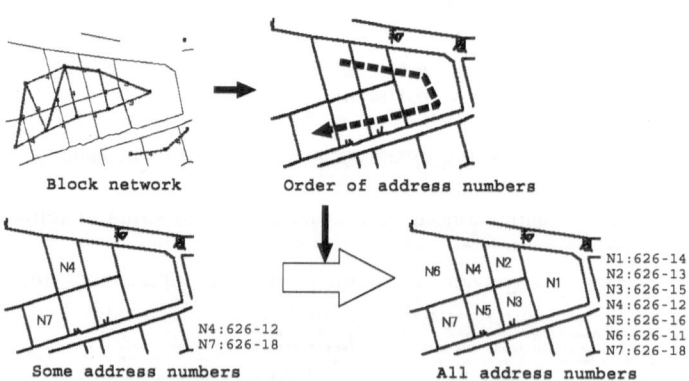

Fig. 1. Address estimation procedure

Block network consists of nodes and edges: the nodes are equivalent to individual house blocks, while the edges are connections between two neighboring house blocks. From our observation over house maps, it is necessary to estimate the order of address numbers with respect to checking up not only whether two house blocks are neighboring with each other but also what kind of connection patterns two neighboring house blocks have. Therefore, the edge in the block network associates with one connection pattern. We define the normal connection patterns in Figure 2: *Include, Overlap, Attach-1, Attach-2, Attach-3* and *Attach-4*. Most of connection patterns in house maps can be categorized into these normal connection patterns.

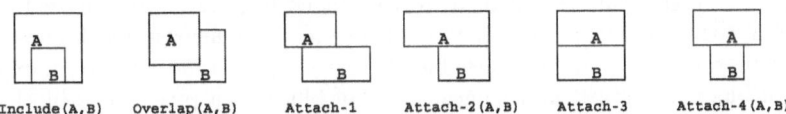

Include(A,B)   Overlap(A,B)   Attach-1   Attach-2(A,B)   Attach-3   Attach-4(A,B)

Fig. 2. Normal connection patterns: *A and B mean house blocks touched with each other. In all normal patterns except for Attach-1 and Attach-3, the block order is described as (A,B): "Overlap(A,B)" means that A overlaps B; "Include(A,B)","Attach-2(A,B)" or "Attach-4(A,B)" represent bigger block A is attached to smaller block B according to "Include","Attach-2" or "Attach-4"*

3   Composition of Block Network

In this section, we explain how to compose the block network, based on connective relationships among house blocks, from house map images. Since house blocks are organized from various shapes of polygons, foreground block line pixels around them do not provide sufficient information to recognize house blocks. Therefore, it is difficult to recognize the house blocks and distinguish connective relationships among them by analyzing only foreground pixels of block lines. We overcome this problem with not only foreground pixels but also background pixels. By using background pixels, we calculate the relation between block line segments and house blocks. The relation, which we call the area pointer, is the key information in extracting block lines as composite line segments of a house block and making up the connection between two neighboring house blocks. Figure 3 illustrates our processing flow in the composition process of block network.

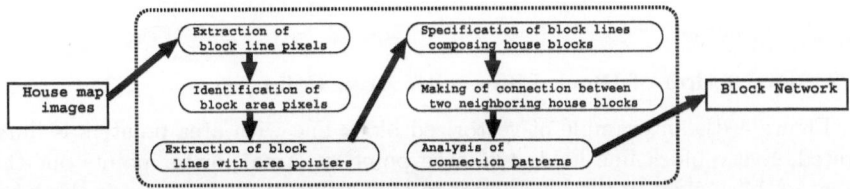

Fig. 3. Processing flow

3.1   Recognition of House Block Areas

In this phase, each house block area is recognized as a set of pixels. All house block areas and other areas(i.e. road areas, noise areas, etc.) are gathered into one image. We call this image the area map (Figure 4(c)). In area maps, each pixel has its own label. This label is assigned in order to distinguish one area from another. The area map is very important because every pixel has area information about which area it belongs to, and enables to refer to house block areas in X-Y coordinates. Since vectorized block lines are also represented by the X-Y coordinate, it is easy to access house block areas from block lines.

The recognition phase of house block areas is divided into two steps: extraction of block line pixels and identification of block area pixels. The block line pixels are extracted as a large pixel set whose members consist of connective foreground pixels [3]: it is the pixel set that can be enclosed with a minimum large rectangular box. Figure 4(b) shows the block line image, in which all foreground pixels are block line pixels. Since block lines in house maps are separated in many cases from other components such as characters, this method is effective. In the next step, pixels of house block areas are identified. The pixel set in block line images which has the proper size of minimum rectangular box is regarded as house block area [3]. For each pixel in house block areas, labels are assigned. All pixels included in one area have different label values from pixels in another area.

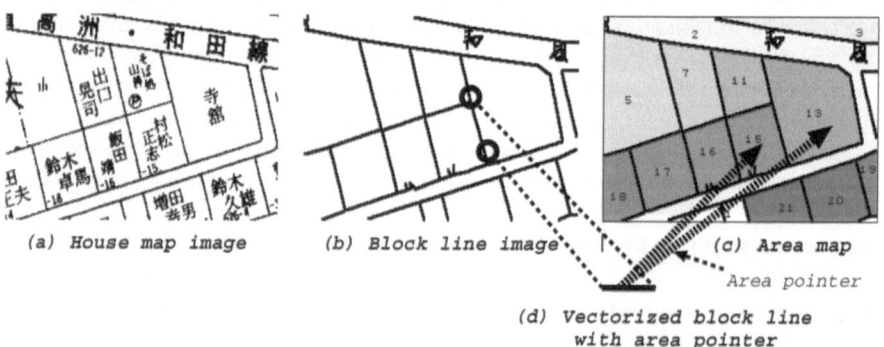

(a) House map image   (b) Block line image   (c) Area map
                                                          Area pointer

(d) Vectorized block line
with area pointer

Fig. 4. Block line image, area map, and vectorized block line with area pointer

3.2   Extraction of Block Lines with Area Pointers

In Figure 4(d), an example of vectorized block line with area pointers is illustrated. Every block line holds two area pointers. Area pointer points out the areas on both sides of the block line, and the value of area pointer is the label value in area map. The area pointer is calculated by scanning area map from the middle point of block line toward the vertical direction against this block line. The extraction step of block lines with area pointer is described below.

1. Vectorize block line image and extract block lines. We use U.E.Ramer's vectorization method [8].
2. For each block line, the following 2(a) and 2(b) are performed.
   (a) Scan the area map from the middle point of block line toward both vertical directions.
   (b) Get the label value from the scanned area map. This label value is the value of area pointer.

3.3   Extraction of Connective Relationships among House Blocks

This phase is divided into three steps: specification of block lines composing the house block, connection between two neighboring house blocks, and analysis of connection patterns. Area pointers play an important role in the former two steps. In the specification step of block lines composing the house block, block lines with one of two area pointers pointing out the house block $H_n(n = 1..N$(number of house blocks)) are selected as the block lines composing the house block H_n. The set of block lines L_n composing the house block $H_n(n = 1..N)$ with the label value h_n in area map is calculated by the following procedure.

1. Select the block line $l_k(k = 1..K$(number of block lines)).
2. If $p1(l_k) = h_n$, then $p1(l_k)$ is added to L_n; otherwise if $p2(l_k) = h_n$, then $p2(l_k)$ is added to L_n;
   Here, $p1(l_k)$ and $p2(l_k)$ are both area pointers of the block line l_k.

At the second step, we make up connection between two neighboring house blocks. The house block H_{n1} is identified to have a connection with the house block H_{n2} when at least one block line in the house block H_{n1} has area pointers pointing out H_{n2}. Here, the following procedure checks up whether the house block H_{n1} has the connection with H_{n2} or not.

1. Select the block line $l_k \in L_{n1}(L_{n1}$ is the set of block lines composing the house block H_{n1}).
2. If $p1(l_k) = h_{n2}$ or $p2(l_k) = h_{n2}$, then H_{n1} has the connection with H_{n2}.

The third step analyzes the connection patterns between two neighboring house blocks according to six normal patterns shown in Figure 2. We use the angle at corner of house block area as the representation of connection pattern. As we would like to categorize the connection pattern as shown in Figure 2, the angle is approximated into 90, 180 or 270. A couple of angles at common corners of two neighboring house blocks(for example (90,90)) is the element of connection pattern. The connection pattern P between two neighboring house blocks, $H1$ and $H2$, is calculated as follows.

1. Extract the common corner $c_m(m = 1..M$(number of common corners)) between $H1$ and $H2$.
2. Calculate $\theta_{H1}(c_m)$ and $\theta_{H2}(c_m)$ which are both the angle at c_m; $\theta_{H1}(c_m)$ is the angle in $H1$ and $\theta_{H2}(c_m)$ is so in $H2$.

3. Approximate the angle $\theta_{H1}(c_m), \theta_{H2}(c_m)$ to 90, 180 and 270 as follows.

$0 \leq \theta_{H1}(c_m), \theta_{H2}(c_m) < 135 \Rightarrow \alpha_{H1}(c_m), \alpha_{H2}(c_m) = 90$
$135 \leq \theta_{H1}(c_m), \theta_{H2}(c_m) < 225 \Rightarrow \alpha_{H1}(c_m), \alpha_{H2}(c_m) = 180$
$225 \leq \theta_{H1}(c_m), \theta_{H2}(c_m) < 360 \Rightarrow \alpha_{H1}(c_m), \alpha_{H2}(c_m) = 270$

4. Add the couple of approximated angles $p_m(\alpha_{H1}(c_m), \alpha_{H2}(c_m))$ to P, except for (180,180).

The connection pattern P calculated by the above procedure consists of the following elements p_m: (90,90), (90,180), (180,90), (90,270), (270,90). Figure 5 illustrates p_m graphically.

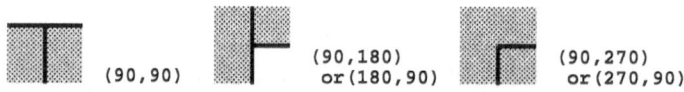

Fig. 5. Elements of connection pattern: *dotted area is house block area to generate elements of connection pattern*

The connection pattern P is categorized into six normal patterns according to the following conditions. In the following description, A and B are neighboring house blocks with each other.

Include(A,B): $|P| \geq 3$[1]; and P has neither (180,90) nor (90,180). A is the house block with $(\exists c_m)(\alpha_A(c_m) = 270)$[2]; B is the other.
Overlap(A,B): $|P| \geq 3$; and P has (180,90) or (90,180). A is the house block with $(\forall c_m)(\alpha_A(c_m) \neq 270)$[3]; B is the other.
Attach-1(A,B): $P = \{(180, 90), (90, 180)\}$. Either house block can be A or B.
Attach-2(A,B): $P = \{(180, 90), (90, 90)\}$ or $P = \{(90, 180), (90, 90)\}$. A is the house block with $(\exists c_m)(\alpha_A(c_m) = 180)$; B is the other.
Attach-3(A,B): $P = \{(90, 90), (90, 90)\}$. Either house block can be A or B.
Attach-4(A,B): $P = \{(180, 90), (180, 90)\}$ or $P = \{(90, 180), (90, 180)\}$. A is the house block with $(\exists c_m)(\alpha_A(c_m) = 180)$; B is the other.

4   Experimental Result

In this section, we evaluates our method through experiments. Figure 7 is the block network composed from the house map image shown in Figure 6(a), through our method. The house map image illustrated in Figure 6(a) is the

---

[1] $|P|$ means the number of elements in P.
[2] $(\exists c_m)(\alpha_A(c_m) = 270)$ shows that c_m exists: at the c_m, approximated angle in the block A is 270.
[3] $(\forall c_m)(\alpha_A(c_m) \neq 270)$ means that no c_m has the approximated angle 270 in the block A.

black-and-white house map image input by scanner at the resolution of 400dpi. The size of this image is 572 x 527 pixels and the scale is 1 to 1,500.

Table 1 shows the experimental result for 5 house map images. Hatched items are the results acquired by using manually extracted block line pixels, that is, by using block line pixels without noises. "Block line" means the ratio of automatically extracted block line pixels to manually ones. "House block" is the success ratio of recognized house block areas. "Connection" stands for the detected connection among neighboring house blocks. "Pattern" represents the connection patterns.

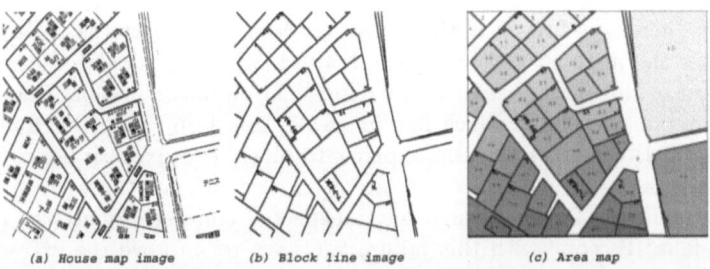

(a) House map image   (b) Block line image   (c) Area map

Fig. 6. Experimental result: house map image, block line image, and area map

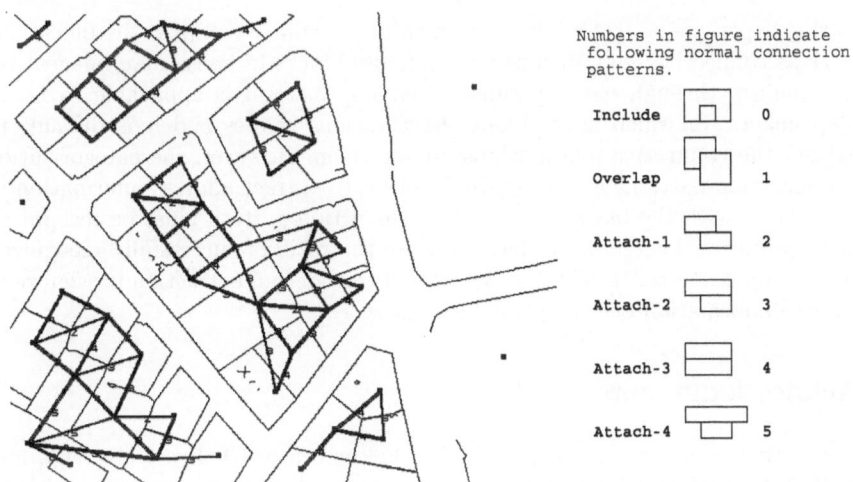

Fig. 7. Experimental result: block network

In this experimental result, we can confirm good results in "House block" and "Connection" in spite of the success ratio of "Block line". Our method recognizes house blocks and makes up the connection between two neighboring house blocks precisely even if some noises appear on block line pixels. However,

Table 1. Experimental result for 5 house map images(%)

	Block line		House block		Connection		Pattern	
Map1	87.0	....	96.8	96.8	94.3	94.3	82.9	88.6
Map2	90.2	....	97.9	97.9	97.6	97.6	92.2	97.0
Map3	96.2	....	98.0	98.0	98.0	98.0	79.0	83.9
Map4	96.4	....	96.0	96.0	96.0	96.0	78.3	83.3
Map5	93.5	....	96.2	96.8	93.4	96.1	88.7	95.3

we can not get a good result in the analysis of connection patterns. This analysis phase uses the angle at corners of the house block area calculated from block lines. Most of the analysis failures are dependent on noises in block line images. Our extraction method of block line images is based on connective foreground pixels and it is easy to attach noise pixels to block line pixels. If noises exist in block line images, invalid block lines are generated through the vectorization of block line images. This generates the unexpected connection patterns and the analysis fails. To cope with this failure, we have to improve the extraction of block line images.

5   Conclusion

In this paper, we addressed an experimental method to compose the block network as connective relationships among house blocks in house map images. We can confirm through our experiment that our method is applicable to house map images, in which house blocks have various shapes and it is difficult to extract the connective relationships among them. However, the categorization of connection patterns is inaccurate. In order to extract address information in accordance with the block network, the connection pattern must be recognized more precisely. Therefore, we have to raise the ratio of successfully recognized connection patterns. In addition, we should consider an extraction procedure of address information based on this block network.

Acknowledgments

The authors are very grateful to Prof. T.Fukumura of Chukyo University, and Prof. Y.Inagaki and Prof. J.Toriwaki of Nagoya University, and also wish to thank our research members for their cooperations and discussions.

References

1. O.Shiku et al.: Character Extraction from Map Image. Trans. on IPSJ. **34-2** (1993) 273-280 [in Japanese] 81
2. T.Watanabe, R.Zhang: Recognition of Character Strings from Color Urban Map Images on the Basis of Validation Mechanism. Proc. of ICDAR'97. **2** (1997) 805-808 81
3. T.Shimasaki, T.Watanabe: Extraction of Character Strings from House Maps. Proc. of MVA'98. (1998) 297-300 81, 84
4. T.Naruse, T.Watanabe, Q.Luo, N.Sugie: A Structure Recognition Method of Table-Form Documents on the Basis of the Information of Line Segments. Trans. on IEICE. **J75-D-II-8** (1992) 1372-1385 [in Japanese] 81
5. T.Sobue, T.Watanabe: Identification of Item Fields in Table-form Documents with/without Line Segments. Proc. of MVA'96. (1996) 522-525 81
6. A.Shio, Y.Aoki: Sketch Plan: A Prototype System for Interpreting Hand-Sketched Floor-Plans. Trans. on IEICE. **J82-D-II-3** (1999) 431-439 [in Japanese] 81
7. N.Yokokura, T.Watanabe: Layout-based Approach for Extracting Constructive Elements of Bar Graphs. Proc. of GREC'97. (1997) 119-126 81
8. U. E.Ramer: An Interative Procedure for the Polygonal Approximation of Plane Curve. Proc. of CGIP. (1972) 244-256 85

Part III

Graphic Document Analysis

A Tabular Survey
of Automated Table Processing

Daniel Lopresti[1] and George Nagy[2]

[1] Bell Labs, Lucent Technologies Inc.
600 Mountain Avenue, Room 2D-447, Murray Hill, NJ 07974
`dlopresti@lucent.com`
[2] Department of Electrical, Computer, and Systems Engineering, Rensselaer
Polytechnic Institute
Troy, NY 12180-3590
`nagy@ecse.rpi.edu`

Abstract. Tables are the only acceptable means of communicating certain types of structured data. A precise definition of "tabularity" remains elusive because some bureaucratic forms, multicolumn text layouts, and schematic drawings share many characteristics of tables. There are significant differences between typeset tables, electronic files designed for display of tables, and tables in symbolic form intended for information retrieval. Although most research to date has addressed the extraction of low-level geometric information from scanned raster images of paper tables, the recent trend toward the analysis of tables in electronic form may pave the way to a higher level of table understanding.

Recent research on table composition and table analysis has improved our understanding of the distinction between the logical and physical structures of tables, and has led to improved formalisms for modeling tables. The present study indicates that progress on half-a-dozen specific research issues would open the door to using existing paper and electronic tables for database update, tabular browsing, structured information retrieval through graphical and audio interfaces, multimedia table editing, and platform-independent display.

Although tables are not a conventional format for conveying the primary content of technical papers, here we attempt to subdue our natural garrulity by adopting this genre to communicate what we have to say about tables entirely in tabular form.

Atul K. Chhabra and D. Dori (Eds.): GREC'99, LNCS 1941, pp. 93–120, 2000.

Table 1. *Motivation and definitions.* The study of tables and forms is gaining momentum because of their suitability for electronic information exchange [36]. In this paper we experiment with tables as a means of conveying information that is usually presented in narrative form. Our tables also serve to illustrate formatting and transformations that can be applied to tables. But the medium is NOT our only message

Why tables?	Prevalent means of communicating structured data Content may include words, numbers, formulas, even graphics Metadata represented by alignment and rulings Adapted to computerized composition Underlying paradigm for spreadsheets and relational databases Bridge between textual and graphic representations
What is a table?	2-D cell assembly for presenting information Regular, repetitive structure along at least one axis [41] Datatype determined by either horizontal or vertical index
What is a form?	Isothetic layout for collecting information One-to-one mapping between indices and data No implication of regularity [41]
What is table analysis?	Information extraction follows table detection and localization Geometric analysis to isolate cell contents Table structure determined simultaneously If needed, OCR translates cells and headers into symbolic form Interpretation requires understanding context
Rationale for this study	Importance of converting tables from one medium to another Rapid growth of tables in various digital formats Desirability of medium-independent query algorithms Interdependence of table composition and interpretation Advent of new applications that require table interpretation Need for research to address neglected table topics

Table 2. *Table of contents.* Table processing draws on established techniques of both text and graphics image analysis, but also requires new research. Starting with a review of current document image analysis, this study leads to a perspective on the relationship between prospective applications and open research areas

Table processing in context
 A document taxonomy
 Schema for document and table image analysis
 Growth of table papers

Characterization of tables
 Table jargon
 Table representation
 Dimensionality of tabular structures
 Wang's formal model (genetic code)
 Logical/physical dichotomies in the literature

Methodology
 Methods for extracting table geometry
 Functional/logical analysis
 Sources of difficulty

Conclusions
 Applications and research tasks
 References

Appendix: challenging examples
 A nice table
 Multi-column headers
 A very small table
 U.S. Army Divisions in Europe
 Crystal structure
 Analysis of the vote
 ICDAR'99 conference schedule
 Alexandar Graham Bell's schedule
 Vocoder algorithms
 Lucent stock watch
 NY Stock Exchange results
 Road centerline striping standards
 Pickup truck evaluation
 The Periodic Table
 A non-table table

Table 3. *A document taxonomy.* The objective of image analysis and the kind of ancillary data that can facilitate it depends on the document type. Most current DIA applications require processing only documents of a single type

Type	Example	DIA Task	Ancillary Data
plain text	Moby Dick, Gettysburg Address	extract correct word order	English lexicon & grammar
newspaper, magazine	NY Times, Vogue	separate and reassemble articles; pointers to illustrations, *tables*	publication-specific format
scholarly & technical text	IEEE-PAMI, Dr. Dobbs Journal	index: author, title, page; pointers to refs, figs, *tables*, footnotes, equations	abbreviations, acronyms, units
formal text	program listing, chess, bridge, cookbook	extract executable, or compilable, form	program, chess syntax
letter, memo, envelope	information request, complaint, reservation	extract routing info; index: sender, date, subject	directories
directory	telephone directory, street index	extract name-attribute pairs	previous edition
structured list	organization chart, table of contents, catalog	recover hierarchy; cross-references	previous edition
business form	order, invoice, subscription, survey, IRS-1040	link field content to DBMS; convert to SGML or XML format	formatted data, DBMS, lexicons, workflow
engineering drawing	assembly or part drawing; isometric	convert to CAD format	part lists, drawing stds
schematic diagram	circuits, utility maps	extract net list or convert to CAD format	P-SPICE, cable inventory
map	topographic quad, street map, road map	convert to GIS format	gazetteer, other maps, GIS
table	*airline schedules, stock quotes*	*construct formal model: headers ↔ entries*	*airline, stock abbreviations, previous edition*

Table 4. *Example of a table operation.* The manipulation of rows and columns is a common requirement. The transformation of Table 3 that is illustrated here alters the table to focus attention of the presence of tables in most types of documents. Some documents ("ISA") are best viewed in their entirety as tables or forms

Type	*Example*	*Tabular Content*
plain text	Moby Dick, Gettysburg Address	none
newspaper, magazine	NY Times, Vogue	stock quotes, temperatures
scholarly & technical text	IEEE-PAMI, Dr. Dobbs Journal	quantitative information
formal text	program listing, chess, bridge, cookbook	repetitive items
letter, memo, envelope	information request, complaint, reservation	delivery schedule, price lists
directory	telephone book, street index	name-attribute pairs
structured list	organization chart, table of contents, catalog	ISA
business form	order, invoice, subscription, survey, IRS-1040	ISA
engineering drawing	assembly or part drawing, isometric	title block, revisions
schematic diagram	circuits, utility maps	component values
map	topo quad, street map, road map	legend
table	*airline schedules, stock quotes*	*ISA*

Table 5. *Common operations in document image analysis.* Tables are in a sense intermediate between mostly-text and mostly-graphics documents. It is therefore instructive to consider the methods of image analysis that have been found useful in these better-established applications. They are organized here bottom-to-top, with the output of the lower-level operations serving for input to the higher-level operations

Process Level	Document Type	
	Mostly-text	*Mostly-graphics*
Pixels	Preprocessing Representation Noise reduction Binarization Skew detection, zoning Character segmentation Script, language, font rec'n Character scaling	Preprocessing Representation Noise reduction Binarization Thinning Vectorization
Primitives	Glyph recognition CC's, strokes Characters, diacritics, punctuation Words	Primitive recognition Straight-lines, curve segments Junctions and nodes Loops Characters
Structures	Text recognition Word segmentation Text line reconstruction Table analysis Morphological content Lexical context Syntax, semantics	Structure recognition Text fields Legends Label attribution Dimensions Graphics symbols Aerial and texture features Beautification (constraints)
Documents	Page layout analysis Text/non-text Physical components Logical components Functional components Compression	Interpretation Component recognition Connectivity analysis CAD/GIS layer separation Database attribute extraction Compression
Corpus	Information retrieval Indexing Search Security, authentication, privacy	DBMS, CAD, GIS interface Validation Update Search

Table 6. *A second example of a table operation.* Condensing the contents of cells and collapsing cell boundaries is useful for accessing tabular information with small displays (palm tops, cell phones). A very small display is illustrated in Fig. 3. A condensed version of Table 5 is shown below

Process Level	Document Type	
	Mostly-text	*Mostly-graphics*
Pixels	Preprocessing	Preprocessing
Primitives	Glyph recognition	Primitive recognition
Structures	Text recognition	Structure recognition
Documents	Page layout analysis	Interpretation
Corpus	Information retrieval	DBMS, CAD, GIS interface

Table 7. *Abstraction in table processing.* As in the case of other types of documents (Tables 5 and 6), the interpretation of tables can be considered at several levels of abstraction. The lowest (image) level is absent in tables prepared for digital media

Level	Elements
Image	pixels
Morphology	geometry: grid, rules, spacing: characters
Syntax	2-D hierarchy; Wang model [51]; text
Semantics	relational data base; natural language processing
Pragmatics	update, retrieval

Table 8. *Growth of table papers.* A simple table that needs lots of context for interpretation! The recent increase in the accessibility of tables in electronic form may be responsible for the sharp growth of table-oriented research

Years	# of Pubs
$\leq$ 1989	11
1990-94	14
1995-98	35

Table 9. *Table papers in the literature.* Relatively few papers attempt to extract semantic information ("content tags")

Analysis	Scanned image	Geometry	[2], [3], [4], [5], [1], [6], [8], [9], [18], [19], [20], [17], [26], [28], [32], [39], [40]
		Cell content analysis	[7], [21], [23], [30], [34], [43], [45], [46], [49], [52], [57]
	Coded text		[25], [29], [42], [41] [13], [24], [27]
Synthesis	Computer		[31], [33], [35], [51]
	Traditional		[10], [22], [48], [54], [55], [56]
Tools	Spreadsheet Database Agents NLP Speech		[37], [38] [14] [16], [45] [13] [12], [44], [47], [50]
Applications	Federal Register Wall Street Journal email		[15] [42] [53]

Table 10. *Table jargon.* Items in Boxhead and Stub are also called Headers, Headings, Labels, Spanning labels, Indices, Captions. There are many books on preferred typesetting practices for tables (see "Traditional" in Table 9). For instance, it was recommended that double-rulings be printed in two passes to avoid gaps at corners

Stub header	← Boxhead →				
↑			↖	↑	↗
Stub	Cell		←	Block	→
↓			↙	↓	↘

Table 11. *Tables can be recursive.* However, by convention subdivisions increase from top to bottom, and from left to right

Tables	can be			
recursive	Tables	can be		
	recursive	Tables	can be	
		recursive	Tables	can be
			recursive	...

Table 12. *Table-form documents.* "Table" and "form" are sometimes used interchangeably, but a clear distinction exists

Tables	Forms
For output	For input
Frame and content created simultaneously	Frame created before content
Tabular structure	Rectilinear structure
Machine-printed	Machine- or hand-printed
Sometimes unique	Frame rarely unique, content often unique

Table 13. *Table representation.* Note: low level can be displayed, intermediate level can be edited, high level can be queried. XML encoding is gaining ground for forms used in commercial transactions, but it is not clear how easy it is to encode meaningfully tables intended for wider use in less specific contexts

Level of Representation		
Low ("morphology")	*Intermediate* ("syntax")	*High* ("semantics")
PNM/PBM GIF TIF (CCITT, JBIG) PostScript PDF	Rich Text Format Troff, LaTeX HTML MS Word, Excel MatLab Wang Model	Relational DBMS ODA SGML XML

Table 14. *Level of representation.* Rotation is another example of a useful operation. The ordering by level of abstraction is more obvious here than in Table 13

Level	Representation
Low[1] ("morphology")	PNM/PBM, GIF, TIF (CCITT, JBIG), PostScript, PDF
Intermediate[2] ("syntax")	Rich Text Format, Troff, LaTeX, HTML, MS Word, Excel, MatLab, Wang Model
High[3] ("semantics")	Relational DBMS, ODA, SGML, XML

---

[1] Can be displayed.
[2] Can be edited.
[3] Can be queried.

Table 15. *The Genetic Code I.* Wang [51] developed an abstract data type for tables. It is essentially a forest where each node, except the leaves, are categories called "labeled domains." The categories can be nested. The leaves are the cell contents. The concept of labeled domains is similar to the Dewey Decimal System for library catalogues. In the example below, there are three trees, corresponding to the first, second, and third positions in the genetic code. The entries are amino acids. Each amino acid is specified by the three category labels. In a more complex table, each entry would be specified by a set of "root-to-frontier" paths through the category trees

Codon Position				Codon Position			
1st	2nd	3rd	Amino Acid	1st	2nd	3rd	Amino Acid
U	U	U	Phenylalanine	A	U	U	Isoleucine
U	U	C	Phenylalanine	A	U	C	Isoleucine
U	U	A	Leucine	A	U	A	Isoleucine
U	U	G	Leucine	A	U	G	Methionine
U	C	U	Serine	A	C	U	Threonine
U	C	C	Serine	A	C	C	Threonine
U	C	A	Serine	A	C	A	Threonine
U	C	G	Serine	A	C	G	Threonine
U	A	U	Tyrosine	A	A	U	Asparagine
U	A	C	Tyrosine	A	A	C	Asparagine
U	A	A	Stop	A	A	A	Lysine
U	A	G	Stop	A	A	G	Lysine
U	G	U	Cysteine	A	G	U	Serine
U	G	C	Cysteine	A	G	C	Serine
U	G	A	Stop	A	G	A	Arginine
U	G	G	Tryptophan	A	G	G	Arginine
C	U	U	Leucine	G	U	U	Valine
C	U	C	Leucine	G	U	C	Valine
C	U	A	Leucine	G	U	A	Valine
C	U	G	Leucine	G	U	G	Valine
C	C	U	Proline	G	C	U	Alanine
C	C	C	Proline	G	C	C	Alanine
C	C	A	Proline	G	C	A	Alanine
C	C	G	Proline	G	C	G	Alanine
C	A	U	Histidine	G	A	U	Aspartic acid
C	A	C	Histidine	G	A	C	Aspartic acid
C	A	A	Glutamine	G	A	A	Glutamic acid
C	A	G	Glutamine	G	A	G	Glutamic acid
C	G	U	Arginine	G	G	U	Glycine
C	G	C	Arginine	G	G	C	Glycine
C	G	A	Arginine	G	G	A	Glycine
C	G	G	Arginine	G	G	G	Glycine

Table 16. *The Genetic Code II.* Wang calls the number of categories the "dimension" of the table. The Genetic Code is three-dimensional, regardless of its physical layout. In the rendering below, the cells are arranged to minimize the repetition of cell entries. The "size" of a table is the product of the number of lowest-level categories, here $4 \times 4 \times 4 = 64$

UUU	Phenyl-	UCU	Serine	UAU	Tyrosine	UGU	Cysteine
UUC	alanine	UCC		UAC		UGC	
UUA	Leucine	UCA		UAA	Stop	UGA	Stop
UUG		UCG		UAG		UGG	Tryptophan
CUU		CCU	Proline	CAU	Histidine	CGU	Arginine
CUC		CCC		CAC		CGC	
CUA		CCA		CAA	Glutamine	CGA	
CUG		CCG		CAG		CGG	
AUU	Isoleucine	ACU	Threonine	AAU	Asparagine	AGU	Serine
AUC		ACC		AAC		AGC	
AUA		ACA		AAA	Lysine	AGA	Arginine
AUG	Methionine	ACG		AAG		AGG	
GUU	Valine	GCU	Alanine	GAU	Aspartic	GGU	Glycine
GUC		GCC		GAC	acid	GGC	
GUA		GCA		GAA	Glutamic	GGA	
GUG		GCG		GAG	acid	GGG	

Table 17. *The Genetic Code III.* Here the first and third categories are laid out vertically, and the second category horizontally. Many other possible permutations exist. Wang also developed software for creating different tabular layouts for the same logical table. She found that most of the several hundred tables in standard texts and monographs that she examined fit her model, except for the frequent presence of footnotes. Wang's main contribution is the separation between the logical and physical aspects of a table

First	*Second Position*				*Third*
Position	U	C	A	G	*Position*
	Phe	Ser	Tyr	Cys	U
U	Phe	Ser	Tyr	Cys	C
	Leu	Ser	Stop	Stop	A
	Leu	Ser	Stop	Trp	G
	Leu	Pro	His	Arg	U
C	Leu	Pro	His	Arg	C
	Leu	Pro	Gln	Arg	A
	Leu	Pro	Gln	Arg	G
	Ile	Thr	Asn	Ser	U
A	Ile	Thr	Asn	Ser	C
	Ile	Thr	Lys	Arg	A
	Met	Thr	Lys	Arg	G
	Val	Ala	Asp	Gly	U
G	Val	Ala	Asp	Gly	C
	Val	Ala	Glu	Gly	A
	Val	Ala	Glu	Gly	G

Table 18. *Strategies for extracting table geometry.* (Issues: Hierarchical vs. flat structure? Skew invariance? Start with cells or with external frame?)

		Model-driven		Data-driven	
		Top-down	Bottom-up	Top-down	Bottom-up
Primitives	Rulings	√	√	√	√
	White space	√	√		
	Text	√	√	√	√
	Cell		√		√

Table 19. *Logical/functional analysis.* In contrast to the data-driven analysis described in Table 18, here the analysis is model-driven

Table syntax	Green and Krishnamoorthy [19,18,20]
Structure description tree	Watanabe, Quo, and Sugie [52]
Cohesion domain template	Hurst [27]
OSM	Embley, Kurtz, and Woodfield [14], Haas [21]
Abstract data type	Wang [51]
Relational algebra	Codd [11]

Table 20. *Some sources of difficulty.* The Appendix has examples that illustrate many of the problems that would have to be solved in developing a broad-gauge table-understanding system. Note, however, that none of the example tables are particularly difficult from the standpoint of human perception, though some require either specialized knowledge (Figs. 5 and 9) or the appropriate mindset (Figs. 12 and 13)

Morphology	Violations of tabular layout
	Incomplete gird rulings
	Close-spaced or misaligned cells
	Misplaced or oddly-oriented headers
	Multi-text-line cells
Syntax	Multi-dimensional structure
	Unusual layout
	Combined tables
	Split tables
	Footnotes[4]
Semantics	OCR or other errors in text
	Synonyms, abbreviations
	Incomplete headers
	Missing data-definition dictionary
	Iconic cell contents

---

[4] Wang surveyed nearly 900 tables and found that 40% contain footnotes [51], pg. 154.

Table 21. *Applications and research problems.* We have identified several classes of potential applications for table processing and some research problems on which little work has been reported so far. We have also formed opinions of the relative difficulties of the tasks involved. The ways in which the applications and problems interrelate are depicted below. Unless we make headway on performance evaluation, including acquisition of statistically adequate test material, it will be difficult to evaluate progress on any of the other tasks

	Query mechanisms	Audio navigation	Table subdivision	Table spotting	Table clustering	Conversion to abstract form	Overcoming recognition errors	Performance evaluation
Large-volume, homogeneous conversion						•	•	•
Large-volume, mixed conversion				•	•	•	•	•
Individual database creation	•		•	•	•	•	•	•
Tabular browsing	•	•	•	•	•	•	•	•
Audio access to tables	•	•	•	•	•	•	•	•
Table manipulation			•		•	•	•	•
Table modification for display			•		•	•	•	•

References

1. A. Abu-Tarif. Table processing and table understanding. Master's thesis, Rensselaer Polytechnic Institute, May 1998. 100
2. J. F. Arias, S. Balasubramanian, A. Prasad, R. Kasturi, and A. Chhabra. Information extraction from telephone company drawings. In *Proceedings of the Conference on Computer Vision and Pattern Recognition*, pages 729–732, Seattle, Washington, June 1994. 100
3. J. F. Arias, A. Chhabra, and V. Misra. Efficient interpretation of tabular documents. In *Proceedings of the International Conference on Pattern Recognition (ICPR'96)*, volume III, pages 681–685, Vienna, Austria, August 1996. 100
4. J. F. Arias, A. Chhabra, and V. Misra. Interpreting and representing tabular documents. In *Proceedings of the Conference on Computer Vision and Pattern Recognition*, pages 600–605, San Francisco, CA, June 1996. 100
5. J. F. Arias and R. Kasturi. Efficient techniques for line drawing interpretation and their application to telephone company drawings. Technical Report CSE TR CSE-95-020, Penn State University, August 1995. 100
6. S. Balasubramanian, S. Chandran, J. F. Arias, R. Kasturi, and A. Chhabra. Information extraction from tabular drawings. In *Proceedings of Document Recognition I (IS&T/SPIE Electronic Imaging'94)*, volume 2181, pages 152–163, San Jose, CA, June 1994. 100

7. L. Bing, J. Zao, and X. Hong. New method for logical structure extraction of form document image. In *Proceedings of Document Recognition and Retrieval VI (IS&T/SPIE Electronic Imaging'99)*, volume 3651, pages 183–193, San Jose, CA, January 1999. 100

8. S. Chandran and R. Kasturi. Structural recognition of tabulated data. In *Proceedings of the Second International Conference on Document Analysis and Recognition (ICDAR'93)*, pages 516–519, Tsukuba Science City, Japan, October 1993. 100

9. A. K. Chhabra, V. Misra, and J. Arias. Detection of horizontal lines in noisy run length encoded images: The FAST method. In R. Kasturi and K. Tombre, editors, *Graphics Recognition – Methods and Applications*, volume 1072 of *Lecture Notes in Computer Science*, pages 35–48. Springer-Verlag, Berlin, Germany, 1996. 100

10. *The Chicago Manual of Style*. The University of Chicago Press, 1982. 100

11. E. Codd. A relational model of data for large shared data banks. *Communications of the ACM*, 13(6), June 1970. 104

12. M. J. DeHaemer, G. Wright, and T. W. Dillon. Automated speech recognition for spreadsheet tasks: Performance effects for experts and novices. *International Journal of Human-Computer Interaction*, 6(3):299–318, 1994. 100

13. S. Douglas, M. Hurst, and D. Quinn. Using natural language processing for identifying and interpreting tables in plain text. In *Proceedings of the Symposium on Document Analysis and Information Retrieval (SDAIR'95)*, pages 535–545, Las Vegas, NV, April 1995. 100

14. D. Embley, B. Kurtz, and S. Woodfield. *Object-oriented Systems Analysis: A Model Driven Apprach*. Yourdon Press, 1992. 100, 104

15. M. Garris, S. Janet, and W. Klein. Federal Register document image database. In *Proceedings of Document Recognition and Retrieval VI (IS&T/SPIE Electronic Imaging'99)*, volume 3651, pages 97–108, San Jose, CA, January 1999. 100

16. P. Gray, S. Embury, W. Gray, and K. Hui. An agent-based system for handling distributed design constraints. In *Proceedings of Agents'98*, 1998. 100

17. E. A. Green. *Model-based analysis of printed tables*. PhD thesis, Rensselaer Polytechnic Institute, May 1996. 100

18. E. A. Green and M. Krishnamoorthy. Model-based analysis of printed tables. In *Proceedings of the Third International Conference on Document Analysis and Recognition (ICDAR'95)*, pages 214–217, Montréal, Canada, August 1995. 100, 104

19. E. A. Green and M. Krishnamoorthy. Model-based analysis of printed tables. In *Proceedings of the First International Workshop on Graphics Recognition (GREC'95)*, pages 234–242, PA, 1995. 100, 104

20. E. A. Green and M. Krishnamoorthy. Recognition of tables using table grammars. In *Proceedings of the Symposium on Document Analysis and Information Retrieval (SDAIR'95)*, pages 261–277, Las Vegas, NV, April 1995. 100, 104

21. T. B. Haas. The development of a prototype knowledge-based table-processing system. Master's thesis, Brigham Young University, December 1997. 100, 104

22. R. Hall. *Handbook of Tabular Presentation*. The Ronald Press Company, New York, NY, 1943. 100

23. Y. Hirayama. A method for table structure analysis using DP matching. In *Proceedings of the Third International Conference on Document Analysis and Recognition (ICDAR'95)*, pages 583–586, Montréal, Canada, August 1995. 100

24. O. Hori and D. S. Doermann. Robust table-form structure analysis based on box-driven reasoning. In *Proceedings of the Third International Conference on Document Analysis and Recognition (ICDAR'95)*, pages 218–221, Montréal, Canada, August 1995. 100

25. J. Hu, R. Kashi, D. Lopresti, and G. Wilfong. Medium-independent table detection. In *Proceedings of Document Recognition and Retrieval VII (IS&T/SPIE Electronic Imaging'00)*, San Jose, CA, January 2000. To appear. 100

26. T. Hu. Recognizing table entries in a scanned document. Master's thesis, Rensselaer Polytechnic Institute, October 1993. 100

27. M. Hurst and S. Douglas. Layout and language: Preliminary investigations in recognizing the structure of tables. In *Proceedings of the International Conference on Document Analysis and Recognition (ICDAR'97)*, pages 1043–1047, August 1997. 100, 104

28. K. Itonori. A table structure recognition based on textblock arrangement and ruled line position. In *Proceedings of the Second International Conference on Document Analysis and Recognition (ICDAR'93)*, pages 765–768, Tsukuba Science City, Japan, October 1993. 100

29. T. G. Kieninger. Table structure recognition based on robust block segmentation. In *Proceedings of Document Recognition V (IS&T/SPIE Electronic Imaging'98)*, volume 3305, pages 22–32, San Jose, CA, January 1998. 100

30. W. Kornfeld and J. Wattecamps. Automatically locating, extracting and analyzing tabular data. In *Proceedings of the 21st International ACM SIGIR Conference on Research and Development in Information Retrieval*, pages 347–348, Melbourne, Australia, August 1998. 100

31. M. Krishnamoorthy. TBL, an easy to use table description language. Internal document, Rensselaer Polytechnic Institute, 1992. 100

32. G. Kyriazis. Analysis of digitized tables. Senior project report, Rensselaer Polytechnic Institute, 1990. 100

33. L. Lamport. *LaTeX: A Document Preparation System*. Addison-Wesley, Reading, MA, 1985. 100

34. A. Laurentini and P. Viada. Identifying and understanding tabular material in compound documents. In *Proceedings of the Eleventh International Conference on Pattern Recognition (ICPR'92)*, pages 405–409, The Hague, 1992. 100

35. M. Lesk. Tbl – a program to format tables. In *UNIX Programmer's Manual*, volume 2A. Bell Telephone Laboratories, Murray Hill, NJ, 1979. 100

36. D. Lopresti and G. Nagy. Automated table processing: An (opinionated) survey. In *Proceedings of the Third IAPR International Workshop on Graphics Recognition*, pages 109–134, Jaipur, India, September 1999. 94

37. *Lotus 1-2-3 User's Handbook*. Ballantine Books, New York, NY, 1984. 100

38. *Microsoft Excel User's Guide*. Microsoft Corporation, Redmond, WA, 1990. 100

39. G. Nagy, M. Krishnamoorthy, S. Seth, and M. Viswanathan. Syntactic segmentation and labeling of digitized pages from technical journals. *IEEE Transactions on Pattern Analysis and Machine Intelligence*, 15(7):737–747, 1993. 100

40. G. Nagy and S. Seth. Hierarchical representation of optically scanned documents. In *Proceedings the International Conference on Pattern Recognition (ICPR)*, pages 347–349, 1984. 100

41. C. Peterman, C. H. Chang, and H. Alam. A system for table understanding. In *Proceedings of the Symposium on Document Image Understanding Technology (SDIUT'97)*, pages 55–62, Annapolis, MD, April/May 1997. 94, 100

42. P. Pyreddy and W. B. Croft. TINTIN: A system for retrieval in text tables. Technical Report UM-CS-1997-002, University of Massachusetts, Amherst, January 1997. 100

43. M. A. Rahgozar and R. Cooperman. A graph-based table recognition system. In *Proceedings of Document Recognition III (IS&T/SPIE Electronic Imaging'96)*, volume 2660, pages 192–203, San Jose, CA, January 1996. 100

44. *The 1.7 Tag Set Usage Guide.* Recording for the Blind and Dyslexic, Princeton, NJ, 1994. 100

45. D. Rus and D. Subramanian. Customizing information capture and access. *ACM Transactions on Information Systems*, 15(1):67–101, 1997. 100

46. J. H. Shamalian, H. S. Baird, and T. L. Wood. A retargetable table reader. In *Proceedings of the International Conference on Document Analysis and Recognition (ICDAR'97)*, pages 158–163, August 1997. 100

47. R. Sproat, J. Hu, and H. Chen. EMU: an e-mail preprocessor for text-to-speech. In *Proceedings of the IEEE Workshop on Multimedia Signal Processing*, pages 239–244, Los Angeles, CA, December 1998. 100

48. E. R. Tufte. *The Visual Display of Quantitative Information.* Graphics Press, Cheshire, CT, 1983. 100

49. E. Turolla, Y. Belaid, and A. Belaid. Form item extraction based on line searching. In R. Kasturi and K. Tombre, editors, *Graphics Recognition – Methods and Applications*, volume 1072 of *Lecture Notes in Computer Science*, pages 69–79. Springer-Verlag, Berlin, Germany, 1996. 100

50. M. A. Walker, J. Fromer, G. D. Fabbrizio, C. Mestel, and D. Hindle. What can I say?: Evaluating a spoken language interface to email. In *Proceedings of the Conference on Human Factors in Computing Systems (CHI)*, pages 582–589, Los Angeles, CA, April 1998. 100

51. X. Wang. *Tabular abstraction, editing, and formatting.* PhD thesis, University of Waterloo, 1996. 99, 100, 102, 104

52. T. Watanabe, Q. L. Quo, and N. Sugie. Layout recognition of multi-kinds of table-form documents. *IEEE Transactions on Pattern Analysis and Machine Intelligence*, 17(4):432–445, 1995. 100, 104

53. S. Whittaker and C. Sidner. Email overload: exploring personal information management of email. In *Proceedings of the Conference on Human Factors in Computing Systems (CHI)*, pages 276–283, Vancouver, British Columbia, Canada, April 1996. 100

54. P. Wright. Using tabulated information. *Ergonomics*, 11(4):331–343, 1968. 100

55. P. Wright. Understanding tabular displays. *Visible Language*, 7:351–359, 1973. 100

56. P. Wright. The comprehension of tabulated information: some similarities between prose and reading tables. *NSPI Journal*, XIX(8):25–29, October 1980. 100

57. K. Zuyev. Table image segmentation. In *Proceedings of the International Conference on Document Analysis and Recognition (ICDAR'97)*, pages 705–708, August 1997. 100

Appendix: Table Examples

In this appendix, we present a number of examples of paper and electronic tables.

TABLE 1
A BRIEF SURVEY OF GEOMETRIC PAGE-LAYOUT ANALYSIS METHODS

No.	Author	Year	Approach	Features
1	Wahl et al. [11]	1982	Run length smoothing	Time consuming and skew sensitive
2	Nagy et al. [12]	1984	X-Y tree cut	Skew sensitive; Assumes rectangular blocks
3	Wang et al. [13]	1989	Run length smoothing and recursive X-Y cut	Newspaper analysis; Sensitive to skew
4	Fujisawa et al. [14]	1990	Top-down	Japanese patent documents
5	Fisher et al. [15]	1990	Run length smoothing and connected component extraction	Identifies text and nontext zones; Skew sensitive
6	Pavlidis et al. [16]	1991	Column oriented projection	Identifies text and nontext regions; Accommodates moderate skew
7	Baird [17]	1992	Global-to-local strategy	Accommodates different languages; Skew correction;
8	Jain et al. [18]	1992	Gabor filtering	Multichannel texture features from gray-scale images; Time consuming
9	Lebourgeois et al. [19]	1992	8x 3 window filtering	Unconstrained documents; Skew not considered
10	Pavlidis et al. [20]	1992	Horizontal smearing and bottom-up	Accommodates small skew; Fixed parameters
11	Akindele et al. [21]	1993	White space tracing	Polygonal blocks; Only text zones considered
12	Amamoto et al. [22]	1993	Morphological operation on white space	Identifies horizontal and vertical writing; Skew not considered
13	Ittner et al. [23]	1993	White space and minimum spanning tree	Language and orientation free; Large computation
14	O'Gorman [24]	1993	k-nearest neighbor clustering	Can handle arbitrary orientation with high accuracy; Large computation
15	Antonacopoulos et al. [25], [26]	1994	Contours from white tiles	Finds nonrectangular and skewed regions; Error in classifying large fonts
16	Zlatopolsky [27]	1994	Connected component extraction	Multiple skewed document; Sensitive parameters
17	Doermann [28]	1995	Wavelet multiscale analysis	Segments nonblock-nested pages; Gray-scale image processing; High computational complexity
18	Drivas et al. [29]	1995	Connected component grouping	Skew correction with a time consuming algorithm
19	Ha et al. [30]	1995	Connected component-based projection profile	Faster than pixel-based projection profile; Skew sensitive
20	Sylwester et al. [31]	1995	trainable X-Y cut	Relatively robust; Skew and noise free
21	Tang et al. [32]	1995	Modified fractal signature	Handles documents with high geometrical complexity; Gray-scale image processing; Time consuming
22	Jain et al. [33], [34]	1996	Masks and neural network	Handles documents with multiple languages; Gray-scale image processing; Time consuming
23	Kise et al. [35]	1996	Background thinning	Skewed nonrectangular layout; Bounding box is not very tight
24	Liu et al. [36]	1996	Adaptive top-down and bottom-up	Nonrectangular regions; Skew free
25	Yamashita et al. [37]	1996	Run length smearing and adaptive thresholding	Less sensitive to font size and spacing; Skew free

Fig. 1. A table with considerable text comparing document layout analysis methods.[5] Except for multi-line cells, this table has no irregular features that would complicate analysis. There are three categories: Citation, Method, and "No.", but the first two are implicit at the root level and only evident from the subcategory labels

---

[5] From "Document Representation and its Application to Page Decomposition" by A. K. Jain and B. Yu, *IEEE Transactions on Pattern Analysis and Machine Intelligence*, March 1998, pg. 297.

[6] From one of the author's Casio DataBank 150 watch.

NAME		ADDRESS					TELNO		
First	Last	#	Street	City	State	Zip	Area-Code	#	Extension
...			...				...		

Fig. 2. Multiple column headers, where the top header subsumes several headers at the next level, are common. This makes it difficult to separate "domains" and "subdomains" (Wang's terminology) for subsequent analysis. Style manuals recommend avoiding horizontal rulings (*The Government Printing Office Style Manual* has over thirty pages of guidelines on "tabular work")

Fig. 3. A very small table.[6] In the scanned image shown, low and irregular contrast would complicate pixel-level analysis. However, the watch is only an example of a small digital display, from which the information would be obtained in computer-readable form rather than by optical scanning. At the logical level, lack of space precludes headers: the only clues are the usual functions of a watch, and the formatting of the entries

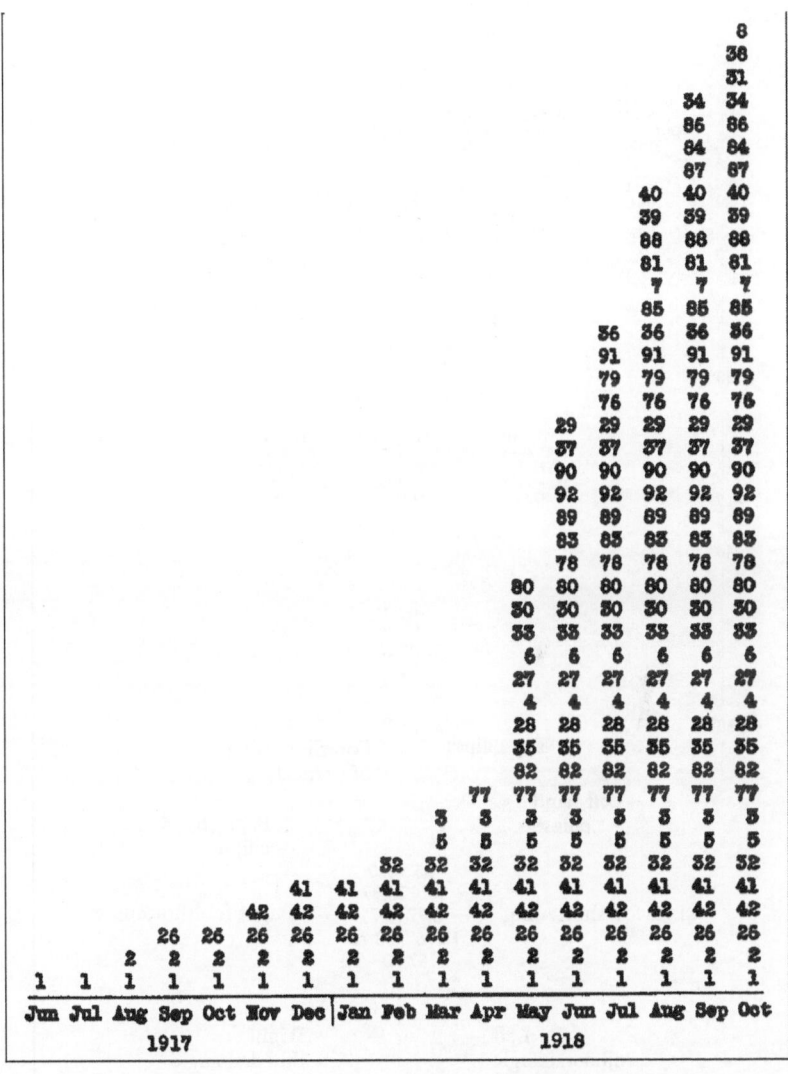

Fig. 4. A table showing the stationing of U. S. Army Divisions in France during WWI.[7] The use of blanks makes this table look like a graph, which complicates extraction of the tabular structure. Note the vestigial ruling between "Dec 1917" and "Jan 1918."

---

[7] From *The Visual Display of Quantitative Information* by Edward R. Tufte, Graphics Press: Cheshire, CT, 1983, pg. 141.

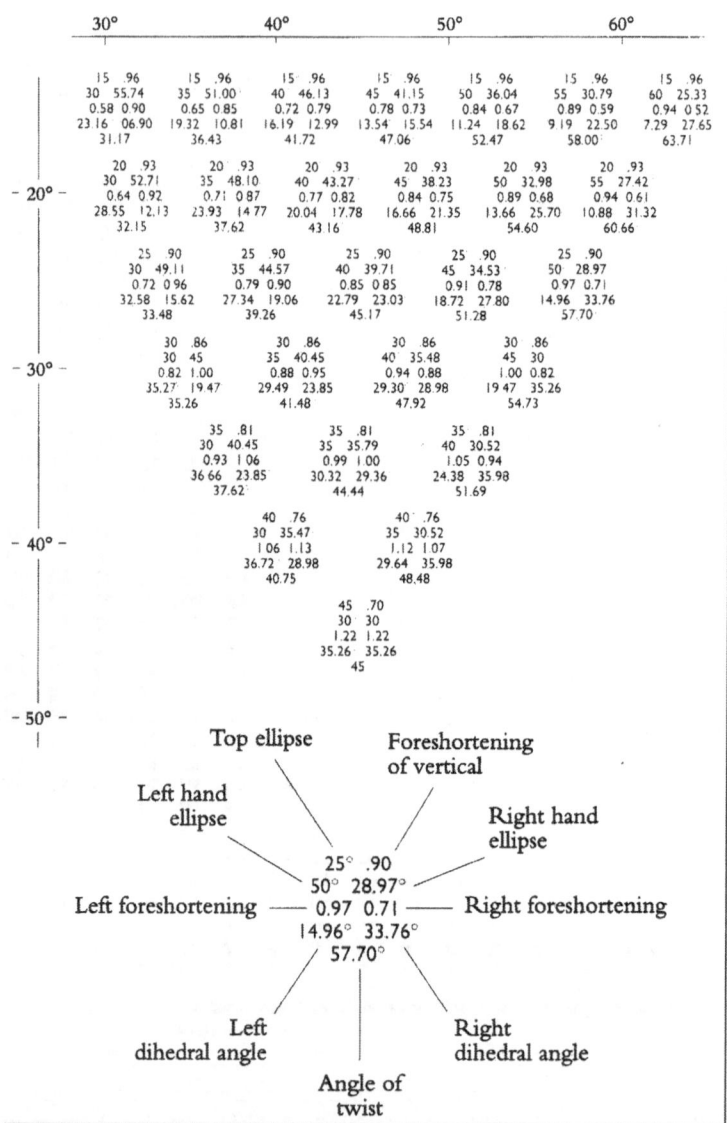

Fig. 5. A table presenting nine parameters for a cube in triametric projection.[8] This table may also be classified as a diagram. The last cell in the third row is recursively expanded in the bottom half. It would be difficult to define the Wang dimensionality of this example because it lacks rectilinear structure

---

[8] From *Visual Explanations* by Edward R. Tufte, Graphics Press: Cheshire, CT, 1997, pg. 85.

How Different Groups Voted for President

Based on 12,782 interviews with voters at their polling places. Shown is how each group divided its vote for President and, in parentheses, the percentage of the electorate belonging to each group.

	CARTER	REAGAN	ANDERSON	CARTER-FORD In 1976
Democrats (43%)	66	26	6	77-22
Independents (23%)	30	54	12	43-54
Republicans (28%)	11	84	4	9-90
Liberals (17%)	57	27	11	70-26
Moderates (46%)	42	48	8	51-46
Conservatives (28%)	23	71	4	29-70
Liberal Democrats (9%)	70	14	13	86-12
Moderate Democrats (22%)	66	26	6	77-22
Conservative Democrats (8%)	53	41	4	64-35
Politically active Democrats (3%)	72	19	8	—
Democrats favoring Kennedy in primaries (13%)	66	24	8	—
Liberal Independents (4%)	50	29	15	64-29
Moderate Independents (12%)	31	53	13	45-53
Conservative Independents (7%)	22	69	6	26-72
Liberal Republicans (2%)	25	66	9	17-82
Moderate Republicans (11%)	13	81	5	11-88
Conservative Republicans (12%)	6	91	2	6-93
Politically active Republicans (2%)	5	89	6	—
East (32%)	43	47	8	51-47
South (27%)	44	51	3	54-45
Midwest (20%)	41	51	6	48-50
West (11%)	35	52	10	46-51
Blacks (10%)	82	14	3	82-16
Hispanics (2%)	54	36	7	75-24
Whites (88%)	36	55	8	47-52
Female (49%)	45	46	7	50-48
Male (51%)	37	54	7	50-48
Female, favors equal rights amendment (22%)	54	32	11	—
Female, opposes equal rights amendment (15%)	29	66	4	—
Catholic (25%)	40	51	7	54-44
Jewish (5%)	45	39	14	64-34
Protestant (46%)	37	56	6	44-55
Born-again white Protestant (17%)	34	61	6	—
18-21 years old (6%)	44	43	11	48-50
22-29 years old (17%)	43	43	11	51-46
30-44 years old (31%)	37	54	7	49-49
45-59 years old (23%)	39	55	6	47-52
60 years or older (18%)	40	54	4	47-52
Family income				
Less than $10,000 (13%)	50	41	6	58-40
$10,000-$14,999 (14%)	47	42	6	55-43
$15,000-$24,999 (30%)	38	53	7	48-50
$25,000-$50,000 (24%)	32	58	8	36-62
Over $50,000 (5%)	25	65	8	—
Professional or manager (40%)	33	56	9	41-57
Clerical, sales or other white-collar (11%)	42	48	8	46-53
Blue-collar worker (17%)	46	47	5	57-41
Agriculture (3%)	29	66	3	—
Looking for work (3%)	55	35	7	66-34
Education				
High school or less (39%)	46	48	4	57-43
Some college (28%)	35	55	8	51-49
College graduate (27%)	35	51	11	46-55
Labor union household (26%)	47	44	7	59-39
No member of household in union (62%)	35	55	8	43-55
Family finances				
Better off than a year ago (16%)	53	37	8	30-70
Same (40%)	46	46	7	51-49
Worse off than a year ago (34%)	25	64	8	77-23
Family finances and political party				
Democrats, better off than a year ago (7%)	77	16	6	69-31
Democrats, worse off than a year ago (13%)	47	39	10	94-6
Independents, better off (3%)	45	36	12	—
Independents, worse off (9%)	21	65	11	—
Republicans, better off (4%)	18	77	5	3-97
Republicans, worse off (11%)	6	89	4	24-78
More important problem				
Unemployment (39%)	51	40	7	75-25
Inflation (44%)	30	60	9	35-65
Feel that U.S. should be more forceful in dealing with Soviet Union even if it would increase the risk of war (54%)	28	64	6	—
Disagree (31%)	56	32	10	—
Favor equal rights amendment (46%)	49	38	11	—
Oppose equal rights amendment (35%)	26	68	4	—
When decided about choice				
Knew all along (41%)	47	50	2	44-55
During the primaries (13%)	30	60	8	57-42
During conventions (8%)	36	55	7	51-48
Since Labor Day (8%)	30	54	13	49-49
In week before election (23%)	38	46	13	49-47

Source: 1976 and 1980 election day surveys by The New York Times/CBS News Poll and 1976 election day survey by NBC News.

Fig. 6. A table analyzing voter preferences in the 1980 U. S. Presidential Election.[9] Some of the category labels, like political affiliation and gender, are implicit. Therefore any automated interpeter would require a built-in understanding of demographic categories

---

[9] From *The Visual Display of Quantitative Information* by Edward R. Tufte, Graphics Press: Cheshire, CT, 1983, pg. 179. Tufte notes: "This type of elaborate table, a *supertable*, is likely to attract and intrigue readers through its organized, sequential detail and reference-like quality. One supertable is far better than a hundred little bar charts."

Monday, September 20, 1999		
Track A Convention Hall A	**Track B** Convention Hall B	**Track C** Chanakya Hall
08:30 10:00	OPENING SESSION(Mo-1) Banquet Hall	
10:00	COFFEE BREAK Pool Side	
10:30 12:30	MULTIMEDIA DOCUMENT PROCESSING Mo-2A	CHARACTER RECOGNITION Mo-2B	DOCUMENT IMAGE PROCESSING - I Mo-2C
12:30	LUNCH Pool Side	
13:30 14:30	POSTER PRESENTATION Mo-3A	POSTER PRESENTATION Mo-3B	POSTER PRESENTATION Mo-3C
13:30 15:30	POSTER SESSION-I (Mo-3) Banquet Hall (Coffee served at 14:30)	
16:30 17:30	INFORMATION RETRIEVAL Mo-4A	POSTAL AUTOMATION Mo-4B	FONT RECOGNITION Mo-4C
19:00 21:00	CONFERENCE RECEPTION Banquet Hall	

Fig. 7. ICDAR'99 schedule.[10] This schedule, which was perfectly clear to the conference attendees, has many irregularities to confuse automated analysis. The information in each column may be a title or a location. Times are shown inconsistently on the left. By introducing a cross-track category for social functions, it would be possible to rationalize the structure

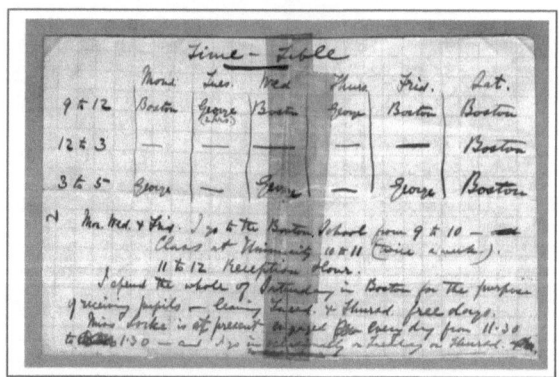

Fig. 8. A handwritten table showing a personal schedule.[12] In handwritten tables like this, both structure extraction and text interpretation are difficult and error-prone. We have seen no work on handwritten tables, but much effort has been devoted to block-lettered tables in engineering drawings and to hand-filled forms. In successful applications a considerable amount of context is available to guide interpretation

---

[10] From http://www.cedar.buffalo.edu/ICDAR99/Program/page12.html.

[12] From the Library of Congress archive of the Alexander Graham Bell family papers, http://memory.loc.gov/ammem/bellhtml/bellhome.html.

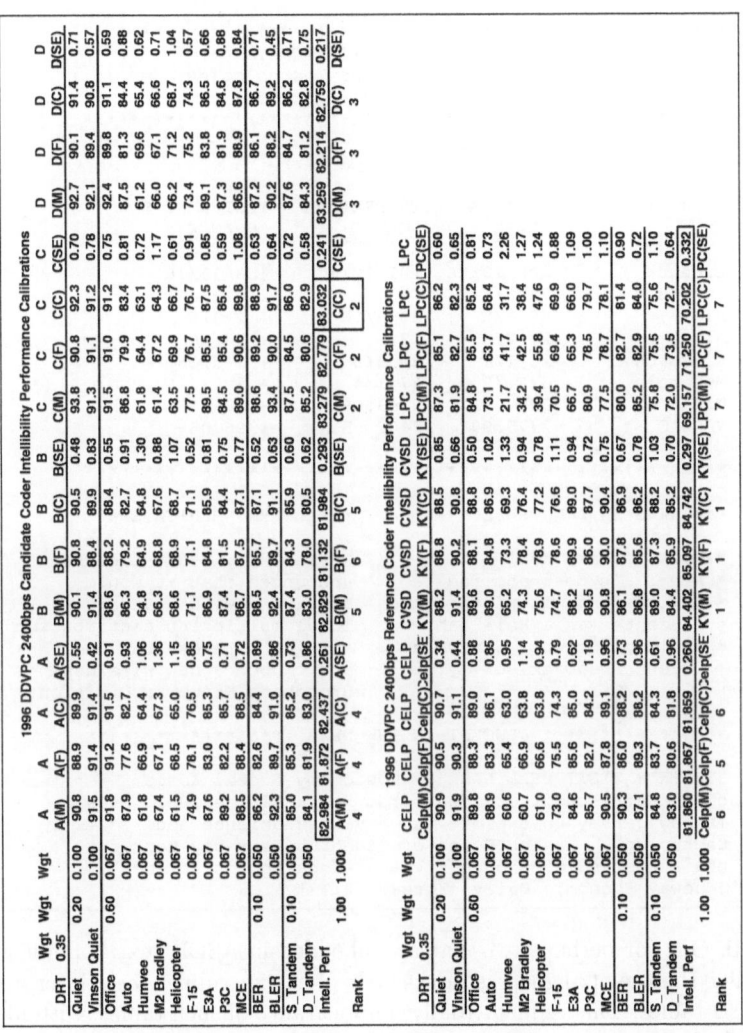

Fig. 9. A wide, wrapped table giving the performance of various voice coding schemes.[13] The identical leftmost columns and different column headers confirm that this is a split table. Distinctions like that between "Quiet" and "Vinson Quiet" require expert interpretation. The abbreviations are the least of the difficulty, since they could be expanded with table look-up. One of the columns with Rank 2 is selected for special consideration

---

[13] From "A New Federal Standard Algorithm for 2400bps Coded Voice." Note the extra, inexplicable (in this context) box surrounding the performance and rank figures for the entry in the middle of the first part of the table. http://www.plh.af.mil/ddvpc/24results.htm.

```
*********************************************************
                 LUCENT TECHNOLOGIES TODAY
             For the People of Lucent Technologies
                    Friday, February 12, 1999
*********************************************************


                  ***   STOCK WATCH   ***

             TODAY'S     YESTERDAY'S     YESTERDAY'S
              OPEN          CLOSE          CHANGE

Lucent      100 13/16    101 1/16       + 3 13/16
Ascend       73 5/8       74 7/8        + 2 3/8
AT&T         87 1/2       88 3/16       + 2 3/8
Alcatel      21 7/8       22            + 13/16
Ericsson     26 1/4       26 3/8        + 1 5/16
Motorola     67 1/2       67 1/4        + 1 13/16
DJIA        9367.32      9363.46        + 186.15
NASDAQ      2375.99      2405.55        + 96.05


*********************************************************

*** NEWS IN A NUTSHELL ***        *** LUCENT HERITAGE ***

* New software tool          On Feb. 17, 1998, Lucent
* America's most admired      announced that it would
* Switch lands in winter games  acquire Hewlett-Packard's
* Students visit Bell Labs    local multipoint distribution
* World of Science Seminars   service wireless business
* Client feedback survey      and launch a new Wireless
                              Broadband Networks Division.


***************    LUCENT IN THE NEWS    *****************

STUDENTS VISIT BELL LABS -- Hosted by Lucent Korea,
elementary school students from Korea visited Bell Labs
in New Jersey to explore its advanced science and
technology.  Lucent Korea provided the six-day tour for
the students to encourage their education in science.
[Naeway Economic Daily (Korea), 2/12]
```

Fig. 10. One (or perhaps two) tables embedded in ASCII text.[14] Some general rules, like the use of aligned asterisks or hyphens for rulings, help interpretation of ASCII tables. The frequent (daily?) appearance of such tables, with identical layout but different content, may justify developing specialized algorithms for extracting the information. An important open problem is the detection and isolation of such tables in ASCII text

---

[14] From *Lucent Technologies Today*, February 12, 1999.

NEW YORK STOCK EXCHANGE

NYSE INDEXES

NEW YORK (AP) — Closing New York Stock Exchange indexes:

	Close	Chg.
Comp	610.49	—0.19
Indus	761.19	—0.24
Transp	494.71	—5.62
Utility	439.68	+0.75
Finance	549.34	—0.34

WHAT THE NYSE MARKET DID

	Yester-day	Prev. day
Advanced	1,240	1,185
Declined	1,743	1,829
Unchanged	563	568
Total issues	3,546	3,582
New highs	36	58
New lows	96	90

DOW JONES AVERAGES

NEW YORK (AP) — Final Dow Jones averages yesterday:

STOCKS

	Open	High	Low	Last	Chg.
Ind	9902.28	10005.95	9796.99	9890.51	—13.04
Trn	3337.44	3376.11	3242.21	3275.68	—62.80
Util	303.91	306.48	300.13	303.22	—0.72
Stk	3030.50	3061.77	2985.30	3014.68	—16.16

30 Indus	61,210,600
Tran	8,544,700
Utils	8,781,600
65 Stk	78,536,900

BONDS

	Close	Chg.
DJ AIG Futures	80.34	+1.46
10 Industrials	105.87	—0.30
10 Public Util	102.63	+0.70
20 Bonds	104.25	—0.16

STOCK SALES

Approx final total	663,291,980
Previous day	922,200,000
Week ago	727,270,000
Month ago	718,530,000
Year ago	631,350,000
Two years ago	451,970,000
Year to date	43,374,202,000
To date one year ago	33,969,170,000
To date two years ago	28,938,520,000

BOND SALES

Approx final total	$13,626,000
Previous day	$14,377,000
Week ago	$12,090,000
Month ago	$11,232,000
Year ago	$10,034,000
Two years ago	$22,323,000
Year to date	$759,113,000
To date one year ago	$1,050,662,000
To date two years ago	$1,431,008,000

MOST ACTIVE NYSE STOCKS

NEW YORK (AP) — Sales, closing price and net change of the 15 most active New York Stock Exchange issues trading at more than $1:

Name	Volume	Last	Chg.
AmOnline s	30,279,300	130	+10 3/4
US Filter	18,371,300	30 3/8	—1/8
Compaq	16,316,100	30 1/8	—5/8
MediaOne	13,143,800	68 1/2	+7 3/4
AT&T	9,387,300	77 3/4	—1 7/8
CHS El	7,415,500	3 15/16	—2 1/16
WarnLm s	7,113,300	66 15/16	—3 3/4
PhilMor	5,984,700	41 13/16	+5/16
IBM	5,948,300	167	—1 9/16
RiteAid	5,777,200	26 3/4	+1 1/8
MicrnT	5,774,300	53	+2 1/2
Lucent	5,254,300	101 1/8	+3/8
CBS	5,094,100	38 5/8	+1 1/16
DataGn	4,661,200	12 15/16	+2 1/8
TycoInt	4,530,500	75 7/16	+3/8

STANDARD & POOR'S

NEW YORK (AP) — Standard and Poor's stock indexes yesterday:

	High	Low	Last	Chg.
S&P 100	653.19	648.44	649.55	—0.56
S&P 500	1303.84	1294.26	1297.01	—2.28
MidCap	363.76	359.82	360.80	—1.51
Indust	1565.34	1552.88	1556.42	—2.67
Transpt	716.73	707.36	708.28	—8.45
Utilities	245.12	243.81	243.99	—0.96
Financial	142.66	141.59	142.22	—0.15
SmallCap	160.66	158.57	158.70	—1.71

Fig. 11. Tables of daily financial results.[15] Some of the quantities are in thousands, others in sixteenths of a dollar. "Industrials" is abbreviated in several ways. The information is condensed and stylized. However, like the previous table, this one can be expected to appear in the same form day after day. Although market information may already available in a completely structured form, like a database, computer queries for other information may require table interpretation

[15] From *The Trenton Times*, March 23, 1999, pg. D2.

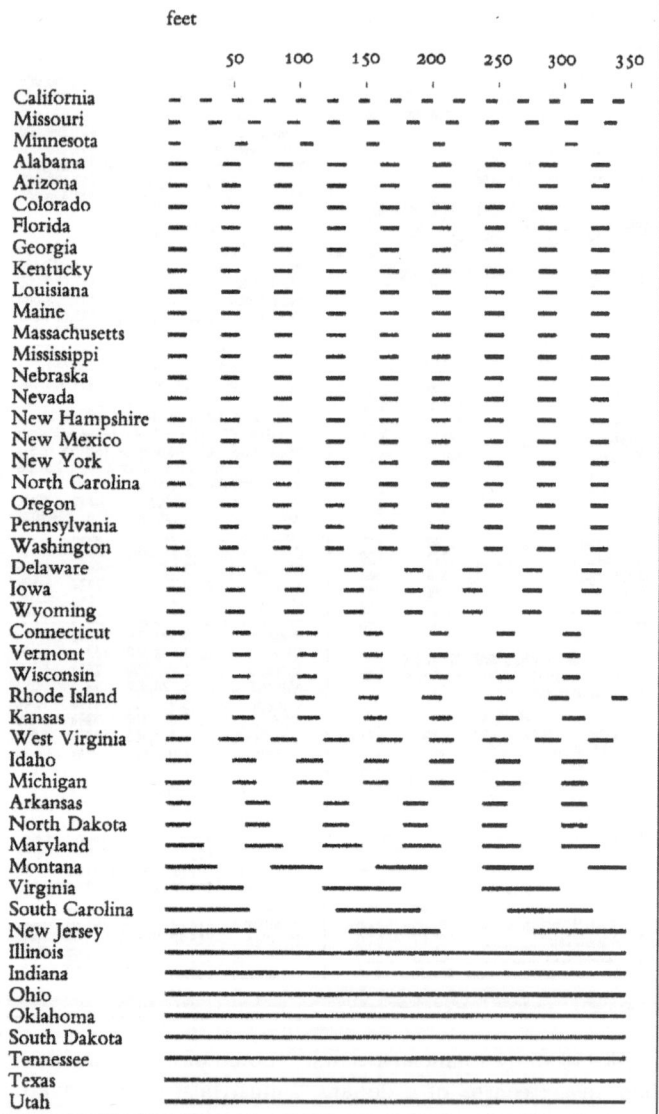

Fig. 12. A table showing standards for painting line stripes on road pavement.[16] This ingenious presentation conveys concisely and visually the length of yellow lane dividers in different states. Automated interpretation is out of the question!

---

[16] From *The Visual Display of Quantitative Information* by Edward R. Tufte, Graphics Press: Cheshire, CT, 1983, pg. 144.

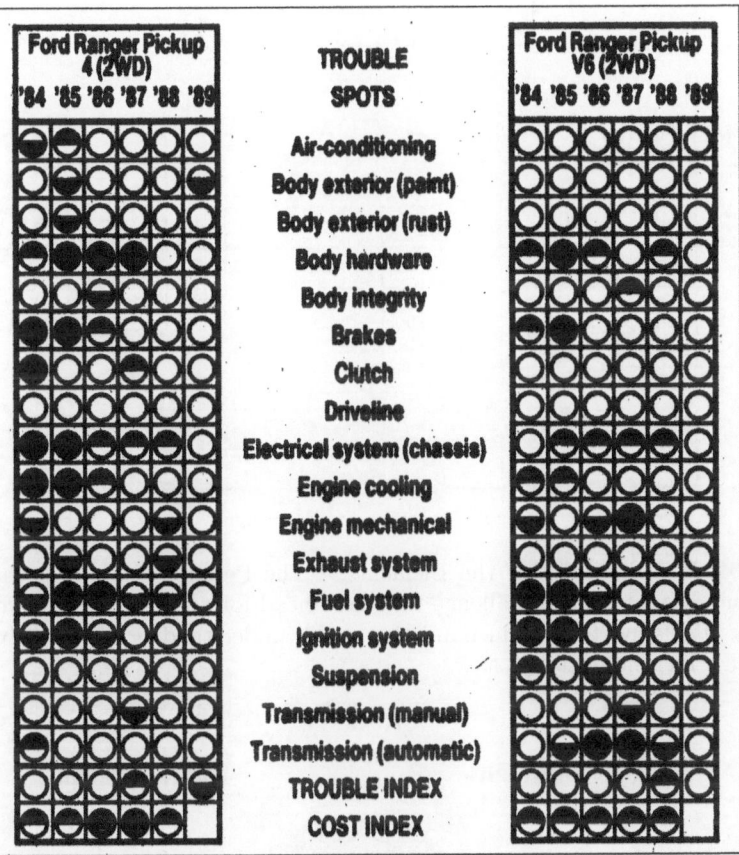

Fig. 13. A table summarizing the reliabilities of two pickup truck models.[17] The use of graphic symbols for cell entries, as in this consumer guide, is not unusual. The legend for the symbols may be far removed from the table itself

---

[17] From *Consumer Reports 1991 Buying Guide Issue*, Consumers Union: Mount Vernon, NY, 1990, pg. 159.

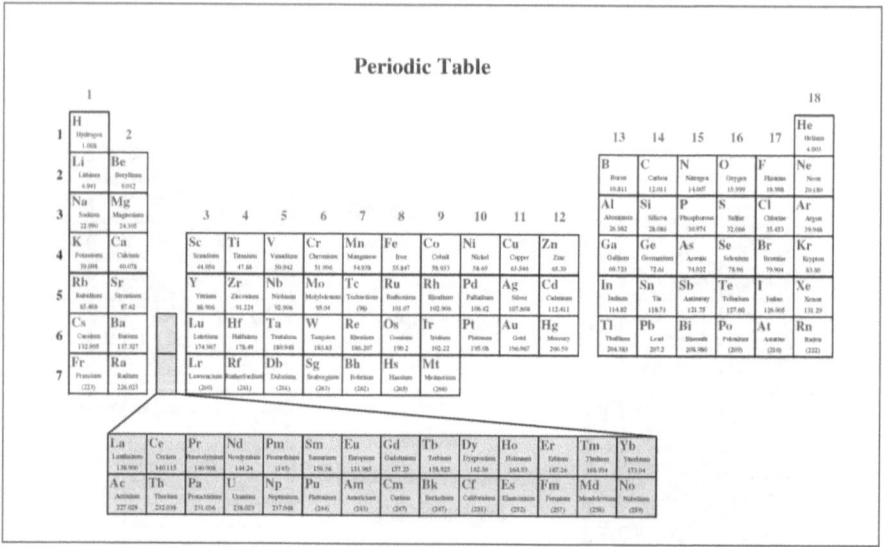

Fig. 14. Periodic Table of the Elements.[18] The Periodic Table is perhaps an extreme example of the challenge that lies ahead for automated table interpretation. It is good to keep in mind that a full understanding of this table may require a lifetime of study

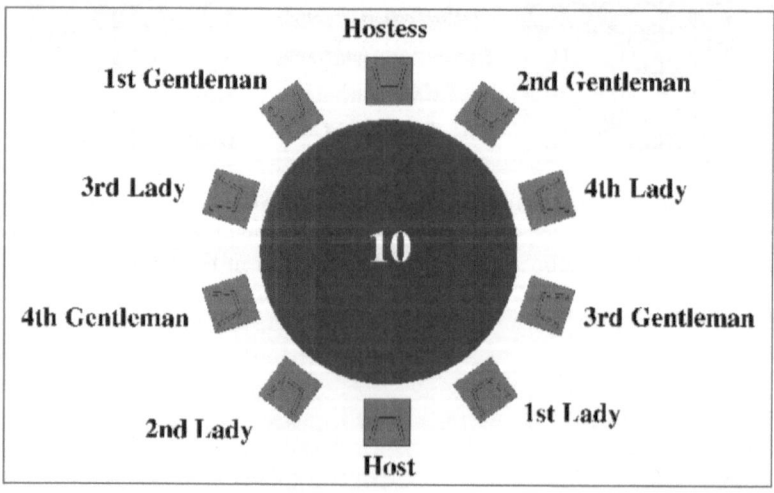

Fig. 15. An example of the wrong kind of "table."[19]

---

[18] From http://www.trends.net/~mu/misc.html.

[19] From http://www.eglin.af.mil/protocol/tainment/table1.htm.

Model-Based Graphics Recognition

Marc Vuilleumier Stückelberg[1] and David Doermann[2]

[1] CUI, University of Geneva, CH-1211 Geneva 4, Switzerland
mvuilleu@cui.unige.ch
[2] LAMP, University of Maryland, College Park, MD 20742, United States
doermann@cfar.umd.edu

Abstract. In this paper, we illustrate the use of a novel probabilistic framework for document analysis on typical problems of document layout analysis and graphics recognition. Our system uses an explicit descriptive model of the document class to find the most likely interpretation of a scanned document image. In contrast to the traditional pipeline architecture, our system carries out all stages of the analysis with a single inference engine, allowing for an end-to-end propagation of the uncertainty.

1. Introduction

Traditionally, graphics recognition systems involving high-level semantics combine pattern recognition algorithms and a symbolic parser in well separated, sequential stages, without any feedback. Items found in the bitmap image are classified using a pattern recognition module, and then rule-based inferences or graph-based inferences are used to recover a structured interpretation. Before, between and after these two main modules, ad-hoc modules are used to preprocess the image, build a list of connected components, locate symbols, and organize the recognition process.

However, a new trend is calling for integrated systems that could address the limitations of the traditional approach, mainly the poor handling of errors at the early stages of the recognition process. This is true in particular for the domain of musical score recognition (MSR) [1,2,3,4,5,6]. The first successful attempt to integrate pattern recognition with top-down reasoning was limited to the subtask of note recognition [7]. Some years later, the document image decoding (DID) approach [8] was successfully applied to a simplified model of the music notation[9], eventually integrating all stages of MSR into a single optimization process. Patterned after the use of hidden Markov models in speech recognition, DID produces an estimate of the original message coded in the document according to a maximum a posteriori decision criterion. Given a Markov model of a music image source and a music symbol set, DID uses a generalized Viterbi decoder to recover the most likely sequence of symbols that might have generated the bitmap image. Among many interesting aspects, it is segmentation-free, it allows for the integration of a noise model within the optimization process, it maximizes a well-defined objective function, and it allows for a complete separation of the document model from the recognition algorithms.

Atul K. Chhabra and D. Dori (Eds.): GREC'99, LNCS 1941, pp. 121-132, 2000.

Despite its unique qualities, DID has not emerged as a preeminent technique for graphics recognition, possibly because the size of the underlying Markov model grows prohibitively fast when handling exceptional cases. Moreover, although heuristics have been found to reduce the computational cost of the optimal decoding procedure to a very acceptable level for line-based text decoding, it is unlikely that such powerful heuristics exist for complex graphics recognition problems such as MSR.

1.1. The Proposed Approach

In [10], we presented a probabilistic framework for document analysis and recognition that lets us find the most likely interpretation of a scanned document image according to a descriptive model of the document class. It addresses some of the limitations of DID, while compromising few of the goals of DID. We look for the maximum a posteriori of an objective function representing the likelihood of the document interpretation, and use a task-specific model of the document to decode. The model is completely separated from the recognition engine. As in DID, our approach is principally grounded on stochastic attribute grammars and hidden Markov models, and is segmentation-free.

To facilitate both the knowledge modeling and the recognition task, we moved from a generative (source) model to a descriptive recognition model. This is a major departure from previous work, although our recognition model is still loosely equivalent to a source model when considered as a set of constraints. The objects in our model are defined using arbitrary parameters rather than using the strict sidebearing model. Moreover, we do not limit observations to predefined templates, and we separate the measures (that can be performed on the document) from the prior model (that predicts the value of such measures). In contrast to the non-overlapping symbol constraint of DID, our model allows for the decoding of an image by successive refinements and re-analysis of the same pattern at different stages of the process, as long as the different underlying models are approximately independent. Finally, we do not directly compute the global optimal solution at once, but we search for it in the subspace defined by the combinations of all locally optimal solutions.

We view the task of document understanding as the search for the optimal description of a bitmap image, where a description is defined as an instantiation of an expert-defined model describing a class of documents. A description is said to be optimal if it has the maximal a posteriori likelihood given the bitmap image. The posterior likelihood of a description is defined as the product of the posterior likelihood over all objects that are part of the description, and the posterior likelihood of an object is defined as the product of the posterior likelihood of all its attributes given the measures and models that link the attributes to the bitmap image.

1.2. The System Architecture

As shown in Fig. 1, the system architecture consists of three stacked layers that cooperate with each other. Data originates in the bitmap image, and is transformed into a more efficient surface-based representation. Feature detectors use this representation to perform on demand the measurements relevant to each concept of the document object model. The instantiation of a document object according to measured parameters produces a new perception, resulting in an atomic step in the top-level parser. The parser directs the recognition process by triggering and chaining these steps until the user's goal is met, or the alternatives provided by the document object model are exhausted.

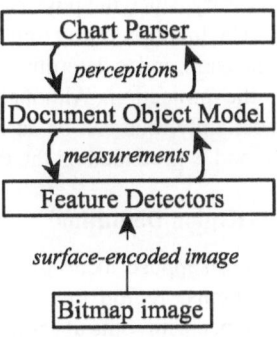

Fig. 1. The global system architecture.

The document model is a task-oriented model that defines objects and how they are to be recognized. Each model is defined by a set of object definitions, and each object is made up of a collection of attributes that have to be given a value. An attribute is defined either as a parameter of the object, an arbitrary region of the image, a measure, a model, an inference, a component object or a relation to another object. Attributes might be expressed as a function of other attributes of the same object. The whole model is simply expressed as a set of mathematical formulas and stored in a text file (a concrete example is given in Section 5). This approach provides an objective, explicit recognition model that can be discussed and compared independently of the details of the recognition engine that process these definitions.

The recognition engine takes as input a document model, and finds the description with the maximum a posteriori likelihood for a given bitmap image (or collection of bitmap images). Our recognition engine searches globally for the most likely description in the subspace defined by combinations of locally most likely object descriptions. The inner search for the optimal object description is carried out by inferences on parametric attribute value distributions, always focusing on the most likely value while keeping a precise estimate of the uncertainty. The outer search for the most likely combination of object descriptions is handled by an active chart parser (also known as Earley parser), a commonly used tool for working with context-free grammars. Functional constraints on the attributes are verified on the most likely parse trees only, to take advantage of the polynomial-space parse-forest representation as long as possible [11].

In this paper, we show how several typical subtasks of document and graphics recognition can be handled in this generic framework, and give sample formulas that can be put in a declarative model to perform them. In Section 2, we show how to segment a page up to the level of small components. Section 3 discusses the classification of such components, and Section 4 proposes one way to further decompose such components in graphical primitives. We conclude with some open problems and directions for future work.

2. Page Layout Analysis

Page layout analysis is the task of decomposing a region of an image into smaller subregions, so that each subregion holds a meaningful part of the object represented in the original region.

We will restrict this discussion to the case where each region can be represented by a one-dimensional list of non-overlapping rectangular subregions. The methodology can readily be extended to more general structures, but in most of the cases this is not necessary, since the physical structure of all documents tends to be that simple.

The traditional way of handling this analysis is to project an image measure on one dimension, and to determine the optimal split in subregions according to some properties of the projection. Although this is usually done without paying attention to the uncertainty, this can be easily extended to get a probability-weighted structure. Our method is grounded on the Bayesian probability theory.

2.1. Region Definition

We suppose to be given the four coordinates (*left*, *right*, *top* and *bottom*) of a rectangular region to be split. As these coordinates might result from a previous inference with some uncertainty, they are not numbers but random variables, that follow a given distribution. For now, we assume that this distribution is unimodal and parametric, for instance a normal distribution $N(\mu,\sigma)$. We can then define a bidimensional function that represents this region as:

$$reg(x, y) := P(left < x < right) \, P(top < y < bottom)$$

This function maps each pixel coordinates $\langle x, y \rangle$ to the probability that the pixel belongs to the region. It can be computed analytically very easily for most parametric distributions, using the cumulative probability function associated with the distribution of each boundary.

Our implementation starts with prior attention regions such as the one defined above, where the parameters *left*, *right*, *top* and *bottom* are considered as normal distributions and estimated from a set of samples taken from 400 pages of scanned music scores. Further regions are inferred together with their uncertainty, as described in Section 2.4.

Fig. 2. A typical region for a staff system highlighted in black, with the gray level representing the uncertainty.

2.2. Measure Definition

The measures typically used to split a region are the one-dimensional moments of the image. The use of such projective measures for MSR has been extensively explored in [12]. Assuming that our document image is given by a function $img(x, y)$ that maps each pixel coordinates $\langle x, y \rangle$ to the probability that the pixel is black[1], the one-dimensional moments of order p are defined as [13]:

$$hm_p(y) := \sum_x x^p \, img(x, y) \qquad vm_p(x) := \sum_y y^p \, img(x, y)$$

---

[1] This probability value can be set to the gray level when a grayscale scan is available, or to zero/one for a bi-level image. Alternatively, a low-level noise model can be included in this probability function.

The zeroth-order moment ($p = 0$) is commonly referred to as the *projection profile* and reflects the expected number of black pixels in each row/column. From the first- and second-order moments, one can easily obtain the center of mass and the moment of inertia of each row/column, which are often pertinent to the task of splitting a region.

Two modifications to this definition are required to integrate it in our probabilistic framework. First, we should only take into account the pixels that belong to the region of interest. This can be done by multiplying $img(x, y)$ by $reg(x, y)$, implicitly assuming that these two factors are independent. Second, we should consider the moments themselves as random variables, since they are functions of random variables. As they are defined as a sum of individual contributions from each pixel, we can reasonably apply the *central limit theorem* and assume they follow a normal distribution, with variance estimated by:

$$\mathrm{Var}(hm_p(y)) := \sum_x (x^p)^2 \; img(x, y) \; reg(x, y) \; (1 - img(x, y) \; reg(x, y))$$

The formula for the vertical moments is similar. Viewing moments as normal random variables can be viewed as adding error bars to the moment histograms. Note that all these moment measures can be performed very efficiently on a run-length encoded image with piece-wise linear approximation for the bi-dimensional functions $img(x, y)$ and $reg(x, y)$.

2.3. Model Definition

Once we have a measure and its associated uncertainty, we need a model to formally relate them with the split. We use a hidden Markov model (HMM) [14] for this task, as it provides us with a probability-grounded interpretation of our ordered data. We model the expected observations by parametric (normal or Gamma) distributions, and we model the state durations using Gamma distributions (which actually makes the model pseudo-Markov). The initial parameters of the model are determined empirically, but they can be re-estimated later from a training set using the Baum-Welsch or the Segmental k-Means algorithms.

As our observations are not numeric values but random variables, we need a special version of the HMM evaluation procedure. When the state-conditional observations are modeled using normal distributions however, one can simply add the variance of each observation to their own variance and thereby get a correct estimate with almost no additional computing cost.

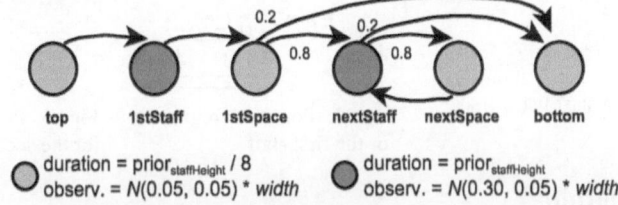

Fig. 3. Sample 6-states left-right HMM used to analyze the horizontal projection profile of a staff system (interpolated at 10 dpi) in order to separate the first staff from the others.

The theoretical *precision* of the model cannot easily be determined, since it will depend on the relevance of the model for the observed data. In practice, experiments show that the precision of an intuitively hand-crafted model such as the one illustrated above is around 5%. However, as the model hardly never overestimates its own reliability, the 5% fuzziness is correctly propagated as uncertainty and therefore does not affect the quality of the global interpretation.

2.4. Inference Definition

The next step is to determine the distribution of the split position according to the measure and model obtained in the previous steps. The simplest way to do this would be to apply the Viterbi algorithm to get the most likely cut. Unfortunately, this is not sufficient, as we need an estimation of the full distribution of the possible cuts. We therefore combine it with a Monte-Carlo estimation procedure.

We assume to be given a prior π on the expected position *pos* of the cut relative to the edge of the region (typically a Gamma distribution). Each sample of this distribution represents an hypothesis on the position of the cut, which likelihood given the measures can be estimated using the HMM (by setting a prior on the HMM state distribution at position *pos*). We can therefore estimate the posterior distribution of the cut parameter by:

$$P(pos \mid HMM, hm_0) \propto P(hm_0 \mid HMM, \text{state}(pos) = \text{cut})\, \pi(pos)$$

We model this posterior by a mixture distribution, whose parameters are estimated using an EM-based procedure patterned after AutoClass II [15]. The resulting distribution can then be used as a random variable for the next region definition, as explained in Section 2.1. Alternatively, instead of working with the full mixture distribution, we can process each mode individually as a separate hypothesis, the most likely first. As the correct split is most of the time included in the most likely mode, this tends to reduce the computational cost.

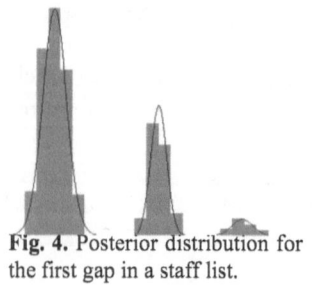

Fig. 4. Posterior distribution for the first gap in a staff list.

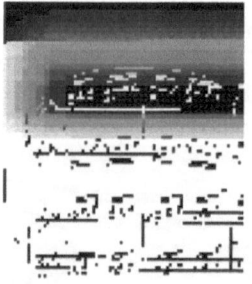

Fig. 5. Posterior region for the first staff

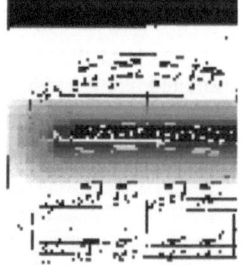

Fig. 6. Posterior region for the second staff.

3. Classification

Classification is the task of attributing an object of a given category to one of its subcategories, possibly to apply a specific recognition procedure later on.

This is usually handled by first extracting out of an object image an observation vector that includes relevant measures to discriminate between the subcategories, then using a classifier to determine the actual subcategory of the object.

3.1. Region and Measure Definition

The image region of an object to be classified is identical to what has been described in Section 2.1. It is defined as a bi-dimensional function $reg(x, y)$ that rates the importance that should be given to each pixel when doing the measurement on the image. The attention region is obtained from the preceding page layout analysis steps, as described in Section 2.

One-dimensional moments are appropriate measures for classification, but there are other alternatives. Two-dimensional moments give a compact representation of the global geometrical properties of a shape such as size, aspect ratio, orientation, moments of inertia and kurtosis that can be used to distinguish between significantly different shapes [13]. They can be extended to our probabilistic framework as easily as one-dimensional moments:

$$E(m_{pq}) := \sum_x \sum_y x^p y^q \, img(x, y) \, reg(x, y)$$

$$Var(m_{pq}) := \sum_x \sum_y (x^p)^2 (y^q)^2 \, img(x, y) \, reg(x, y) \, (1 - img(x, y) \, reg(x, y))$$

When moments are insufficient to distinguish between shapes, the image region can be resampled to a predetermined grid representation (with gray levels representing the uncertainty in the pixel values) and be used directly as an observation vector for a neural network.

The kind of measurement to use for each classification task has been determined empirically.

3.2. Classifier Definition

Classifiers can be roughly separated in two classes: those modeling the between-class discriminant function (such as neural networks and decision trees) and those modeling each class-conditional distribution separately and using Bayes rule to determine actual class (such as HMM-based classifiers and all statistical classifiers using an explicit class-conditional model). Whereas these two kinds have been used indifferently in document recognition, we tend to favor the latter as they do not only find the most likely class but also give a Bayesian estimate of the probability of each class given the observation vector. However, under precise circumstances, some types of neural networks can also produce an estimate of the class probabilities [16], and we can therefore also use them in our framework.

Neural networks that give a probability as output cannot be hand-coded as is possible with HMMs for instance. Once a network structure is chosen, the weights and biases of the cells have to be determined by a training procedure. If the output of the network is to be interpreted as a probability, the output of the network should be processed by a *softmax* function and the error function used for the training should be the *mean square* or the *entropy* error for instance [16]. We use a quasi-Newton algorithm for optimizing the network parameters. Defined this way, neural networks are a very convenient and versatile tool for performing classification in our framework. However, in order to give good performance they still require a good training set, which is not yet available for music symbols for instance.

Class-conditional probability modeling is sometimes easier, and might be hand-crafted without a training set. Once a first classifier is set up, it can be used to automatically build a training set, which can then be used (after a manual validation) to re-estimate statistically significant values for the model parameters or to train a neural network.

The class-conditional observation probability $P(Obs \mid C_i)$ is defined separately for each class, using a HMM or an explicit parametric multivariate distribution. A class prior is also given, although it is not a very sensitive factor as the class-conditional distribution tends to have much greater variations than typical prior values. The system then computes the posterior class probability according to Bayes rule:

$$P(C_i|Obs) = \frac{P(Obs|C_i)\,P(C_i)}{\sum_j P(Obs|C_j)\,P(C_j)}$$

3.3. Combination of Classifiers

It is often useful to combine several classifiers to enhance the discrimination between subcategories. For instance, in our music recognition model, we distinguish between the different possible clefs using HMM-based class-conditional models of both the horizontal and the vertical projection profile. In such a simple case, both class-conditional probability estimations can be assumed to be independent since they are based on (almost) independent observations. We can therefore simply multiply them before applying Bayes rule.

In a more general case, there might be a correlation between the classifiers, which might be difficult to model correctly. One possible approach for solving this problem could be to consider them as competing models, and use yet another classifier to determine how likely is each model to classify the current observation. We did not yet investigate this issue.

3.4. Optional Components

Some graphical objects might have optional components. For instance, our definition of a staff list (as modeled in Section 2.3 and formally defined later in Section 5) as "a staff followed by a staff list" cannot be recursively applied forever: the next staff list is optional. A straightforward way to handle such cases is to define two subcategories of the object, one with the optional component and one without it. However, this is not very convenient to express in a model, and gets even more complex when there are multiple optional components, leading to an exponential number of subcategories. We solved this problem by allowing in the definition of the objects a probability function to be specified for the presence of each of its component. For instance, given a prior staff *height* and the estimated boundaries of the next staff list given by the random variables *pos* and *bottom*, we define:

$$P(next) := P(bottom - pos > height)$$

The inference system handles the alternative cases as if they were explicit subcategories, the most likely first.

4. Graphics Decomposition

Graphics decomposition is the task of locating and identifying the primitive components of a known graphic shape, when top-down method (as described in Section 2) cannot any more be applied to further decompose the graphics.

Graphics decomposition is usually performed through sophisticated vectorization techniques, but unfortunately, we are not aware of any vectorization algorithm that can handle an image with uncertainty associated to each pixel, and produce a probabilistic result. We therefore use simpler techniques, but ones which can be expressed all the way using probability distributions. We did not yet tackle the problem in all its aspects, but only considered some tasks relevant to music recognition, and in particular to the understanding of a note group.

One fundamental task is to locate line segments. We use the Hough Transform (HT) [17] to simultaneously determine the slant and the offset of possible line segments around an expected angle. As done previously for the moments, we weight each source pixel by its probability. The parameter distributions for each line can then be estimated from each local peak on the HT. Once the slant and offset of a line segment are known, we can build a region to represent it, similarly to what we did in Section 2.1 (we here assume a non-vertical line, but the complement is straightforward), either as an ideal zero-width line:

$$line(x, y) := reg(x, y) \int_{-\infty}^{\infty} p_{offset}(y - ax)\, p_{slant}(a)\, da$$

or as a slanted rectangular region, much easier to compute when all random variables follow normal distributions:

$$line(x, y) := P(left < x + slant\, y < right)\, P(top < y - slant\, x < bottom)$$

We then perform a projection profile on this region to determine the starting and ending points of the line segment(s), with regards to what is expected within the current object. We can easily classify the line as plain, dotted or dashed using a HMM-based classifier on this projection profile.

In order to understand note groups, we also have to locate the note-heads and other localized objects (such as flat and sharps) that might be found in a group. Closed (black) note-heads can easily be detected by resampling the image to a lower resolution (the resampling acts as a low-pass filter), but open (white) note-heads cannot be reliably found in this way. Template matching can be used instead, but it tends to be quite intolerant to variations of shapes. As all localized symbols have to be written either on a staff line or between two staff lines, we chose to first use a horizontal projection profile to determine which staff lines could possibly hold a symbol, then define a rectangular region between and across these lines (taking the skew into account as in the formula above) and use a vertical projection profile to detect each individual symbol with a HMM. This method seems to nicely tolerate variations of shape, but we still have to develop it further to see if all possible cases are properly handled.

As for the grouping of the primitives according to the musical notation rules, we rely on the stochastic grammar-like structure of our recognition model to find the most likely interpretations. Our parser ensures a maximal complexity in $O(n^3)$ of the number of primitive detected for the group, typically a small number.

5. Sample Object Definition

Here is an example definition of one object of our musical score recognition model, to give a precise idea of how the models described above are actually specified. All document recognition expertise, heuristics and ad-hoc rules are explicitly written in the model (see for instance the definition of the HMM parameters *white*, *data* and *spc*). This allows us to use a totally generic inference engine, and to give an objective sight on all our modeling assumptions. This would also allow a third party to understand our model, reuse it and customize it to fit particular needs.

```
OBJECT staffList
GIVEN
    img : Image;                           // the bitmap image
    left, right, top, bot : Distribution;  // staff system dimensions
    hgt : Distribution;                    // prior staff height
REGION
    reg : PiecewiseLinearInterpolation [ img, 10 Dpi ];
    reg(x,y) := P(left < x < right) * P(top < y < bot);
MEASURE
    hpp : Histogram [ Approximate, 20 Dpi ]; // horiz projection profile
    hpp(y) := Sum(reg(x,y) * img(x,y));
PARAMETER
    width := right - left;
    // we assume around 5% black between staves
    white := Gauss(E(width) * 0.05, E(width) * 0.05);
    // we assume around 30% black in staves
    data := Gauss(E(width) * 0.30, E(width) * 0.05);
    spc := hgt / 8;                        // inter-staff space
MODEL
    chn : HiddenMarkovModel [ 6 States, GammaDuration, GaussianFeature ];
    chn.Observations := hpp;
    chn.Names := [ "topwhite", "first", "firstspc", "other", "otherspc",
"botwhite" ];
    chn.Features := [ white, data, white, data, white, white ];
    chn.Durations := [ spc, hgt, spc, hgt, spc, spc ];
    chn.InitialProbabilities := [ 1, 0, 0, 0, 0, 0 ];
    chn.FinalProbabilities := [ 0, 0, 0, 0, 0, 1 ];
    chn.Transitions := [[   0,      1,      0,      0,      0,      0     ]
                        [   0,      0,      1,      0,      0,      0     ]
                        [   0,      0,      0,      0.8,    0,      0.2   ]
                        [   0,      0,      0,      0,      0.8,    0.2   ]
                        [   0,      0,      0,      1,      0,      0     ]
                        [   0,      0,      0,      0,      0,      1     ]];
PARAMETER
    ref := E(top) + StdDev(top);       // upper boundary for staff split
INFERENCE
    hgt' : GammaDistribution;
    p(hgt' | chn) :=% P(chn | chn(E(ref) + hgt) = "firstspc") * p(hgt);
PARAMETER
```

```
      sep := Gauss(E(ref + hgt'), StdDev(hgt'));
COMPONENT
      first : staff;                                    // the first staff
      first := parse(img, left, right, top, sep);
      next : staffList;                                 // the next staves
      next := parse(img, left, right, sep, bot, hgt);
      P(next) := P(bot - sep >= hgt);
END OBJECT
```

6. Conclusion

We have shown that common techniques for document recognition can be formulated into an explicit document recognition model. This model can be interpreted using random variables to represent each quantity. When processed by an appropriate inference engine, it leads to a document recognition process where probabilities are handled from one end to the other, avoiding unrecoverable mistakes typical of the traditional pipeline architecture. Our first experiments on a wide variety of scanned music scores (400 pages taken from various sources) show that combining simple measures with probabilistically grounded models lead to a robust system, removing the need for so commonly used ad-hoc tricks. In particular, page layout analysis and classification tasks appear to be fully tractable within this framework.

There are still a number of issues that we have to address, in particular, graphics decomposition and the detection of large objects such as slurs. Given our experience with this inference framework, we are confident that it is indeed possible and fruitful to explicitly write down a complete probabilistic model for musical score recognition, as well as many other instances of the graphics recognition problem.

References

[1] D. Bainbridge and N. Carter. Automatic Reading of Music Notation, in H. Bunke and P.S.P. Wang editors, Handbook of Character Recognition and Document Image Analysis, World Scientific, 1997.

[2] D. Blostein and H. Baird. A Critical Survey of Music Image Analysis, in H. Baird, H. Bunke and K. Yamamoto editors, Structured Document Image Analysis, Springer Verlag, 1992.

[3] N. Carter, R. Bacon and T. Messenger. The acquisition, Representation and Reconstruction of Printed Music by Computer: A Review. Computers and the Humanities, 22:117-136, 1988.

[4] D. Bainbridge. Extensible Optical Music Recognition. Ph.D. Thesis, University of Canterbury, 1997.

[5] B. Coüasnon and J. Camillerapp. Using Grammars to Segment and Recognize Music Scores. IAPR Workshop on Document Analysis Systems, Kaiserslautern, Germany, 1994.

[6] H. Fahmy and D. Blostein. A Graph Grammar for High-Level Recognition of Music Notation. Proceedings of ICDAR'91, Saint Malo, France, 1991.

[7] H. Kato and S. Inokuchi. A Recognition System for Printer Piano Music Using Musical Knowldge and Constraints, in H. Baird, H. Bunke and K. Yamamoto editors, Structured Document Image Analysis, Springer-Verlag, 1992.

[8] G. Kopec and P. Chou. Document Image Decoding Using Markov Source Models. IEEE Trans. on Pattern Analysis and Machine Intelligence, 16(6):602-617, June 1994.

[9] G. Kopec, P. Chou and D. Maltz. Markov Source Model for Printed Music Decoding. Journal of Electronic Imaging, 5(1):7-14, January 1996.

[10] M. Vuilleumier Stückelberg and D. Doermann. On Musical Score Recognition using Probabilistic Reasoning. Proceedings of ICDAR'99, Bangalore, India, September 1999.

[11] J. Maxwell III and R. Kaplan. The Interface between Phrasal and Functional Constraints. Computational Linguistics, 19(4):571-589, 1994.

[12] I. Fujinaga. Optical Music Recognition using Projections. M.S. Thesis, McGill University, Montreal, Canada, 1988.

[13] R. Prokop and A. Reeves. A Survey of Moment-Based Techniques for Unoccluded Object Representation and Recognition. Computer Vision, Graphics and Image Processing, 54(5):438-460, September 1992.

[14] L. Rabiner and B.-H. Juang. Fundamentals of Speech Recognition. Prentice-Hall, 1993.

[15] P. Cheeseman et al. AutoClass: A Bayesian Classification System. Fifth Int. Workshop on Machine Learning, Ann Arbor, 1988.

[16] C. Bishop. Neural Networks for Pattern Recognition. Oxford University Press, 1995.

[17] J. Illingworth and J. Kittler. A Survey of the Hough Transform. Computer Vision, Graphics and Image Processing, 44(1):87-116, January 1988.

A Client-Server Architecture for Document Image Recognition

Atul K. Chhabra[1], Juan F. Arias[1],
Theo Pavlidis[2], Phoebe X. Pan[2], and Pedro V. Sanders[2]

[1] Verizon Communications
500 Westchester Avenue, White Plains, NY 10604, USA
atul.k.chhabra@verizon.com
[2] Department of Computer Science, State University of New York at Stony Brook
Stony Brook, NY 11794, USA
t.pavlidis@ieee.org

Abstract. We propose a client-server architecture for deploying document image recognition applications, especially graphics recognition applications, in large organizations. An example of such an application is presented. We discuss advantages of client-server techniques over the currently available stand-alone tools for document image recognition.

1 Introduction

In most disciplines, a vast majority of documents and drawings still exist only in hard copy form (paper, microfilm, etc.). Invariably, crucial factors in the success of a business include the ability to quickly retrieve and edit the documents, the ability to extract useful information from the documents, and the ability to query all documents by their content. The first step in providing such capabilities is to raster scan all hard copy documents. The next logical step is the conversion of the raster documents into the appropriate intelligent computer representation. For text documents, this implies converting the raster images to ASCII data using techniques such as page layout analysis & decomposition and OCR followed by full text indexing. For graphical documents such as engineering drawings, the conversion involves line drawing interpretation – text-graphics separation, raster to vector conversion, higher-level graphics recognition, and OCR. For interconnected drawings, this should be followed by logically connecting the recognized graphical entities. Although the techniques discussed in this paper are equally applicable to the process of recognition and conversion of both text and graphical documents, we concentrate only on graphical documents here. Specifically, we focus on the conversion of engineering drawings.

Frequently, the price tag for manual, one-time, mass conversion of hard copy or raster documents into intelligent graphical data is extremely high. Several systems for engineering drawing analysis and recognition have been proposed in the 1990's [1,2,3,4,5,6]. The difficulty of this task is apparent from the fact that despite these published systems, no commercial tool exists for high level drawing

Atul K. Chhabra and D. Dori (Eds.): GREC'99, LNCS 1941, pp. 133–142, 2000.

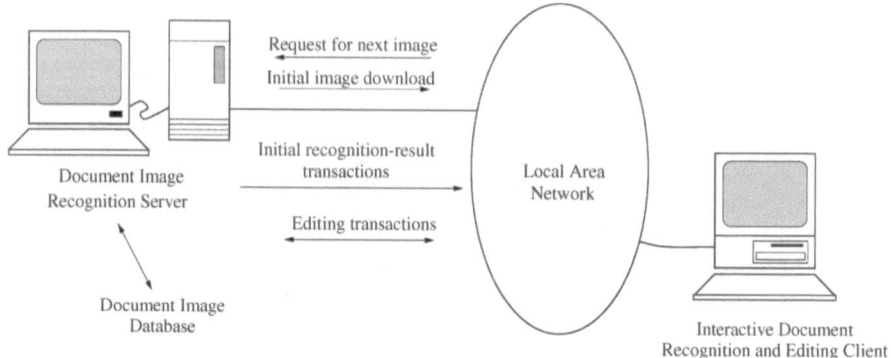

Fig. 1. Client-server architecture for a document recognition system

recognition. Commercial tools limit themselves to raster-to-vector conversion (e.g., [7,8]); they do not attempt high level drawing interpretation. These tools take a raster image and convert it to a CAD file. Both the research prototypes and the commercial tools for graphics recognition attempt to be general purpose tools. In a majority of graphics recognition applications, the accuracy of the recognition can be improved tremendously by customizing the tools using domain knowledge. The conversion tools need to be goal directed for good performance. Moreover, due to the inherent difficulties in automatically interpreting complex line drawings, it is always necessary to have a person in the loop, monitoring the conversion process and making corrections as necessary. A small correction at an early stage in the conversion of a drawing can often yield much more accurate results at later stages. Therefore, to cut down on extensive manual editing, it is quite important for the conversion process to be interactive. Another driver for interactive drawing image conversion is the frequent need for just-in-time conversion (as opposed to one-time mass conversion).

This paper focuses on a method of deploying interactive drawing image recognition tools in a large organization. Specifically, we propose using the client-server model, a technique that is already pervasive in enterprise database applications and several world wide web applications. In client-server database applications, desktop computers connect to database servers over local area networks to query and retrieve relevant information from the database; the type of data transferred between the client and the server is mostly plain text. For deploying graphics recognition tools with a client-server architecture, one has to overcome the hurdle of sending images back and forth between the clients and the server, over a network with limited bandwidth. The worst method to implement a client-server image recognition application is by using X-windows. X-windows carries a huge network traffic overhead when dealing with image based applications. For simple events such as 'expose', the image content of the entire window is transferred over the network. The sluggishness of X-windows based client-server imaging applications is unbearable when working over a slow network connection, such as a modem connection. We propose a client-server architecture where the client starts off by requesting the next image from the server, the server provides a copy of the image (in compressed form), and all the remaining work involves only ASCII transactions between the client and the server (Figure 1). Although we discuss this architecture only in the context of engineering drawing recognition, the technique is just as valid and applicable for a wide variety of interactive image processing and computer vision applications.

Most research prototypes for graphics recognition have been developed on some variant of the Unix operating system. The authors developed one such system for converting telephone company drawings [9,10,11,12,13,14]. This system was developed on the Sun Solaris operating system using an X-windows based interface. This is a problem because the industry has become entrenched in low cost personal computers running Windows 95/98. The client-server architecture presented here offers an elegant solution to this problem. It allows one to run the recognition software on Unix servers and the graphical editing software on client PC's.

2   Interactive, Client-Server Drawing Conversion System

In this section, we illustrate a client-server architecture for the tabular drawing recognition system of [12,13]. Our first experience with a small client-server image processing application is summarized in [15].

Systems for interpreting images of engineering drawings most often work upon a pixel map of drawing images (i.e., one byte per pixel). For ANSI 'E' size drawings scanned at 300 dpi, this requires about 160 MBytes of memory to hold one copy of the image. More efficient programs work on the bitmap representation of an image. That cuts down the image size to about 20 MBytes. This is still a large amount of memory, especially if the software needs to use several intermediate copies of the image. For such systems, running one copy of the recognition process ties up most system resources. Running several copies is extremely difficult. Such software also slows down due to large amounts of data transfer involved. Therefore, these systems are not suited to running on an image recognition server that serves several clients.

We built our line drawing recognition systems using very fast and memory efficient line finding techniques [16,17]. The fast methods enable us to build an interactive system. The memory efficient nature of the line finding methods puts them in a good position for deployment on a network server. One such image recognition server can serve several clients. In other words, the server can run several instances of the drawing recognition software with a moderate amount of memory. To make the drop in speed (with several recognition processes running simultaneously) less noticeable, we can use a multi-processor server.

We designed the system such that all the recognition happens on the recognition server, and all the user interaction and correction happens on client PC's. The client application requests an initial download of the next image from the server. Soon after the image download, the recognition results are also transmit-

Table 1. Client-server communication protocol for the table recognition application. This is the list of commands that a client can send to the image recognition server

Command	Description
RD char *filename*	Read the specified image file
FL	Find lines
FT	Find tables
FX	Find text
AL int *x1* int *y1* int *x2* int *y2*	Add a line with the given coordinates
DL int *line_id*	Delete line with the given id.
JL int *line_id1* int *line_id2*	Join lines with the given ids.
SD int *line_id* int *state*	Set a line as ditto line or not, according to state
SE int *box_id* int *state*	Set a box as empty or full, according to state
QT	Quit

ted to the client as a sequence of ASCII transactions. Subsequently, the client and the server exchange several graphical editing transactions in both directions.

Tables 1 and 2 list the types and syntax of transactions initiated from the client and the server respectively. The set of transactions is designed specifically for interactive recognition and graphical editing of tabular drawings. These transactions are domain specific. However, they can easily be extended to cover any specific drawing, document, or image domain.

The communication channel used for transmitting the transactions is the socket interface. The server process creates a socket, maps it to a local address, and waits for client requests. Each client request for image recognition starts a new recognition process on the server and a communication channel is established between the process and the client.

The image recognition server is written in the C language. It runs on Sun Solaris or Linux Operating systems. We are developing two prototype clients for monitoring and editing the recognition results. One is written using the C++ language for a PC running Windows (95/98 or NT), and the other uses the Java language that can run on any platform. Screen shots of the two prototypes are shown in Figure 2. The Java language offers portability and ease of maintenance of applications. However, currently the Java language lacks support for displaying and manipulating large compressed images. Therefore, our current implementation of the client software in Java only displays the results of graphics recognition. It does not show the image. Hopefully, this support will be added to the language soon. In case this doesn't happen soon enough, we will have the C++ client software to fall back on.

The constraints that we have to work within are as follows – we have to make use of the existing computer and network infrastructure; we do not have the luxury to require powerful desktop computers for every user. Figure 3 il-

Table 2. Client-server communication protocol for the table recognition application. This is the list of commands that the image recognition server can send to the recognition and editing client

Command	Description
OK	Operation performed
AI int int_id int x int y	Add intersection
DI int int_id	Delete intersection
AX int $text\_id$ int x int y char $string$ float $conf$	Add a text string with the given confidence
AL int $line\_id$ int $x1$ int $y1$ int $x2$ int $y2$	Add line
SD int $line\_id$	Set line as a ditto line
AB int box_id int x int y int w int h int $type$ int $state$ int $table$	Add box
DB int box_id	Delete box

lustrates how we plan to deploy the client-server graphics recognition software in the existing infrastructure. The existing infrastructure provides the telephone company engineers and drafters with engineering, drafting, and drawing management software applications and a host of other enterprise applications. We plan to provide engineers and drafters the ability to convert a raster image into intelligent computer data by just an incremental installation of an image recognition server and Java client software (that possibly runs from within a web browser – so the client software doesn't even have to reside on the client machine).

3 The Client Interface

Here we briefly describe some salient features of the C++ client interface. Using this interface, the operator is able to see both the original scanned document and the results of the conversion. We decided to create two scrolling windows, one displaying the original document and the other the conversion. The two windows are completely synchronized; any time the user scrolls one of the them, the other scrolls by the same amount. Also when an area is selected on one, a corresponding area is selected on the other. While the client side was written using the Microsoft Visual C++ environment and the Microsoft Foundation Classes (MFC), these two windows were written using the Win32 API because of their special nature. The application also includes a toolbar (created through MFC) and other auxiliary windows, including one displaying the complete document at a highly reduced scale.

Editing operations include "Add Line", "Extend Lines", "Split Line", "Erase Lines", "Edit Text", "Move Text", etc. A key issue in CAD systems is whether a selection should be made first and then an operation applied (object-verb method) or whether an operation will be selected first and then objects will be selected (verb-object method). The former method is the one most commonly

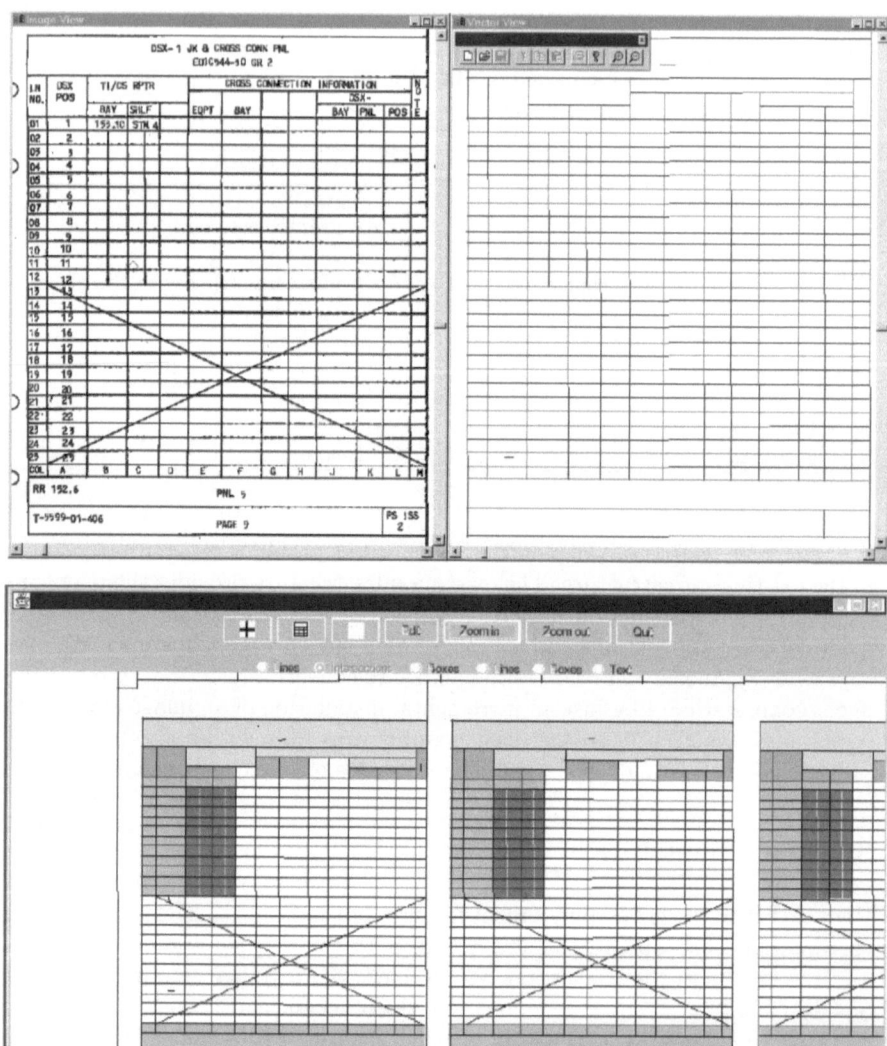

Fig. 2. Screen shots of two prototype client applications for monitoring and graphical editing of tabular image recognition. Top: the C++ PC client software; bottom: the Java PC client software

used in text editors, but for drawings editors this is not the case. We decided, wherever applicable, to offer both options.

For clarity we discuss the strategies for a specific operation: "Erase Lines." The user may select one or more line segments by enclosing them with a rect-

Existing Drawing Management & Engineering Infrastructure

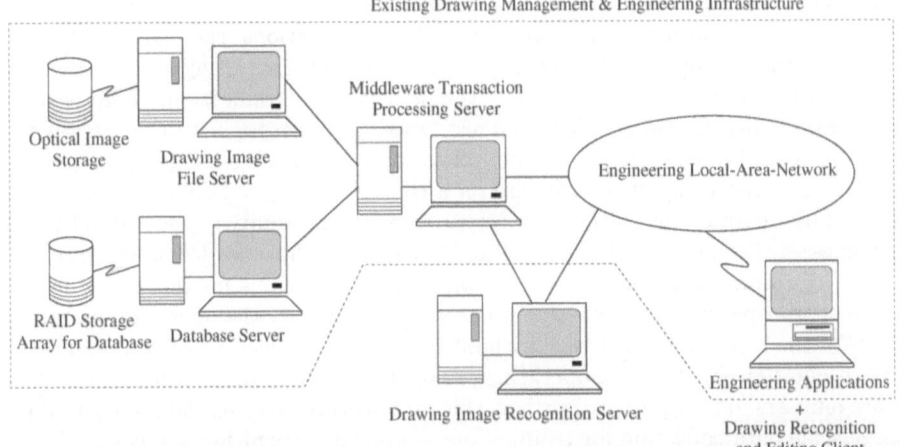

Fig. 3. The image recognition server and the document recognition and editing client, as they fit in an existing infrastructure for engineering and drawing management applications

angle. Then when the user clicks on the "Erase Lines" button, all line segments contained entirely within the rectangle are erased. Alternatively, the user may click first on the "Erase Lines" button in which case the cursor icon is changed to reflect the erase operation. When the user clicks on a a line, the line is highlighted and after a second click it is erased. The double-click operation reduces the chances of errors. The second mode is more convenient when the lines to be erased are far from each other. While we allow for multiple selections (using the SHIFT key), this is not practical unless the lines are in the same view.

The most novel feature of the GUI is the use of pattern recognition methods to provide intelligent response to the user. In particular, the user does not have to specify the positions exactly with the mouse. The program selects nearby intersections or other special locations for the intended locations of a point.

4   Advantages of Client-Server Architecture for Interactive Engineering Drawing Conversion

As stated above, the two basic requirements to implement a drawing conversion system using a client-server architecture are that the graphics recognition algorithms be interactive (i.e., fast) and be designed for very efficient use of memory. As long as these two requirements are met, the client-server architecture offers the following benefits.

The work load is split between the client and the server. The server does the graphics recognition and the client does the monitoring and correction of the intermediate and the final results. Since the client does not need to do any computing, it is possible to use cheap PC's as clients. Since we designed the communication protocol as mostly ASCII transactions, there is very little network traffic generated by the application. In fact, in testing done using a 10 Base-T ethernet LAN connection versus a modem connection, there is no noticeable difference in the performance (speed) of the application except for the longer initial delay in the modem scenario for a one-time image download.

Running the recognition software on a central server, and collecting the results of user corrections on the same server, gives us the ability to learn about the weaknesses of the recognition algorithms. We can use this knowledge to improve the recognition algorithms, and can update the algorithms on the server in a manner transparent to the users. Similarly, we can modify the operating parameters of the recognition software without disrupting the users. We can upgrade the recognition software and operating parameters without re-installing any software on users' desktop PC's. Further, this architecture gives us the ability to do large scale data collection for training our character recognition software.

The database transactions to fetch the next image to be converted, and to check in the converted data file into the database, are completely transparent to the client PC. The database transactions take place between the image recognition server and the middleware or database server. Similarly, the client PC does not to know where to get the drawing image from. The image recognition server negotiates that with the middleware or image file server and downloads the image to the client PC.

For image recognition software developed on Unix (or any non-Windows 95/98/NT platform), this architecture obviates the need to port large amount of code to the Windows environment.

Disdvantages of X-window emulation solutions have been mentioned above. Essentially, X-windows impose a heavy network traffic overhead for any image based application. Our client-server solution generates minimal network traffic. By designing the client and the server ourselves, we control the granularity of the network traffic. We control what tasks are performed on the client and what work is done on the server. Moreover, from the user interface point of view, X-window emulation is an unacceptable solution for people well versed in using PC's with Windows 95/98/NT.

Finally, since the communication between client and server is transaction based, it is possible to log all transactions (in both directions) for all images that go through the conversion process. Subsequently, it is possible to reconstruct the interactive drawing conversion session for a given drawing by looking at the transaction log for that drawing. This can help the developers to monitor the conversion process for debugging purposes and to pin point areas in which the users are making excessive mistakes (this knowledge can be used for better user training).

References

1. R. Kasturi, S. T. Bow, W. El-Masri, J. R. Gattiker, and U. B. Mokate. A system for interpretation of line drawings. *IEEE Trans. Pattern Analysis and Machine Intelligence*, 12(10):978–992, 1990. 133

2. D. Antoine. CIPLAN: A model-based system with original features for understanding French plats. In *Proc. 1st International Conference on Document Analysis and Recognition*, pages 647–655, St. Malo, Paris, 1991. 133

3. D. Antoine, S. Collin, and K. Tombre. Analysis of technical documents: The RE-DRAW System. In H. S. Baird, H. Bunke, and K. Yamamoto, editors, *Structured Document Image Analysis*, pages 385–402. Springer Verlag, Berlin/Heidelberg, 1992. 133

4. S. H. Joseph and T. P. Pridmore. Knowledge-directed interpretation of mechanical engineering drawings. *IEEE Trans. Pattern Analysis and Machine Intelligence*, 14(9):928–940, 1992. 133

5. P. Vaxivière and K. Tombre. CELESSTIN: CAD conversion of mechanical drawings. *IEEE Computer Magazine*, 25(7):46–54, July 1992. 133

6. L. Wenyin and D. Dori. Automated CAD conversion with the machine drawing understanding system. In *Proc. IAPR Workshop on Document Analysis Systems*, pages 241–259, Malvern, PA, USA, October 1996. 133

7. I/Vector (Vectory) ver. 3.8 Raster to Vector Conversion Software. Graphikon, Berlin, Germany, and IDEAL Scanners & Systems, Rockville, MD, USA. http://www.graphikon.com. 134

8. VPstudio ver. 6 rev. 2 Raster to Vector Conversion Software. Softelec, Munich, Germany, and Austin, TX, USA. http://www.softelec.com. 134

9. J. F. Arias, A. Prasad, R. Kasturi, and A. Chhabra. Interpretation of telephone company central office equipment drawings. In *Proc. 12th IAPR International Conference on Pattern Recognition*, pages B310–B314, Jerusalem, Israel, October 1994. 135

10. J. F. Arias, S. Balasubramanian, A. Prasad, R. Kasturi, and A. Chhabra. Information extraction from telephone company drawings. In *Proc. IEEE Conference on Computer Vision and Pattern Recognition*, pages 729–732, Seattle, Washington, June 1994. 135

11. J. F. Arias, R. Kasturi, and A. Chhabra. Efficient techniques for telephone company line drawing interpretation. In *Proc. of 3nd Int. Conf. on Document Analysis and Recognition*, pages 795–798, Montréal, Canada, August 1995. 135

12. J. F. Arias, A. Chhabra, and V. Misra. Interpreting and representing tabular documents. In *Proc. of CVPR*, pages 600–605, San Francisco, CA, June 1996. 135

13. J. F. Arias, A. Chhabra, and V. Misra. Efficient interpretation of tabular documents. In *Proc. International Conference on Pattern Recognition*, volume III, pages 681–685, Vienna, Austria, August 1996. 135

14. H. Luo, R. Kasturi, J. F. Arias, and A. Chhabra. Interpretation of lines in distributing frame drawings. In *Proc. International Conference on Document Analysis and Recognition*, volume I, pages 66–70, Ulm, Germany, August 1997. 135

15. J. F. Arias, A. Chhabra, and V. Misra. A practical application of graphics recognition: Helping with the extraction of information from telephone company drawings. In K. Tombre and A. Chhabra, editors, *Graphics Recognition – Algorithms and Systems*, volume 1389 of *Lecture Notes in Computer Science*, pages 314–321. Springer-Verlag, Berlin, Germany, 1998. 135

16. A. K. Chhabra, V. Misra, and J. Arias. Detection of horizontal lines in noisy run length encoded images: The FAST method. In R. Kasturi and K. Tombre, editors, *Graphics Recognition – Methods and Applications*, volume 1072 of *Lecture Notes in Computer Science*, pages 35–48. Springer-Verlag, Berlin, Germany, 1996. 135

17. J. F. Arias, A. Chhabra, and V. Misra. Finding straight lines in drawings. In *Proc. International Conference on Document Analysis and Recognition*, volume II, pages 788–791, Ulm, Germany, August 1997. 135

Multi-Dimensional Interval Algebra with Symmetry for Describing Block Layouts

Ankur Lahoti, Rohit Singh and Amitabha Mukerjee
{lahoti,rohitsi,amit}@iitk.ac.in

Dept of Computer Science, Indian Institute of Technology, Kanpur, INDIA

Abstract. Describing the relative positions of Rectangular boxes on a page is a fundamental task in document layout processing. T ypically , this is achiev ed by comparing quantitativ e values of the endpoints of the rectangle. Such a representation expresses a property that is basic for the "in terval" as a conjunction of relations for the "point". In this w ork, w e adopt a qualitative interval projection model to describe the relativ e positions of such blocks using interval algebra, which defines the spatial relation of two points only in terms of precedence, coincidence and post-occurrence. Such relations have not been found very meaningful in document or other media layout con texts since they cannot capture symmetry.

In this w ork, w e propose an extension of interval algebra by defining secondary operators (e.g. "centered") which are expressed in terms of basic in terval algebra operators. By extending the ordering of intervals to higher dimensions, Multidimensional Interval Algebra can capture the notion of tangency and alignment betw een blocks while retaining the relativ e size information. We present several examples from the document domain to show that this information is sufficient to iden tify the layout of block structured formats. While this representation does not provide any immediate benefit to document analysis per se - the fact that it provides a compact yet complete vocabulary enables its use in abstraction tasks such as learning the grammar of a document sets by studying a series of examples.

1 Qualitative Modeling of Block-Structured Images

Many artificial objects such as document pages, video frames, w eb pages, images, etc. use rectangular boxes as the building block. In documents, the relative positions of blocks suc h as the heading, paragraphs, columns is described in the *do cument layout*, as opposed to the contents, fonts, or other markup characteristics. The lay out of a document or other media is important in forming a preliminary expectation of the content - for example, to identify where a page n umber may be on a page. In addition to its importance in document recognition, la yout analysis is also becoming relev ant in conten t based image and video retrieval.

Quantitativ e descriptors with exact co-ordinates are too precise for expressing relationships like alignment and tangency. Given the relativ e positions of

Atul K. Chhabra and D. Dori (Eds.): GREC'99, LNCS 1941, pp. 143-154, 2000.

nearby blocks, the exact location of a block (specified quantitatively) is, often, unimportant. Another difficulty is the reliance on a global coordinate frame such as the page frame in defining positions- objects further from the origin often have their errors amplified. The notion of Qualitative Position [6, 1], on the other hand, is designed precisely to capture such relative descriptions. Qualitative position descriptions are based on Interval Logic and provide an efficient, complete and robust formalism for expressing the relative positions of points or intervals along a one dimensional space, or that of rectangular blocks in a two-dimensional document. For example, the relative position of a time-point a with respect to another b along an can be expressed as -, 0, or +, which distinguish, respectively, precedence, coincidence, and post-occurrence. Thus *relation (a/b)* = + is simply saying that a occurs after b. This description clearly ignores every aspect of their positions except for alignment. For corporal spatial objects such as intervals whose endpoints are points, qualitative descriptions are a mechanism which are precise only for tangency and alignment information, and bundle all interim positions as a single descriptor. As we show below, media layout analysis requires precisely this type of information and surprisingly little else. Note that these relations require an ordering direction, which is simple for points in time, but not so convenient for spatial issues. Fortunately in the limited domain of documents and other multimedia formats, there is a known ordering in both the vertical and the horizontal directions: top to bottom, and for most cultures, left to right.

In this paper we show how such models of qualitative spatial reasoning can be used to describe rectangular blocks with particular reference to the document formalism but the same concepts can be used for other structures as well with relatively little modification.

The main benefit of using such representations are akin to that of using a better notation in algebra - it provides insights into the structure of the objects we are studying. In practical terms, the fact that the set of descriptors is small and the inter-relations are open provides an efficient mechanism for describing a document layout in human-friendly terms and, computationally, for abstracting a description or a grammar from of an example set of document layouts.

1.1   Interval Algebra

Interval algebra [1] was developed in the context of temporal intervals, which are ordered along a one-dimensional space. The same concept can also be applied in structures in two-dimensional space [5]. In two dimensional space, the idea can be directly applied to spaces that are orthogonal, such as documents and other multimedia layouts. In the case of blocks in a document layout, we can consider the projections of these blocks along two orthogonal axes and model these separately as one-dimensional intervals. Interval logic then provides a set of tools for modeling the qualitative position and size of different blocks in the document.

There are various versions of interval algebra depending on whether the entities considered are intervals [1] or points [9]. But, fundamentally, these distinctions are not important and in this notation we use a combined point-interval algebra capable of reasoning about both points and intervals. Traditional interval algebra does not provide for a measure of size, however, focusing only on relative positions. But, while analyzing documents, relative size is also of importance. However, interval algebra does provide for a test of *equality* between two intervals. In the following we show how this test can be used to handle the requirements for modeling symmetry and centered-ness. We begin by describing the point-interval algebra used for this purpose [5].

If we consider a point a and an interval B then a can be before, inside or after B, along with the two tangency positions where a can coincide with the back of B or its front . The five relations thus defined are: - (before), b (coincide with back), i (inside), f (coincide with front), and + (after). Relations between two intervals A and B can now be defined as the ordered 2-tuple of relations for the two endpoints of A with respect to B. Thus, the statement *relation $A/B =$* if is another way of saying that A is smaller than B and aligned at the front. The relation is expressed more compactly as A if B.

Qualitative Spatial Reasoning [5, 3] extends this notion to that of higher dimensional spaces. Multidimensional Interval Algebra simply uses interval algebra along each axis of an orthogonally aligned rectangular system. Thus the relation between two rectangloid entities in a D-dimensional space is a D-vector of interval relations defined by their unique projections along each orthogonal axis. Thus, in the Fig. 1: A $\left(\begin{smallmatrix} - \\ -i \end{smallmatrix}\right)$ B.

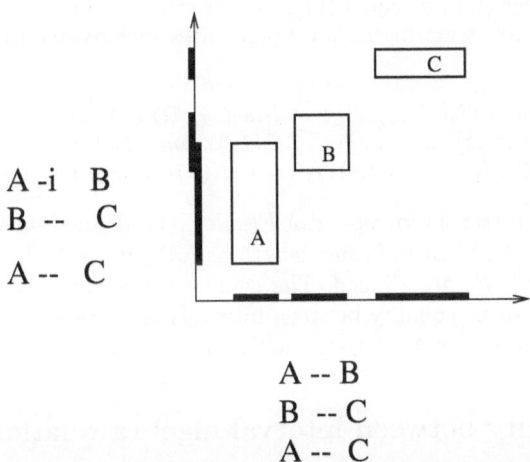

Fig. 1. *Interval Algebra in 2-Dimensions.* For example, along the y-axis, the relation between (A) and (B) is -i, i.e. with respect to (B) the start point of (A) is '-' and its endpoint is 'i'.

Such relations have been used for identifying block structures in documents as in [2]. In this work, we use this notion to define the grammar for any class of block structured media documents. We also point to an approach for using this approach in capturing the structural similarity within a class of documents. A context-free grammar is derived from a set of document images, which can then be used to determine if a new document belongs to this class or not. For example, conference organizers can use this tool to determine if submissions follow the norms.

The advantage of using qualitative models is that unlike *ad hoc* abstractions of quantitative data, the set of relations is **complete** within the assumption that relative positions are unimportant unless involving tangency.

1.2   Symmetry Relations

One of the problems of interval algebra is that it is only concerned with the relative positions of the end points of the interval, and not so much with the sizes. Where two objects do not have a common boundary or complete overlap, e.g. in relations like –i or ++, it is not possible to infer the relative sizes. In spatial reasoning however, the sizes of distant objects may also be of importance. In document analysis there is the need for determining symmetry.

This difficulty arises only if we consider intervals as fixed at their position along the directional axis. However, spatial objects can be moved or can be moved relatively by moving the viewing apparatus. Thus it is possible to compare the size of objects that are not aligned. In this work we use a procedural operator *Flush* which returns an imaginary interval that is aligned with another at the back point. Now one can immediately determine whether the first interval is smaller (bi), larger (b+) or equal (bf).

Now one can construct higher-level predicates such as *centered* in the following fashion:

$$SameSize((\mathcal{I}_\infty), (\mathcal{I}_\in)) \Leftrightarrow Flush_{(\mathcal{I}_\in)}((\mathcal{I}_\infty))\{\ \mathtt{bf}\ \}(\mathcal{I}_\in)$$
$$CenteredSmaller((\mathcal{A}), (\mathcal{B})) \Rightarrow (\exists(\mathcal{I}_\infty))(\exists(\mathcal{I}_\in))SameSize((\mathcal{I}_\infty), (\mathcal{I}_\in)) \bigwedge ((\mathcal{I}_\infty)\ \mathtt{bi}$$
$$(\mathcal{B})) \bigwedge ((\mathcal{I}_\infty)\ \mathtt{-b}\ (\mathcal{A})) \bigwedge ((\mathcal{I}_\in)\ \mathtt{if}\ (\mathcal{B})) \bigwedge ((\mathcal{I}_\in)\ \mathtt{f+}\ (\mathcal{A}))$$

where the flush-translation operator $Flush_{(\mathcal{B})}()$ is defined such that $Flush_{(\mathcal{B})}(\mathcal{A})$ returns an interval $(\mathcal{X})$ of the same length as $(\mathcal{A})$ but such that the back end-points of $(\mathcal{X})$ and $(\mathcal{B})$ are aligned. The centered predicate essentially uses the **bf** operator to test for equality between intervals, and states that A is centered on B iff the sub-intervals A−B to the left and right are equal.

2   Transitivity between interval-algebra relations

The relations between blocks within a document expressed by the formulation of interval-algebra are transitive in nature. This is useful in certain cases when the relation between the two objects may not be known directly. Here with the given information on relations as $A\ r_1\ B$ and $C\ r_2\ B$, we would like to infer the relation between the intervals A and C. Thus, given a relation A (b+)B and C (if)B, we can infer that A (−+) C.

Table 1 gives a comprehensive description of the transitivity relations between two intervals A and B in terms of the two endpoints of A.

$\frac{C/B}{a/B}$	++	f+	i+	if	ii	bi	bf	b+	−+	−f	−i	−b	−−
+	?	>	>	+	+	+	+	>	>	+	+	+	+
f	−	b	i	f	+	+	f	i	i	f	+	+	+
i	−	−	<	<	?	>	i	i	i	i	>	+	+
b	−	−	−	−	−	b	b	b	i	i	i	b	+
−	−	−	−	−	−	−	−	−	<	<	<	<	?

Table 1. Transitivity Table : Given the relation of point (a) w.r.t interval (B), and the relation of (C) w.r.t (B), can infer the position of a w.r.t (B). The symbols <,> and ? are disjunctions of (−,b,I), (i,f,+) and (−,b,i,f,+) respectively.

The transitivity rules can also be extended to multi-dimensional space by applying them independently along the orthogonal axes (Fig. 1).

3   Document Layout Description Grammar

One of the main advantages of interval algebra over traditional approaches are the compactness and human-readability of the notation. Consider the title and the author block in the image below. For example, compare a statement like

$$(rect_1.x1 − rect_2.x1 = rect_2.x2 − rect_1.x2) \wedge (rect_1.y4 < rect_2.y1)$$

with

Authors ($^c_-$−) Title

where the relation "c" is *centered* and −− indicates the entire interval is *before* the other (in the y-direction).

Based on this notation, one can now build a descriptive grammar for the structure of such documents as in 2:

R1:   Title ($^{cs}_{ii}$) Frame
R2:   Authors ($^{cs}_{ii}$) Frame
R3:   Authors ($^c_{--}$) Title
R4: AbstractTitle ($^{c,ii}_{--}$) Authors
R5:   Abstract ($^{c,-+}_{-}$) Authors
R6: AbstractTitle ($^{cs,bi}_{++}$) Abstract
R7:   Heading ($^{-i}_{--}$)Abstract
R8:   Para ($^{i+}_{--}$) Heading

Fig. 2. *A Sample Input Image and Its symmetric Block Structure*

Document Grammar Reconciliation

The first task in document description using interval algebra is to identify the block structure of the document, given the document image. By using well-known techniques like RLSA [10] and histogram analysis it is traditional to obtain a block characterization of a document image. The quantitative block positions can be matched with a known grammar such as the example above - i.e. a set of qualitative interval relations. At this point, a certain tolerance of error in the block positioning is required because it is unlikely that the exact typesetting information will be reproduced accurately. Fig. 5 shows the identified block structure of a simple document. Alternately, for generating a description, the quantitative data may be converted into interval relations which can then be matched with the grammar learned so far.

In matching the rules to the quantitative block structure or vice-versa, it is assumed that the blocks are listed from the top right to bottom left and that the relations are also ordered in the same fashion. Thus the title relations are usually the first seen in a title page.

4   Template Learning

In this work we observe that a description of a document instance is a conjunction of relations between the constituent blocks. This permits us to use the old concept of Version Spaces [7] which works well with conjunctive descriptions. In this model, for each positive instance of the document format shown the hypothesis corresponding to the block-layout grammar is generalized. Since the input models used are only positive examples, there is at present no need for specialization. However this can be incorporated, for example, to prune undesirable formatting elements. Fig. 3 shows the generalized grammar rule for three one-column input documents.

Fig. 3. *A Sample Set of 3 One-Column Input Images and their corresponding Block Structures.* All of these correspond to the same grammar as in Figure 2.

The objective is to develop a set of unified grammar rules consistent with all the input document images. The grammar should reconcile with all the input documents and at the same time should not conform to more documents. Since the relative positions may differ, we have to take the disjunction of two or more rules and try to find the minimal expression for this disjunction. In some cases, we may look for a more general relation expressing all the sub-relations.

5   Unified Grammar Generation

The aim of this paper is realized in three stages each of which can individually be used as separate modules.

5.1   Segmentation of blocks in the documents by image processing

This module accepts a document image as input that is processed by applying horizontal and vertical projections to identify the higher level block structure of the document. It outputs the block-segmented image of the input document. The algorithm deals with the segmentation of blocks at two levels- a coarser level block-structure is obtained by applying RXYC and RLSA which is then fine-tuned by applying certain typesetting heuristics. Fig. 4 describes a step-by-step procedure for block-segmenting a document image.

5.2   Reconciliation of the Block structure

The objective of this module is to match the block-structured document image with the given grammar. The grammar specification is a conjunction of rules for the relationship between the blocks of the document. The set of grammar rules describing the document are ordered in keeping with the ordering defined on the blocks identified in the document. The specifications for the grammar definition are adopted from the concept of interval-algebra [2]. Thus the grammar rules give a qualitative description of the document image.

The matching is done by running a linear trace through the set of grammar rules and verifying the relations between the respective blocks. A certain degree of tolerance is used while matching the rules with the respective blocks.

5.3   Generating unified grammar for a generic class of documents

This is the final phase which accepts a set of document images and outputs the unified grammar that conforms to all the input documents. The algorithm applied generates all the possible relations between the blocks of the documents. These individual descriptions of the documents are minimized using the transitivity relations between the interval-algebra descriptions.

Currently, the unified grammar rules can be derived only for the set of documents having the same number of block segments. A one-to-one correspondence between the respective blocks in each of the documents is established with the help of the ordering of blocks. With this correspondence being established, the disjunction of all the relations between the same blocks in all the documents is taken and added to the set of rules for the universal grammar. The conjunction of all the disjunctive grammar rules is again minimized to get the minimal set of rules for the grammar describing the generic class of documents belonging to the family to which the input documents belong.

The algorithm for the minimization of the grammar rules is implemented in Prolog. The rules are chosen one by one and added to the final list. Any grammar rule that is derivable from the current final list of rules is eliminated from the set. When there are no more rules left in the input set then the final list is the minimal list of rules describing the document/documents.

6   Results

The results of the image processing phase are quite close to the actual block structure that is observed in a document image. Except a few discrepancies in identifying lists as a single block or identifying title as two blocks (when there is a large font difference in the title and the text) or deciphering the position of the blocks in the document page the results are satisfying.

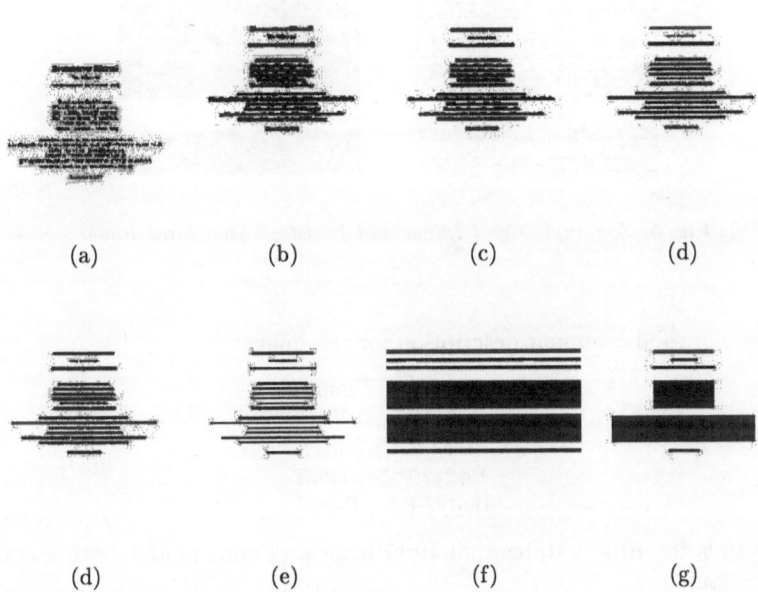

(a)   (b)   (c)   (d)

(d)   (e)   (f)   (g)

Fig. 4. *Steps in Processing of a sample page* The original image (a) is blocked out at a fine scale by RLSA (b) and histogramming (c) to remove extra pixels (d). Gaps are removed and homogenized (e) before processing to a coarser scale vertically (f) based on which the paragraphs are formed (g).

6.1   Results of the Grammar Reconciliation Phase

Here is a document image that is accepted as the input to this module (Fig 5). The resulting block-structured image is obtained as the result of the first part and is matched with the supplied grammar entered by the user.

Fig. 5. *A Sample Input Image and Its Block Structured Image*

This is a valid grammar description for the image:

$$\text{Hdr1 } \left({}^{ii}_{ii}\right) \text{ Frame}$$
$$\text{Body1 } \left({}^{b+}_{--}\right) \text{ Hdr1}$$
$$\text{Hdr2 } \left({}^{bi}_{--}\right) \text{ Body1}$$
$$\text{Body2 } \left({}^{b+}_{--}\right) \text{ Hdr2}$$
$$\text{Body2 } \left({}^{cs}_{--}\right) \text{ Body1}$$

In words the Rule 1 states that Hdr1 is inside Frame , along both x and y directions.
Now if we modify the Rule 1 of the grammar as :

$$\text{Hdr1 } \left({}^{cs}_{ii}\right) \text{ Frame}$$

The modified grammar does not match the document as the Hdr1 is not *Centrally symmetric* with respect to the Frame and is rejected.

6.2   Choosing Tolerances

One of the open issues that needs to be explored further is of choosing intervals appropriately for the scale of discourse [8]. In this task, as with most systems that perform document recognition, a number of such tolerances (for the X-Y segmentation) have to be identified by trial and error during the image segmentation steps. It is possible that more formal approaches [4, 8] toward handling tolerances in interval algebra would be able to provide a better mechanism for determining the tolerances automatically.

6.3 Sample Results of the Unified Grammar Generation Phase

The result obtained is the minimized unified grammar of individual grammars for the documents generated from the same module.

Fig. 6. *Sample Input set of block-structured Images*

The blocks are ordered lexicographically from the top left and result in the following description.

$$6 \left({}^{cs}_{--} \right) 8 \wedge 7 \left({}^{cs}_{--} \right) 8 \wedge 4 \left({}^{cs}_{--} \right) 7 \wedge 5 \left({}^{cs}_{--} \right) 7$$
$$1 \left({}^{cs}_{--} \right) 6 \wedge 2 \left({}^{cs}_{--} \right) 6 \wedge 3 \left({}^{cs}_{--} \right) 6 \wedge 1 \left({}^{cs}_{--} \right) 8$$
$$2 \left({}^{cs}_{--} \right) 8 \wedge 3 \left({}^{cs}_{--} \right) 8 \wedge 4 \left({}^{cs}_{--} \right) 8 \wedge 5 \left({}^{cs}_{--} \right) 8$$
$$6 \left({}^{bi}_{--} \right) 8 \wedge 7 \left({}^{bf}_{--} \right) 8 \wedge 4 \left({}^{ii}_{--} \right) 7 \wedge 5 \left({}^{ii}_{--} \right) 7$$
$$1 \left({}^{i+}_{--} \right) 6 \wedge 2 \left({}^{++}_{--} \right) 8 \wedge 3 \left({}^{i+}_{--} \right) 8$$

Their unified minimal grammar is represented as follows:

$R1$: Title $\left({}^{cs}_{ii} \right)$ Frame
$R2$: Authors $\left({}^{cs}_{ii} \right)$ Frame
$R3$: Authors $\left({}^{c}_{--} \right)$ Title
$R4$: AbstractTitle $\left({}^{cs}_{--} \right)$ Authors
$R5$: Abstract $\left({}^{c}_{--} \right)$ Authors
$R6$: AbstractTitle $\left({}^{cs}_{++} \right)$ Abstract
$R7$: Heading $\left({}^{-i,cs}_{--} \right)$ Abstract
$R8$: Para $\left({}^{b+,cb}_{--} \right)$ Heading

7   Conclusion

In this paper we have used Multidimensional Interval Algebra for two tasks: that of identifying the different blocks given a document grammar, and that of generating a unified grammar for a set of documents belonging to the same document class. The latter task is one of the emerging areas in document analysis, and the former task is important for a number of domains such as video processing, visual language compilation, VLSI layouts etc. The methodology of Qualitative Spatial Reasoning provides a powerful tool for abstracting much of this information. The current implementation is only demonstrative and more complete implementations will be needed to handle a number of additional issues such as that of inlaid figures, equations, or lists. However, the grammar for such structures can also be defined using the structures of interval algebra.

The final task of generating a unified grammar given a set of documents is an important aspect that will grow in importance with the large volume of documentation coming on-line and the need for maintaining and testing for conformity of format between such documents.

References

[1] James F. Allen. Maintaining knowledge about temporal intervals. *CACM, November 1983. Also in "Readings in knowledge representation", ed. Ronald J. Brachman and Hector J. Levesque, Morgan Kaufman, 1985*, 26(11):832–843, 1983.

[2] Hiroko Fujihara and Amitabha Mukerjee. Qualitative reasoning about document structures. In *Symposium on Document Analysis and Information Retrieval, Las Vegas, March 16-18, 1992*, 1992.

[3] Daniel Hernandez. *Qualitative Representation of Spatial Knowledge*. Springer Verlag Lecture Notes in Artificial Intelligence, vol.LNCS804, 1994.

[4] Yumi Iwasaki, Adam Farquhar, Vijay Saraswati, Daniel Bobrow and Vineet Gupta. Modelling Time in Hybrid Systems: How fast is "instantaneous"? In *IJCAI-95, p. 1773-1780*

[5] Gene Joe and Amitabha Mukerjee. Qualitative spatial representation based on tangency and alignments. Technical Report Texas A&M University Technical Report 90-014, July 1990, 54 pages, TexasA&M-CS, 1990.

[6] Benjamin Kuipers. Mit press, cambridge, ma, artificial intelligence series, 1994,452 pp, 1994.

[7] Tom M Mitchell. Version space: a candidate elimination approach to rule learning. In *Proceedings of the seventh international joint conference of Artificial Intelligence, IJCAI-81, August 1981*, pages 29–37, 1981.

[8] Amitabha Mukerjee and Frank Schnorrenberg. Reasoning across scales in space and time. In *AAAI Symposium on Principles of Hybrid Reasoning, November 15-17 1991, Asilomar , CA*

[9] Van Beek, Peter and Cohen Robin AI::Temporal Interval-Logic Complexity Transitivity Approximate. In *Exact and Approximate Reasoning About Temporal Relations Computational Intelligence, v.6:133-44*

[10] Wong K. Y., Casey R. G. and Wahl F. M. Document Analysis System. In *IBM J. of Res. Develop.* 26(6):647-656, 1982.

Identification of Person Objects
in Four-Scenes Comics of Japanese Newspapers

Tomoyuki Yamada and Toyohide Watanabe

Department of Information Engineering,
Graduate School of Engineering, Nagoya University
Furo-cho, Chikusa-ku, Nagoya 464-8603, Japan
tyamada@watanabe.nuie.nagoya-u.ac.jp
watanabe@nuie.nagoya-u.ac.jp

Abstract. Four-scenes comics in Japanese newspapers are composed of four related pictures and organize one story based on current social topic. Though the subject to extract person objects from such pictures and identify the same objects among different scenes is one of graphics recognition issues, it is not easy to perform this subject successfully because individual objects are deformed more tremendously than these in the ordinarily investigated graphics recognition. In this paper, we address an extraction and identification subject of person as the first step for understanding the story of four-scenes comics in Japanese newspaper. Our technique for extracting person objects in each scene is to infer person objects from the hair areas, and our idea for identifying the same person object among different scenes is to apply the distance distribution among component pixels to the distinction of person objects. This paper discusses our experimental method and shows the recognition result clearly through experiments.

1   Introduction

The subjects which extract the meaningful data from paper-based documents and make it possible to manipulate the extracted data as operative objects in electronic-formed documents are looked upon as interesting and worthy issues, and have been investigated for various kinds of documents until today. In particular, the graphics recognition focuses on the extraction/interpretation problems of objects which are not well defined from a viewpoint of declarative specification for features of individual composite elements : map recognition, logic/electronic/electric-circuit recognition, mechanical-part recognition and so on are typical[1,2]. However, the same or similar approaches are not always applicable to interpret all these drawings because the structural features may be analytic in some drawings but in other drawings the constructive relationships among composite elements or among objects may be not clear. The approaches/methods appropriate to the geometric, spatial, structural, representative feature of individual drawings must be desirably established[3,4].

Four-scenes comics in Japanese newspapers, which are addressed in this paper, are usually composed of four related pictures and organize one story based

Atul K. Chhabra and D. Dori (Eds.): GREC'99, LNCS 1941, pp. 155–163, 2000.
© Springer-Verlag Berlin Heidelberg 2000

on a topic for current sociality. Figure 1 shows some examples. In this figure, some objects are illustrated in different scenes, but these shapes, sizes, locations, directions, whole-part relationships, and so on are tremendously deformed and changed: of course, in one scene some objects may be disappeared; and in another scene some objects may be variously depicted from different projections of three-dimensional objects. In addition to the conventional difficulty such as the overlay and intersection among objects, the feature that all line segments are written by hands is remarkably observed. At least, it is not easy to extract individual objects smartly from each scene and identify exactly the same object among a few scenes.

In this paper, we address an experimental method to extract person objects independently from each scene and identify the same person objects among these extracted ones through a four-scene comic. Our idea is to first extract the hair area as one of most reliable composite elements for finding out person objects wholly and then infer person objects from the hair area as the first searching point, in the extraction phase of person objects. Also, in the identification phase of the same person objects the analysis method based on the distance distribution among composite elements is applied.

Fig. 1. Example of four-scenes comics in Japanese newspaper MAINICHI (depicted by Mr. Sadao Shoji)

2   Framework

Our objective is to extract person objects in each scene and identify the same person objects through four-scenes. Four-scenes comics in Japanese newspapers are characterized by the following features in addition to the ordinarily investigated graphics/drawings.

- Each object is remarkably deformed;
- Individual composite elements are written by hand;
- Not only structural features of individual objects (including composite elements), but also constructive relationships among objects are not explicitly depicted;
- The composite elements or objects, which are necessary to expand the story, take rules to represent each scenes and organize four-scenes systematically;
- In order to illustrate the phenomena actually, the painter-specific drawing techniques are applied under the pseudo-representation;.

Moreover, we can observe many typical drawing features in Figure 1. Of course, in four-scenes comics utterances from actor objects and explanations for situations are complementarily used, but we do not discuss this view here.

With respect to the extraction and identification of person objects, our basic recognition strategy focuses on the hair area, which is in many cases painted by black color, and searches the face, body, hands and foots from the hair area continuously. Of course, these components are not explicitly organized by handwriting line segments; some line segments are often interrupted by others or not connected directly to others. Our recognition process is shown in Figure 2, and is divided into two phases : extraction of person objects ; and identification of same person objects. In Figure 2, the characteristic pixel is defined as a point in hand-writing line segments to approximate un-straight lines as vectors.

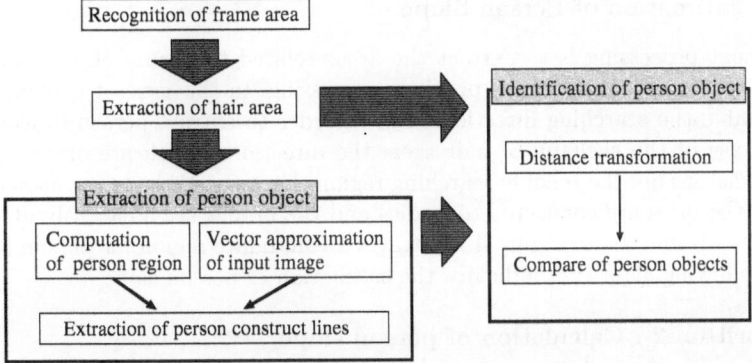

Fig. 2. Processing flow

3   Extraction of Person Object

The extraction phase of person objects in each scene is organized procedurally from finding out first the hair area, painted by black color, as most reliable composite element for distinguishing person objects. Of course, this assumption is not always valid because some person objects may be not associated with black-painted hairs or may be neither depicted with hair areas nor depicted with hair areas or face components.

3.1   Extraction of Hair Area

The extraction of hair area is the first procedure for all other processings in our recognition approach. We define the hair area as an area of continuously black-painted pixels whose number is more than an experimental threshold value. The algorithm is as follows:

[**Algorithm-1 : Extraction of hair area**]
Step 1 : Replace black pixel, neighboring to white pixel, by white pixel by means of shrinking processing;
Step 2 : Repeat Step 1 by n times $(n \geq 1)$;
Step 3 : Replace white pixel, neighboring to black pixel, by black pixel by means of expansion processing;
Step 4 : Repeat Step 3 by $n + m$ times $(m \geq 1)$.

Here, the reason that the number of expansion processings is more than that of shrinking processings is to collect and merge several areas of distributed black pixels into one related area together. Figure 3 is a result of extracted hair areas. Although the result does not represent exactly only the corresponding areas, it is successful approximately.

3.2   Estimation of Person Slope

The next processing is to extract the areas related to person objects with respect to the hair areas in the previous processing. In this case, it is effectual to determine the searching directions first in order to extract person objects. We make use of the skeleton of hair area: the directions which are orthogonal to the skeletons are the reliable searching regions because the hairs are attached to faces, the faces are connected to bodies and the bodies are adjacently attended with hands and foots. Figure 4 illustrates a comdidate region for person object. The following algorithm indicates the estimation of person slope.

[**Algorithm-2 : Calculation of person slope**]
Step 1 : Transform distance about hair area;
Step 2 : Extract skeleton;
Step 3 : Shrink and expand extracted skeletons;
Step 4 : Compute slopes of individual line segments;

Step 5 : Select maximum length of line segment from them, and look upon it as slope.

Next, the person region must be inferred on the basis of skeleton of hair area. The algorithm is as follows:

[Algorithm-3 : Computation of person region]
Step 1 : Compute left-upper and right-upper points of hair area;
Step 2 : Compute width of hair area;
Step 3 : Set left and right sides of person regions.

Fig. 3. Hair area   Fig. 4. Person region

3.3   Extraction of Characteristic Pixel

The characteristic pixels are looked upon as points in hand-writing line segments, which assign some remarkable features to drawn lines in the direction, structure and so on. For example, currently T-form, +-form and L-form are candidates on hand-writing pictures. Namely, these forms correspond to crosses or corners. Of course, the terminal points of interrupted line segments are characteristic pixels. Figure 5 shows typical examples of characteristic pixels with respect to 8-neighboring images.

The following three conditions for characteristic pixels are satisfied:

[Condition-1 : Characteristic pixel]

1. Number of neighboring pixels is more than 3 (for cross pixel)
2. Number of neighboring pixels is 1 (for end pixel)
3. Number of neighboring pixels is 2 and curvature is more than threshold value (for corner pixel).

Here, the curvature is a cosine value for angle between two line segments, as shown in Figure 6. The algorithm for extracting characteristic pixels is as follows:

[Algorithm-4 : Extraction of characteristic pixel]
Step 1 : Count up number of neighboring pixels;
Step 2 : Compute the curvature using Algorithm-5;
Step 3 : Define the pixels, which satisfy Condition-1, as characteristic pixels.

Also, the algorithm for computing the curvature is:

[Algorithm-5 : Computation of curvature]
Step 1 : Select pixels whose number of neighboring pixels is 2;
Step 2 : Search $k(k \geq 1)$ pixels in two directions; stop if pixels to be searched are not found out;
Step 3 : Compute cosine of angle between two searched lines.

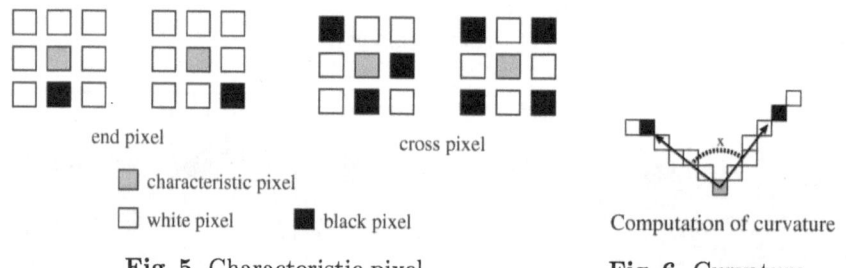

end pixel   cross pixel

☐ characteristic pixel

☐ white pixel   ■ black pixel   Computation of curvature

Fig. 5. Characteristic pixel   **Fig. 6.** Curvature

3.4 Vectorization

Using the characteristic pixels, hand-writing line-based drawings are vectorized. Basically, two neighboring characteristic pixels in one hand-writing line segment are transformed into one straight line segment. The algorithm is as follows:

[Algorithm-6 : Vector approximation]
Step 1 : Select one characteristic pixel "s";
Step 2 : Trace black pixel from "s" to another characteristic pixel "e";
Step 3 : Approximate traced black pixel to line segment connecting between "s" and "e";
Step 4 : Repeat these steps until all of black pixels are traced.

3.5 Extraction of Person Object

The final processing in the extraction phase of person objects is to select the vectorized line segments in the estimated person region and distinguish only reliable line segments as composite elements of person objects. The algorithm is as follows:

[Algorithm-7 : Extraction of person object]
Step 1 : Search both terminal points of vectorized line segments;
Step 2 : Select appropriate line segments as candidates if either of terminal points is contained in person region;
Step 3 : Repeat these steps for all of line segments, related to person region.

4   Identification of Person Object

In this identification phase of the same person object, the objective is to find out the same person objects from four different scenes. Of course, all scenes do not always contain the same persons and also the pictorial representations are changeable in many cases.

4.1   Distance Transformation

We transform the distance for hair areas in order to compute the distribution of the distance of hair area. The algorithm is as follows:

[Algorithm-8 : Distance transformation]
Step 1 : Put label "0" on all of white pixels and label "1" on all of black pixels;
Step 2 : Change pixel label to "$k + 1$" if pixel label adjacent to a black pixel is more than or equal to "k";
Step 3 : Repeat Step 2 by one step from "$k = 1$" while label is changed.

4.2   Identification of Person Object

We make up the list of the distribution obtained by transforming the distance and compare the features among graphs for each person object(Figure 8). We use the graphs obtained from these results. However, we can compare more obviously if we use the graph of the difference of distance transformation but not the graph of distance transformation. The algorithm is as follows:

[Procedure-1 : Identification of person object]
Step 1 : Compute difference *average* between graphs A and B. Here, "x" is pixel label of distance transformation and "N" is greatest value of "x":

$$average = \sum_{x=0}^{N}(Ay[x] - By[x])/N;$$

Step 2 : Compute difference *comparison* between *average* and difference between graphs A and B

$$comparison = \sum_{x=0}^{N}|average - (Ay[x] - By[x])|/N;$$

Step 3 : Judge that person expressed by two graphs is same if *comparison* is less than threshold value.

In Figure 7, "x" is the distance data and "y" is the number of pixels in "x". And Figure 8 is the graph to differentiate Figure 7.

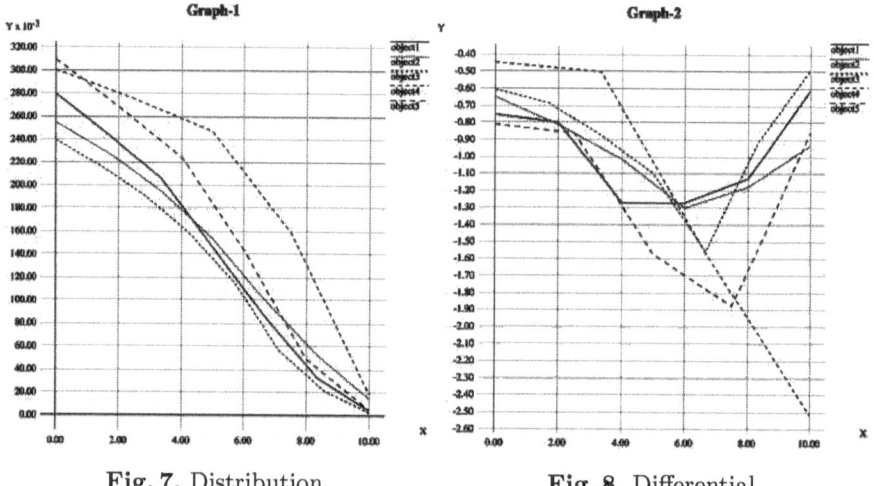

Fig. 7. Distribution   **Fig. 8.** Differential

5 Experiment

We experimented the extraction and identification process of person objects for sixteen comics. The input image is 900 × 300 pixels.

Extraction of person object : We show the result in Table 1. Also, Figure 9 is successful examples and Figure 10 is failure examples.

Table 1. Extraction result of person object

persons	extracted persons	ratio
113	87	77%

Fig. 9. Successful examples   **Fig. 10.** Failure examples

The extraction result is not sufficient. However, we appreciate that our method is effective though its extraction strategy is very simple. Of course, the basic idea is too strongly dependent on the strategy that the hair area is a key to extract person objects. As we can observe in Figure 10 some errors was generated.

Identification of person object : We show the result in Table 2.

Table 2. Identification result of person objects

number	persons	same persons	identified persons	ratio
16	113	46	15	34%

Also, the identification result is not always successful. Another similarity concept must be introduced in place of hair slopes.

6 Conclusion

In this paper, we discussed a method for extracting and identifying person objects on four-scenes comics of Japanese newspapers. In this method, the recognition results in the extraction and identification of person objects are insufficient. However, in comparison with the traditionally developed graphics recognition subjects, the comics interpretation is very difficult because all drawings are deformed and drawn by hands. This experiment is the first step for improving our approach. One current idea is to analyze each object on the basis of closed regions, which will be indicated as meaningful objects, using Snake method [5]. However, the closed regions are not always observed practically. The first step is to resolve this problem technically. Maybe, it is so useful that some model for comics drawings and some understanding knowledge should be investigated.

References

1. S. H.Joseph, T. P.Pridmore: Knowledge-Directed Interpretation of Mechanical Engineering Drawings. IEEE Trans. on PAMI. **9-18** (1992) 928-940   155
2. N. P.Carter: Segmentation and Preliminary Recognition of Madrigals Notated in White Mensural Notation. Machine Vison and Applications. **3-5** (1992) 223-229   155
3. A.Yoshitani, K.Ikeda, M.Minoh: Recognition and Identification of Line-Drawn Faces. Proc. of the Autumn Annual Meetings'92 **D-285** (1992) 271-287 [in Japanese]   155
4. J.Yashiki, K.Ikeda, M.Minoh: Recognition of Faces in a Drawing through Element Candidates' Vote. Research Report of IEICE. **PRU-93-12** (1994) 17-24 [in Japanese]   155
5. S. R.Gunn, M. S.Nixon: A Robust Snake Implementation: A Dual Active Contour. IEEE Trans. on PAMI. **1-19** (1997) 63-68   163

Part IV

Graphic Symbol and Shape Recognition

Symbol and Shape Recognition

L. P. Cordella and M. Vento

Dipartimento di Informatica e Sistemistica - Universita' di Napoli "Federico II"
Via Claudio, 21 – 80125 Napoli, Italy
{cordel,vento}@unina.it

Abstract. The different aspects of a process for recognizing symbols in documents are considered and the techniques that have been most commonly used during the last ten years, in the different application fields, are reviewed. Methods used in the representation, description and classification phases are shortly discussed and the main recognition strategies are mentioned. Some of the problems that appear still open are proposed to the attention of the reader.

1   Introduction

A significant part of many documents is made of entities which can be classified as symbols, i.e. as sets of graphic signs or shapes which are entrusted with the task of ideally and/or synthetically represent something. In the framework of document processing, symbols are characterized by the semantics attributed to them and by the rules used to build them. In fact, symbols are generally not free shapes, but they are formed according to rules, whose knowledge can help for their recognition. From an operative point of view, it is worth noting that, on the contrary of other entities (e.g. characters making up a piece of text, which are singled out only after the text region has been delimited in its whole), symbols are generally distributed over the document, thus the procedure to search for them has to be in some way peculiar. From this point of view, isolated characters or short strings may be considered symbols.

From the point of view of symbol recognition, the documents of interest for automatic processing can be roughly grouped into three large families:

- Technical Drawings, including Electrical and Electronic Circuits, Logic Diagrams, Flow Charts, Mechanical Drawings, Architectural Drawings, Facility Drawings (also referred as Utility Maps) which for their part include documents such as Electric Power Maps, Gas and Telephone Maps, Piping and Instrument Diagrams.
- Maps, including Geographic, Topographic, Cadastral and Hydrographic maps.
- Others, including a miscellany of documents containing special types of symbols, such as Musical Scores, Mathematical Symbols, Logos, Structured Chemical Formulas.

Atul K. Chhabra and D. Dori (Eds.): GREC'99, LNCS 1941, pp. 167-182, 2000.

Within this large variety of documents, there is a still larger variety of entities that are considered symbols. Symbols can be simple 2-D (substantially) binary shapes, made by sets of line segments possibly forming loops so as foreground regions of various shapes; they can be complex gray level or color shapes like for some logos, so as simple silhouettes within a frame, like for some geographic symbols. Characters, present together with graphics in almost every drawing or map, are symbols above all, although they are generally specially treated.

In any case, symbols may appear isolated, or embedded in a net of lines. Moreover, they can touch, partially overlap each other, or intersect other line. The problems with symbol recognition depend not much on their intrinsic shape variability or on the complexity of the features characterizing them, but on the fact that they are more or less embedded in a context which is often very crowded. Often symbols must be located in an apparent clutter of other signs.

To rely on a priori knowledge about the nature of the document is generally necessary to locate candidate symbols or regions of interest where to apply specific recognition techniques. It is therefore not surprising that a number of different approaches have been devised for the different application fields considered.

On the other hand, the whole field of image recognition (both by man or machine) is characterized by the fact that many of the analysis methods developed are very application dependent. This is due to the fact that the characteristics of images belonging to different application areas may be quite different and such that their interpretation requires specific knowledge. Even for a human being, the skill for interpreting, e.g. a geographic map, requires the knowledge of criteria and conventions which led to its production, as well as to have developed a set of methods and strategies which the experience taught to be especially effective for extracting the information held by the document. Methods and strategies used in one case may reveal effective also in case of images of a different type, but to solve some problems peculiar to a given type of images, methods may be needed which can seldom be exported outside that image type. It is not a case that often the right interpretation of an image can be given only after having attributed it to a type (or having received information about its type) and thus having made implicit or explicit reference to the techniques for accessing its informative content.

Although it remains unavoidable that peculiar problems require peculiar treatment, there are, however, methods and tools for automatic image analysis which can be used in different frameworks, so that a substantial part of the analysis process of any particular class of images could be built up with a suitable combination of them. With special reference to the problem of symbol and shape recognition in a document, a number of techniques have been tested in the past years. Many of them can be profitably used with different types of symbols in different contests. Particular contests will always require special processing.

Generally speaking, the process leading to the interpretation of an image evolves through three main phases: during the first, that will be called here Representation Phase, the scope is to put the image in a form more suitable for the subsequent processing so as to locate and outline the entities of interest. The second phase is devoted to give a description of the located entities, while the third phase attempts to classify them. Of course, a strategy has to be defined for controlling the whole recognition process.

In the ideal case, one could devise a strategy according to which:

- The document is first preprocessed in order to obtain a more convenient representation of it; the type of preprocessing may at least partly depend on the type of document.
- Then symbols are searched for in the representation, on the basis of some general features possibly shared by all the symbols: this process produces a number of candidate symbols.
- Each candidate symbol is described in terms of more detailed features so as to obtain a feature vector or a structural description.
- Finally the description is feed into a classification stage which attributes it to a class (i.e. recognizes the description as that of a specific symbol which has been previously learned or which exists in a database of prototypes).

This scheme, with variants, has been actually used by many researchers in various applications. As for graphic documents, specific actions are performed during each of the mentioned phases with the aim of locating and processing symbols. Processes in which the three phases mentioned above are not simply distinguishable, or some of them are merged, have of course been proposed. A desirable feature of a recognition system would also be that of having the capacity to going back to a previous phase, to try to improve the results, in case a decision cannot be reliably taken. However, this feature is rarely present in actual recognition systems.

A number of good review papers completely or partly dedicated to problems related to symbol recognition in documents, have been presented in the last few years [1-9]. In the following, the field will be shortly reviewed from a different point of view. Some of the techniques which, in the three mentioned phases, are more commonly used, or have been proposed, for processing symbols will be shortly discussed, attempting to understand which are applicable to different kinds of documents and are well established as regards the obtainable results, and which are tailored to specific application fields.

2   Representation Phase

At the lowest level of the vision process, the information is usually processed without using any knowledge about the considered image. The aim is that of extracting the information which is retained more significant for the next analysis (e.g., sharp intensity variations). The result of preliminary processing is generally still an image, which is one of the possible representations of the original one (alternative with respect to row data). Successive processing steps can lead to further representations, with the scope of achieving a more convenient way to supply those information about an image which are considered necessary and sufficient for a given processing task.

The main aims of the representation phase are to reduce noise and amount of data, to outline the image components and to represent them in such a way that not significant differences among their various instances are smoothed. However, not always information can be aggregated in a single way or independently of semantics. In some cases, the representation phase can be intended as a first step towards the abstraction process leading from a specimen of a class to the prototype of that class. Information about the image representation is stored in a suitable data structure.

With reference to documents containing symbols, techniques widely applicable in this phase are binarization, thinning, polygonal approximation, run length coding, curve fitting, connected component labeling, mathematical morphology operations, Hough or other transformations, etc.

An idea of the frequency with which different techniques have been used in the different symbol recognition systems reported in the reference list of this paper can be got from Table I, where the approximate percentage of systems using each different technique is shown, for each different phase. The sum of the percentages is not necessarily equal to 100, because different techniques are sometimes used within the same recognition system; e.g. a representation may be used for locating candidate symbols or regions including them and a different one for recognition purposes. Same systems illustrated in more than one paper have been considered only once. The reference list includes papers published during the last ten years in the application fields considered: technical and facility drawings [10-33], maps of various types [34-46], musical scores [47-51], logos [52-55] and others [56-59].

Documents are generally scanned at a spatial resolution ranging from 150 to 400 dpi, but low resolution is preferred whenever possible. In the large majority of cases, documents are intrinsically black and white images, so the first step is their binarization. This may not be convenient with some color maps and logos. For good quality documents, binarization is presently not a problem. Although a number of thresholding and edge detection algorithms are available [60],[61], low contrast or degraded documents may still constitute a problem.

After binarization and some very preliminary processing (e.g., black and white noise cleaning), the most common choices are:

- to operate directly on the bit map
- to transform the bit map into a run-length coded image (referred also as a LAG)
- to thin the image and represent it as a graph or a linked list (this step is often performed later in the process)

Whatever the choice made, a common initial step is Connected Component Labeling. Connected component labeling is used for a number of purposes: generally it is a way for segmenting a document into regions among which to select those corresponding to potential symbols or including symbols. When applied on the foreground it allows locating components among which to search for isolated symbols. An alternative point of view is using it to clear the field of everything is certainly neither a symbol nor is connected to symbols (especially used as a first step for candidate character location). Connected component labeling applied on the background allows finding regions bounded by lines, i.e. loops. This technique is widely used in electronic circuit drawings. Of course symbols must then be selected among all loops found. In order to separate symbols made by thick foreground regions from the rest of the drawing (supposed to be made of thin lines) mathematical morphology operations have been used.

At a certain point of the analysis process, the thin parts of the drawing are often vectorized before further processing. This is also a widely employed method for image segmentation since, by suitably grouping the obtained vectors, it is possible to segment symbols from the rest of the document. Thinning [62] followed by polygonal approximation is the most common vectorization method. It has to be noted that the thinning algorithms more often used are based on contour peeling or on the iterative application of masks. The so obtained skeletons do not hold information on local thickness which can instead be useful, e.g. for discriminating filled symbols from empty ones (loops). Skeletons of the Medial Axis Transform type [63] preserve this information and are reversible. However, all of the above techniques can introduce shape distortions at the crossing and junction of lines and generally oblige to adopt more complex processing, not always effective, in the following stages. Several algorithms, which claim to have eliminated or at least reduced this problem, have been proposed in the last ten years. Some of them try to avoid that the distortions arise [64-74], other try to correct the distortions [75-81]. To our knowledge, however, no such algorithms came into common use. This may also depend on the fact that details on the algorithms such to allow their actual implementation have rarely been given. Vectorization can also be achieved starting from run length coding of the image or with other techniques like mesh crossing. Such different approaches should avoid the thinning side effects, but in fact may equally give place to several problems. Some authors prefer not to pass through vectorization, but to divide the drawing into primitive strokes and to work on this kind of representation.

Given a digital line, e.g. obtained by thinning, it is simplest to describe its geometric characteristics if it is transformed into a sequence of pieces of regular curves. This allows simpler structural descriptions of sets of such pieces. Digital curve fitting in its simplest form is polygonal approximation. Fitting with higher order functions can been used for obtaining a compact and effective representation of some sort of regular shapes, like circular arcs and more generally conical curves. An alternative way for detecting some regular shapes is the Hough transform that has been used to check collinearity of points [15],[50], e.g. for detecting character strings or separating connecting lines from symbols, and, by suitably choosing the representation plane, to highlight circular shapes [33].

A problem often present in this phase is the separation of symbols from lines and other symbols that possibly cross, overlap or touch them. Such situations are a standard in music documents, are very common in geographic, cadastral and topographic maps, may happen with technical drawings, but are generally less dramatic in logical circuit drawings. Effective methods have been proposed for some special case [82], but the general problem is still open.

Table 1. Frequency with which different techniques or features have been used in the different symbol recognition systems reported in the reference list of this paper. The approximate percentage of systems using each different technique or feature is shown, for each different phase. The sum of the percentages is not necessarily equal to 100, because different techniques are sometimes used within the same recognition system

	%
REPRESENTATION PHASE	
Run length based representations (LAG etc.)	15
Connected component labeling	69
Thinning and polygonal approximation (graph)	58
Thin-thick separation	12
Internal and/or external contours	12
Distance transform (3-4, Voronoi)	8
Wavelet transform	4
Hough transform	15
DESCRIPTION PHASE	
Geometric and topologic features (n. of vectors, global shape descriptors such as A, P, shape factors, x-y projections, etc.)	38
Moment invariants	15
Fourier Transform	8
Structural descriptions	23
Syntactic descriptions	4
Other (morphol. functions, special transforms)	12
CLASSIFICATION PHASE	
Template matching	46
Decision tree	12
Neural net	15
Graph matching	8
Syntactic parser	4
Statistical classifier	15
Heuristic techniques	27
RECOGNITION STRATEGY	
Bottom-up	85
Top-down	15

3   Description Phase

It is possible to associate to this phase the methods which, starting from a representation of the image, give a symbolic description of it. According to the strategy adopted in the previous phase, such description may be of different level. Indeed, some kind of representation may already imply a description scheme.

A description may regard the whole image or the different subparts of it selected as candidate symbols. In the former case the data structure supporting the description has to be analyzed in order to find the substructures corresponding to symbols. This process can directly arrive to symbol classification, so including the next phase, or it can just suggest some candidates that have to be validated in the successive recognition step. In the latter case the description of each subpart is passed to the recognition module. In any case there is a problem of feature extraction and of selection of the data structure that support the description.

Since the largest family of symbols used in maps and technical drawings is made of simple geometric shapes and of their combinations, topological or geometric features are generally used for description. At preliminary steps of the analysis process simple and often global features are used, while at successive steps different or more detailed features are introduced. Recent reviews on shape analysis and the feature extraction problem can be found in [83], [84].

Different instances of a symbol, like of any other visual entity, almost never appear identical to a given prototype. This is especially true if they are represented directly by row data. Their shape may be corrupted by noise or there may be differences due to position, orientation and size. For certain types of documents, it is quite common that symbols touch or overlap other graphics. It is then convenient to select the features characterizing the representation of a symbol at a level sufficiently abstract to overcome the variability of its different instances. A particular representation may render some features more accessible than others, but is still susceptible of different descriptions, as a function of scope or of number of classes. If a description has to be used to faithfully reproduce the described entity, then it has to be quantitative and very detailed. On the contrary, for recognition purposes, it is more convenient to use few qualitative features, especially if there are few different classes and the variability inside a class is high. A description has to be oriented to the scope and be possibly stable, concise, sensitive, unique and accessible. For shape recognition purposes, descriptions should be invariant with respect to affine transformations (translation, rotation, scale changes). A list of the features most frequently used for symbol description can be found in Table I.

Among data structures, graphs are used to support structural descriptions of graphics and symbols. Graphs are especially suitable for representing structural information. They can be simple linked lists of pixels or line adjacency graphs, but can also describe polylines by associating graph nodes to the segments of the polygonal and graph edges to the spatial relations between adjacent segments. Graphs of this type are commonly used in methods based on the hypothesis that symbols are represented in terms of straight components as happens for the majority of technical drawings. More generally, Attributed Relational Graphs (ARG's) are a good support for structural descriptions of images: nodes and edges, with their associated attributes, describe respectively the components of interest and the interconnections among them. This is the case when higher level components, e.g. arcs or primitive shapes, are also used for representing the entities of interest.

However, descriptions are also frequently given in terms of vectors of "unstructured" measures (features) executed on the symbols. Generally such features do not include relations between parts. Examples of this kind of descriptors are geometric moments.

4   Classification Phase

In principle, classification implies training for prototype learning, a knowledge base and the skill for using this information together with contextual information. When the output of the description stage is a vector, a variety of well established statistical or neural network classifiers (K-NN, Back-Propagation, Learning Vector Quantization, etc.) are in use. Template matching, with different variants, is a simple technique often applied in the context of symbol recognition, in spite of the limitations generally imposed by the representation, as rotation and scale dependence, so that its applicability is limited to a few domains in the context of symbol recognition. It has been used for recognizing symbols in geographic maps [36], [37], [45] and is the first choice for logo recognition [52], [54], [55].

Logos are generally very conspicuous patterns easily identifiable in a document and often located in key points (upper-left or upper right in the page). Logos generally do not appear rotated. Because of these peculiarities logos are generally treated with simple techniques in the phase of segmentation and attention is focused on classification. Candidate logos can be extracted by simple algorithms using a priori-knowledge regarding the position in the page, the size, the fact that are made by graphics not embedded in text, and so on. Correlation between the image and a logo prototype has also been used. Logos are also described by feature vectors. Examples of used features are wavelet coefficients and geometric moments. Geometric moments are global shape features interesting in logo recognition because of their property of being insensitive to local deformations. Sometimes these features are used only in the first stage of the classifier. When different logos having similar appearance exist in the domain, the classification stage is carried out using more local features or multi-stage classifiers. Classification is carried out by feature based classification paradigms as statistical classifiers and neural networks.

Methods adopting graph descriptions carry out recognition by graph-matching algorithms. Isomorphism, graph-subgraph isomorphism and other similar techniques are generally adopted for finding occurrences of symbols in images described by graphs. In practice, inexact matching algorithms are the only effective because of noise and symbol shape variability (namely in case of hand-drawings). Error-correcting algorithms try to achieve the isomorphism by using, during the matching process, some predefined editing operations such as node and/or branch insertion, node merging, attribute value modification, etc.. Error-correcting isomorphism can be used for evaluating the distance between the sample graph and the prototype graph as the minimum cost of the transformations applied to one of the graph to obtain the other one (distance-based methods).

The computational complexity of graph matching techniques is, in general, rather high, even if for some classes of graphs, efficient algorithms have been proposed. In any case a reduction of time complexity and memory occupation has been obtained by using suitable look-ahead rules during the matching process [85]. Alternatively, a reduction of computational complexity has been achieved by pre-compiling the database of prototypes [11]. The latter technique is convenient when a single graph has to be matched against a large database of prototype graphs each made of a few nodes and edges and achieves a significant reduction of matching time, to the detriment of memory occupation.

All the above techniques require that a set of prototypes have been defined. The most common way of obtaining prototypes is their definition by an expert of the application domain. This approach is feasible when the application requires a few prototype graphs of small size, but becomes more and more impractical when the number of prototypes and/or the graph size increase. The automatic generation of the prototypes is a complex problem in the most general case and only in the recent past some methods, working under specific hypotheses, have been proposed.

Frequencies of use of the most diffused classification methods employed in the recognition phase are listed in Table I. Hierarchical classification schemes, in different forms, are adopted in about 30% of systems.

5   Recognition Strategies

The process for recognizing symbols can be carried out according to a top-down or a bottom-up strategy. Bottom-Up strategies start from the lowest level representation (the bit-map) and evolve through representations of higher and higher level till to the final comparison between the sample and the set of the prototypes. Ascending to higher levels of abstraction Bottom-Up methods do not use a model of the object to be found. Top-Down strategies, vice versa, start from a model of the objects to be found and try to fit the model into the data. In successive iterations the process is refined by verifying the presence of more detailed features of the object to be found, described in the model. In practice bottom-up approaches have been used in more than 80 % of the recognition systems reviewed in this paper.

Among top-down approaches, verification based methods (hypothesize and test) use contextual knowledge and constraints, first to formulate and then to verify interpretation hypotheses [34]. The initial recognition of some features produces hypotheses instead of final recognition decisions. These approaches are basically designed to extract only the data of interest and then are especially valuable in a database environment where a specific query is asked about the raster image. They could be convenient in cluttered documents, since do not necessarily require that the objects of interest are preliminarily isolated or that other overlapping or touching graphics are removed.

They are especially suitable for taking advantage of the available knowledge base and of contextual information. Contextual reasoning is based on the assumption that all the objects in a map are interrelated. A typical strategy alternates a top-down process to generate search actions, a bottom-up process to recognize objects and a process to verify the results [35]. The detection of an object generates expectations about other objects in its neighborhood and then new search actions. This mechanisms allow consistency check: if attributing an object to a class implies the existence of another object, the verification of its existence reinforces the classification or, in the opposite case, may suggest to try a new classification or to try a different segmentation of the object.

Top-down approaches have been used for detecting symbols in maps and technical drawings (e.g., 12, 34, 35,) and revealed profitable for processing musical scores. A musical score is a complex document including a variety of graphic signs, lines, symbols and text that touch and overlap each other in many different ways. Some symbols are connected to form more complex symbols in a variety of different combinations. The main problems arise from these overlaps and connections that make segmentation a difficult task. There are a number of components in a musical score: staves, note heads (both filled-in and empty dots) with their possible appendixes, stem and beams, various symbols for modifying the note values, for specifying pauses etc. and finally text. Almost all the approaches start by detecting and eliminating the staves. For recognizing staves a bottom-up approach can apply thinning, polygonal approximation, and a final approximation of the polylines with single lines, standing for the staves. A top-down approach [48] starts from the assumption that staves are perfect straight lines, are five, are equally spaced and cannot be broken (in the model). A set of procedures estimates the distance of the staves in the given document, determines columns of five points belonging to the staves and then traces the set of five straight lines representing the staves.

6   Conclusions

The most commonly used techniques for symbol recognition have been shortly reviewed. Some problems requiring peculiar treatment have been mentioned. Considering the literature appeared on the subject during the last ten years, several problems appear still open and many questions can be consequently asked. Some of them are listed below.

What is the most convenient scanning resolution for the different applications? From 150 to 400 dpi have been used within the same field. Which are the acceptable recognition rates, error rates and reject rates for the different applications and what is the most appropriate way of measuring them: e.g., for each single document or in the average over a set of documents? Should errors be grouped according to their type?

Among the many techniques that are in use for symbol representation, description and recognition in the different application fields, which are the best for each given application area? Several of them are well established as regards the obtainable results and could be applied in different contexts. To what an extent are they transportable from one to another area?

There is the need for comparing both whole systems and different techniques for achieving the same subtask. Methods tested on a few drawings of different characteristics and quality, as it is often made, can neither be significantly evaluated nor compared between them, but where are the databases for testing different methods? Objective criteria should be adopted for evaluating system performance. How to assess accuracy, flexibility and efficiency of a system? How performance is affected by scale (i.e. number of symbols and, size of the document)? Given a system, what is the cost of updating it (the addition of new symbols requires total or partial readjustment)? How to evaluate the cost to benefit ratio for different applications?

References

1. K. Chhabra: Graphic symbol recognition: an overview. Proc. GREC'97, Nancy, France (1997) 244-252
2. D Blostein: General diagram recognition methodologies. Proc. GREC'95, University Park, PA (1995) 200-212
3. K. Tombre: Analysis of engineering drawings: state of the art and challenges. Proc. GREC'97 (1997) 54-61
4. J.F. Arias and R. Kasturi: Recognition of Graphical Objects for Intelligent Interpretation of Line Drawings, in Aspects of visual form processing. C. Arcelli, L. P. Cordella and G. Sanniti di Baja Ed.s, World Scientific (1994) 11-31
5. L. O'Gorman: Basic Techniques and Symbol-Level Recognition - An overview. in Graphics recognition –Methods and applications, (Proc. GREC'95) Vol. LNCS 1072, Springer (1996) 1-12
6. K. Tombre, C. Ah-Soon, P. Dosch, A. Habed and G. Masini: Stable. Robust and Off-the-Shelf Methods for Graphics Recognition, Proc. ICPR'98 (1998) 406-408
7. Y.Y. Tang, S.W. Lee and C.Y. Suen, Automatic Document Processing: a Survey. Pattern Recognition Vol. 29 N. 12 (1996) 1931-1952
8. T. Kanungo, R. Haralick, and D. Dori: Understanding engineering drawings: A survey. Proc. First Int. Workshop on Graphics Recognition, The Pennsylvania State University, PA, USA (1995) 119-130
9. D. Blostein and H. Baird: A critical survey of music image analysis. in Structured document image analysis, H. Baird, H. Bunke, K. Yamamoto Ed.s, Springer (1992) 405-434
10. C.S. Fahn, J.F. Wang, J.Y. Lee: A topology based component extractor for understanding electronic circuit diagrams. CVGIP, 44 (1988) 119-138
11. B. Messmer and H. Bunke: Automatic learning and recognition of graphical symbols in engineering drawings. In R. Kasturi and K. Tombre, editors, Graphics Recognition: Methods and Applications, Selected Papers from First International Workshop on Graphics Recognition (1995) Vol. LNCS 1072 123-134. Springer, Berlin (1996)
12. A.D. Ventura and R. Schettini: Graphic symbol recognition using a signature technique. Proc. 12th ICPR, Jerusalem Vol. 2 (1994) 533-535
13. B. Yu: Automatic understanding of symbol-connected diagrams. Proc. of Third IAPR International Conference on Document Analysis and Recognition, ICDAR'95, pages 803-806, Montreal, Canada, August 1995

14. Okazaki, T. Kondo, K. Mori, S. Tsunekawa, and E. Kawamoto: An automatic circuit diagram reader with loop-structure-based symbol recognition. IEEE Transactions on Pattern Analysis and Machine Intelligence Vol. 10N. 3 (1988) 331-341

15. R. Kasturi et al.: A System for Interpretation of Line Drawings. IEEE Transactions on Pattern Analysis and Machine Intelligence Vol. 12 N. 10 (1990) 978-992

16. A.Hamada: A new system for the analysis of schematic diagrams. In Proc. of the Second International Conference on Document Analysis and Recognition-ICDAR'93, pages 369-372, Tsukuba Science City, Japan, October 1993

17. T. Cheng, J. Khan, H. Liu and D.Y.Y. Yun: A Symbol Recognition System, Proc. ICDAR'93 (1993) 918-921

18. S. Kim, J. Suh, and J. Kim: Recognition of logic diagrams by identifying loops and rectilinear polylines. In Proc. of Second International Conference on Document Analysis and Recognition-ICDAR '93, pages 349-352, Tsukuba Science City, Japan, October 1993

19. Y.H. Yu, A. Samal, and S. Seth: Isolating symbols from connection lines in a class of engineering drawings. Pattern Recognition Vol. 27 N. 3 (1994) 391-404

20. Y.H. Yu, A. Samal, and S. Seth, A system for recognizing a large class of engineering drawings, Proc. ICDAR'95 (1995) 791-794

21. K. Abe, Y. Azumatani, M. Kukouda, and S. Suzuki: Discrimination of symbols, lines, and characters in flow chart recognition. Proc. 8th ICPR, Paris, France (1986) 1071-1074

22. F.C.A. Groen, A.C. Sanderson, and J.F. Schlag: Symbol recognition in electrical diagrams using probabilistic graph matching. Pattern Recognition Letters Vol. 3 N. 5 (1985) 343-350

23. B. Pasternak: The role of taxonomy in drawing interpretation. Proc. ICDAR'95 (1995) 799-802

24. P. Vaxiviere and K. Tombre, Celesstin: CAD conversion of mechanical drawings. Computer Vol. 25,7 (1992) 46-53

25. Y. Aoki, A. Shio, H Arai, K. Odaka: A prototype system for interpreting hand-sketched floor plans. Proc. ICPR'96 (1996) 747-751

26. J. Llados, J. Lopez-Krahe, E. Marti': Hand-drawn document understanding using the straight line Hough transform and graph matching. Proc. ICPR'96 (1996) 497-501

27. J. Llados, G. Sanchez, E. Marti': A string based method to recognize symbols and structural textures in architectural plans. Proc. GREC'97 (1997) 287-294

28. Ah-Soon, Symbol detection in architectural drawings. Proc. GREC'97 (1997) 280-286

29. J.F. Arias, C. Lai, S. Surya: R. Kasturi and A. Chhabra, Interpretation of telephone system manhole drawings. PRL, 16 (1995) 355-369

30. J.F. Arias, R. Kasturi and A. Chhabra: Efficient techniques for telephone company line drawing interpretation. Proc. ICDAR'95, Montreal (1995) 795-798

31. M. Furuta, N. Kase, and S. Emori: Segmentation and recognition of symbols for handwritten piping and instrument diagram. Proc. 7th ICPR, Montreal, Canada (1984) IEEE Publ. 84CH2046-1, 626-629

32. O.D. Trier, T. Taxt, and A.K. Jain: Recognition of digits in hydrographic maps - binary versus topographic analysis. IEEE Transactions on Pattern Analysis and Machine Intelligence Vol. 19 N. 4 (1997) 399-404

33. R. Mullot, J.-M. Ogier, F. Brisepierre, Y. Lecourtier and M.F. Collinas: An Original Approach for Extracting Circular Shapes from Technical Charts. Proc. ICPR'96 (1996) 813-817

34. G. Myers, P. Mulgaonkar, C. Chen, J. DeCurtins, and E. Chen: Verification-based approach for automated text and feature extraction. in Graphics Recognition: Methods and Applications, R. Kasturi and K. Tombre Ed.s, Selected Papers from First Int. Workshop on Graphics Recognition Vol. LNCS 1072 190-203, Springer, Berlin (1996)

35. J. den Hartog, T. ten Kate and J. Gebrands: Knowledge based segmentation for automatic map interpretation. in Graphics Recognition: Methods and Applications, R. Kasturi and K. Tombre Ed.s, Selected Papers from First Int. Workshop on Graphics Recognition (1995) Vol. LNCS 1072 159-178, Springer, Berlin (1996)

36. De Stefano, F. Tortorella, and M. Vento: Morphological functions for symbol recognition on geographic maps. Proc.ICRCV'92,Singapore (1992) CV-21.3.1-5

37. C. De Stefano, F. Tortorella, and M. Vento: An entropy based method for extracting robust binary templates, Machine Vision and Applications Vol. 8 N. 3, 1995, 173-178

38. H. Samet and A. Soffer: Legend-driven geographic symbol recognition system. Proc. 12th ICPR, Jerusalem Vol. 2 (1994) 350-355

39. Soffer and H. Samet: Negative Shape Features for Images Databases Consisting of Geographical Symbols. Proc. 3rd International Workshop on Visual Forms, World Scientific (1997) 569-581

40. L. Boatto, V. Consorti, M. Del Buono, V. Eramo, A. Esposito, F. Melcarne, and M. Meucci: Detection and Separation of Symbols Connected to Graphics in Line Drawings. Proc. 11th ICPR Vol. II, The Hague, The Netherlands (1992) IEEE Comp. Soc. Press (1992) 545-548

41. L. Boatto et al.: An interpretation system for land register maps. Computer, July 1992, 25-33

42. H. Yamada, K. Yamamoto, and K. Hosokawa: Directional mathematical morphology and reformalized Hough transformation for the analysis of topographic maps. IEEE Transactions on Pattern Analysis and Machine Intelligence Vol. 15 N. 4 (1993) 380-387

43. K. Yamamoto, H. Yamada, and S. Muraki: Symbol recognition and surface reconstruction from topographic map by parallel method. Proc. 2nd Int. Conf. on Document Analysis and Recognition (ICDAR '93) Tsukuba Science City, Japan (1993) 914-917

44. O.A. Morean and R. Kasturi: Symbol identification in geographical maps. Proc. 7th ICPR, Montreal, Canada (1984) IEEE Publ. 84CH2046-1, 966-967

45. E. Reiher et al.: A System for Efficient and Robust Map Symbol Recognition. Proc. ICPR'96 (1996) 783-787

46. J.M. Ogier, R. Mullot, J. Labiche and Y. Lecoutier: An Interpretation Device Can Not Be Reliable Without Any Semantic Coherency Analysis of the Interpreted Objects – Application to French Cadastral Maps. Proc. ICDAR'97, Ulm (1997) 532-

47. R. Randriamahefa, J. Cocquerez, C. Fluhr, F. Pepin, and S. Philipp: Printed music recognition. In Proc. Second IAPR International Conference on Document Analysis and Recognition, ICDAR '93, pages 898-901, Tsukuba Science City, Japan, October 1993

48. K.Todd Reed and J.R. Parker: Automatic computer recognition of printed music. Proc. ICPR'96 (1996) 803, 807

49. J. Armand: Musical score recognition: A hierarchical and recursive approach. In Proc. Second IAPR International Conference on Document Analysis and Recognition, ICDAR '93, pages 906-909, Tsukuba Science City, Japan, October 1993

50. H. Miyao and Y. Nakano: Note symbol extraction for printed piano score using neural networks. IEICE Transactions on Inf.& Syst., E79-D(5):548-554, May 1996

51. I. Leplumey, J. Camillerapp, G. Lorette: A robust detector for music staves. Proc. ICDAR'93 (1993) 902-905

52. D.S. Doermann, E. Rivlin and I Weiss: Logo recognition using geometric invariants. Proc. ICDAR'93 (1993) 894-897

53. M. Corvi, E. Ottaviani: Multiresolution logo recognition. in Aspects of visual form processing, World Scientific, (Proc. 3rd Int. Workshop on Visual Form, Capri, Italy) (1997) 110-118

54. F. Cesarini, M. Gori, S Marinai, G. Soda: A Hybrid system for locating and recognizing low level graphic items. in Graphics Recognition: methods and applications, (papers from GREC'95) Vol. LCNS1072, Springer (1996) 135-147

55. P. Suda, C. Bridoux, B. Kammerer, G. Maderlechner: Logo and word matching using a general approach to signal registration. Proc. ICDAR'97 (1997) 61-65

56. N.A. Murshed, F. Bortolozzi: Recognition of electronic components in circuit layouts using the fuzzy ARTMAP neural network. Proc. GREC'97 (1997) 267-272

57. L. Wenyin, D. Dori: Generic graphics recognition of engineering drawing objects. Proc. GREC'97 (1997) 70-80

58. M. Minoh, T. Munetsugu, and K. Ikeda: Extraction and Classification of Graphical Symbol Candidates Based on Perceptual Organization. Proc. 11th ICPR Vol. II, The Hague, The Netherlands (1992) IEEE Comp. Soc. Press (1992) 234-237

59. Z. Xeujun, L. Xinyu, Z. Shengling, P. Baochang and Y.Y. Tang: On-Line Recognition of Handwritten Mathematical Symbols. Proc. ICDAR'97, Ulm (1997) 645-648

60. Y.J. Zhang: A survey on evaluation methods for image segmentation. Pattern Recognition Vol. 29 N. 8 (1996) 1335-1346

61. P.K. Sahoo, S. Soltani, A.K.C. Wong and Y.C. Chen: A survey of thresholding techniques. CVGIP Vol.41 (1988) 233-260

62. L. Lam, S.W. Lee and C.Y. Suen: Thinning methodologies-A comprehensive survey. IEEE Trans. PAMI Vol.14, n.9 (1992) 869-887

63. A. Rosenfeld: Axial Representations Of Shape. Computer Vision Graphics and Image Processing Vol. 33 156-173 (1986)

64. R.M. Brown, T.H. Fay, and C.L. Walker: Handprinted symbol recognition system, Pattern Recognition. Vol. 21 (1988) 91-118

65. R. Plamondon et al.: Validation of preprocessing algorithms: a methodology and its application to the design of a thinning algorithm for handwritten characters. Proc. ICDAR'93 Tsukuba, Japan (1993) 287-290

66. V.K. Govindan and A.P. Shivaprasad: A pattern adaptive thinning algorithm. Pattern Recognition Vol.20 N. 6 623-637, (1987)

67. X. Li and A. Basu: Variable-resolution character thinning. Pattern Recognition Letters Vol.12 241-248 (1991)

68. M. Frucci and A. Marcelli: Line Representation of Elongated Shapes. Lecture Notes in Computer Science, Berlin: Springer-Verlag Vol. 970 643-648 (1995)

69. F.Leymaria and M.D. Levine: Simulating the grassfire transform using an active contour model. IEEE Trans. on PAMI Vol.14. no.1 56-75 (1992)

70. G. Dimauro, S. Impedovo and G. Pirlo: A new thinning algorithm based on controlled deletion of edge regions. IJPRAI 969-985

71. C. Chouinard and R. Plamondon: Thinning and Segmenting handwritten characters by line following. Machine Vision and Applications Vol. 5 185-197 (1992)

72. D. Kalles and D.T. Morris: A novel and reliable thinning algorithm. IVC Vol.11 N. 9 588-603 (1993)

73. F.L. Bookstein: The line skeleton. CVIP Vol.11 123-137 (1979)

74. J.W. Brandt and V.R.Algazi: Continuous skeleton computation by Voronoi diagram. CVGIP:IU Vol. 55 N. 3 329-338 (1992)

75. A. Sirijani and G.R. Cross: On representation of a shape's skeleton. Pattern Recognition Letters Vol.12 149-154 (1991)

76. S. Lee and J. C. Pan: Off-line tracing and representation of signatures. IEEE Trans. on Systems, Man and Cybernetics Vol. SMC-22 N. 4 (1992) 755-771

77. S.W. Lu and H. Xu: False stroke detection and elimination for character recognition. Pattern Recognition Letters Vol. 13, 745-755 (1992)

78. G. Boccignone, A. Chianese, L.P. Cordella, A. Marcelli: Recovering dynamic information from static handwriting, Pattern Recognition. 26, 3 (1993) 409-418

79. G. Boccignone, A. Chianese, L.P. Cordella, A. Marcelli: Using skeletons for OCR. in Progress in image analysis and processing, V. Cantoni et al. Eds., World Scientific (1990). 275-282

80. L.P. Cordella, A. Marcelli: An alternative approach to the performance evaluation of thinning algorithms for document processing applications. in Graphics Recognition: Methods and Applications, R. Kasturi and K. Tombre Ed.s Vol. LNCS 1072 190-203, Springer, Berlin (1996)

81. O. Hori and S. Tanigawa: Raster-To-Vector Conversion by Line Fitting Based on Contours and Skeletons. Proc. ICDAR'93 (1993) 353

82. L. A. Fletcher and R. Kasturi: A robust algorithm for text string separation from mixed text/graphics images. IEEE Trans. on PAMI Vol.10 N. 6 (1988) 910-918

83. D. Trier, A. K. Jain, and T. Taxt: Feature extraction methods for character recognition - a survey. Pattern Recognition Vol. 29 N. 4 641-662, Apr. 1996

84. S. Loncaric: A Survey of Shape Analysis Techniques. Pattern Recognition Vol. 31 N. 8 (1998) 983-1001

85. L.P. Cordella, P. Foggia, C. Sansone and M. Vento: Subgraph transformations for the inexact matching of attributed relational graphs. Computing, 12 (1998) 43-52

Synthesis of Representative Graphical Symbols by Computing Generalized Median Graph

Xiaoyi Jiang, Andreas Münger, and Horst Bunke

Department of Computer Science
University of Bern, Switzerland
{jiang,muenger,bunke}@iam.unibe.ch

Abstract. Median is a general concept of capturing the essential information of a given set of objects. In this work we adopt this concept to the problem of learning, or synthesis, of representative graphical symbols from given examples. Graphical symbols are represented by graphs. This way the learning task is transformed into that of computing the generalized median of a given set of graphs, which is a novel graph matching problem and solved by a genetic algorithm.

1 Introduction

In the last years the automatic processing and analysis of graphical data has become the focus of intensive research. There are numerous applications based on the detection and recognition of graphical symbols [6]. An important issue in this context is that of learning graphical symbols.

The discipline of machine learning is concerned with algorithms by which a system can automatically construct models, knowledge, or skills from the outside world. Generally, there are different categories of approaches to machine learning, like learning in neural networks, symbolic learning from examples, case-based learning, explanation-based learning, or reinforcement learning. For a general introduction to the area of machine learning and an overview, the reader is referred to [4].

In object prototype learning we consider a set of noisy samples of the same object and want to infer a representative model. In the present paper we consider the learning, or synthesis, of representative graphical symbols from given examples. In the context of prototype learning the concept of median of a set of given objects turns out to be very useful.

Graphs are a powerful and versatile tool useful in pattern recognition, computer vision and related areas. In particular, they have been applied to various problems in graphics recognition [3,7,8,9,10]. For our purpose of learning graphical symbols we represent graphical symbols by means of graphs. Hence, the learning task is transformed into that of median graph computation, which is a novel graph matching problem and has been investigated recently in [5].

The rest of the paper begins with an introduction of the median concept in general. Then, we define the generalized median graph and briefly describe a

Atul K. Chhabra and D. Dori (Eds.): GREC'99, LNCS 1941, pp. 183–192, 2000.

genetic algorithm for its computation. The application to synthesis of representative graphical symbols is presented in the next section. Finally, some discussions conclude the paper.

2   Concept of Median

Assume that we have a set S of patterns in an arbitrary representation space U and a distance function $d(p, q)$ to measure the dissimilarity between any two patterns $p, q \in U$. An important technique for capturing the essential information of the given set of patterns is to find a pattern $\bar{p} \in U$ that minimizes the sum of distances to all patterns from S, i.e.

$$\bar{p} = \arg\min_{p \in U} \sum_{q \in S} d(p, q).$$

The pattern $\bar{p}$ is called the *generalized median* of S. If the search is constrained to the given set S, the resultant pattern

$$\hat{p} = \arg\min_{p \in S} \sum_{q \in S} d(p, q)$$

is called the *set median* of S. In general there is no unique solution for both set and generalized median.

Average and median are two widely used concepts in statistics. As a matter of fact, they represent the generalized median of a set of real numbers for the distance function $d(p, q) = (p - q)^2$ and $d(p, q) = |p - q|$, respectively. The generalized median of strings has also been investigated and found useful in the field of OCR [11]. In this work we are interested in (generalized) median graphs.

3   Generalized Median Graph

In this paper we consider directed and labeled graphs. Formally, a labeled *graph* is a 4-tuple, $G = (V, E, \alpha, \beta)$, where V is the finite set of nodes, $E \subset V \times V$ is the finite set of edges, $\alpha : V \to L_N$ is the node labeling function, and $\beta : E \to L_E$ is the edge labeling function. L_N and L_E are the sets of node and edge labels, respectively.

In order to measure the dissimilarity of two graphs G_1 and G_2, we define six graph edit operations, namely, the insertion, deletion, and substitution of both nodes and edges. A cost is assigned to each of these edit operations. Then, the *edit distance*, $d(G_1, G_2)$, of G_1 and G_2 is simply defined as the minimal cost, taken over all sequences of edit operations that transform G_1 into G_2. The computation of this edit distance is a well-known NP-complete problem, which is sometimes called *error-correcting graph isomorphism*, or simply *graph matching*. For a more formal introduction of graph matching see [12].

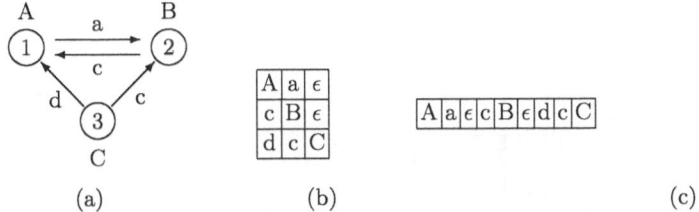

(a)   (b)   (c)

Fig. 1. Chromosome representation of a graph by linearization of its adjacency matrix: (a) original graph; (b) adjacency matrix; (c) chromosome

Let $S = \{G_1, G_2, \ldots, G_k\}$ be a set of given graphs with labels from L_N and L_E. Let U be the set of all graphs that can be constructed using these labels. The *generalized median graph* $\overline{G}$ is defined by

$$\overline{G} = \arg\min_{G \in U} \sum_{G_i \in S} d(G, G_i). \tag{1}$$

The computation of generalized median graphs is a novel graph matching problem and turns out to be exponential both in the number of graphs and in the size of the graphs.

An optimal algorithm using A*-search for the generalized median graph computation problem was described in [13]. It is based on the idea of iteratively enumerating potential candidates G for the generalized median graph $\overline{G}$ of a set of input graphs $S = \{G_1, \cdots, G_k\}$. If G has a fixed number, n, of nodes, then all possible mappings of the nodes of G to the nodes of the G_i's can be systematically enumerated. Thus, for fixed n, the graph G that has the smallest sum of edit distances to the G_i's can be found. Furthermore it can be proved that the generalized median graph of any set S of graphs cannot have more nodes than the sum Σ of all the nodes of the G_i's in set S. Hence, by iteratively increasing the number of nodes of the candidate graph G, starting with 1 and terminating at Σ, $\overline{G}$ of S can be found. Unfortunately, this solution suffers from a very large computational complexity, which is exponential in the sum of the nodes of all graphs in set S. An experimental evaluation on a powerful workstation has shown that already for a small number of small graphs the generalized median graph cannot be computed any longer due to combinatorial explosion.

Genetic algorithms [2] are a particular class of stochastic optimization algorithms, partly motivated by concepts from the theory of biological evolution. Numerous successful applications of genetic algorithms have been reported recently, including applications in graph matching [1,14]. We have developed a genetic algorithm to solve the generalized median graph problem. In the following we only give a brief description of the algorithm and the reader is referred to [5,13] for the full details.

For the development of a genetic algorithm we have to specify a graph representation by means of chromosomes, a fitness function, and crossover and mutation operator. A straightforward chromosome representation is derived from

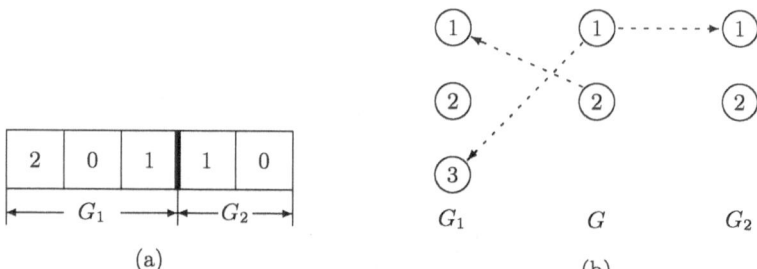

2	0	1	1	0

$\longleftarrow G_1 \longrightarrow \!\!\longleftarrow\! G_2 \!\longrightarrow$

(a)

(b)

Fig. 2. A candidate median graph G represented by a chromosome (a) and its graphical illustration (b)

first representing G by its adjacency matrix and then linearizing the adjacency matrix, for example, by concatenating its rows. An example is shown in Figure 1.

This chromosome representation, however, has a serious drawback. In each iteration and for each individual chromosome in a population, representing a candidate G for the generalized median graph, we have to compute $d(G, G_i)$ for each graph G_i in set S, which is exponential in the size of G. Hence, we end up with a procedure that still has a very high computational complexity.

To avoid the high computational complexity resulting from the chromosome representation shown in Figure 1, we have adapted another solution. Rather than just coding a candidate graph G in a chromosome and finding the optimal mapping between G and the G_i's separately, we encode the graph G as well as all the mappings to the G_i's directly in a chromosome. Thus, not only generating a potential candidate G for the generalized median graph, but also computing the optimal mappings between G and the G_i's in set S is accomplished by the genetic algorithm.

Each chromosome is an array of integers that represents the transformations from a candidate graph G to each of the G_i's. The length of the array is equal to the total number of nodes in the different input graphs. Each node has a corresponding position in the array. The number at a specific position in a chromosome tells us how the corresponding node v of some G_i is generated by transforming the candidate graph G. The number 0 denotes an insertion of v into G, while any other number $n \geq 1$ means that v is substituted from the candidate graph node n. Suppose we have two graphs, G_1 and G_2, of three and two nodes, respectively. Then the size of the array will be five. Its first three (last two) positions represent the nodes of G_1 (G_2). For instance, the chromosome in Figure 2(a) is interpreted as follows. The implicitly defined candidate graph G has two nodes. When transforming G into G_1, the first (second) node of G is substituted by the third (first) node of G_1, and the second node of G_1 is inserted. Similarly, when transforming G into G_2, the first node of G is substituted by the first node of G_2, while the second node of G_2 is inserted and the second node of G is deleted. A graphical illustration of this mapping is given in Figure 2(b).

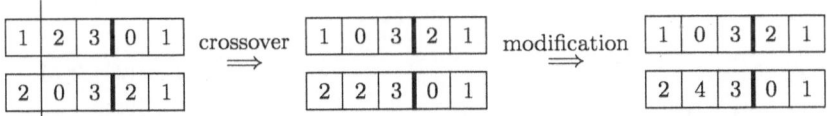

Fig. 3. Modification procedure for the crossover operator

The candidate generalized median graph G, as specified by such a chromosome, is only partially complete; the labeling of nodes and the specification of edges and their labeling are still missing. However, these missing informations can be uniquely completed in low-polynomial time such that the sum of edit distances defined by (1) is minimized among all possible completions, see [5] for more details. By uniqueness we do not mean a single minimal completion. As a matter of fact, several minimal completions of identical sum of edit distances may exist in general, and an arbitrary one can be selected. This minimal sum of edit distances defines at the same time the fitness function. The smaller the value is, the larger is the fitness of a candidate. The advantage of this chromosome representation over the naive approach exemplified in Figure 1 becomes now obvious; the fitness function can be computed much more efficiently.

The single-point crossover operator commonly used in genetic algorithms has to be extended in our algorithm. From both chromosomes to be crossed, we cut off a tail of the same, randomly chosen length. To perform the crossover, the tails are simply exchanged. Doing this, however, it can happen that the transformations represented by the resulting chromosomes become inconsistent. In this case the chromosomes have to be modified. In the example shown in Figure 3, the inconsistency occurs in the lower chromosome. Both the first and second node of G_1 are mapped to the second node of G. The modification is accomplished by randomly changing the relevant position(s) of an inconsistent chromosome until it becomes consistent. Mutation is accomplished by randomly changing the numbers in the array. Again, a consistency test and, if necessary, a modification similar to the crossover operator are carried out.

For the population initialization we assume that the given graphs G_i's are a good approximation for the unknown generalized median graph and therefore directly use them to form the initial population. In this case the chromosomes of the initial population correspond to transformations that represent the given input graphs, i.e. transformations that minimize the sum of edit distances of a particular graph G_i to all other G_j's.

4   Synthesis of Representative Graphical Symbols

If graphs are used for object representation, then one possibility of object prototype learning is to compute the generalized median graph of a set of sample graphs of a given object. We illustrate this approach by synthesizing represen-

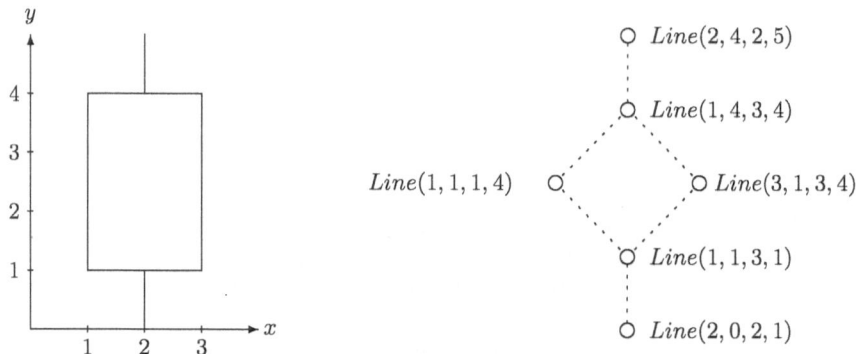

Fig. 4. A symbol (left) and its graph representation (right)

tative graphical symbols. The symbols used in our experiments are shown in Figure 5.

A symbol is represented by a labeled graph. Each line segment of a symbol is modeled as a vertex associated with the label *Line*. The label *Line* has four attributes that correspond to the coordinates of the two end points of the line segment. In Figure 4 an example is shown to illustrate this representation scheme. Notice that no edges are used in the graph representation and the dashed lines connecting vertices indicate merely the connectivity relationship between the line segments in the original symbol in order to ease the understanding of this particular graph. In addition no topological information such as crossing, touching, and close-but-not-touching between line segments is explicitly represented in our graphs. Instead, they contain the complete geometry of symbols. If necessary, however, topological relationships can readily be induced from the geometrical representation.

We have manually generated samples used in our experiments. Five samples of each symbol are shown in Figure 5, together with the representative symbol corresponding to the computed generalized median graph. These examples demonstrate the ability of generalized median graphs to provide a good overall representation of objects by smoothing out the individual imprecisions in the noisy samples. It is also evident that for the purpose of learning representative graphical symbols the generalized median outperforms the set median in general.

Basically, our generalized median graph algorithm assumes that the input graphs correspond to noisy samples of the same symbol. Therefore, it is interesting to investigate its behavior in the case of outliers, see Figure 6. In the first row, A1-5/B1 represents the result by taking all five samples of symbol A and, as an outlier, the first one of symbol B. Similarly, two and three outliers, respectively, are involved in A1-5/B1-2 and A1-5/B1-3. While symbols A and B are similar, the second row demonstrates the results from combining A's with samples of the totally different symbol C. Finally, results from using two outliers

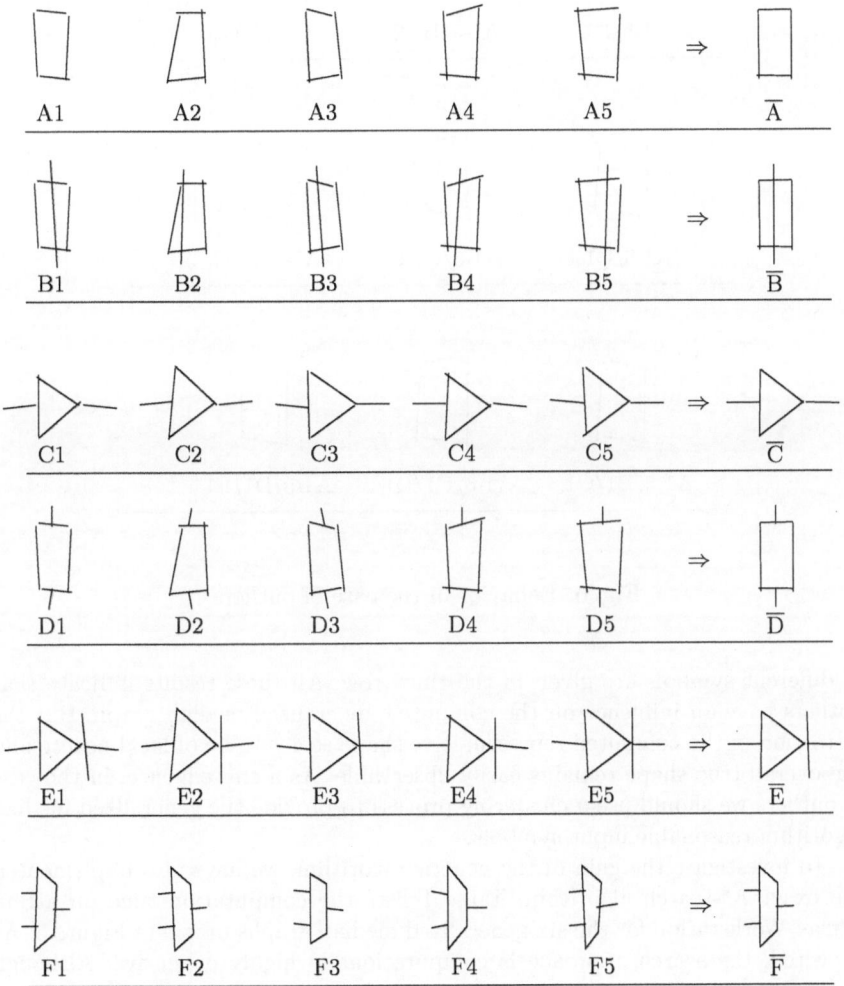

Fig. 5. Symbol A to F (from top to bottom): Five noisy samples of each symbol (left) and the representative symbol corresponding to the generalized median graph (right)

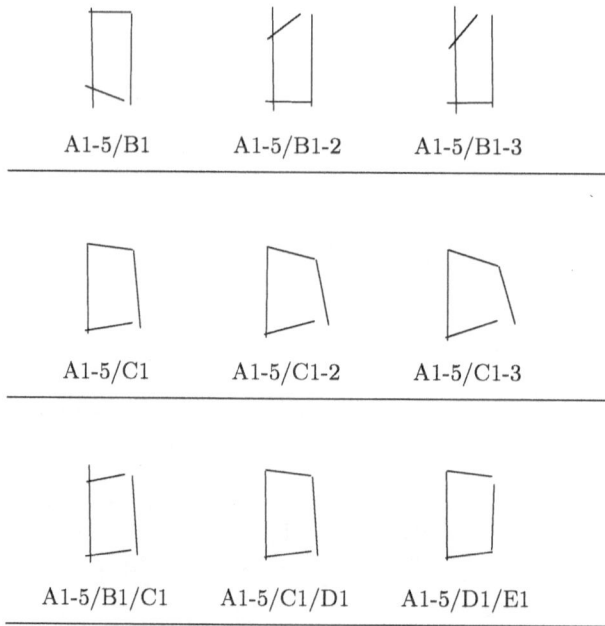

Fig. 6. Behavior in the case of outliers

of different symbols are given in the third row. All these results indicate that outliers have an influence on the computed generalized median graph. But the distortion in the computed representative shape seems to be of local nature and the overall true shape remains easily observable. As a consequence, in the case of outliers we should use a clustering process to provide the generalized median algorithm reasonable input symbols.

To investigate the gain of the genetic algorithm, we have also implemented the exact A*-search algorithm. Table 1 lists the computation time on a Sun Ultra4 Workstation for the six generalized median graphs drawn in Figure 5. As expected, the search approach is computationally highly expensive. Although the genetic algorithm provides only approximate solutions in general, it has computed the true median graphs in all cases.

5 Conclusions

Median is a general concept of capturing the essential information of a given set of objects. In statistics the generalized median of numbers corresponds to the two fundamental concepts average and median. Also, median strings have found their application in practice. In this work we have adopted the median concept

Table 1. Computation time (seconds): combinatorial search vs. genetic algorithm (GA)

	symbol A	B	C	D	E	F
search	6	127	93	1219	1232	13725
GA	0.06	0.08	0.09	0.11	0.10	0.12

to the problem of learning, or synthesis, of representative graphical symbols from given examples. Graphical symbols are represented by graphs. This way the learning task is transformed into that of computing the generalized median of a given set of graphs.

The computation of generalized median graphs is a novel graph matching problem and turns out to be exponential both in the number of graphs and in the size of the graphs. Exact algorithms like the A*-search approach briefly described in Section 3 are prohibitively expensive in nature. For this reason a genetic solution has been suggested. We have shown the practical usefulness of both the generalized median concept for the learning task under consideration and the proposed approximative computational approach. In particular, the experimental results have demonstrated the ability of generalized median graphs to provide a good overall representation of objects by smoothing out the individual imprecisions in the noisy samples.

References

1. A. D. J. Cross, R. C. Wilson, and E. R. Hancock, Inexact graph matching using genetic search, *Pattern Recognition*, 30(6): 953–970, 1997. 185
2. D. E. Goldberg, *Genetic algorithms in search, optimization and machine learning*, Addison-Wesley, 1989. 185
3. A. H. Habacha, Structural recognition of disturbed symbols using discrete relaxation, *Proc. of 1st Int. Conf. on Document Analysis and Recognition*, Saint Malo, France, 170–178, 1991. 183
4. A. Hutchinson, *Algorithmic Learning*, Oxford University Press, 1994. 183
5. X. Jiang, A. Münger, and H. Bunke, Computing the generalized median of a set of graphs, *Proc. of 2nd ICPAR Workshop on Graph-based Representations*, Haindorf, Austria, 115–124, 1999. 183, 185, 187
6. R. Kasturi and K. Tmobre (Eds.), *Graphics Recognition: Methods and Applications*, Springer-Verlag, 1996. 183
7. P. Kuner and B. Ueberreiter, Pattern recognition by graph matching: combinatorial versus continuous optimization, *Int. Journal of Pattern Recognition and Artificial Intelligence*, 2(3): 527–542, 1988. 183
8. S. Lee, Recognizing hand-written electrical circuit symbols with attributed graph matching, in H. S. Baird, H. Bunke, and K. Yamamoto (Eds.), *Structured Document Analysis*, 340–358, Springer-Verlag, 1988. 183
9. S. W. Lee, J. H. Kim, and F. C. A.Groen, Translation-, rotation-, and scale-invariant recognition of hand-drawn symbols in schematic diagrams, *Int. Journal of Pattern Recognition and Artificial Intelligence*, 4(1): 1–25, 1990. 183

10. J. Lladós, G. Sánchez, and E. Martí, A string based method to recognize symbols and structural textures in architectural plans, *Proc. of 2nd IAPR Workshop on Graphics Recognition*, Nancy, France, 287–294, 1997. 183

11. D. Lopresti and J. Zhou, Using consensus sequence voting to correct OCR errors, *Computer Vision and Image Understanding*, 67(1): 39-47, 1997. 184

12. B. T. Messmer and H. Bunke, A new algorithm for error-tolerant subgraph isomorphism detection, *IEEE Trans. on Pattern Analysis and Machine Intelligence*, 20(5): 493–504, 1998. 184

13. A. Münger, *Synthesis of prototype graphs from sample graphs*, Diploma Thesis, University of Bern, 1998. (in German) 185

14. Y.-K. Wang, K.-C. Fan, and J.-T. Horng, Genetic-based search for error-correcting graph isomorphism, *IEEE Trans. on Systems, Man and Cybernetics – Part B: Cybernetics*, 27(4): 588–597, 1997. 185

Deformable Template Matching within a Bayesian Framework for Hand-Written Graphic Symbol Recognition

Ernest Valveny and Enric Martí

Computer Vision Center – Computer Science Department,
Universitat Autònoma de Barcelona
Edifici O - Campus UAB. 08193 Bellaterra. Spain
{ernest,enric}@cvc.uab.es

Abstract. We describe a method for hand-drawn symbol recognition based on deformable template matching able to handle uncertainty and imprecision inherent to hand-drawing. Symbols are represented as a set of straight lines and their deformations as geometric transformations of these lines. Matching, however, is done over the original binary image to avoid loss of information during line detection. It is defined as an energy minimization problem, using a Bayesian framework which allows to combine fidelity to ideal shape of the symbol and flexibility to modify the symbol in order to get the best fit to the binary input image. Prior to matching, we find the best global transformation of the symbol to start the recognition process, based on the distance between symbol lines and image lines. We have applied this method to the recognition of dimensions and symbols in architectural floor plans and we show its flexibility to recognize distorted symbols.

1   Introduction

Bayesian inference and deformable templates have been widely used in many fields of computer vision to reason with uncertainty when prior information about possible values of parameters to be estimated is available. Their application ranges a wide number of computer vision tasks such as object recognition, segmentation, tracking, restoration, etc. [4]. In document analysis, however, and to our knowledge, their use has been restricted to a few applications to hand-written numeral and character recognition [1,5,12].

We argue that a Bayesian framework is also a well-suited method to recognize hand-drawn graphic symbols, such as those found in many kinds of diagrams, maps and line drawings. Hand-drawn symbols are imprecise, with very distorted shapes from their ideal patterns, as it is shown in Fig. 1. Therefore, their recognition must face a high degree of uncertainty. Traditional methods for symbol recognition are generally based on vectorization, feature extraction and structural matching [3,6,8,9,11]. They decrease their efficiency and robustness as long as noise and distortion of hand-drawn symbols increase [2,13] because structural matching cannot recover from feature misdetections and errors introduced

Atul K. Chhabra and D. Dori (Eds.): GREC'99, LNCS 1941, pp. 193–208, 2000.

in feature extraction. Bayesian inference can help to overcome the drawbacks of these methods modelling uncertainty though the combination of prior information and likelihood. Prior information can be easily encoded in symbol recognition through the representation of the symbol with a pattern of its ideal shape and the generation of all its possible deformations from this pattern. Then, prior information provides the degree of fidelity of each deformation to the ideal shape of the symbol. On the other hand, likelihood can be seen as a measure of similarity between a given deformation of the symbol and the image. Combining both concepts we can look for the less deformed shape of the symbol that yields the best fit to the image. Therefore, deformable template matching and Bayesian inference arise as an alternative approach to symbol recognition in front of traditional methods. In a previous work [14] we have proposed to use them to recognize hand-drawn symbols in graphic documents. In this work, we extend and further develop our initial proposal and we face the important issue of matching initialization. We also show more extended results that reinforce the feasibility of the application of this approach to the recognition of hand-drawn symbols.

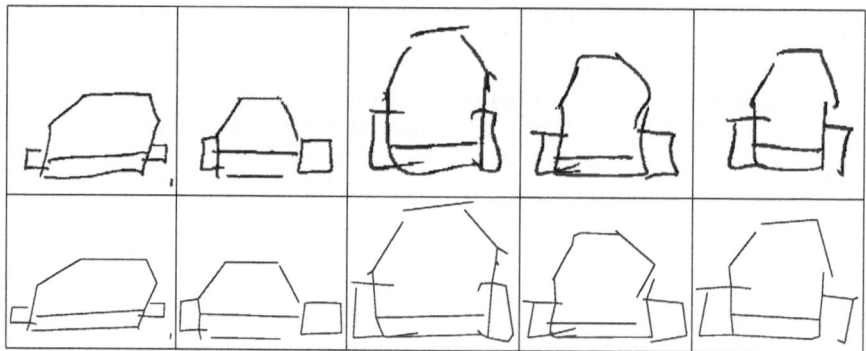

Fig. 1. Some examples of images of symbol *Sofa*. Original image in the top and vectorization in the bottom

In section 2 we explain the general framework of Bayesian inference applied to symbol recognition. In section 3 we describe the application of this general framework to the recognition of hand-drawn lineal symbols. In section 4 we discuss the problem of finding a good initialization of the symbol to get an accurate convergence of the matching algorithm. Section 5 shows some of the experiments carried out and, finally, in section 6, we state the conclusions from our work.

2   Bayesian Formulation of Symbol Recognition

The general problem of symbol recognition can be stated in this way: given an input image I and a set of predefined symbols, $\{S_1, \ldots, S_n\}$, represented by their ideal shapes, symbol recognition provides the symbol S_i that can be best identified in image I.

In a probabilistic framework the correspondence between an image and a symbol can be expressed as $P(S_i|I)$, i.e., the probability that given image I, we can identify symbol S_i in it. Then, symbol recognition consists in finding the symbol S_i which maximises the conditional probability $P(S_i|I)$. Applying Bayes' rule, we can express $P(S_i|I)$ in the following way:

$$P(S_i|I) = \frac{P(I|S_i)P(S_i)}{P(I)} . \tag{1}$$

Assuming that all symbols have the same prior probability, $P(S_i)$ and verifying that $P(I)$ is constant for all symbols, we can deduce that finding S_i which maximizes $P(S_i|I)$ is equivalent to finding S_i which maximizes $P(I|S_i)$.

As a hand-drawn symbol can take many different shapes, we must search over all its possible and valid shape variations when looking for the correspondence between an image and the symbol. We let D_i be any possible deformation of the ideal shape of symbol S_i. Then, $P(I|S_i)$ can be expressed as the marginal probability summing up for all deformations D_i the joint probability of the image and each of the deformations, $P(I, D_i|S_i)$:

$$P(I|S_i) = \int P(I, D_i|S_i)dD_i = \int P(I|D_i, S_i)P(D_i|S_i)dD_i . \tag{2}$$

Then, the probability to be maximized, $P(I|S_i)$, is expressed as the combination of the prior probability of the deformations, $P(D_i|S_i)$, and the likelihood between the image and each of the deformations, $P(I|D_i, S_i)$. Prior probability is the probability that deformation D_i is still a valid representation of symbol S_i. It penalizes excessive distortions by giving them lower probability. Likelihood is the probability that image I corresponds to deformation D_i. It is usually measured by computing the distance between the image and the deformation.

Expression (2) is solved using Laplacian approximation yielding the following expression:

$$P(I|S_i) = k \cdot P(I|\hat{D}_i, S_i) \cdot P(\hat{D}_i|S_i) . \tag{3}$$

where k is a constant and $\hat{D}_i$ is the deformation of the symbol that maximizes $P(I|D_i, S_i) \cdot P(D_i|S_i)$. Usually $\hat{D}_i$ is found searching for the minimum of the negative log of this expression:

$$\begin{aligned}
\hat{D}_i &= \arg\max_{D_i} P(I|D_i, S_i)P(D_i|S_i) \\
&= \arg\min_{D_i} \left(-\log P(I|D_i, S_i) - \log P(D_i|S_i)\right) . \tag{4}
\end{aligned}$$

Making the following equivalences:

$$E_{ext} = -\log P(I|D_i, S_i) \,. \tag{5}$$

$$E_{int} = -\log P(D_i|S_i) \,. \tag{6}$$

$$E = E_{ext} + E_{int} = -\log P(I|S_i) \,. \tag{7}$$

the problem of symbol recognition is reduced to the problem of minimizing an energy function, E, composed of two terms: external energy, E_{ext}, which is related to likelihood and internal energy, E_{int}, which is related to prior probability. External energy plays the role of a force which tries to deform the shape of the symbol as much as possible to get the best match to the input image. On the other hand, internal energy acts like a force that prevents high deformations keeping the shape of the symbol as close as possible to the ideal shape. The minimum of the energy function is the equilibrium point between these two opposite forces. It corresponds to the shape of the symbol that best fits the image with the minimum amount of deformation. The final value of the energy function at this point is related by Eq.(7) to the maximum of $P(I|S_i)$ and by Eq.(1) to the maximum of $P(S_i|I)$. Thus, it is a measure of the degree of correspondence between the input image and the symbol. Then, image can be identified with the symbol with the lowest final energy value.

3   Deformable Template Matching for Lineal Symbols

In this section we describe the application of the general framework introduced in the previous section to the recognition of lineal symbols. Using that framework, there are three main components involved in a deformable template matching approach which need to be defined: first, prior information, i.e., the representation for the symbol and deformations and the definition of the prior probability; secondly, the likelihood between the image and deformations and finally, the matching procedure used to find the minimum of the global energy function.

3.1   Prior Information

As symbols that can be found in drawings are basically composed of lines, we define each symbol as a set of straight lines, not necessarily connected. Each line is represented by the position of its midpoint, its orientation and its length. Deformations of the symbol are generated by translating, rotating and scaling each of the lines. This is an intuitive and natural way to represent symbols and their variations and it yields a set of shapes very close to those produced by handwriting.

We define two kinds of deformations that can be applied to a symbol: global and local deformations. Global deformations apply the same transformation to all the lines of the symbol. Therefore, they do not change the global shape of the symbol. On the other hand, local deformations apply different changes in position, orientation and length to each of the lines. Thus, they can be used to change the global shape of the symbol. Prior probability has only to penalize local deformations while global deformations are assumed to have the same probability.

Prior probability and internal energy are defined assuming that each possible transformation (translation, rotation or scaling) of a line follows a gaussian distribution of zero mean and that all transformations applied to each line are independent. These assumptions allow to express prior probability and internal energy in this way:

$$P(D_i|S_i) =$$

$$\prod_{i=1}^{n} \left(\frac{1}{\sqrt{2\pi}\sigma_{t_{x_i}}} e^{-\frac{t_{x_i}^2}{2\sigma_{t_{x_i}}^2}} \frac{1}{\sqrt{2\pi}\sigma_{t_{y_i}}} e^{-\frac{t_{y_i}^2}{2\sigma_{t_{y_i}}^2}} \frac{1}{\sqrt{2\pi}\sigma_{\theta_i}} e^{-\frac{\sin^2\theta_i}{2\sigma_{\theta_i}^2}} \frac{1}{\sqrt{2\pi}\sigma_{s_i}} e^{-\frac{s_i^2}{2\sigma_{s_i}^2}} \right). \quad (8)$$

$$E_{int} = \sum_{i=1}^{n} \left(\frac{t_{x_i}^2}{2\sigma_{t_{x_i}}^2} + \frac{t_{y_i}^2}{2\sigma_{t_{y_i}}^2} + \frac{\sin^2\theta_i}{2\sigma_{\theta_i}^2} + \frac{s_i^2}{2\sigma_{s_i}^2} \right) + K . \quad (9)$$

Internal energy is derived, as it is shown in expression (6), from the negative log of prior probability, which is defined as a product of gaussian distributions. There is one distinct gaussian for each kind of transformation applied to a specific line. Each line has its own distribution for translation, rotation and scaling. n is the number of symbol lines; t_{x_i}, t_{y_i} are the translations in x and y directions applied to the midpoint of line i; θ_i is the change in orientation applied to the line; and s_i the scaling applied to the length of the line. ; $\sigma_{t_{x_i}}$, $\sigma_{t_{y_i}}$, σ_{θ_i} and σ_{s_i} are the standard deviations for each of the gaussian distributions.

3.2   Likelihood

Likelihood must be a measure of similarity between a given deformation of the symbol and the input image. We have defined it from the distance between the deformation and the pixels of the binary input image. Working over the binary image allows to avoid errors and loss of information induced by skeletonization and vectorization and illustrated in Fig. 1.

The distance function is defined by summing up for all the lines of the deformation, the distance between the line and the closest pixels of the image. For each line of the deformation, we take a regular sample of points along it and we find, for each point, the closest image pixel. Each pair composed of a line point and an image pixel contributes to the distance with two values: the first one is based on the distance between them and the second one on the difference between the orientation of the line and the orientation of the pixel. This orientation is computed through the analysis of a window centered on the pixel. The proportion of points along the line overlapping with inked image pixels is also taken into account. In this way, we promote deformations of the symbol having lines close to the image, with the same orientation of image pixels and overlapping with them.

Then, external energy is made equivalent to this distance function. Likelihood is defined from external energy using a Gibbs distribution:

$$P(I|D_i, S_i) = \frac{1}{Z} e^{-E_{ext}(I,D)} . \tag{10}$$

$$E_{ext} = \frac{1}{n} \sum_{i=1}^{n} \left(\frac{1}{n_i} \sum_{j=1}^{n_i} \left(1 - e^{-\lambda \cdot d(p_j, q_j)} \cdot e^{-\mu |\sin(\theta_i - \alpha_j)|} \right) + \gamma \frac{n_i - \hat{n}_i}{n_i} \right) . \tag{11}$$

where Z is a normalizing constant; n is the number of lines in the symbol; n_i is the number of points sampled along line i; p_j are each of the points sampled along the line; q_j is the image pixel closest to point p_j; θ_i is the orientation of line i; α_j is the orientation of pixel q_j; $\hat{n}_i$ is the number of points of line i overlapping with image pixels; and λ, μ and γ are weighting factors. The use of exponential functions in the factors related to the distance and the difference of orientation allows to control (changing the value of weighting factors λ and μ) how the distance increases when the lines in the deformation moves away from the image pixels, both in distance and in orientation.

3.3   Matching

Matching is defined as a procedure for finding the minimum of the global energy function. It corresponds to the deformation of the symbol that keeps the best compromise between minimum deformation from ideal shape and maximum fit to the input image. The value of the energy function for this deformation gives a measure of the correspondence between the symbol and the image. Therefore, symbol recognition is performed applying matching between the image and all the symbols and selecting the symbol yielding the lowest energy value.

Combination of internal and external energy is a complex, non-linear energy function, with many local minima. Complex algorithms must be used to find a solution close to the global minimum. We have employed a simulated annealing algorithm [7]. This is a well-known general optimization algorithm that allows to avoid local minima searching randomly over the space of parameters. As the algorithm runs, this random search is directed towards low energy areas. In this way, and if good parameter initialization is achieved, convergence to a point close to the global minimum can be reached. The main drawbacks are the unstability of the solution and the computational cost. Due to the random nature of the algorithm, we cannot guarantee that two distinct runs of the algorithm yield exactly the same solution. It depends very much on a good initialization and on a good setting of all the parameters involved in algorithm performance. On the other hand, many iterations are needed to guarantee an stable and robust convergence. Then, computational cost tends to be high. Currently, our attention is not focussed on computational issues but in showing the feasibility of bayesian deformable template matching to recognize symbols with high distortions. Further considerations can be found in sections 5 and 6 where alternative solutions to these problems are discussed.

The matching algorithm starts from an initial representation of the symbol and, at each step, it randomly generates a new deformation by applying local transformations to every line. This new deformation is accepted or rejected depending on its energy value. If energy is lower than energy of previous deformation, it is always accepted because we are moving towards the global minimum. If energy increases, it can also be accepted in order to jump over areas of local minima. Its acceptance depends on the change in energy and on the value of a temperature parameter. First, the following expression is evaluated:

$$e^{-\frac{E_{k+1}-E_k}{T_k}} \ . \tag{12}$$

where E_{k+1} is the value of energy for the deformation at step $k + 1$, E_k is the energy for the deformation at step k, and T_k is the temperature at step k. Then, a random number u between 0 and 1 is generated. The new deformation is accepted only if the computed value in (12) is lower than u. In this way, at the beginning of the algorithm, with high temperatures almost every new state is accepted and we can randomly move over all the space of deformations. As the algorithm runs and we get focussed to areas close to the global minimum, the temperature decreases and the probability of accepting deformations moving towards higher energy values is lower.

Accurate convergence of the algorithm depends very much on two factors: first, the initial value of temperature and its decreasing rate; and secondly, the election of a good starting representation of the symbol. In the next section, we explain how this latter issue is achieved by finding the best global transformation of the symbol that best fits to the image.

4   Initialization of Matching

The goal of this step is to find the global deformation of the symbol closest to the image. This is the optimal point to start the matching between the symbol and the image. Using only global transformations we can get the best possible fit to the image with no change in the global shape of the symbol. Then, matching starts from a shape closer to the image. As a result of that, convergence is easier and smaller changes have to be applied to symbol lines.

This initialization step is performed on the lineal representation of both the image and the symbol in order to speed up the process. We have defined a metric to measure the distance between two lines and the distance between two lineal symbols. Then, initialization consists in finding the global deformation of the symbol yielding the lowest distance to the lineal representation of the image.

First, we will introduce the distance between two lineal symbols and then, we will describe the procedure for finding the best global deformation.

4.1   Distance between Lineal Symbols

A line is defined by the position of its midpoint, its orientation and its length. These three features allow to specify any line in a very natural and intuitive

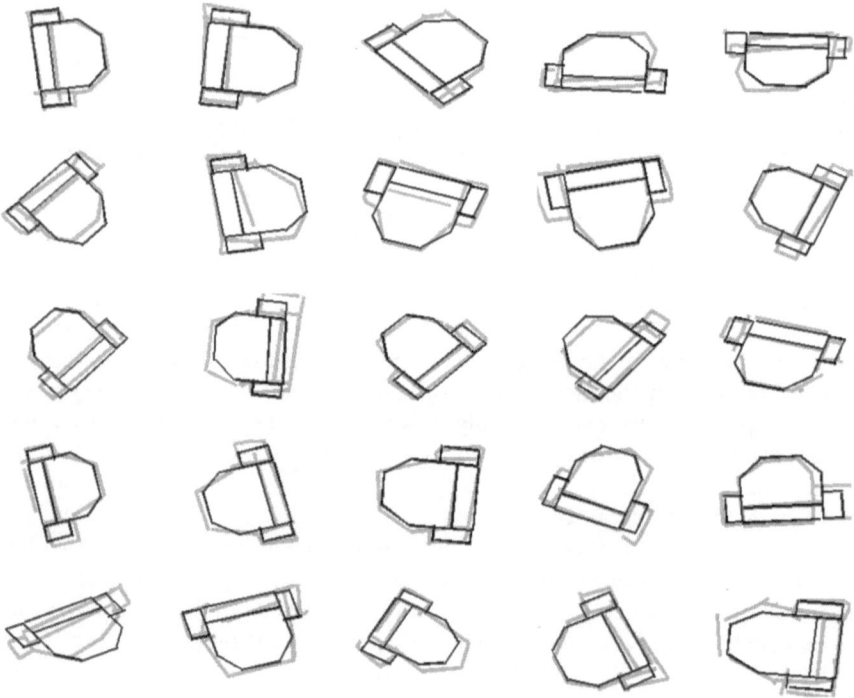

Fig. 2. Initialization of matching for 25 images of symbol *sofa*. Original image in gray and best global deformation in black

fashion. Then, the distance between two lines is based on the difference in midpoint position, orientation and length between them. A line is represented by a vector $L = (P, \alpha, l)$ where P is the position of the midpoint, α is the orientation, and l is the length. Given any two lines $L_1 = (P_1, \alpha_1, l_1)$ and $L_2 = (P_2, \alpha_2, l_2)$, the distance between them is expressed by:

$$d^2(L_1, L_2) = \omega_1 \cdot \|P_1 - P_2\|^2 + \omega_2 \cdot \sin^2(\alpha_1 - \alpha_2) + \omega_3 \cdot \frac{(l_1 - l_2)^2}{(l_1 + l_2)^2} . \quad (13)$$

This measure satisfies the properties of a metric. Moreover, it yields results very close to our visual idea of similarity between lines. The distance increases as lines become more separate and more distinct in orientation and length, factors which contribute to produce more visually distinct lines. Finally, it is an easily computable function, which makes it suitable to derive other measures from it.

The distance between two lineal symbols is then deduced from this definition of distance between two lines. It is defined as the weighted sum of distances between each pair of lines in both symbols. The weighting factor for each pair of lines must be an estimation of the correspondence between the two lines. A priori, we cannot know which line of one symbol is the corresponding line of every line of the other symbol. We estimate this correspondence with a probability distribution based on the distance between the two lines. Closer lines will have higher probability of correspondence. These criteria can be expressed in the following way: given two lineal symbols S_1 and S_2, each of them composed of a set of lines, $S_1 = \{L_1, \ldots, L_{n_1}\}$ and $S_2 = \{L_1, \ldots, L_{n_2}\}$, the distance between the two symbols is defined by:

$$d(S_1, S_2) = \frac{1}{n_1} \sum_{L_i \in S_1} d(L_i, S_2) = \frac{1}{n_1} \sum_{L_i \in S_1} \sum_{L_j \in S_2} P_{ij} \cdot d(L_i, L_j) . \tag{14}$$

$$P_{ij} = \frac{e^{-\frac{d_{ij}^2}{2\sigma^2}}}{\sum_{k=1}^{n_2} e^{-\frac{d_{ik}^2}{2\sigma^2}}} . \tag{15}$$

d_{ij} is the distance between line L_i in S_1 and line L_j in S_2. P_{ij} is the weighting factor for the distance between L_i and L_j and it corresponds to the probability of correspondence between both lines assuming a normal distribution based on the distance between them. It is normalized so that global probability of correspondence of a line in S_1 sums up to 1 for all lines in S_2.

4.2   Finding the Best Global Deformation of Symbol

First, the input image must be vectorized to get its representation as a set of lines. Then, initialization will find the global deformation of the symbol closest to this set of lines. This is achieved looking for the minimum of the distance function between the image and each of possible global deformations. This optimal deformation is identified by the parameters of a global translation, rotation and scaling applied to all the lines of the symbol. Finding these parameters is not a straightforward task as modifying the lines of the symbol also implies modifying the probability of correspondence among symbol lines and image lines.

We have employed an implementation of the *EM* algorithm [10] to get the optimal deformation. With the *EM* algorithm we can fix the probability of correspondence in the expectation step and then, in the maximization step we can find the optimal global transformation with that estimation of the correspondence. These two steps are iterated until convergence is reached.

The algorithm starts from the ideal representation of the symbol and the lineal representation of the input image and it iteratively finds successive deformations of the symbol until the optimal global deformation is reached. At each iteration two steps are applied. The expectation step estimates the probability of correspondence, P_{ij} between each line of the image and each of the lines of the current deformation. The maximization step finds a new global deformation using these estimated probabilities. The parameters of this new deformation are found analytically deriving the expression for the distance between two lineal symbols (14) in two steps: first, the best rotation is found and secondly, best translation and scaling. The variance used in computing P_{ij} is decreased at each iteration. In this way, as the algorithm runs and the deformation is getting closer to the image, correspondence among similar lines is favoured.

Results of the application of this procedure to a set of test images can be seen in Fig. 2. In it we can see 25 images of a symbol, and superimposed in black, the starting initialization of it for every image. It can be seen that this initialization reflects orientation and scaling of the image. In this way, it will be easier to find the best fit when introducing local deformations of the symbol and applying the matching procedure described in section 3.3.

Fig. 3. Example of a hand-drawn architectural drawing

5 Results and Discussion

We have applied this method to the recognition of symbols in hand-drawn architectural drawings. Fig. 3 shows an example of this kind of drawings with the symbols to be recognized. In these drawings, the identification and the recognition of all the symbols play a very important role in the semantic analysis. We

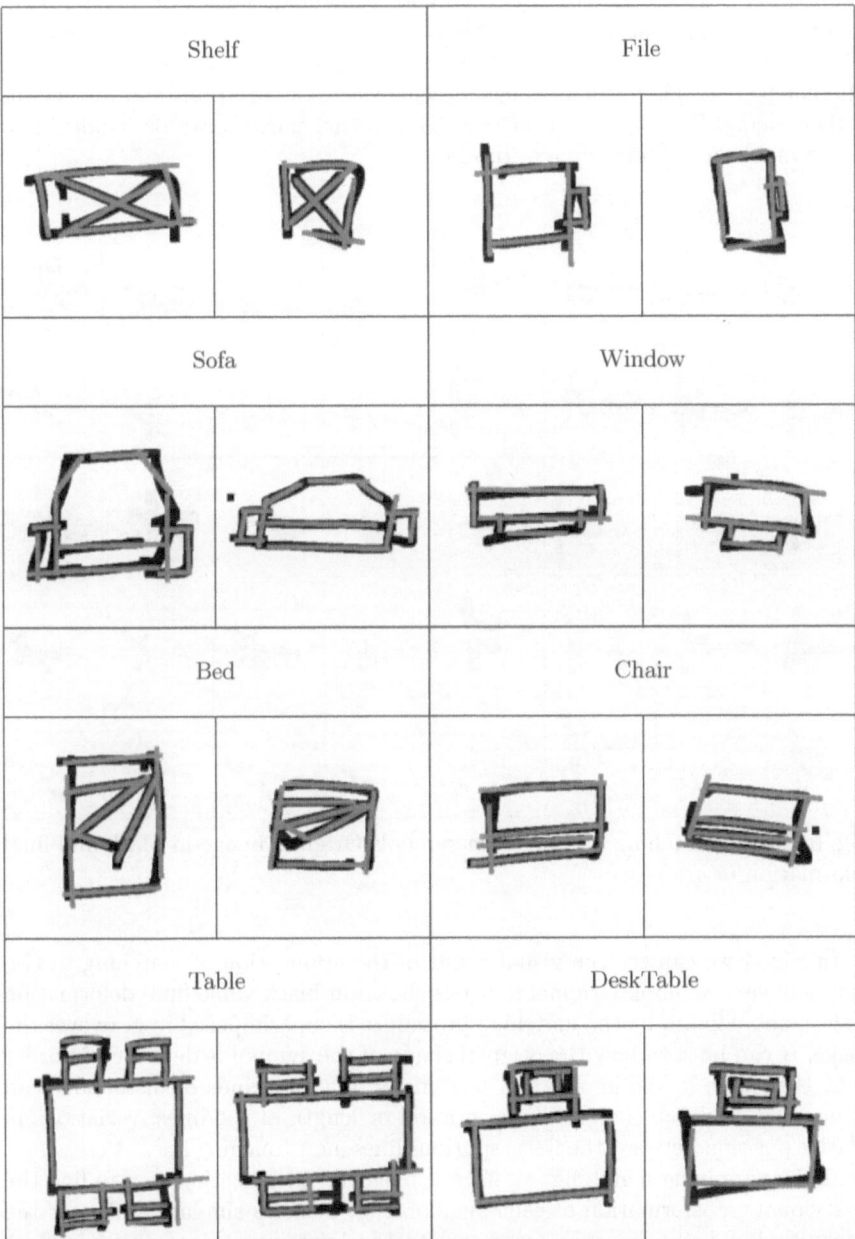

Fig. 4. Visual matching of two images of each symbol. Original image in black and final deformation in gray

have focused on the problem of being able to recognize isolated symbols. We assume that symbols have been located and segmented. Thus, our method relies on a previous segmentation step. This is an issue to be further studied and developed. We have worked with a set of symbols drawn with no constraints by ten different people. These symbols have a wide range of variations and distortions in their shape. Results show that most of the deformations can be handled and that symbols are accurately recognized.

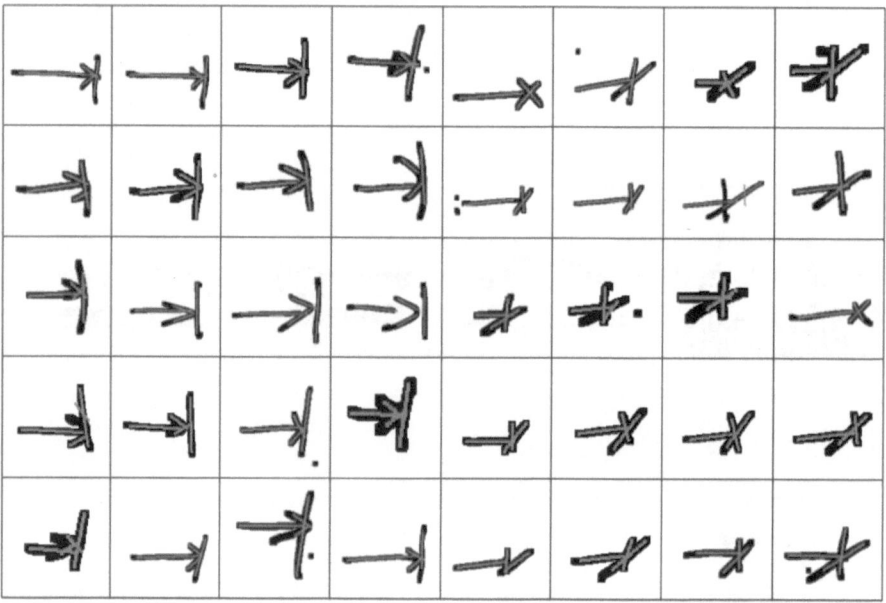

Fig. 5. Visual matching of dimension symbols.Original image in black and final deformation in gray

In Fig. 4 we can see the visual result of the application of matching to two images of each symbol. Original image is shown in black while final deformation of the symbol found by the matching procedure is superimposed in gray over the image. It can be seen how the original shape of the symbol is deformed in order to fit the shape in the image, and how many different kinds of distortions can be handled, such as: changes in orientation or length of the lines, variations in relative position between the lines, spurious lines, non-touching lines at crossings, etc. Before applying matching, we have applied the initialization step to find the best global transformation of each symbol. Fig. 5 shows similar results for the recognition of dimension symbols in architectural drawings. Once again, in most cases, the ideal shape of the symbol is deformed to fit the input image. Only in some few cases, symbol cannot be deformed to adjust it to the input image. These errors can be due to a bad initialization of the symbol and the algorithm or to excessive distortions in the image.

Visual matching is an indicator of the goodness of the fit between the image and the symbol. However, the identification of an image with a symbol is done, as stated in section 2, by analyzing the minimum value of energy after the matching procedure. The graphic in Fig. 6 shows the final energy value found by the matching procedure after comparing 50 images of symbol *sofa* with each of the eight symbols taken into account. The wider line corresponds to values of matching each image with the symbol *sofa*, while thinner lines show the values of matching with the other symbols. It can be seen how, in almost all cases, energy of matching with symbol *sofa* corresponds to the minimum value. The graphic also illustrates that when the energy of matching with symbol *sofa* is too high (due to errors of matching), the image can be confused with some other symbol with lower energy.

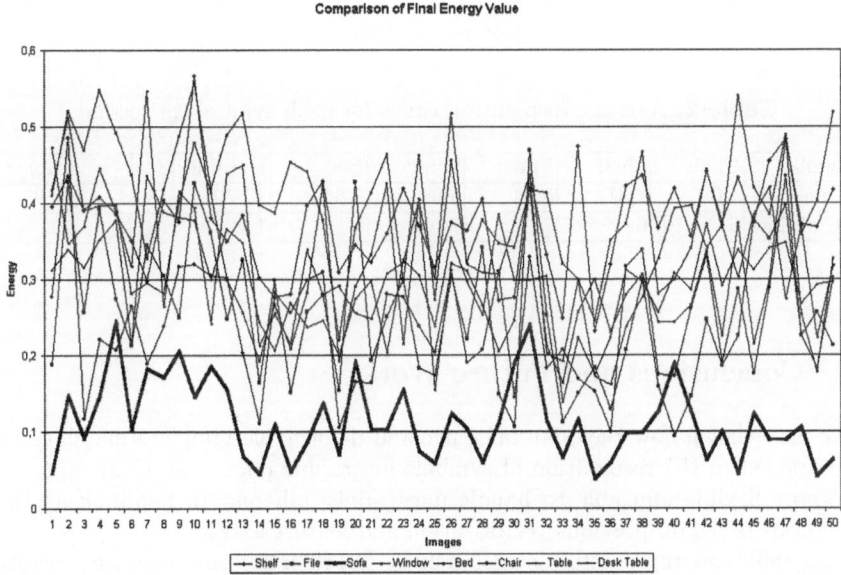

Fig. 6. Comparison of energy for matching of 50 images of a *sofa* with all symbols. The widest line is energy for matching with symbol *sofa*

Table 1 shows the recognition rates achieved with the application of this criterion. We have matched 50 images of each symbol with the model of each of eight symbols, applying first the initialization step and we have identified each image with the symbol with lower minimum energy. The table shows, for each symbol, the percentage of images correctly classified. We have got 85.25% of average accuracy for all symbols. We can see how, in some symbols, as in symbol *window*, the recognition rate is much lower. This fact is due to the confusion of this symbol with two other similar symbols: symbol *file* and symbol *chair*. Confusions are due to errors in matching (bad initialization or excessive distortion) and to the ability of confused symbols (*file* and *chair*) to deform yielding lower energy values.

Finally, Table 2 illustrates the computation time of the algorithm. For each symbol, it shows the average time (in seconds) of matching an image with the symbol. We can see how the complexity is approximately linear with the number of lines in the symbol.

Table 1. Recognition rates for 50 images of each symbol

Shelf	File	Sofa	Window	Bed	Chair	Table	D.Table	**Average**
88%	88%	92%	68%	74%	88%	92%	92%	**85.25%**

Table 2. Average recognition times for each symbol (in seconds)

Symbol	Chair	Shelf	File	Window	Bed	D.Table	Sofa	Table
Time	5,62	7,31	6,04	6,64	9,84	10,79	16,34	28,93
N. of lines	6	6	7	7	8	11	13	20

6   Conclusions and Future Work

We have shown how Bayesian inference and deformable template matching can be applied to the recognition of symbols in graphic documents. This approach is more flexible and able to handle uncertainty inherent to handwriting than methods based on previous vectorization and feature extraction.

Symbols are represented as a set of lines, and their deformations are generated by geometric transformations of these lines which yields very natural distortions, close to those produced by handwriting. Bayesian formulation of matching over the binary image allows to derive an energy function, whose minimization gives the equilibrium point between low deformation and maximum fit. This minimization is not simple. We have employed a simulated annealing algorithm with a previous initialization step to facilitate convergence. The initialization step finds the best global orientation and scaling of the symbol, based on distance between lines of the symbol and lines of the image. Simulated annealing is a random algorithm, so that convergence is not always guaranteed to be stable through successive runs of the algorithm. The complexity of the algorithm is linear with the number of lines in the symbol, although computation time is high.

Our goal was mainly to show the feasibility of bayesian inference and deformable template matching to hand-drawn symbol recognition without taking into account computational issues. However, there are some relevant points to be further studied in order to be able to apply this method to real applications: first, segmentation of symbols in the drawing should be solved in order to locate candidate areas where applying the recognition. Secondly, we are investigating other ways to define internal and external energy yielding an energy function easier to minimize. In this way, we could reduce computation time and we could get more stable convergence. Thirdly, the response of the algorithm of the scalability problem should always be tested with a wider set of symbols and images. Finally, we have assumed independence in the deformations applied to each line; however this assumption is not always true, specially with complex symbols. More accurate representation of prior information about deformations and their associated cost would also allow to improve recognition rates. Generalization to other types of primitives other than straight lines should also be considered.

References

1. K. W. Cheung and D. Y. Yeung. A bayesian framework for deformable pattern recognition with application to handwritten character recognition. *IEEE Transactions on Pattern Analysis and Machine Intelligence*, 20(12):1382–1388, Desember 1998. 193

2. A. K. Chhabra. Graphic symbol recognition: An overview. In K. Tombre and A. K. Chhabra, editors, *Graphics Recognition: Algorithms and Systems*, pages 68–79. Springer Verlag, Berlin, 1998. 193

3. A. H. Habacha. Structural recognition of disturbed symbols using discrete relaxation. In *Proceedings of 1st. International Conference on Document Analysis and Recognition*, pages 170–178, Sep-Oct 1991. Saint Malo, France. 193

4. A. K. Jain, Y. Zhong, and M. P. Dubuisson-Jolly. Deformable template models: A review. *Signal Processing*, 71:109–129, 1998. 193

5. A. K. Jain and D. Zongker. Representation and recognition of handwritten digits using deformable templates. *IEEE Transactions on Pattern Analysis and Machine Intelligence*, 19(12):1386–1391, Desember 1997. 193

6. P. Kuner and B. Ueberreiter. Knowledge-based pattern recognition in disturbed line images using graph theory, optimization and predicate calculus. In *Proceedings of 8th. International Conference on Pattern Recognition*, pages 240–243, October 1986. Paris, France. 193

7. P. J. M. Van Laarhoven and E. H. Aarts. *Simulated Annealing: Theory and Applications*. Kluwer Academic Publishers, 1989. 198

8. S. Lee. Recognizing hand-written electrical circuit symbols with attributed graph matching. In H. S. Baird, H. Bunke, and K. Yamamoto, editors, *Structured Document Analysis*, pages 340–358. Springer Verlag, Berlin, 1992. 193

9. J. Lladós, J. López-Krahe, and E. Martí. A system to understand hand-drawn floor plans using subgraph isomorphism and Hough transform. *Machine Vision and Applications*, 10(3):150–158, 1997. 193

10. G. J. MacLachlan and T. Krishnan. *The EM algorithm and extensions*. John Wiley and Sons, Inc., 1997. 201

11. B. T. Messmer and H. Bunke. Automatic learning and recognition of graphical symbols in engineering drawings. In R. Kasturi and K. Tombre, editors, *Graphics Recognition: Methods and Applications, Selected Papers from First International Workshop on Graphics Recognition, 1995*, pages 123–134. Springer, Berlin, 1996. Volume 1072 of Lecture Notes in Computer Science. 193

12. M. Revow, C. K. I. Williams, and G. Hinton. Using generative models for hand-written digit recognition. *IEEE Transactions on Pattern Analysis and Machine Intelligence*, 18(6):592–606, June 1996. 193

13. K. Tombre. Graphics recognition - general context and challenges. *Pattern Recognition Letters*, 16(9):883–891, 1995. 193

14. E. Valveny and E. Martí. Application of deformable template matching to symbol recognition in hand-written architectural drawings. In *Fifth IAPR International Conference on Document Analysis and Recognition ICDAR'99*, pages 483–486, Bangalore, India, September 1999. 194

A Symbol Classifier Able to Reject Wrong Shapes for Document Recognition Systems

Éric Anquetil, Bertrand Coüasnon, and Frédéric Dambreville

IRISA / INSA-Département Informatique
20, Avenue des buttes de Coësmes - CS 14315, F-35043 Rennes Cedex, France
couasnon@irisa.fr

Abstract. We propose in this paper a new framework to develop a transparent classifier able to deal with reject notions. The generated classifier can be characterized by a strong reliability without loosing good properties in generalization. We show on a musical scores recognition system that this classifier is very well suited to develop a complete document recognition system. Indeed this classifier allows them firstly to extract known symbols in a document (text for example) and secondly to validate segmentation hypotheses. Tests had been successfully performed on musical and digit symbols databases.

Keywords: Document Recognition, Symbol Recognition, Musical Score, Classification, Genetic Algorithm, Radial Basis Function, Neural Networks, Reliability.

1 Introduction

In structured document analysis and especially in graphics recognition systems it is really important to recognize well all the symbols found in those documents. Symbol recognition is usually considered as the heart of a document recognition system [5]. We present in this paper a neural network symbol classifier designed with properties needed for a real interaction with a complete document recognition system.

Indeed, a first classical way of using classifiers consists in presenting only shapes that belong to known classes.

However, in a complete document recognition system it is necessary to extract and identify shapes of known classes from a large dataflow including wrong shapes coming from segmentation problems, noises... Therefore we propose to develop a second kind of classifier able to deal with wrong shapes by implementing a reliable notion of reject.

Moreover, it is possible to specialize this kind of classifier to different groups of classes (letters, digits...) and then to chain them to produce a robust and global identification (Fig. 1). Based on this principle we will present the integration of this second kind of classifier into a complete musical score recognition system.

This system is general enough to point out properties needed by a classifier in a document recognition system. We will first describe the architecture of the

Atul K. Chhabra and D. Dori (Eds.): GREC'99, LNCS 1941, pp. 209–218, 2000.

musical score recognition system we develop. We then explain how to design a classifier able to reject all shapes different from the classes learned before. We end by experimental results on musical and digit symbols databases.

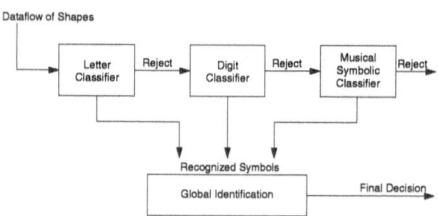

Fig. 1. Using classifiers in a chained way

2   Integration of a Classifier in a Musical Score Recognition System

In the context of musical score recognition, we can consider a distinct between graphic symbols [6]:

- the *symbolics* can be considered as characters as they have a quite ratio stable shape at least on a same document. They could be printed by a "wood type" and contrary to characters in most cases, they do not need to be represented by a single connected component (*e.g.* accidentals, noteheads, some logos, arrowheads...). We also include of course all characters in the *symbolics*;
- the *constructed* are composed of primitives (mostly line segments and some symbolics) plus a set of assembly rules on those primitives. These graphics symbols can have really different shapes on a same document and their size or ratio can contain information (*e.g.* beamed notes, square root...).

A document recognition system needs among other things to firstly be able to extract symbolics from the rest of the document (like text extraction in engineering drawings). This can be done if we can present to the symbolic classifier all the connected components of the document without any selection (Fig. 2). The symbolic classifier must then be able to recognize the components corresponding to a learned class and reject the others.

Secondly it needs to include syntactic or semantic level in the segmentation phase as symbolics are usually badly segmented. They can touch other symbolics or other graphical objects (Fig. 3a). They can also be over-segmented (Fig. 3b). If the system is firstly able to bring context at the segmentation level and secondly able to make re-segmentation hypotheses, it is necessary to have a tool to validate those hypotheses. This validation can be done by the symbolic classifier if it can recognize only well segmented symbolics.

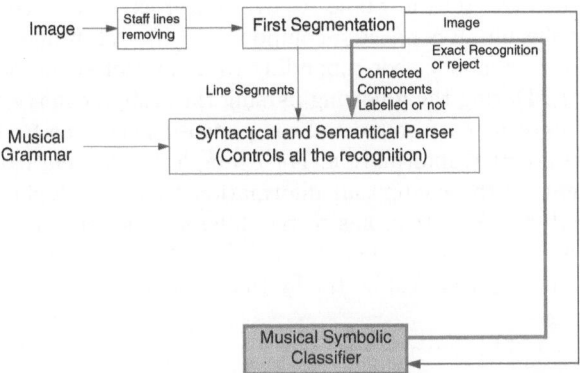

Fig. 2. Using a classifier in a musical score recognition system (first use)

Therefore we propose a symbolic classifier able to reject all shapes different from the classes it learned before. Moreover this classifier has good generalization properties on learned classes.

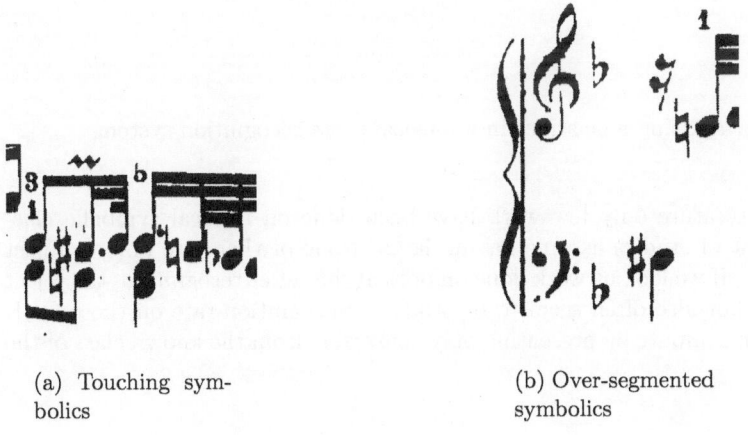

(a) Touching sym-
bolics

(b) Over-segmented
symbolics

Fig. 3. Examples of segmentation problems

To show how this kind of classifier can be included in a document recognition system, we present shortly an application in a musical scores recognition system we develop. This system uses a grammar to formalize the musical knowledge on full scores with polyphonic staves [7]. This grammatical formalism allows to define firstly the needed rules for the constructed recognition and secondly the syntactic and some semantic context on music. The parser produced from the grammar can control the whole recognition process. It starts by calling the symbolic classifier on all connected components (after staff lines removing [12]) to recognize only symbolics corresponding to a connected component well segmented (Fig. 4). During the following parsing the system can try new segmentation on set of unrecognized connected components by coming back to the image level with a contextual information. For example the system can go back in a sub-image knowing the contextual information that it is looking for an accidental (sharp, flat...). It then has to try different segmentation adapted to an accidental and validate one of them with the symbolic classifier (Fig. 4). If none are validated another rule will be try by the parser.

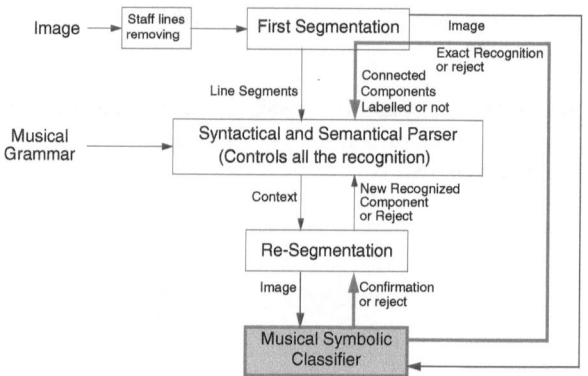

Fig. 4. Using a classifier in a musical score recognition system

In the literature only few work have been done on musical symbolic classifier as most of studies assume having it [2]. None of them are able to reject wrong shape. If we look at work done on optical character recognition, the reject ability does not also often seem to be studied. Recognition rate on those OCR systems were compute by presenting only characters from the known class of the classifier [13].

3   A Framework to Design Reliable Classifier

To develop a classifier with strong reliability, we propose to generate a fully understandable classifier based on Radial Basis Function (RBF) networks [4,9]. Contrary to classical neural networks such as multilayer perceptron that makes after the learning phase a black box system, the RBF neural networks can keep fully understandable depending on the learning strategies.

Basically RBF neural network is structured with three layers. The first layer is composed of input nodes whose number corresponds to the feature space dimension (input vector). The second layer is the hidden layer, composed of units connected directly to all the input nodes. The activation of these hidden units is formalized by radial basis functions. The output layer consists in linear units (one for each classes) fully connected by weighted links to the hidden units.

The proposed framework corresponds to a three level learning strategy to obtain a transparent classifier able to deal with reject notion.

Firstly, we propose to use a hybrid learning process [11] based on two stages to estimate all the parameters of the RBF network. The aim of the first stage is to estimate the hidden units. We propose to use fuzzy clustering [3] to determine in a robust manner the most pertinent prototypes (location and activation fields of the RBF) for each class. As in our previous works [1] we use possibilistic clustering [10] to generate these fuzzy prototypes which represent intrinsically each cluster (Fig. 5). Union of these resulting prototypes composes the hidden layer. Consequently, each unit corresponds to a pertinent area in the chosen feature space to characterize each class of shape to model. The second stage consists in a classical supervised learning to estimate the linear weights of the output layer.

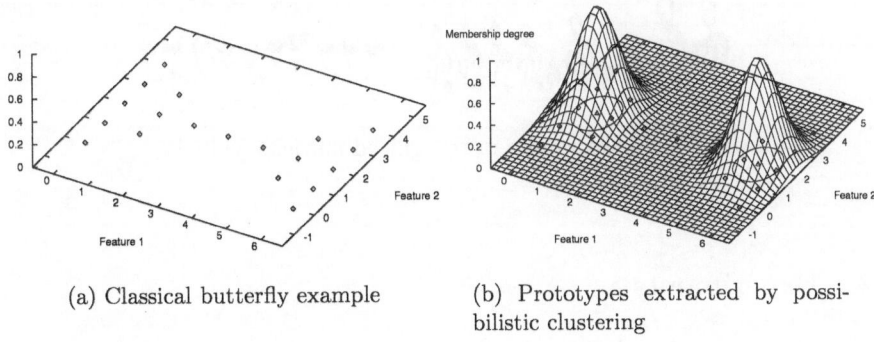

(a) Classical butterfly example   (b) Prototypes extracted by possibilistic clustering

Fig. 5. Example of possibilistic clustering

The second learning level is based on the understandable aspect of the resulting RBF neural network. It consists of estimating, for each hidden unit, the hard limit of their receptive fields to obtain the reliable reject of the wrong shapes that must not be associated with the learning classes. To estimate automatically the optimal activation limit of each hidden unit, we use a learning database composed on many different shapes supposed to be rejected. It is interesting to note, that a second type of reject, corresponding to the notion of confusion, can also be estimated by considering the too close proximity of the best activated units of the output layer.

The last learning level of the proposed framework generates an automatic selection of the best feature space to design the classifier. To obtain a robust and optimal classification, features used to characterize the shapes are very important. Moreover, the feature choice depends on the type of classifier you wanted to generate: reliable, optimal performances, good reject of some special shapes...

To overcome this well-known difficult problem, we propose to use a genetic algorithm [8]. Based on the principle of genetic algorithm, we can optimize efficiently the selection of a subset of features (given an *a priori* feature set) according to the specific type of classifier we wanted to obtain. The type of classification can be quite easily formalized by the right identification of the fitness function of the genetic algorithm.

This framework allows to design a reliable classifier with a complete control of each steps of the building process : RBF neural networks to generate transparent classifier to deal with reject notion; fuzzy clustering for a robust learning phase and genetic algorithms for feature selection.

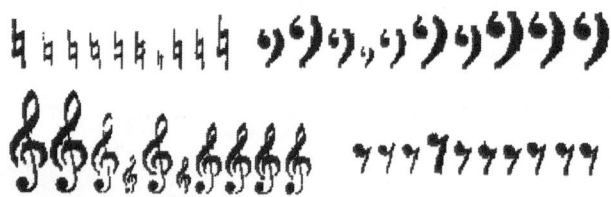

Fig. 6. Examples of recognized musical symbols

4   Experiments

4.1   Computational Complexity

The global learning phase is controlled by a genetic algorithm where each individual corresponds to a subset of features. To evaluate the fitness of all the individuals in the population, it is necessary to generate the corresponding classifier; that means to proceed for each individual the two basic learning phases described before. The fitness of each individual is based on the generalization performances and the reliability of the corresponding classifier. This operation is repeated at each reproduction cycle of the genetic algorithm. Consequently according to the number of individuals in the population (around fifteen in our experiments) and to the size of the data bases used for the basic learning, this global learning phase can be time expensive. Considering our experiments, this global leaning phase can take around three computational days with a classical computer.

Even if the global learning phase is time expensive, it is important to notice that after this learning phase we obtain an optimized classifier with a well defined feature space according to the fixed criterions of reliability and performance. Moreover, the resulting classifier is able to recognize a symbol as fast as a basic RBF network.

2 1 5 5 4 2 7 7 4 1 8 0 9

Fig. 7. Examples of recognized digits

4.2   Experimental Results

These experimental results focus on classifier reliability obtains with the proposed approach. To our knowledge, few experimental results have been published on this particular aspect. In our further works, we will report more global comparisons with other known classifiers according to performance aspect.

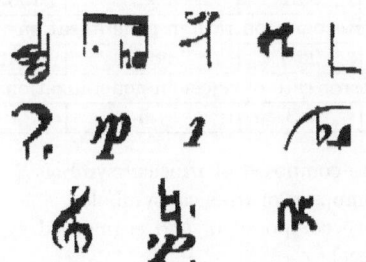

Fig. 8. Some examples of rejected images

To validate the proposed framework that design classifier adapted to document recognition, we report different experimental results obtain on musical and digit symbol databases respectively composed of 13 and 10 different classes. The first database contains 2,100 musical symbols (Fig. 6) and the second 12,000 digit symbols (Fig. 7). The digit symbol database mixes Times and Courier font digits. Moreover we have used two other different databases composed of shapes to reject. The first one contains 1,800 bad segmented musical symbols and various shapes (Fig. 8) and the second one 2,200 printed letters (Fig. 9).

Each of these four databases has been separated in two distinct parts. The first part is used for the learning process and the second part to evaluate the

JTSÎPQBÙ)CJ

Fig. 9. Examples of letters rejected by the digit classifier

generalization performances and the reliability of the classifier considering the reject notion.

For each classification problem (musical and digit symbol), two types of classifier have been generated using the proposed framework. The first one is characterized with a strong constraint of reliability (0% error) and the other one with a tolerance of 1% error.

All reported results (tables 1 & 2) show the good performances of all classifiers designed with the proposed framework.

Table 1. Recognition rates on musical symbols

	Reliability imposed to classifiers (reject sensibility)		Classifier without reject
	0% err L_{bR}	≈ 1% err L_{bR}	
Recognition rate on learning database			
L_m	99.2	99.8	100.0
Recognition rate in generalization			
T_m	96.4	98.8	99.6
Error rate of reject in generalization			
T_{bR}	0.3	1.5	-

L_m: **L**earning database composed of **m**usical symbols

T_m: **T**est database composed of **m**usical symbols

L_{bR}: **L**earning database composed of **b**ad segmented symbols (used to estimate thresholds of **R**eject)

T_{bR}: **T**est database composed of **b**ad segmented symbols (used to evaluate **R**eject performances)

We can notice a good stability of performances in generalization for recognition rates as well as for reject capacity. Moreover table 2 illustrates reject reliability on symbols quite similar (letters for digits, Fig. 9) even if they have not been integrated before in the learning phase.

Finally it is important to notice how well we managed to specialize the classifier comportment according to the reliability we wanted to impose. For instance we can obtain a very strong reliable classifier with 0% of reject error (table 2, columns 1 & 2) or we can focus on an even better generalization rate (99.97%) by authorizing a quite little reject error (1.8%).

Table 2. Recognition rates on digit symbols

	Reliability imposed to classifiers (reject sensibility)				Classifier without reject
	0% err L_{bR}	0% err L_{lR}	≈ 1% err L_{bR}	≈ 1% err L_{lR}	
Recognition rate on learning database					
L_d	99.89	100	100	100	100
Recognition rate in generalization					
T_d	99.85	99.95	99.96	99.97	100
Error rate of reject in generalization					
T_{bR}	0	0	0.4	0	-
T_{lR}	0	0	27.3	1.8	-

L_d: Learning database composed of digit symbols
T_d: Test database composed of digit symbols
L_{bR}: Learning database composed of bad segmented symbols (used to estimate thresholds of Reject (idem table 1))
L_{lR}: Learning database composed of printed letter to estimate thresholds of Reject
T_{bR}: Test database composed of bad segmented symbols (used to evaluate Reject performances)
T_{lR}: Test database composed of printed letter (used to evaluate Reject performances of classifier on printed letter shapes)

5   Conclusion

We proposed in this paper a complete framework to design RBF neural network classifier able to deal with the reject notion. We have underlined that the notion of classifier reliability constitutes an important point to overcome the segmentation problem in the conception of a document recognition system. Based on the optimization process of a genetic algorithm and on the fully understandable structure of the RBF neural networks, the proposed framework permits to control the classifier reliability (reject sensibility). The first experimental results have been reported and show the good performances of the designing classifiers on a significant musical and digit symbol databases.

In our further works, we will report the development of a complete musical document recognition system integrating the presented musical symbol classifier. We will also focus our work on using the reliable classifier we presented in a chained way to easily build global classifiers.

References

1. E. Anquetil and G. Lorette. Automatic generation of hierarchical fuzzy classification systems based on explicit fuzzy rules deduced from possibilistic clustering: Application to on-line handwritten character recognition. In *Information Processing and Management of Uncertainty in Knowledge-Based Systems (IPMU96)*, pages 259–264, 1996. 213

2. D. Bainbridge and N. P. Carter. Automatic reading of music notation. In P. S. P. Wang H. Bunke, editor, *Handbook of Character Recognition and Document Image Analysis*, pages 583–603. World Scientific, 1997. 212

3. J. C. Bezdek. *Pattern Recognition with Fuzzy Objective Function Algorithms*. Plenum Press, New York, 1981. 213

4. C. M. Bishop. *Neural networks for pattern recognition*. Oxford University Press Inc., 1995. 212

5. A. K. Chhabra. Graphic symbol recognition: An overview. In K. Tombre and A. K. Chhabra, editors, *Graphics Recognition, Algorithms and Systems*, number 1389 in LNCS. Springer, 1998. 209

6. B. Coüasnon and J. Camillerapp. Using grammars to segment and recognize music scores. In L. Spitz and A. Dengel, editors, *Document Analysis Systems*. World Scientific, 1995. 210

7. B. Coüasnon and J. Camillerapp. A way to separate knowledge from program in structured document analysis: application to optical music recognition. In *ICDAR, International Conference on Document Analysis and Recognition*, volume 2, pages 1092–1097, Montréal, Canada, August 1995. 211

8. David E. Goldberg. *Genetic algorithms in search, optimization and machine learning*. Addison-Wesley, 1989. 214

9. Simon Haykin. *Neural Networks, a comprehensive foundation*. Prentice Hall, 1997. 212

10. R. Krishnapuram. Generation of membership functions via possibilistic clustering. In *IEEE World congress on computational intelligence*, pages 902–908, 1994. 213

11. R. P. Lippmann. Pattern classification using neural networks. *IEEE Communications Magazine*, 27:47–64, 1989. 213

12. V. Poulain d´Andecy, J. Camillerapp, and I. Leplumey. Kalman filtering for segment detection: application to music scores analysis. In *ICPR, 12th International Conference on Pattern Recognition (IAPR)*, volume 1, pages 301–305, Jrusalem, Israel, October 1994. 212

13. Ching Y. Suen Shunji Mori and Kazuhiko Yamamoto. Historical review of ocr research and development. *Proceedings of the IEEE*, 80(7), July 1992. 212

A Robust Shape Decomposition Method

L. P. Cordella[1], C. De Stefano[2], and M. Frucci[3]

[1] Dipartimento di Informatica e Sistemistica, Università di Napoli "Federico II"
Via Claudio 21, 80125 Napoli, Italy
cordel@unina.it
[2] Facoltà di Ingegneria, Università del Sannio
Piazza Roma, 82100 Benevento, Italy
cladeste@unina.it
[3] Istituto di Cibernetica, CNR, Arco Felice
Via Toiano 6, 80072 Arco Felice, Napoli, Italy
mfr@imagm.cib.na.cnr.it

Abstract. A shape decomposition method for non-elongated figures is proposed. The method allows to obtain structural descriptions that are widely invariant with respect to non-significant shape changes occurring in rotated or noisy instances of a same figure. The detection of the significant parts composing a figure is based on a suitable definition of shape primitives and is performed by exploiting the information associated to the skeleton pixels. In this process the regions having higher perceptive relevance are first identified and extracted from the image. Then, starting from this initial decomposition, the remaining parts of the figure are detected together with the structural relations among them. The proposed decomposition scheme is particularly appropriate for building structural descriptions in terms of attributed relational graphs. The experimental results obtained by using a large set of figures confirmed the robustness of the proposed approach and the stability of the achievable decompositions.

1 Introduction

The problem of describing the shape of an object for its recognition is of paramount importance in computer vision and has received considerable attention in the last decades. Substantial work has been spent on problems concerning the choice of the shape properties to be considered for description and the way to compute them. Classifying objects according to their shape, in fact, requires that objects are described in terms of suitable shape features and then grouped into classes through a supervised or unsupervised classification process.

Samples to be considered similar for the purposes of the considered application should be characterized by suitable uniformity properties in such a way to allow assigning all of them to the same class. At the same time, the properties used should not allow to attribute to the same class samples that should be considered dissimilar.

Atul K. Chhabra and D. Dori (Eds.): GREC'99, LNCS 1941, pp. 219-227, 2000.

This represents one of the main difficulties in many practical recognition problems in which the large shape variability existing among the samples belonging to the same class requires an accurate balance between the two opposite requirements implied by any description process: *generalization* and *specialization*. Pushing too much towards generalization may increase the interclass confusion, while preserving specialization too severely may lead to descriptions unable to manage the shape variability exiting within a same class.

Another significant difficulty encountered in many real applications derives from the fact that the objects to be recognized may appear rotated or affected by a considerable and unpredictable amount of noise. This motivates the need for qualitative as well as quantitative shape description methods that allow to detect the main object components and the structural relations between them: these, in fact, should remain largely invariant under the above changes.

The approaches proposed in the literature for structural shape representation can be divided into two broad categories: *region based* and *boundary based* approaches. The first group includes methods emphasizing figure properties such as symmetry and thickness or features such as number of holes and protrusions. Methods emphasizing salient properties of the figure boundary, such as curvature extrema and inflection points, belong to the second group. Significant examples of region based representations include Blum's Symmetric Axis Transform [1,7] and the related Smoothed Local Symmetries [2]. Well-known methods belonging to the second group include polygonal approximation of a figure contour and representations based on contour segments bounded by minima of curvature [3,4]. However, as it has been discussed in [5], the above approaches are neither mutually exclusive nor unique. In fact it may be very helpful to capture both boundary and region based information in order to improve the effectiveness of a shape description technique [10].

The method presented in this paper represents a contribution in this direction and it has been devised for the shape description of two-dimensional non-elongated figures, i.e. of figures in which the thickness of the component parts plays an important role in describing their shape. We propose a structural description method in which the detection of the significant parts making up a figure is performed by adopting a suitable definition of shape primitives and by exploiting the information associated to the skeleton pixels. In principle the method could be used with a large class of skeletonization algorithms, but the quality of the results may be heavily affected by the properties of the skeleton considered. The skeleton we considered [6] is computed giving special emphasis to the contour propagation information and it exhibits large stability in presence of border noise and invariance under rotation. These features are fundamental to obtain effective results.

The rationale behind our approach is that the information held by the skeleton pixels can be used for detecting the shape primitive composing a figure and for classifying them according to their perceptive relevance. We defined a hierarchical shape decomposition process in which the primitives corresponding to regions having higher perceptive relevance are first identified and extracted from the image. Then, starting from this initial decomposition, the remaining parts of the figure are detected together with the structural relations among them. More specifically, we have considered four types of shape primitives that represent regions differing either for properties such as shape regularity, thickness variation, elongation, etc., or for the way in which they are connected to neighboring regions. The choice of such primitives and the use of a hierarchical process for their detection lead to figure decompositions that are substantially invariant with respect to shape variations existing among figure samples belonging to a same class or due to border noise and rotation. The proposed decomposition scheme is particularly appropriate for building structural descriptions in terms of attributed relational graphs.

The paper is organized as follows: in section 2 the adopted skeletonization algorithm is briefly described, while in section 3, the definition of the primitives and the criteria used to obtain figure decomposition are outlined. Finally, the experimental results are discussed in section 4.

2   The Skeleton

The skeleton is an appealing figure representation that, in the past decades, has received far more attention than any other tool for shape description. The points forming the skeleton can be defined in a number of ways. Some of them can be brought back to the definition given by Blum [1,7], according to which the skeleton of a figure is made of the points which are centers of the maximal discs inscribed in the figure; each point can be labeled with the value of the radius of the associated maximal disc. Such label gives the distance of the point from the background and is representative of the local figure thickness. An alternative point of view is that of considering the boundary of the figure as the source of a grassfire propagating isotropically and with uniform velocity towards the interior. The skeleton points coincide with the quenching points, i.e., with the points where different fire fronts meet. In this case, each quenching point can be labeled with the time at which it is reached by the fire fronts.

Over the years, since this definition was given, various algorithms have been proposed in the literature to compute the skeleton (S) in the digital plane . Although the structure of the skeleton and its properties depend on the adopted algorithm, some of these are considered especially desirable. In particular, S should be "centrally" located within the figure; it should have the same number of components and form the same number of holes of the figure. Moreover, it has to be a linear structure, i.e., the union of simple arcs and curves; its pixels should be labeled with their distance from the background; the points labeled with the largest distance values should be included in S. However, its major drawback is its sensitivity to rotation and to noise in the figure boundary which can give rise to instability of the skeleton structure (e.g., appearance or disappearance of skeleton branches and distortions of existing branches). This is basically due to two factors: the use of non-Euclidean metric in the computation of the distance labels and the Blum's skeleton definition, according to which the skeleton pixels are the centers of the maximal discs. A pixel p is a center of a maximal disc, only if it does not belong to a minimal path between a neighbor of p and the background. According to this definition, to decide if p is a skeleton pixel, it is sufficient an analysis of the distance labels associated to p and to its neighbors. Even if small perturbations of the boundary due to border noise or to figure rotation imply small variations of distance labels, this may affect the process of skeleton pixel selection in a significant way. To eliminate both spurious and not significant branches, a pruning process can be performed. However this process, generally based on the analysis of the trend of the distance labels associated to the branch pixels, may be not devoid of side effects.

To tackle these deficiencies, we have adopted an original skeletonization algorithm that uses a rather different approach for selecting the skeletal pixels [6,8]. To compute the distance labels of the figure pixels, a (d1,d2)-weighted distance [9], i.e. an approximation of the Euclidean metric, is chosen. The algorithm has been developed by considering a grassfire transform in which the selection of the skeleton pixels is achieved by combining boundary and region information. Such a transform associates to a pixel p of the input figure its distance label together with information about intensity and direction of the fire fronts that reach p starting from each of its neighbors belonging to the current boundary. The intensity of each front originated by a neighbor q of p is given by the distance label associated to q, while its direction is given by the position of q with respect to p. Note that the boundary information associated to p is represented by intensity and direction of propagation of the fire fronts hitting p, while region information is encoded into the distance label associated to p.

Boundary information is used to perform a look-ahead operation which first verifies the existence of directions along which the fire front can further propagate starting from p, i.e. directions such that a minimal path between a neighbor q of p and the background pass through p. For any of such directions it is then checked whether q is more internal than p. If no such directions can be detected or no neighbors of p in the detected directions are more internal than p, then the different fire fronts hitting p collide frontally and p is considered a quenching pixel. This means that the boundary information attached to p indicates that at least two opposite boundary sides collapse in p (e.g., see Fig. 1a and Fig. 1b). On the contrary, if it exists a direction in which a neighbor q of p is more internal than p, p is assumed to be the origin of one fire front which propagates on q. As it can be simply shown, according to our definition, p can propagate on q even if p does not belong to the minimal path between q and the background. Hence, if p is a propagating pixel, it is not considered a skeleton pixel even if it is the center of a maximal disc. This may happen for example when the fire fronts hitting p have been originated either by a protrusion of the figure boundary (see Fig. 1c) or by an inflection as in presence of a neck (see Fig. 1d). However a propagating pixel will always belong to the skeleton if it is needed to preserve skeleton connectedness.

In conclusion, the main feature of the adopted skeletonization algorithm is that the generation of spurious and not significant branches is better controlled and thus considerably reduced with respect to similar algorithms. This is due to the fact that the attribution of a pixel p to the skeleton is essentially based on relative direction and intensity of the fire fronts hitting in p, while the analysis of the distance labels of the neighbors of p is not a tie for the attribution of p to the skeleton pixels (i.e., centers of maximal discs must not necessarily belong to the skeleton). A further advantage of the method is that the successive pruning process can use boundary information in order to increase its effectiveness.

Hence, the use of a global propagation mechanism allows extracting a skeleton that exhibits, to a large extent, stability in presence of noisy borders and invariance under rotation.

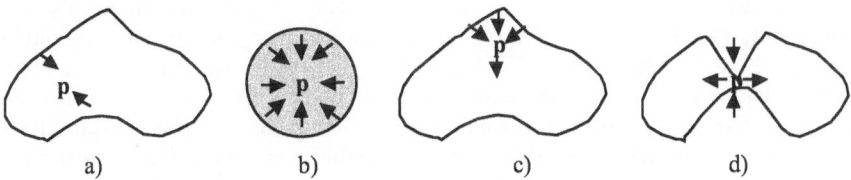

a)   b)   c)   d)

Figure 1. Four types of boundary propagation patterns across a pixel p are shown. The directions of the fire fronts hitting p or starting from p are shown

3   Shape Decomposition

As mentioned above, our method performs figure decomposition in the sense that the significant regions composing a figure are detected and classified according to their perceptive relevance. However, the main purpose of the approach is to achieve decompositions that are insensitive to the variations of the skeleton structure (relative to either pixel labels or skeleton shape) due to border noise or figure rotation. Such variations, although significantly reduced because of the skeletonization technique used, cannot be completely avoided. For this reason we have proposed a hierarchical decomposition process in which the shape primitives corresponding to regions less sensitive to noise (hereafter called *First Class Primitives*) are first detected. The detection of the remaining regions composing the figure (*Second Class Primitives*) is performed by exploiting information relative to both pixel labels and properties of the previously detected primitives.

First Class Primitives (FCP) are obtained by connecting sequences of skeleton pixels having almost equal labels. They share the property of having uniform or at most smoothly varying thickness. In particular, two different types of shape primitives having this property have been defined:

- *type A* - These primitives represent regions that are perceived as the most significant parts composing a figure. A region of this type is either an isolated region or a region that is overlapped to regions having smaller thickness or is connected to other regions by necks.
- *type B* - These primitives correspond to regions that must be overlapped to at least one region with higher thickness. This aspect represents the main distinction between primitives of type A and B. In fact a primitive of type A represents a confluence region of the figure (in which other regions having smaller thickness flow into), while a primitive of type B corresponds to a region that must flow into at least one region with higher thickness.

It is worth noting that, due to skeleton variations, many small pixel sequences having equal labels may be generated and, according to our definition, may be candidate to represent FCP's. As a consequence, in order to detect the actual FCP's, a set of criteria, based on both region elongation and relations with adjacent regions, has been defined. The pixels sequences not selected in the first step of the decomposition process and those discarded by applying the previous criteria, are candidate to represent Second Class Primitives (SCP).

SCP's are characterized by a thickness that changes monotonically and significantly along their main symmetry axis. This property makes such primitives perceptively very different from FCP's because they typically represent elongated parts of larger regions or connections between regions having higher perceptive relevance. Moreover, a further distinction is needed inside this class of primitives, because they are characterized by high shape variability and are highly influenced by noise. Some of them, in fact, might represent *additional* regions of the figure, not essential for its description, since they could appear or disappear in rotated or noisy instances of the same figure. A specific set of criteria, based on both relative elongation and size, has been defined for evaluating their reliability. On the basis of such criteria, two different types of shape primitives belonging to this class have been defined: primitives having a high reliability will be called of *type C*, less reliable ones will be called of *type D*.

Finally, in order to increase the effectiveness of the decomposition method, a reconstruction process of the regions belonging to the First Class is performed. In fact, some of the regions represented by SCP's might be disregarded since largely overlapped to one or more regions previously identified and thus having poor perceptive relevance. As a consequence, only candidate sequences of skeleton pixels not covered by these reconstructed regions are considered as actual occurrences of SCP's.

Let us now describe more formally the different steps in which the decomposition process is organized:

Step 1: Selection of skeleton pixels candidate to represent First Class Primitives
A skeleton pixel p is selected if at least one of the following conditions holds:
– p is a branch point or an end point whose neighbors have distance labels less than p;
– p belongs to a sequence of skeleton pixels whose distance labels vary smoothly.

Step 2: Merging
Sequences of skeleton pixels selected at step 1 are allowed to merge only if the thickness variation is lower then a threshold T_V or the distance between the sequences is lower then a threshold T_D.

Step 3: Unfolding at branch points
In order to unfold branches merging in the same branch point p, a set of criteria based on the distance labels associated to p and to its neighbors has been defined. Such criteria take also into account the information relative to either the trend of the distance labels in the neighborhood of p, or the detection of selected skeleton pixels in the neighborhood of p.

Step 4: Detection of actual occurrences of primitives of type A
If the set of selected skeleton pixels coincides with the whole skeleton, i.e. the figure has an elementary shape, then this set represents a primitive of type A and no further

process is required. Otherwise each sequence of selected pixels, delimited only by sequences of not selected pixels whose distance labels decrease, is confirmed as representative of a region of type A.

Step 5: Detection of actual occurrences of primitives of type B
In this step, any sequence S of selected skeleton pixels not representing primitives of type A, is considered. If S has a length greater than a given threshold T_L then it is confirmed as representative of a region of type B otherwise it is disregarded.

Step 6: Detection of actual occurrences of Second Class Primitives
The pixel sequences not selected in the step 1 and those discarded in the step 5 are candidate to represent SCP's. However, some of these sequences might represent only junctions between different regions not corresponding to meaningful parts of the figure. In order to decide whether such a sequence represents or not a junction, the regions relative to all the FCP's previously identified must be reconstructed. To this aim, it is sufficient to apply a Reverse Distance Transform to the corresponding skeleton pixels: sequences not recovered by the reconstructed regions are considered primitives of the Second Class.

Step 7: Detection of type C and D primitives
Each sequence S of skeleton pixels corresponding to a SCP is analyzed and the difference h between the distance labels associated to the extrema of S is computed, as well as the length l (number of pixels) of S. The sequence S is considered as a primitive of type C if:

$$l > T1 \quad \text{or} \quad T2 < h \leq l \quad \text{where T1 and T2 are given thresholds (with T1 > T2);}$$

otherwise S is labeled as a primitive of type D in order to indicate that the represented region is not essential for the description of the figure.

4   Experimental Results and Discussion

The robustness of the proposed approach and the stability of the achievable decompositions with respect to rotation, noise and shape variations, has been tested on a set of about 1000 not elongated figures. About 100 silhouettes representing natural and artificial shapes, such as animals and mechanical pieces, were considered at several rotation angles and size ratios. Rotation was performed either before or after digitization. In fig. 2 some examples of figures differently rotated and shaped are shown. Figure skeletons overlapped on input bit maps are shown on the left and the relative decompositions are given on the right. Over the tested database, a decomposition error less than 3 % was achieved. Errors were estimated by presenting the results of automatic decomposition to human observers and asking for their agreement.

Note that figure components are represented by only a small number of skeleton pixels. This implies that the union of the component regions does not necessarily coincide with the input figure, and then a perfect figure reconstruction is generally not achieved. However, it has to be outlined that the purpose of the proposed method is that of decomposing a figure in terms of a given set of primitives for the purpose of a successive process of description and recognition. As it is well known, the main feature of any decomposition process is that of allowing descriptions that are as much as possible invariant with respect to not significant shape changes occurring among figure samples belonging to the same class. However, the loss of information can be controlled, so as to guarantee that pixels not recovered by the union of the component regions do not constitute distinctive features of the input figure.

Let us also note that certain regions, like the ones indicated by the arrows in fig. 2a, are classified as primitives of type D. Having fair descriptive power, they could disappear after rotation, as it happens in fig. 2b.

The decomposition scheme is especially suitable to build structural descriptions in terms of attributed relational graphs whose nodes are the component regions and whose arcs represent relations between adjacent regions. Node attributes specify the type of primitive and its reliability when applicable, as well as information about the shape of the represented region. Arc attributes specify spatial relations and type of connection between components. The effectiveness of the above description scheme for figure recognition is still being tested.

References

1.   H. Blum: Biological shape and visual science (part I), Journal of Theoretical Biology, vol. 38, (1973) 205-287.
2.   M. Brady and H. Asada: Smoothed local symmetries and their implementation, International Journal of Robotic Research, 3, 3, (1984).
3.   D. D. Hoffman and W. A. Richards: Parts of recognition, Cognition, vol. 18, (1985) 65-96.
4.   H. Freeman: Boundary encoding and processing, Picture Processing and Psychopictorics, B. S. Lipkin and A. Rosenfeld eds., Academic Press, (1970) 241-263.
5.   K. Siddiqi, B. Kimia: Toward a Shock Grammar for Recognition, Technical Report LEMS-143, Brown University, (1995).
6.   M. Frucci and A. Marcelli: Efficient skeletonization of binary figures through (d1,d2)-erosion and directional information. In C. Arcelli, L.P. Cordella and G. Sanniti di Baja eds.: Aspects of Visual Form Processing, World Scientific, Singapore, (1994) 221-230.
7.   H. Blum: A transformation for extracting new descriptors of shape. In W. Wathen-Dunn ed.: Models for the Perception of Speech and Visual Form, MIT Press, Cambridge, (1967) 362-380.
8.   M. Frucci and A. Marcelli: Parallel skeletonization by directional information, IEEE Proc. Int. Conf. Image Processing, Austin (USA), (1994) 681-685.
9.   G. Borgerfors: Distance transformations in digital images, CVGIP, vol. 34, (1986) 344-371.
10. H. Rom and G. Medioni: Hierarchical decomposition and axial shape description, IEEE trans. PAMI, vol.15, no. 10, (1993) 973-981.

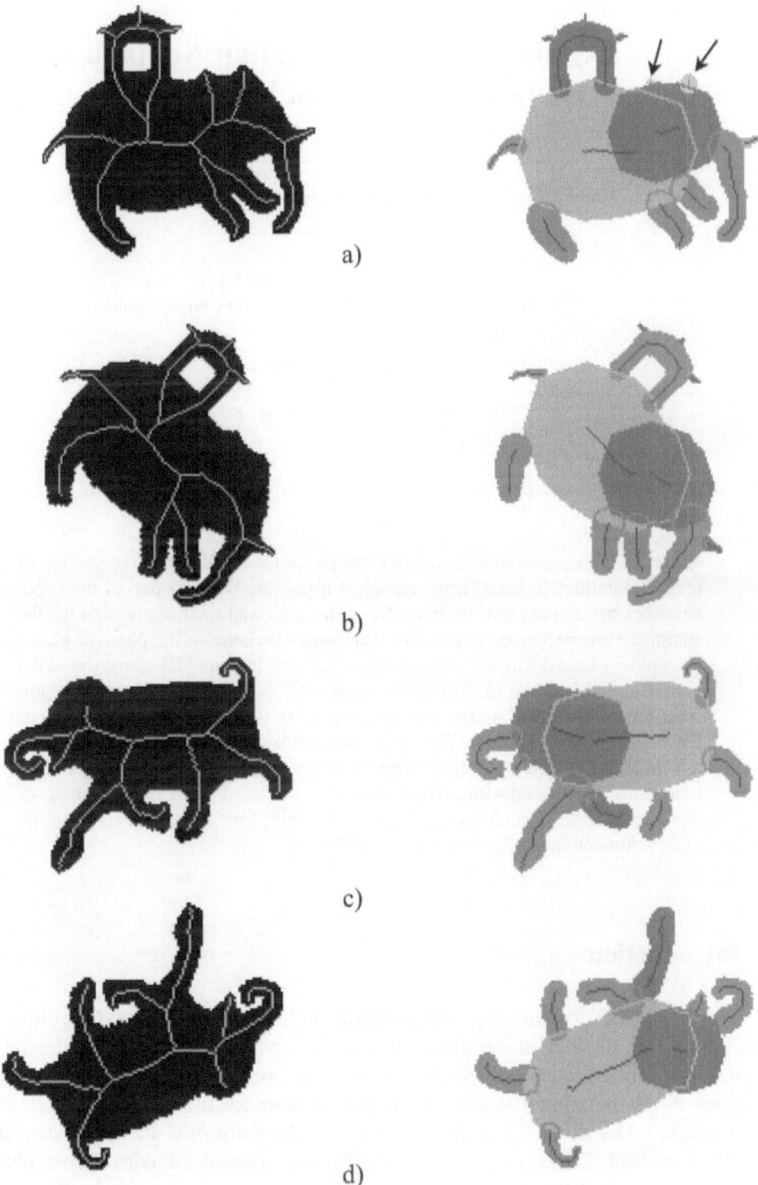

Figure 2: Some examples of figures differently rotated and shaped: skeletons overlapped on bit-maps (left) and the relative decompositions (right) are shown. a) The arrows indicate type D primitives

A Structural Representation Adapted to Handwritten Symbol Recognition

Jean-Yves Ramel[1], Guillaume Boissier[2], and Hubert Emptoz[2]

[1] GRACIMP - ICTT, Bât. 401 - INSA de Lyon
20, av. A. Einstein, 69621 Villeurbanne Cedex, France
ramel@gprhp.insa-lyon.fr

[2] Reconnaissance de Formes & Vision, Bât. 403 - INSA de Lyon
20, av. A. Einstein, 69621 Villeurbanne Cedex, France
emptoz@rfv.insa-lyon.fr

Abstract. This paper presents a new strategy for localization and recognition of graphical entities in handwritten chemical formulas. The first part of the paper describes the context of this study. Next, the tools and methods needed for the automatic interpretation are defined. Our system includes a first phase of global perception of the document followed by a phase of incremental extraction of the graphical entities. The phase of global perception constructs a structural representation of the drawing and provides a precise description of all the shapes present in the initial image. Thereafter, this representation constitutes the main resource that will be used by different processes (specialists) achieving the interpretation of the drawing. The knowledge extracted from the intermediary representation (a structural graph) is used instead of the bitmap image material to drive the interpretation process.

1. Introduction

Very little works treats the interpretation of freehand drawings. The difficulties stemming from the lack of standardization and the artist's broad freedom undoubtedly explain the limited interest these documents have so far aroused. The present article explains the functioning of a machine reading system for off-line handwritten chemical formulas. The different modules making up the automatic reading system developed are presented with examples of results. Our system includes a first phase of global perception of the document followed by a phase of incremental extraction and recognition of the graphical entities. The phase of global perception constructs a structural representation of the image that provides a precise description of all the shapes (and their relationship) present in the initial drawing. Thereafter, this representation constitutes the main resource that will be used by different processes achieving the interpretation of the drawing. The actions done by the different special-

Atul K. Chhabra and D. Dori (Eds.): GREC'99, LNCS 1941, pp. 228-237, 2000.
© Springer-Verlag Berlin Heidelberg 2000

ists are scheduled in order to read and understand the content of the drawing. The knowledge extracted from the representation is used instead of the bitmap image material to drive the interpretation process. So, a solution is progressively constructed and, all along the process, and remains consistent with the effective context.

2. Interpreting Freehand Drawings

2.1. Specificity of Freehand Drawings

Each type of document has its own structure [1], selected so that the information transmitted is easily understood and reusable by the readers. Within these documents, freehand drawings form a particular category; they are made up of fluctuating lines, solid areas, hatched areas, text, etc. They always contain a large quantity of information, can be very complex, and their field of application is extremely vast. Shapes to recognize are generally polygons, lines, circles, and other elementary geometric objects. The overall objective is thus to extract attributes relative to elementary objects so as to provide a description of the spatial relations existing between the components (inclusion, link, intersection, etc.). The fluctuating quality of the lines requires setting up specific line-recovery and -improvement algorithms before or during the recognition phase. Research done in this field [2][3] emphasizes, moreover, the difficulty of this task, even for a human reader. The classical techniques of vectorizationng [4][5], text localization, and curve localization can only be used after the modifications so that they take into account this fluctuating aspect of freehand lines [6][7].

2.2. How to Analyze Freehand Drawings ?

For the reading of chemical symbols [8][9], classic architectures generally include, therefore, a module for extracting text, a vectorization module (extracting segments of straight lines), and a module for extracting curves or circles. After text zones are localized, they are submitted to an OCR module. All these modules are working on the same static original image. At a higher level can be found an aggregation/recognition module (of the symbols) and a module which verifies the coherence of the extracted data.

The proposed system proceeds in two distinct phases :

- Instead of using always and only the static bitmap image to realize the segmentation and the interpretation, we have decided to use a structural representation. This intermediary description of the image will constitute the unique resource and will be able to evolve at any moment during the processing.
- To analyze the drawing, some different processes (the specialists) are activated sequentially and progressively, they contribute to simplify (by deleting recognized elementary objects) and to improve the representation of the image (by appending high level objects) . These specialists recognize ("catch") the elementary primitives

by modifying their attributes, they constitute more complex entities (polygons, text, chemical elements,...) and thus, they make the representation evolve. The management of all these recognized objects is therefore achieved and allows the specialists to take into account already extracted entities.

3. Construction of the Structural Representation

Vectors

A binary shape is described in the same way by its contour or its constituent black-area pixels. A datum on its direction can be obtained by a local study of its contours. The thickness, corresponding to the distance between the two boundaries of the line, is especially relevant for the study of the straight lines. These reasons have led us to select the description of shapes by the contours through the primitive Vector. Thus, a polygonal approximation of the contours of the shapes making up the initial image will provide an ordered sequence (by contour tracking) of the vectors.

The vectors obtained are stored in a chained list respecting the order supplied by contour tracking. Then, as we analyze freehand drawing, we have to improve the selection performance of the control points and to decrease the variability according to the threshold chosen, the boundaries are studied at different levels of detail. This entails the polygonal approximation phase proceeding iteratively (always using the same approximation algorithm) on the control points thus obtained.

The number of control points is thus reduced by fusion of certain segments obtained during the successive stages. This procedure is repeated until it reaches stabilization, in other words, until not a single fusion is possible. The number of iterations before stabilization varies generally between two and five, depending on the contour's characteristics (curvature, noise, photocopy, ...).

The representation of the image as *Vector* chains (SV sequence) matching contours of shapes limits the loss of information and gives a very reliable approximation of the drawing, but it is not easily put to use and does not provide enough information on the structure of the document.

Quadrilaterals

To obtain and easily handle the additional data, we had to define a more advanced description tool. The nature of the shapes to extract prompted the choice of the *Quadrilateral* A step pairing *Vectors* of the SV sequence establishes *Quadrilateral* primitives. Each *Quadrilateral* is defined by a pair of *Vectors* (each belonging to one of the two opposite boundaries of a thin shapes). As the Quadrilateral is a flexible primitive, we did not have to extract the text contained in the image beforehand. To obtain a more robust description of the thin shapes, the construction of the Quadrilaterals was carried out in several stages:

- Pairing *Vectors* (of SV) to construct the *Quadrilaterals* and updating SV,
- Sorting *Quadrilaterals* according to their proximity so as to reconstruct a "chronology" of the line,

- As we analyze freehand drawing, fusion of certain neighboring *Quadrilaterals*.

Improving the robustness of the pairing algorithm requires selecting the longest vector V1 from the list of vectors remaining unpaired, then searching for the vector nearest each of V1's extremities (depending on the Euclidean distance between points) which verifies certain criteria. Conditions of pairing criteria, each corresponding to a physical property of the lines, must be met for two vectors to be matched. These criteria are chosen "empirically" but respect the intuitive definition of a line.

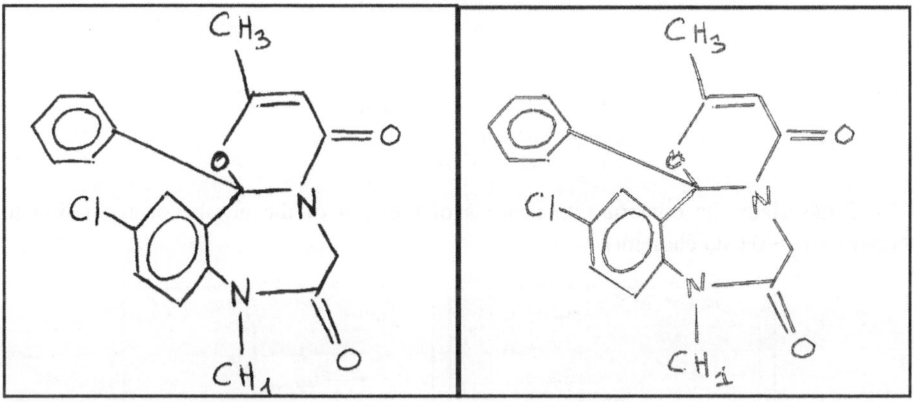

Fig. 1. Image of the Quadrilaterals

The group of *Quadrilateral* objects finally obtained (SQ) is representative of the thin shapes present in the initial document (in other words, everything for freehand drawings); this step must not be considered a true document vectorization step, but rather as the method we have chosen to obtain an initial description of a handwritten drawing using a set of primitives that is very easy to manipulate (Fig. 1).

Vectors matching no others correspond to the contours of solid shapes (in images containing such patterns).

Structural graph

To recognize high level elements (chemical symbols : liaisons, polygons, and chains), we found it necessary to organize the data extracted so as to use the context more appropriately during interpretation. A graph representation is the best qualified to link the different objects making up a drawing in relation to their neighborhood; it is also the most suitable to translating the structural relationships between primitives.

The lines (quadrilaterals) extracted are the nodes of the graph and arcs linking these nodes translate the relationships existing between the primitives. The graph represents the global structure of a document. Constructing a graph means calculating a zone of influence for each primitive. Arcs will describe the nature of the links between the primitive being studied and those belonging to its zone of influence. The table below (Table 1) lists the types of relationships used to construct the graph.

Table 1. Type of relationship between objects

Type of relationship between objects	Example
T junction → T	
Intersection → X	
Parallel relation → //	
L junction → L	
Two successive lines → S	

Fig. 2 describes the construction process of the part of the graph corresponding to Quadrilateral 0 (SQ element).

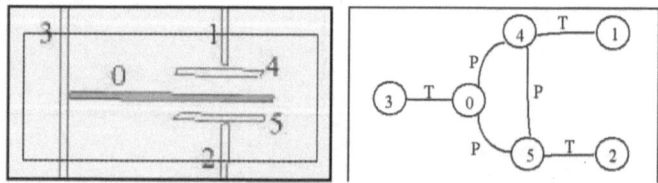

Fig. 2. Zone of influence of the Quadrilateral 0 and the corresponding graph

Fig. 3 shows the structural graphs obtained, representative of chemical formulas. We can notice that, for chemical elements, most of the relationships between lines must be L-junctions or Parallel relations (no T or X junctions). This remarks has enables us to realize a "Redraw" function that analyzes the graph (transforming T, X, S junctions) to obtain a better representation of the lines constituting the drawing. For the first image (Fig. 3), the textual components have been taken out to improve the readability of the graph.

Over and above the description in graph form, each quadrilateral has different attributes which characterize its neighborhood as much as possible. In particular, to each of the two extremities is associated a number corresponding to the number of lines with this same point as its extremity. Consequently, an isolated line is characterized by two integers with the value 1. This allows, for example, easy localization of liaison-type chemical elements (see below).

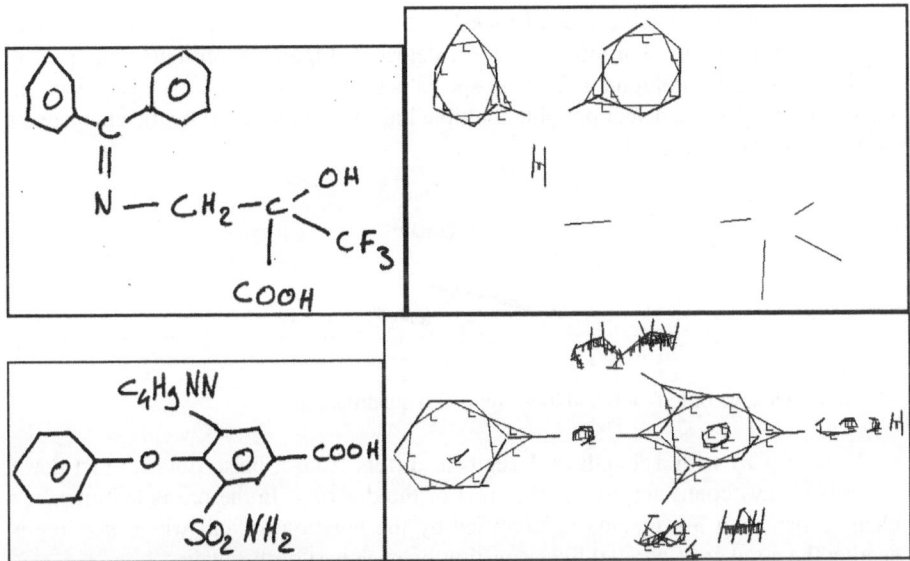

Fig. 3. Example of the graph obtained

4. Reading by Analysis of the Structural Representation

Different modules called specialists serve the purpose of interpreting a document. Each of them uses the constructed representation (structural graph) to focus on precise zones of the drawing (hypothesis generation) which are studied in detail (verification) to advance the analysis.

4.1. Chemical Elements Recognition

The study of the relationships between lines (making up the chemical formula) obtained with the constructed graph allows different specialists to localize and recognize different constituents of a chemical formula.

The **Liaison** specialist (in charge of recognizing chemical elements constituted by parallel lines) analyzes (in the structural graph) type-'P' arcs and associated quadrilaterals as well as quadrilaterals with "free" extremities (see explanation above). This grouping identifies liaisons (Ln) and their characteristics (Fig. 8).

Polygon and Chain specialists both operate in much the same manner since a polygon is actually no more than a closed chain (non-concave in our case). Their operation rests on two recursive procedures: look-left and look-right, capable of scanning the structural graph representing the image, starting from a line and searching for a neighboring line, respectively either more to the left or more to the right of the current line (as illustrated in Fig. 4).

Thus, if after n recursive runs of look-left we return to the starting line (quadrilateral), then a polygon of n sides has been detected. Figures 8 presents examples of results provided by Polygon and Chain specialists. When a polygon is recognized, its interior is analyzed to detect possible multiple liaisons (symbolized by the characters # or ⊗ on the result images).

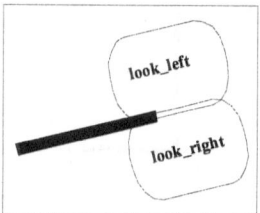

Fig. 4. Search zone of look-left and look-right for a quadrilateral

A chain (Cn) with a length of 1 segment differs from a liaison by the fact that a chain is always connected to an other part of the drawing. In the presented images, a chain drawn with 3 segments is identified by the notation : Cnnn where n is representing the number of parallel lines constituting each part of the chain.

4.2. Text Localization and Recognition

Another module is responsible for extracting text zones. In our representation (graph), the size, shape, and arrangement of the quadrilaterals are representative of the texture of the initial image. Text zones are characterized by groups of short quadrilaterals. They are detected by their physical proximity without taking their orientation and their relationship (arc attribute) into account. Even though other shapes produce quadrilaterals with similar characteristics, local analysis of these groups of quadrilaterals and their neighborhood allows construction of focusing zones (which may contain handwritten text) without resorting to connected components of the image. Starting from each quadrilateral cluster (sub-graph), it is possible to generate a virtual text component formed by the rectangle encompassing the group of quadrilaterals brought together to form the cluster. Fig. 5 shows examples of focus zones.

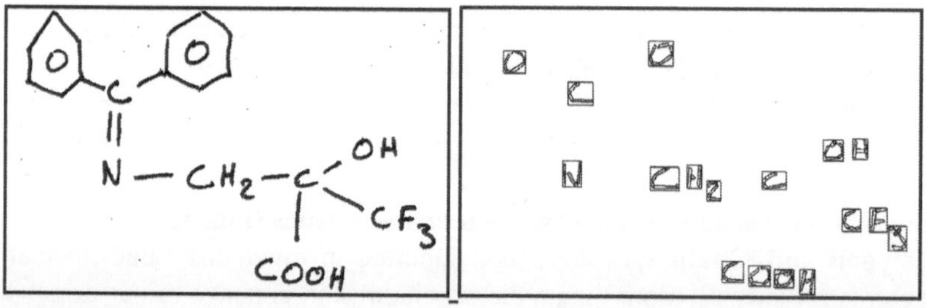

Fig. 5. Virtual text-components

Coupling this information with that provided by the study of connected components present in the initial image, the model makes a decision and classifies each zone into one of the following categories: text, non-text, non-decision. For non-decision zones, studying the size and position of the virtual text-components in relation to the text zones already localized, leads to a comparison with the context, and certain ambiguities can thus be resolved. Finally, in case doubt persists, an OCR module can be called in or, in an interactive system, the user can be questioned to make other decisions.

Our method of recognition combines three techniques. First of all, it draws on a classic method based on Pattern Matching applied after normalization. Each reference model of a character is composed of a table with 8 x 10 "slots" (Fig. 6).

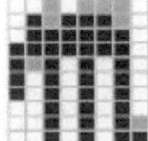

Each slot can be in the following states:
- Black (or 1): the character compared must include one black slot in the same place;
- White (or 0): the character compared must include one white slot in the same pla e

Fig. 6. Reference model of the character m

We corroborate this technique with a study of right half-profiles of the normalized character. In order to improve the discrimination between two characters even further, we combine these classic methods with the study of "significant" quadrilaterals (lines) which comprise a character. We label "significant" quadrilaterals those which are included in the studied text zone, and whose length is greater than or equal to 1/3 (empirically established threshold) of the length or height (depending on inclination) of the text zone (Fig. 7). A "rule base" has been defined which, for each character, sets the number of quadrilaterals which should have one of the four following orientations: horizontal, vertical, right diagonal, left diagonal. Orientations of "significant" quadrilaterals are set from the average angle (between 0° and 180°) formed with the horizontal.

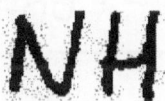 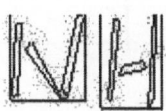 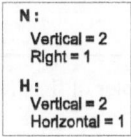

Fig. 7. Characters N & H, corresponding significant quadrilaterals; and a part of the rule base

4.3. Evaluations of this System

For the text recognition, results vary enormously in relation to the drawer's level of application. That is why we have preferred showing images which have been used for the evaluations specified in the article. The recognition rate evaluated (with a base comprising 328 models) is approximately 95%.

Concerning the extraction of the graphic parts (chemical elements), the recognition rate on images such as those presented in Fig. 8 is close to 97%. Figure 8 presents examples of complete results.

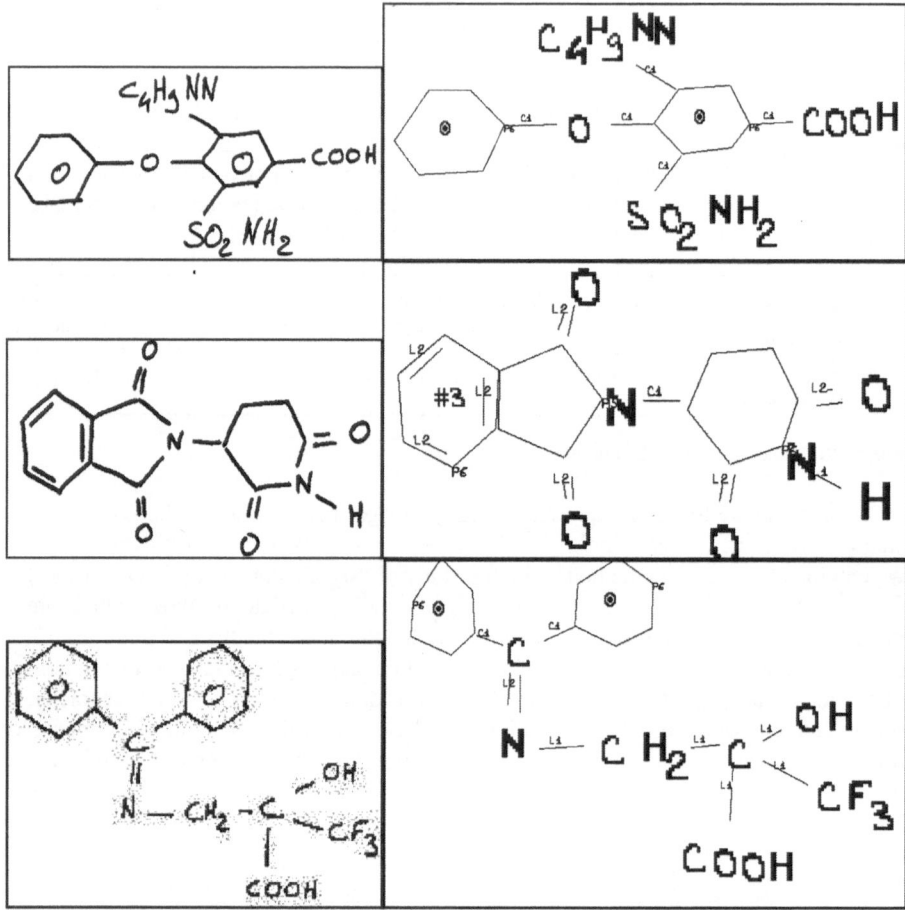

Fig. 8. Examples of final results

5. Conclusion

For this application of chemical formula recognition, sensitive points seem to be localizing text zones in the image, and in particular choosing the threshold which defines the greatest authorized size for a quadrilateral part of a text area. As expected, the recognition rate of handwritten characters is not impressive. It was therefore necessary to define certain hypotheses in order to improve the performance at this level: each potential writer should possess a personal model base, and characters that are linked together are to be avoided. Localization of polygons is acceptable when they are closed or quasi closed. When the spaces between extremities are too large, the polygon is localized as several chains. Here also the threshold defining the maximum distance between extremities was difficult to establish. Our system treats off-line documents with a resolution of 300 dpi. It passes from the image of a freehand draw-ing (a cluster of black and white pixels) to a structured representation of the image (structural graph). Then, from this representation, it recognizes handwritten text, lo-calizes multiple liaisons, polygons, chains, and saves the results obtained in vectorial form.

Our system includes two steps. The first step corresponds to the construction of a simple and sufficient structural representation using elementary primitives (vectors, quadrilaterals) and providing a precise description of all the shapes and their relation-ship in the initial raster image. During the second step, the actions realized by the different specialists can be coordinated in order to read and understand a document content using the previously built representation instead of the image. Most often, management of recognized entities (polygons, text, ...) raises problems by increasing the complexity of the recognition of the other elements in the bitmap image. Our rep-resentation and its evolution mechanism (append/delete objects) solve this difficulty and enable detection of objects that are elements in several entities.

References

[1]   Tombre, K. Technical drawing Recognition and understanding : From Pixel to se-mantics. In : *Pro-ceedings of the Workshop on Machine Vision and Application. Tokyo, December 1992*. p. 393-401.

[2]   Poirier, F., Julia, L., & Faure, C.. Tapage : édition de tableaux sur ordinateur à stylo. Vers une désignation naturelle. *Proceedings of IHM93, 1993*. p. 45-49.

[3]   Galindo, D., Faure, C. Perceptually based representation of network diagrams *Pro-ceedings of the International Conference on Document Analysis and Recognition, Ulm, 1997*. Vol. 2. p. 352-356.

[4]   Ramachandran, K. Coding method for vector representation of engineering drawings. In : *Proceedings of the IEEE*, 1980, Vol. 68, N° 7, p. 813-817.

[5]   Pavlidis, T. A vectorizer and feature extractor for document recognition. *Computer Vision, Graphics and Image Processing*, 1986, Vol. 35, p. 111-127.

[6]   Roosli, M. and Monagan, G. A high quality vectorisation combining local quality measures and global constraints. In : *Proceedings of the 3rd International Conference on Document Analysis and Recognition, Montreal (Canada), august 14-16, 1995.* Vol. 1, p. 243-248.

[7]   Tanigawa, S., Hori, O. and Shimotsuji, S. Precise line detection from an engineering drawing using a figure fitting method based on contours and skeletons. In : *Proceed-ings of the 12th International Conference on Pattern Recognition, Jérusalem (Israël), 9-13 octobre, 1994.* Vol. 2, p. 356-360.

[8]   Casey, R., & Nagy, G. Document analysis : a broader view *Proceedings of the First International Conference on Document Analysis and Recognition, Saint-Malo (France), september,* 1991.

[9]   Casey, R., & Al. Optical recognition of chemical graphics *Proceedings of the 2rd International Conference on Document Analysis and Recognition, 1993.* p. 628-631.

Combination of Invariant Pattern Recognition Primitives on Technical Documents

Sébastien Adam [2,3], Jean-Marc Ogier [2], Claude Cariou [1],
Joël Gardes [3], Rémy Mullot [2], and Yves Lecourtier [2]

[1] LASTI-Groupe Image, ENSSAT,
6 rue de Kerampont, 22305 Lannion
Claude.Cariou@enssat.fr
[2] PSI-LA3I, Université de Rouen,
76 821 Mont Saint Aignan
{Sebastien.Adam,Jean-Marc.Ogier,Remy.Mullot}@univ-
rouen.fr
[3] CNET - DES/OLI - 6,
Avenue des Usines BP 383 90 007 Belfort Cedex
joel.gardes@cnet.francetelecom.fr

Abstract. This paper deals with a particular aspect of a technical document interpretation device: the recognition of multi-oriented and multi-scaled characters and symbols. The adopted methodology is based on original descriptors, relying on the computation of the Mellin Fourier Transform. These descriptors are then combined with classical invariant through the use of Genetic Algorithms. The application frame of this study is the interpretation of the documents of the French telephonic operator France-Telecom for which the recognition of symbols constitutes a crucial point for a robust interpretation.

1 Introduction

Many research laboratories are currently working on character recognition and some of them have even marketed systems. However, the quality of their performances drops dramatically when the text is noisy or when its orientation and/or size changes. In this paper, we address the problem of pattern recognition in this particular case, where patterns are available at any orientation and scale factor. Specifically, we describe the design of a sub-system used for the automatic interpretation of technical documents (archived as paper maps) of the French telephonic network.

The automatic processing of technical documents in a way to produce digital (and as « intelligent » as possible) archives is a formidable task for industrial companies. This is not only due to the difficulty of passing from a paper support to a vectorized and interpreted one, but also due to the huge amount of technical maps already archived and still updated. For example France Telecom (a french telephonic operator)

Atul K. Chhabra and D. Dori (Eds.): GREC'99, LNCS 1941, pp. 238-245, 2000.

estimates to over 2.4 million documents the volume of archived maps of the french telephonic network. A reliable document interpretation, whatever the strategy and the knowledge representation that is used, should not be efficient without robust and high quality low-level techniques. These ones are designed to process digital images (given by scanning a paper map) in order to produce reliable information to a higher description level. Among low-level processing techniques, one finds filtering (often impulse noise removal), segmentation (often binarization), recognition of alpha-numeric characters and/or specific symbols (sometimes under geometrical invariance constraints).

In this communication, we present an approach of the latter point, in the context of the interpretation of telephonic network maps. Specifically, the constraints are the following :

- The recognition of a character / symbol should be invariant under rotation and scale changes (i.e. similitude). Indeed, many character strings and symbols are available in any orientation and scale.
- The recognition should be robust to pattern misplacement. Overlapping or interconnected character / symbols should be retrieved and recognized.

As an example, figure 1 shows a small portion of a technical document where multi-oriented characters and symbols appear. Thus, the aim of this study is to try to determine the most efficient primitives in regard with our similitude constraints, and to evaluate the interest of the combination of these primitives in order to reach an optimal classification rate.

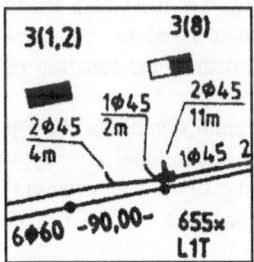

Fig. 1. An example of map

2   The Proposed System

2.1   General Structure

The general structure of the proposed system for similitude invariant pattern recognition relies on the use of original gray-level pattern descriptors proposed in [1] and in their combination with other efficient primitives [2][3], by using genetic algorithms. In order to have quite representative results, two classification strategies have been retained for this study : the LVQ (*Learning Vector Quantization*) and a 1NN's approach.

The analysis of technical documents, after high resolution scanning (400 dpi), is performed within processing of isolated patterns : using a tool for the extraction of connected patterns and other shape descriptive parameters [4], one identifies each isolated pattern within the image. Each pattern is analyzed in a simple manner in order to decide of its accessibility to the classification procedure (i.e. if it is a interpretable one). On each of the retained patterns, a set of invariant descriptors is computed and sent as entry of the LVQ/1NN, yielding an identification of the pattern in terms of class. Of course, the use of a LVQ for classification requires at first a careful calibration step, which is to be performed by using a large learning base.

In the next section, we will give a description of the primitives retained for this study.

2.2   The Retained Primitives

Justifications. Many studies deal with the symbol/character recognition problem. As a consequence many types of primitives have been developed and studied (one can find a good state of art in [5]) and it is quite difficult to have an objective point of view in regard with the classification rate without testing each one in the considered problem : indeed, the presented classification rates are generally excellent but the tests conditions are so various that they are not comparable.

For our study, the choice of the primitives was motivated by the following points :

- at first, we have retained primitives for which theoretical aspects and experimental results are not debatable (Zernike moments and Mellin Fourier invariants are both based on the decomposition in orthogonal function and their performance are excellent in regard with other techniques).
- secondly, we have tried to retain complementary primitives, the complementarity being considered either on the local/global description (respectively Fourier Mellin invariants and Zernike moments) or on the structural/statistical description (respectively circular primitives and moments)

The Fourier-Mellin Transform and Related Invariants. This point constitutes a great contribution of this paper since the Mellin Fourier invariants, as far as we know, have never been used for character/symbol recognition problem, in the context of technical document analysis. The major assets of this approach have been detailed in [1]. For a given gray-level 2-D pattern, the set of similitude invariant descriptors is computed from the Fourier-Mellin transform (FMT) applied at a characteristic point of the pattern called the center of development (CoD). Here we chose the centroid of the pattern as the CoD, although this choice is not the only one possible.

Let $f(r, \theta)$ be a function (the shape) expressed in polar coordinates. The Analytic Fourier Mellin Transform is defined as the Fourier transform for the specific group of positive similitudes $\mathbf{R}_+^* \times S^1$ [6] :

$$\tilde{M}_f(\upsilon,q) = \int_{\rho=0}^{+\infty} \int_{\theta=0}^{2\pi} \rho^{-i\upsilon+\sigma_0} \exp(-iq\theta) f(\rho,\theta) \frac{d\rho}{\rho} d\theta \tag{1}$$

with $q \in \mathbf{Z}$, $\upsilon \in \mathbf{R}$, and $\sigma_0 \in \mathbf{R}_+^*$

from the following set of invariant quantities can be computed :

$$I_f(\upsilon,q) = \tilde{M}_f(\upsilon,q) \left[\tilde{M}_f(0,0) \right]^{-1+i\frac{\upsilon}{\sigma_0}} \left[\tilde{M}_f(0,1) \right]^{-q} \left| \tilde{M}_f(0,1) \right|^q \tag{2}$$

One can show easily that if $g(\rho,\theta) = f(\alpha\rho, \theta+\beta)$, then $I_g(\upsilon,q) = I_f(\upsilon,q)$.

The two important properties of the AFMT-derived invariants are their completeness and the convergence of the L_p measure with these invariants.

The setting up of the discrete AFMT ($\upsilon = p \in \mathbf{Z}$) for digital images enhances the problem of Cartesian to polar coordinates. This problem may be solved by applying, at the CoD of the pattern, a bank of 2-D digital filters the IRs of which form the basis of the discrete AFMT [7]. If the given result is only an approximation of the TFMA, the advantage of this approach relies in the possible use of the 2-D FFT in the case of overlapping patterns [1].

Zernike Moments. In the literature, many authors highlight the superiority of the Zernike moments when dealing with the characterization of multi-oriented and multi-scaled shapes [2][7]. In the context of our study, 24 moments have been used, corresponding to the orders three to six of Zernike polynomials (see eq.3). These ones were normalized through Belkasim's method [8]

$$V_{nm}(x,y) = R_{nm}(x,y) e^{jm\tan^{-1}(x,y)} \tag{3}$$

with $j = \sqrt{-1}$, $n \geq 0$, $|m| \leq n$, $n-|m|$ is even

$$R_{nm} = \sum_{s=0}^{(n-|m|)/2} \frac{(-1)^s (x^2+y^2)^{(n/2)-s} (n-s)!}{s!(\frac{n+|m|}{2}-s)!(\frac{n-|m|}{2}-s)!} \tag{4}$$

Circular primitives. This kind description of the shapes [9] is generally presented as very competitive in comparison with classical techniques (Hu moments, for instance [10]). In our case, we have retained circular primitives developed by [3] because of their promising results. This second kind of description is based on a more local analysis of the shape. After the pattern detection, a set of circles centered on its centroïd is computed and overlaid on the shape. The overlapping angles for each of these circles are then calculated and arranged. This process permits to obtain a rotation invariant vector of 100 descriptors corresponding to the juxtaposition of 10 circles.

3   Experimental Results – Comparison and Combination

In this part, we will first provide a comparison between primitives presented in the above part in regard with our document analysis problem. Two classifiers are compared in order to improve robustness of the system. Then, in the second section, we will give the strategy that we have adopted for finding a combination of the most relevant primitives in order to optimize the classification rate.

3.1   Recognition of Isolated Characters: A Comparison Between Primitives

The recognition of isolated and clean patterns on binarized digital images of the French telephonic network can be split in two parts. At first, in order to validate the methodology, we have applied our technique on a set of "clean " characters, issued from a database especially provided for this application (figure 2). In the second part, we considered a set of 20000 characters issued from real France Telecom Documents (figure 1). This set was divided in two parts : a learning set composed of 10000 samples and a test set of 10000 labeled shapes. For the industrial application, the characters which have used were not rotated version of existing shapes : the considered shapes were extracted from real France Telecom documents through a very heavy labeling process. The classification results, obtained with LVQ and 1NN procedures are summarized in the table 1 (classification rate).

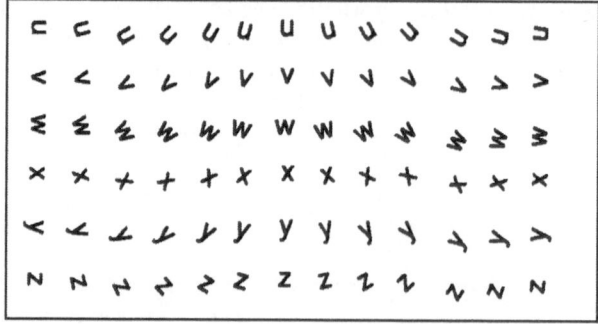

Fig. 2. A set of the clean data base

Concerning the Mellin Fourier invariants, all experimental results have been obtained by computation of a 18-complex invariant points AFMT ($-2 \leq p \leq 2$; $0 \leq q \leq 3$), yielding 33 non-redundant invariant per pattern.

Table 1. Results of the classification for the different primitives (Recognition Rate)

	Clean Data Base		Real Data Base	
LVQ	FM Transform	97%	FM Transform	86.1%
	Zernike moments	75,51%	Zernike moments	74,07%
	Circular primitives	73,61%	Circular primitives	68,05%
1NN'S	FM Transform	97.5%	FM Transform	87.55%
	Zernike moments	80,93%	Zernike moments	78,46%
	Circular primitives	77,51%	Circular primitives	71,54%

This comparison of these different approaches shows the global quality of each of these primitives and, one of the most important point is that it highlights the superiority of the Fourier Mellin Invariants with recognized techniques. Considering the large number of classes, it was difficult to introduce in this paper the confusion matrix. However, an analysis of this confusion matrix shows that that the confusions are coherent since they concern similar shapes such as "m" and "E" (which are quite similar for our fonts if we consider a rotation of 90 degrees and a scale factor) or "N" and "Z". These particular cases do not invalidate the general methodology since this kind of problem is generally solved thanks to contextual information. Within our interpretation strategy, this contextual information is to be provided by the global interpretation system.

3.2   Recognition of Isolated Characters: A Combination of Primitives

Even if the results obtained with the previously presented primitives are satisfying, a combination of these primitives may be interesting in regard with our objective. At first, we have tried to concatenate all our primitives in order to constitute a new vector and study the interest of this proposition. The corresponding results show a slight improvement of the classification rate (the recognition rate reaches 88,5 % for the real data base and the 1NN's classifier). Nevertheless, considering the dimensionality malediction problem, we have tried to determine if an optimal combination of different relevant primitives may be computed. The determination of the optimal combination of primitives comes as a classical optimization problem.

In the context of a wide representation space, features selection methods are numerous in the literature. Considering the specificity of our problem, i.e. non linearity and non derivability constraints, only three kinds of optimization techniques were applicable : simulated reannealing, Genetic algorithms, and exhaustive research. Technique. Considering the large number of available primitives, exhaustive research has been rejected because of computational constraints. One can find a good comparative study in [11], which lead us to genetic algorithms (G.A.), which are considered by [12] to be a powerful tool, specifically when dimensionality of the feature space is greater than 20. Because of its adaptive nature and it's learning capacity, we have retained this method in order to give a dynamic aspect to our features selection. Thus, in the context of our future industrial application, we may respond efficiently to the strong variability of the shapes. Many G.A. versions are proposed in the literature, each of them corresponding to small refinements, in order to improve convergence speed. In our context, we only use fundamental G.A.

As in [12], a possible combination of the optimization problem is represented by a binary chromosome in which each bit reflects the presence or the absence of a primitive. After a random initialization of the population, the three usual operators (selection, crossover, and mutation) are used successively until a particular stopping criterion is verified. The first obtained results are very encouraging since only a few generations are sufficient to improve the recognition rate of 3 % on the real France Telecom data base, in comparison with the rate obtained with the whole available primitives. The analysis of the confusion matrix, that is difficult to insert in this paper because of the large number of classes, shows that the using of the G.A. does not change many things in the confusions which are observed. As a consequence, one must highlight here that this improvement comes with a consequent reducing of the number of primitives to be extracted. Nevertheless, numbers of parameters still have to be adjusted and we are currently working on the choice of a cost function in order to consider the time problem.

4   Conclusion

The recognition of multi-oriented and multi-scaled patterns is performed in order to help the automatic interpretation of technical paper documents, with application to the vectorization of the French telephonic network. The developed tool relies on the use of the Fourier-Mellin transform, the Zernike moments and circular primitives integrated in a selection process through genetic algorithms. This shape description, together with a robust classification strategy (LVQ/1NN), provides at the moment very encouraging results. This strategy has now to be included in a global interpretation device taking into account feature extraction problem.

5   References

1. S. Adam , J.M. Ogier , C. Cariou, R. Mullot, J. Gardes, Y. Lecourtier, *Multi-Scaled and Multi Oriented Character Recognition : An Original Strategy*, Proceedings of ICDAR 99, Bangalore,India, 45-48, 1999
2. M. Teague, *Image analysis via the general theory of moments,* Journal of Optical Society of America, **70**, 920-930, 1980.
3. E. Menu, L. Lefrere, Y. Lecourtier, A New Method of Distorsion Invariant Character Recognition, Proceedings of IAPR 1992, La Hague, Vol. 2, 599-602, 1992.
4. J.-M. Ogier, *Contribution à l'analyse automatique de documents cartographiques : interprétation de données cadastrales*, Thèse de Doctorat, Université de Rouen, 1994.
5. O. D. Trier, A. K. Jain, T. Taxt, *Features extraction methods for character recognition - A Survey*, Pattern Recognition, **29**, 641-662, 1996.

6.   F. Ghorbel, *A complete invariant description for gray level images by the harmonic analysis approach*, Pattern Recognition Letters **15** , pp 1043-1051, 1994.
7.   A. Khotanzad and Y. H. Hong,, *Rotation Invariant image recognition using features selected via a systematic method*, Pattern Recognition **23** 1089-1101, 1990.
8.   G. Ravichandran, M. Trivedi, *Circular-Mellin Features for Texture Segmentation*, IEEE Trans. on Image Processing, 1995.
9.   S. O. Belkasim, M. Shridar and A. Ahmadi, *Pattern Recognition with moment invariants : A comparative study and new results*, Pattern Recognition **24**, 1117-1138, 1991.
10.   N. Kita, *Object locating based on concentric circular description*, Proceedings of 11th IEEE International Conference of Pattern Recognition, Den Haag, Vol 1, 637-641, 1992.
11.   S. A. Dudani, K. J. Bredding, R. M. McGhee, *Aircraft identification by moment invariants*, IEEE Transaction Computer, **C-26**, 39-45, 1977.
12.   D. Zongker and A. Jain, *Algorithms for Feature Selection : An Evaluation*, Proceedings of ICPR 96, Vol II, 18-22, 1996
13.   W. Siedlecki and J. Sklansky. A Note on Genetic Algorithms for Large-Scale Feature Selection, Pattern Recognition Letters, 10, 335-347, 1989.

Engineering Drawing Database Retrieval Using Statistical Pattern Spotting Techniques

Stefan Müller and Gerhard Rigoll

Department of Computer Science, Faculty of Electrical Engineering
Gerhard-Mercator-University Duisburg, Bismarckstr. 90, 47057 Duisburg, Germany
Phone: ++49/203/379-1140, FAX: ++49/203/379-4363
{stm,rigoll}@fb9-ti.uni-duisburg.de

Abstract. An experimental mechanical engineering drawing database system, which allows a user to retrieve images by presenting sketches or shapes which represent details such as e.g. screws or holes, is presented in this paper. Due to the use of novel augmented pseudo 2-D Hidden Markov Models with filler states, images can be retrieved, where the detail that corresponds to the query is embedded in e.g. hatching or is connected to other elements in the image. The proposed technique achieves a good performance which is demonstrated by a number of query and retrieval examples in this paper.

1   Introduction

In many application areas there is a growing need for the automatic indexing and retrieval of pictorial information. Some of these areas are e.g. large archives in museums or libraries, product catalogs or services searching for images on the World Wide Web. Content based techniques allow the user of an image database system to specify a query in terms of sketches or color distribution rather than textual keywords. Thus, content based access is not dependent on indexing information previously attached to the database elements. There is a number of publications describing systems which use this principle including [1,2,3,4].

In this publication we describe an experimental mechanical engineering drawing database which can be accessed by specifying shapes describing details of interest. Such a query could e.g. correspond to a textual query such as *retrieve those images which contain one or more screws*. It is noteworthy, that in the textual query the exact shape of the screw is not specified yet, which is easier to manage by applying a sketch. Fig. 1 shows a query shape on the left followed by four elements of our database which contain such a shape. The database elements have been scanned from an engineering drawing tutorial [5], whereas the query has been issued by a standard drawing tool (xfig). Fig. 1 represents an optimal retrieval result, which is difficult to achieve, due to the facts that the query shape is connected to other components in the images (see e.g. the rectangle surrounded by hatching) and varies also in scale. Because of these difficulties we propose the use of stochastic modeling techniques in order to build the retrieval

Atul K. Chhabra and D. Dori (Eds.): GREC'99, LNCS 1941, pp. 246–255, 2000.

system. This leads to an integrated approach which assigns probability scores to the elements of the database and performs pattern spotting simultaneously, using the combined segmentation and probability scoring abilities of the Viterbi algorithm within the Hidden Markov Model (HMM) framework. This approach differs from well known two or more stage systems, which first identify elements such as lines, arcs or points and perform image interpretation in a second step (see e.g. [6,7]). Such an approach, however, is difficult to follow whenever it is not possible to perform a segmentation of the drawing into the primitive elementary objects as mentioned above. Alternatively, as demonstrated in [8], the proposed pseudo 2-D HMM-approach enables an integrated segmentation and recognition process. Other publications which propose the use of the combined scoring and segmentation abilities include [4,9].

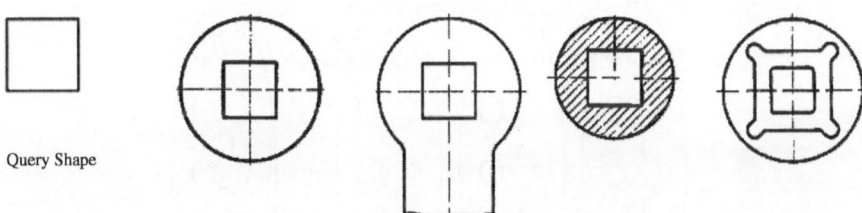

Fig. 1. Query shape and four elements taken from our engineering drawing database. The engineering drawings have been scanned from [5]

This paper is organized as follows: Section 2 gives a brief introduction to the modeling of two-dimensional data based on pseudo 2-D HMMs. Section 3 describes the combined probability scoring and spotting approach, based on the use of filler models. In Section 4 the mechanical engineering drawing database is presented and Section 5 gives the experimental results on this database. A summary is given in the final section.

2   Pseudo 2-D HMMs for Stochastic Modeling of Two-Dimensional Data

Hidden Markov Models are finite stochastic automata and represent one of the most powerful tools for modeling dynamic, time-varying patterns. It is therefore not surprising that they became popular in speech recognition [10]. Their major advantage in time series classification results from their capability to align a pattern along their states using a probability density function (pdf) for each state that estimates the probability that a certain part of the pattern belongs to that state (see [10] for details). In recent years, HMMs have been more and more applied to other pattern recognition problems, especially in on-line handwriting recognition [11], where the recognition procedure is similar to speech recognition. It has also been shown that HMMs can not only be applied successfully to time series problems, but also to pattern recognition problems where the pattern varies in space rather than in time. The problem most closely related to the above mentioned examples is off-line handwriting recognition, where the characters represent a pattern changing in space while moving horizontally from left to right [11]. Therefore, HMMs have been recently also applied to image recognition problems with promising results [12] and the symbol recognition problems mentioned in [8,13] have been tackled using HMMs, too. For our integrated segmentation and scoring approach, we propose the use of pseudo 2-D HMMs (P2DHMM), which are also known as planar HMMs. A P2DHMM is a stochastic automata with a two-dimensional arrangement of the states, as outlined in Fig. 2.

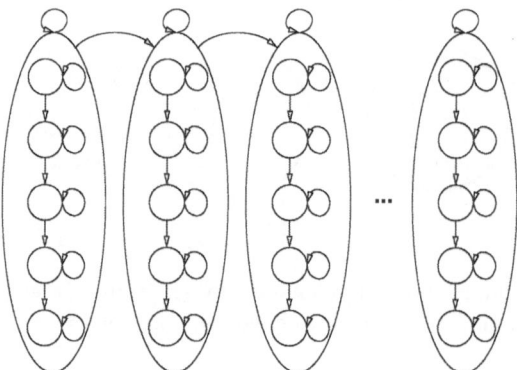

Fig. 2. Pseudo 2-D Hidden Markov Model

The states in horizontal direction are denoted as *superstates*, and each superstate consists of a one-dimensional HMM in vertical direction. P2DHMMs have been already used for character recognition in [9]. If one considers e.g. the query image in Fig. 1 subdivided into e.g. vertical stripes, it is possible to use P2DHMMs for modeling a two-dimensional object in the following manner: Each stripe is aligned to one of the superstates of the P2DHMM, resulting in a horizontal warping of the pattern. Furthermore, within the superstate, the pattern representing the stripe is aligned to the one-dimensional HMM states, resulting in a vertical alignment of the stripe. In a similar way, it is also possible to model two-dimensional data, which is considered as consisting of horizontal stripes.

The P2DHMM shown in Fig. 2 can be trained from data, after features have been extracted, using the segmental k-means algorithm as outlined in Fig. 3. The feature extraction used throughout the paper is based on the discrete cosine transform (DCT). The image is scanned with a sampling window (block) top to bottom and left to right. The pixels in the sampling window of the size 16×16

are transformed using the DCT according to the equation:

$$C(u,v) = \alpha(u)\alpha(v)\sum_{x=0}^{15}\sum_{y=0}^{15} f(x,y)\cos\left(\frac{(2x+1)u\pi}{32}\right)\cos\left(\frac{(2y+1)v\pi}{32}\right) \quad (1)$$

A triangle shaped mask extracts the first 15 coefficients $(u + v \le 4)$, which are arranged in a vector. The result of the feature extraction is a two-dimensional array of vectors $\boldsymbol{O}(x,y)$. An overlap between adjacent sampling windows improves the ability of the HMM to model the neighborhood relations between the sampling blocks. The effect of this overlap is somehow comparable to the use of delta-features in speech recognition, and includes redundant information into the features. Experiments showed that an overlap of 75% in each direction gives the best results. Due to the fact, that a P2DHMM is built for a single query image, this image is shifted in each direction by a few pixels and for each shifted version the array of vectors $\boldsymbol{O}(x,y)$ is calculated, in order to increase the amount of training data. Once the query-model has been trained – and as will be described in Sec. 3 surrounded by filler states – the scoring and segmentation procedure is accomplished by calculating the probability that the database element has been generated by that HMM. For this procedure, the doubly embedded Viterbi algorithm can be utilized, which has been proposed by Kuo and Agazzi in [9]. Alternatively, Samaria shows in [12], that a P2DHMM can be transformed into an equivalent one-dimensional HMM by the insertion of special *end-of-line* states. Thus, these equivalent HMMs can be trained by the Baum-Welch algorithm and the recognition step can be carried out using the standard Viterbi algorithm.

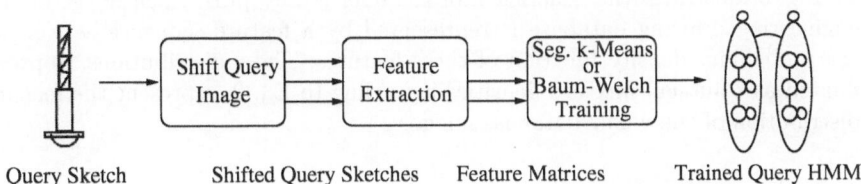

Query Sketch   Shifted Query Sketches   Feature Matrices   Trained Query HMM

Fig. 3. Training procedure for the query HMM

3 Filler Modeling for Combined Probability Scoring and Spotting

As already mentioned in the previous sections, the query shape or detail which is a part of the database images that should be retrieved, is modeled as a pseudo 2-D HMM. In order to represent the remaining part of the database images, this P2DHMM is surrounded by filler states, whose output probability distributions (pdfs) have been adapted to the individual engineering drawings of the database. The structure of the augmented model is illustrated in Fig. 4, where the white circles represent the states of the original pseudo 2-D HMM of the query image (see also Fig. 3), whereas the shaded circles denote the additional filler states. The dotted transitions in Fig. 4 have not been trained and have to be chosen arbitrarily. By setting the transition it is possible to integrate an expected background to query shape ratio. The filler states surrounding the original HMM all share the same pdf, a strategy which is commonly referred to as (state-)tying [14].

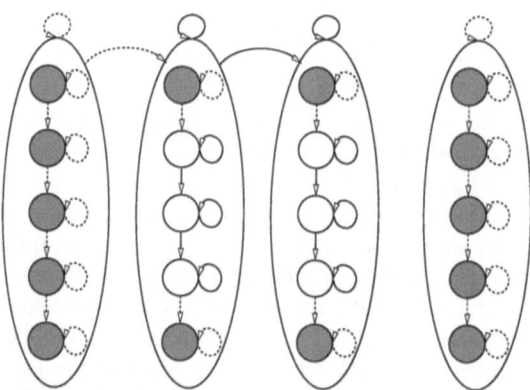

Fig. 4. Augmented P2DHMM with filler states

Fig. 5 illustrates the generation of the filler states' pdfs. Each image of the engineering drawing database is represented by a feature sequence as well as the probability density function of these features. These distributions, approximated as Gaussian mixture densities according to Eq. 2, represent the feature distribution of the whole database image.

$$b\left(\boldsymbol{o}\right) = \sum_{m=1}^{M} c_m \, \mathcal{N}\left(\boldsymbol{o}, \boldsymbol{\mu}_m, \overleftrightarrow{\Sigma}_m\right) \tag{2}$$

Once the query has been presented and the query P2DHMM has been trained, the augmented P2DHMM is built and the filler states' pdf are taken successively from every database element, while presenting the corresponding features, in order to retrieve the matching engineering drawings. While processing the whole database, segmentations as well as probability scores are generated for each engineering drawing by the Viterbi algorithm. Fig. 6 illustrates such a segmentation. On the left hand side of Fig. 6 the query is shown, which is the rough sketch of a screw drawn with a standard drawing tool and on the right hand side the corresponding segmentation of one of the database elements is given. The features taken from the shaded region in Fig. 6 have been aligned to the filler states of the augmented HMM, whereas the features of the non-shaded area have been assigned to the query HMM, which represents the sketch of a screw. Although this segmentation is not perfect, the alignment of the features in the non-shaded region to the states of the query HMM will lead to a high probability score. All database elements are ranked according to this probability score and those e.g. five elements with the highest score are retrieved.

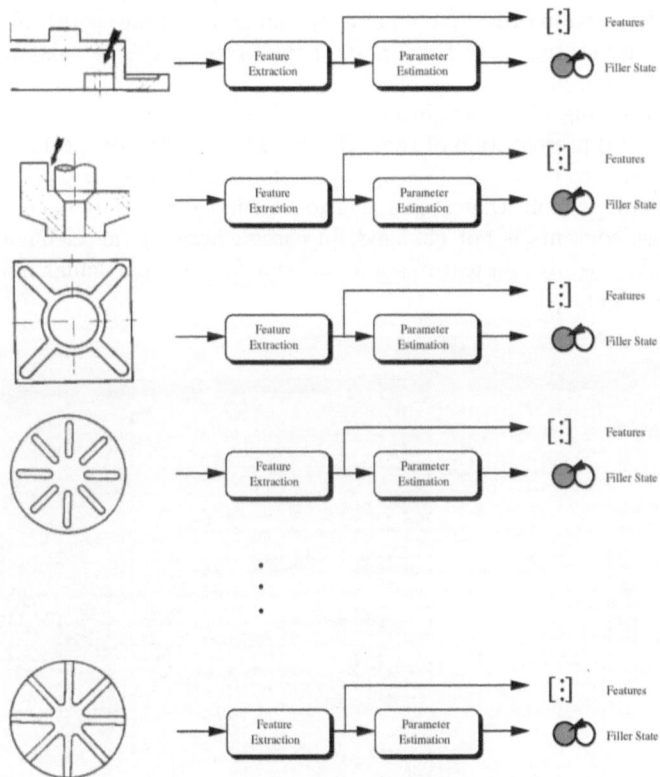

Fig. 5. Processing of the database elements

In order to provide a more detailed explanation of the entire process, the major steps for the image retrieval procedure using augmented P2DHMMs are outlined in the following:

Step 1: Feature extraction and parameter estimation of the pdf for every image in the database, as shown in Fig. 5. The pdf will be used for the filler state if this image is investigated for retrieval.

Step 2: Presentation of a query sketch and training of a P2DHMM for this sketch (see also Fig. 3).

Step 3: Modification of the initial P2DHMM by adding filler states, which results in the augmented structure, as outlined in Fig. 4.

Step 4: For every engineering drawing of the database, segmentations as well
as probability scores are calculated by applying the Viterbi algorithm.
Note that the individual features as well as the corresponding pdfs of the
database elements according to Fig. 5 are used. However, the structure
as well as the non-shaded states of the augmented structure in Fig. 4 are
maintained.

Step 5: Using the segmentations achieved in step 4, the probability scores are
recalculated in order to eliminate the influence of the scores calculated on
the filler states. Note that most of the probabilities calculated in step 4
can be reused.

Step 6: Ranking of the engineering drawings according to the recalculated
score and presentation of those images with the highest probability score.

Step 7: Back to step 2 for the presentation of the next query.

It is important to note that step 1 has to be carried out only once, as long as
the database contents is not changed. In cases where e.g. an element is added
to the database, only the features and the pdf for that particular new element
have to be calculated.

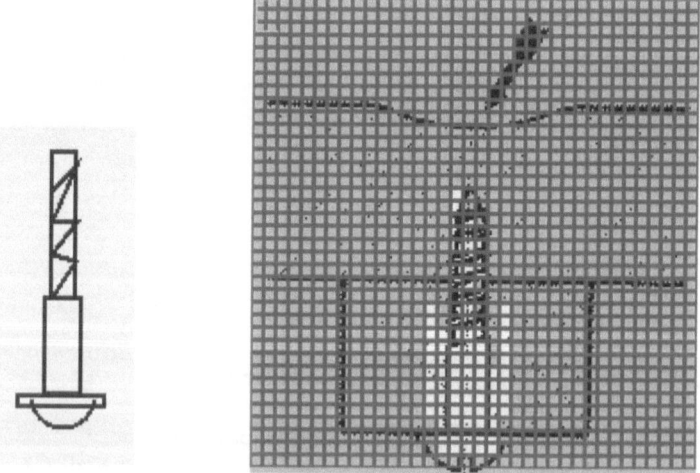

Fig. 6. Query sketch and corresponding segmentation of a database element

4   Database

Our experimental mechanical engineering drawing database currently consists of
56 elements, all of which have been scanned from [5]. For the scanning procedure
a resolution of 300 dpi has been chosen. The size of the images varies from
180×134 up to 258×240 pixels. The use of images with different sizes without the

need for a resizing or scaling step is an additional advantage of the utilization of P2DHMMs. Due to their elastic matching capabilities, no uniform size is needed. Note that all typical preprocessing steps have been omitted here, in particular no despecle step or line thinning step has been carried out.

5   Experiments and Results

In order to evaluate the experimental retrieval system, 10 query shapes have been defined, all of which have been drawn using the standard UNIX drawing package *xfig*. Three of these queries and the corresponding retrieved images are shown in the figures 7, 8 and 9. The query itself is always shown in the upper left part of the figures, followed by those five database elements with the highest probability score (ordered left to right and top to bottom, with decreasing score). We regard the results shown in the figures as good retrieval results, especially when examining Fig. 7, where two images containing screws could be retrieved, although the sketch is very rough and the screws, which have been retrieved, are embedded in hatching and are connected to other lines. Note that just the ranking of the images according to the calculated score is shown, however the segmentation and thus the position of the query in the retrieved images has also been found (see step 4 in Sec. 3). The presentation of the other seven queries showed similar results.

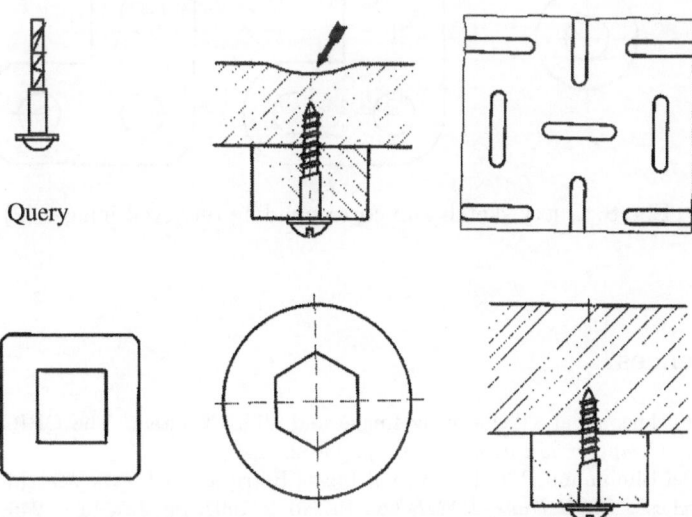

Fig. 7. Query sketch and corresponding retrieved images (1)

6   Summary

A novel approach to the retrieval of engineering drawings based on the use of stochastic models has been presented. Engineering drawing databases can be searched intuitively by presenting sketches or shapes which represent details such as e.g. screws or holes in the drawings of mechanical parts. The query is represented by a pseudo 2-D Hidden Markov Model which is surrounded by filler states. These filler states generate the remaining part of the engineering drawing apart from the query shape or sketch itself. Thus, our approach aims to retrieve those images containing certain details and also locates these details in the retrieved images, even in cases where the query shape is embedded in e.g. hatching or is connected to other parts in the drawing. The proposed technique shows good results, which has been demonstrated by a series of queries.

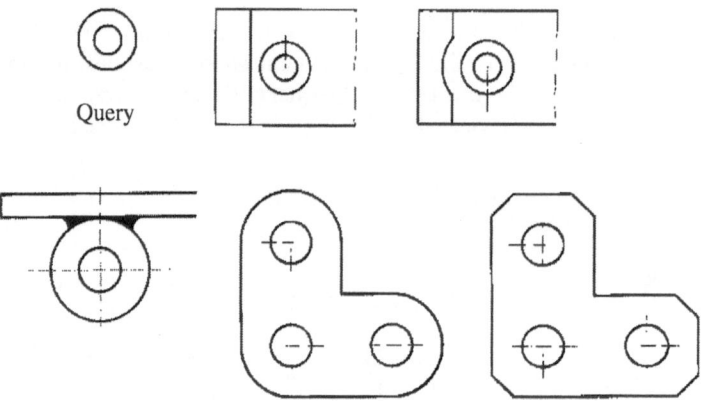

Fig. 8. Query sketch and corresponding retrieved images (2)

References

1. M. Flickner et al., "Query by Image and Video Content: The QBIC System", *IEEE Computer Magazine*, 1995, pp. 23–32. 246
2. A. Del Bimbo and P. Pala, "Visual Image Retrieval by Elastic Matching of User Sketches", *IEEE Trans. PAMI*, Vol. 19, No. 2, 1997, pp. 121–132. 246
3. H.-C. Lin, L.-L. Wang, and S.-N. Yang, "Color Image Retrieval Based on Hidden Markov Models", *IEEE Trans. on Image Processing*, Vol. 6, No. 2, Feb. 1997, pp. 332–339. 246
4. S. Müller, S. Eickeler, G. Rigoll, "Image Database Retrieval of Rotated Objects by User Sketch," In *Proc. IEEE Workshop on Content-Based Access of Image and Video Libraries (CBAIVL)*, Santa Barbara, 1998, pp. 40–44. 246, 247

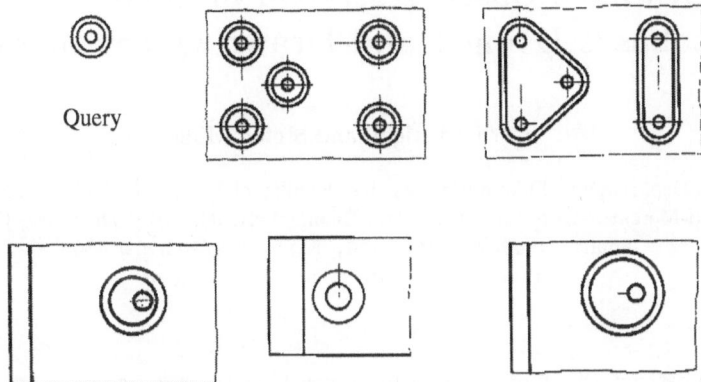

Fig. 9. Query sketch and corresponding retrieved images (3)

5. K.-H. Bode, "Konstruktions-Atlas: Werkstoff- u. verfahrensgerecht konstruieren", Hoppenstedt Technik Tabellen Verl., 1988. 246, 247, 252
6. S. Ablameyko, V. Bereishik, O. Frantskevich, M. Homenko, N. Paramonova, "Algorithms for Recognition of the Main Engineering Drawing Entities", In *Proc. Intern. Conference on Document Analysis and Recognition (ICDAR)*, 1997, Ulm (Germany), pp. 776–779. 247
7. R. Kasturi, S. T. Bow, W. El-Masri, J. Shah, J. R. Gattiker, U. B. Mokate, "A System for Interpretation of Line Drawings", *IEEE Trans. on PAMI*, Vol. 12, No. 10, 1990, pp. 978–992. 247
8. S. Müller, S. Eickeler, Ch. Neukirchen, B. Winterstein, "Segmentation and Classification of Hand-Drawn Pictograms in Cluttered Scenes – An Integrated Approach", In *Proc. IEEE Intern. Conf. on Acoustics, Speech, and Signal Processing*, Phoenix, 1999, pp. 3489–3492. 247, 248
9. S. Kuo and O. Agazzi, "Keyword Spotting in Poorly Printed Printed Documents Using Pseudo 2-D Hidden Markov Models", *IEEE Trans. on PAMI*, Vol. 13, No. 11, 1991, pp. 1172–1184. 247, 248, 249
10. L. R. Rabiner and B. H. Juang, "An Introduction to Hidden Markov Models", *IEEE ASSP Magazine*, 1986, pp. 4–16. 247
11. R. Seiler, M. Schenkel and F. Eggimann, "Off-Line Cursive Handwriting Recognition Compared with On-Line Recognition", In *Proc. IEEE Intern. Conference on Pattern Recognition (ICPR)*, Vol. IV, 1996, pp. 505–509. 247, 248
12. F. S. Samaria, "Face Recognition Using Hidden Markov Models", Ph. D. Thesis, Cambridge University, 1994. 248, 249
13. Y. He and A. Kundu, "2-D Shape Classification Using Hidden Markov Model", *IEEE Trans. on PAMI*, Vol. 13, No. 11, 1991, pp. 1172–1184. 248
14. S.-J. Young, "The General Use of Tying in Phoneme-Based HMM Speech Recognisers", In *Proc. IEEE Intern. Conference on Acoustics, Speech and Signal Processing*, 1992, pp. 569–572. 250

Graphics-Based Retrieval of Color Image Databases Using Hand-Drawn Query Sketches

Gerhard Rigoll and Stefan Müller

Department of Computer Science, Faculty of Electrical Engineering
Gerhard-Mercator-University Duisburg, Bismarckstr. 90, 47057 Duisburg, Germany
Phone: ++49/203/379-1140, FAX: ++49/203/379-4363
{rigoll,stm}@fb9-ti.uni-duisburg.de

Abstract. This paper presents a novel approach to graphics-based information retrieval validated with an experimental system that is able to perform integrated shape and color based image retrieval with hand-drawn sketches which can be presented in rotation-, scale-, and translation-invariant mode. Due to the use of Hidden Markov Models (HMMs), an elastic matching of shapes can be performed, which allows the retrieval of shapes by applying simple sketches. Since these sketches represent hand-made line drawings and can be augmented with color features, the resulting user query represents a complex graphics structure that has to be analyzed for retrieving the image database. The database elements (mostly images of hand tools) are represented by HMMs which have been modified in order to achieve the desired rotation invariance property. Invariance with respect to scaling and translation is achieved by the feature extraction, which is a polar sampling technique, with the center of the sampling raster positioned at the shapes's center of gravity. The outcome of the feature extraction step is also known as a shape matrix, which is a shape descriptor that has been already used occasionally in image processing tasks. The image retrieval system showed good retrieval results even with unexperienced users, which is demonstrated by a number of query sketches and corresponding retrieval images in this paper.

1 Introduction

With the increasing popularity of the use of large-volume image databases in various applications, there is a growing need for an automatic retrieval system in order to access the image database content easily and intuitively. A common criterion for the retrieval of pictorial data is "what object (shapes or images) in the database match or are closely similar to a given shape or image ?" [5]. This type of retrieval is called shape similarity based retrieval. Note that in the context of shape based image retrieval, the shape similarity measure should be invariant to affine transformations (i.e. rotation, scaling, and translation) of shapes and images. This is due to the fact, that humans ignore such variations in images for recognition and retrieval purposes.

Atul K. Chhabra and D. Dori (Eds.): GREC'99, LNCS 1941, pp. 256–265, 2000.

An experimental system that is able to perform shape based image retrieval, thereby ignoring the effects of the affine transformations rotation, scaling and translation, has been presented by the authors in [6]. Due to the use of Hidden Markov Models (HMMs), an elastic matching of shapes can be performed, which allows the retrieval of shapes by applying simple sketches. The database elements (mostly images of hand tools) have been represented by HMMs which have been modified in order to achieve the desired rotation invariance property. Invariance with respect to scaling and translation is achieved by the feature extraction, which is a polar sampling technique, with the center of the sampling raster positioned at the shape's center of gravity (COG). The outcome of the feature extraction step is also known as a *shape matrix*, which is a shape descriptor that has been introduced by Goshtasby in [1] and that has been further evaluated in [8, 9]. The image retrieval by sketch system mentioned above showed good retrieval results even with unexperienced users, which has been demonstrated by a number of query sketches and corresponding retrieved images in [6]. In order to further evaluate the system, a Java-based version has been developed and placed on the World Wide Web (WWW) at http://www.fb9-ti.uni-duisburg.de/demos/query.html. Fig. 1 presents the Java applet, which has been developed in order to apply query sketches. Once

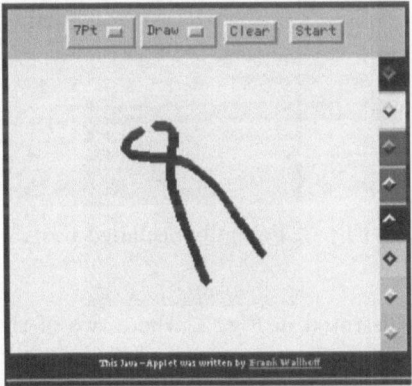

Fig. 1. Java applet for presenting query sketches to our image retrieval system

the sketch has been drawn, data representing the sketch is transmitted to the server and the image database is searched for similar images. Finally, those four images with the highest (probability-) score are send back to the client where the query has been issued and displayed in a separate window. When using the system, the query can be refined and intermediate retrieval results can be kept until the desired results are achieved. The Java-based system demonstrates the elastic matching capabilities of the retrieval system as described in [6].

In order to further improve the retrieval procedure, we added color as a visual cue to the baseline system. Thus, shape and color derived features are integrated into a single model, which can elegantly be achieved through the use of streams within the HMM framework. A section in this paper will introduce this integrated retrieval system. It is noteworthy, that the matching of both visual cues shape and color is measured in a local and thus detailed way. Global similarity measures usually utilize e.g. geometric moments and histograms for the matching of shape and color, respectively. The combination of global similarity measures, namely edge and color histograms, for the task of image retrieval has been presented in [3].

Furthermore, improved modeling techniques leading to a deformation tolerant matching mode will be presented in this paper. The improvements in deformation tolerance have been achieved by applying so-called pseudo 2-D Hidden Markov Models (P2DHMMs) or by alternatively applying weighting factors which have been introduced by Taza and Suen [9] in the context of shape matrices. The deformation tolerant modeling allows for the retrieval of deformed or

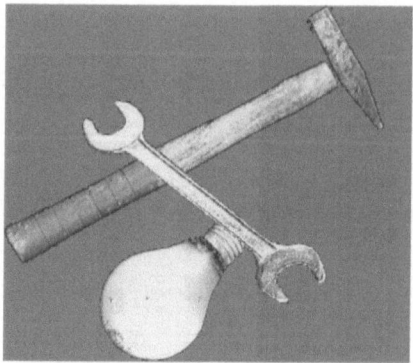

Fig. 2. Partially occluded tools

occluded shapes as illustrated in Fig. 2, where two of the objects are partially occluded.

The organization of this paper is as follows: we recapitulate the elements of our baseline system in Section 2, followed by the description of the enhanced system, which integrates color and shape features, in Section 3. Section 4 presents the modeling techniques, which lead to an improved deformation tolerant shape based retrieval mode and experiments and results on a retrieval task on artificially deformed objects are presented. A summary is given in the final section.

2   Shape-Based Image Retrieval Using HMMs

In [6] a retrieval system, which enables the user to search an image database by presenting simple sketches has been described. After presenting the sketch, a feature sequence is extracted from this pictorial query which is scored by HMMs representing the individual database elements. This sequence is calculated by applying thresholding and lowpass filtering steps and finally by applying a polar sampling step. This sampling step is performed in an adaptive way which results in scale and translation invariance as well as rotation invariance together with the rotation invariant Markov modeling. The polar samples are also known as a *shape matrix*, a shape descriptor introduced by Goshtasby in [1]. A shape matrix with dimension $N \times M$ is generated in the following way:

1: Let O be the center of gravity of the shape, and OA with length R_{max} the maximum radius of the shape
2: set the sampling length $\Delta r = R_{max}/(M-1)$
3: set the angular step $\Delta\varphi = 2\pi/N$
4: take samples from the image I on polar coordinates (r, φ) using the following sampling raster:

$$I_s(n,m) = I(n \cdot \Delta r, m \cdot \Delta\varphi) \tag{1}$$
$$m = 0, \ldots, M-1$$
$$n = 0, \ldots, N-1$$

$I_s(n,m)$ now contains $N \times M$ samples and can be regarded as a shape matrix. Fig. 3 shows the sampling raster as used by the authors.

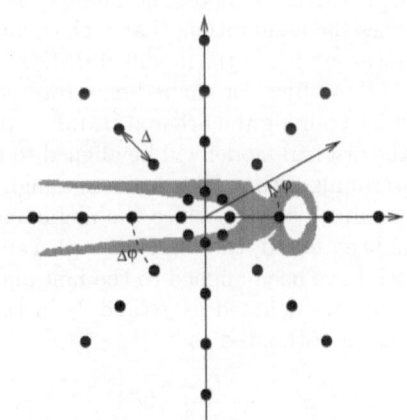

Fig. 3. Polar sampling raster

Note that we made the following changes to the original procedure of generating a shape matrix as described in [1]. As can be seen in Fig. 3, samples are taken at $r = \Delta r/2$ rather than $r = 0$. This has been done in order to avoid redundancy. Furthermore, due to the use of a lowpass filtering step, the shape matrix $I_s(n,m)$ no longer contains only binary values. Binary values have been used in [1, 9] in order to be able to calculate shape distances easily.

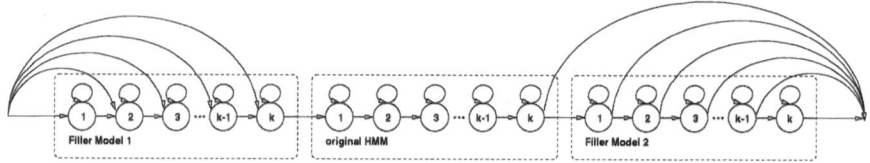

Fig. 4. HMM structure for the rotation invariant modeling of shapes

When using HMMs, a feature sequence $(o_1, \ldots, o_M)$ has to be built. Note that a short introduction to the HMM framework can be found in [6] and a very detailed explanation is given in [7]. The feature sequence is built in the following manner: Each feature vector o contains those samples of $I_s(n, m)$ where $m = const$. The sequence is built by arranging these vectors such that m increases $(m = 0, \ldots, M - 1)$. This feature sequence is already invariant to translation and scaling. In order to achieve rotation invariance, we proposed in [6] the use of modified HMMs, which have been concatenated with so-called filler models. These filler models are copies of an original or initially trained HMM, which are attached in front of or behind the original model, with the first HMM (Filler Model 1) having a modified initial state distribution vector π and the final one (Filler Model 2) being modified so as to allow the HMM to be in any state, once the end of the feature sequence is reached. The components of the vector π are uniformly set to $\frac{1}{k}$, where k denotes the number of states of the original model. This step expresses the assumption, that each (quantized) rotation angle is equally likely. The concatenation of the modified HMMs is illustrated in Fig. 4. If the feature sequence of an object or shape being rotated with respect to the (unrotated) shape used for training the original HMM, is presented twice to the concatenated HMMs, the original model will be aligned to the unrotated part of the sequence by the Viterbi algorithm. This leads to a high probability $Pr(O|\lambda)$ if the two objects have similar shapes. Once the alignment of the sequence to the Markov Models has been found, the rotation angle can be estimated by the number of features which have been aligned to the first and second filler model. These numbers of features are denoted as f_1 and f_2 in the following and thus the rotation angle $\varphi^\star$ can be estimated as

$$\varphi^\star = \frac{f_1}{f_1 + f_2} \cdot 360° \tag{2}$$

As described in [6], every image of the database is represented by a rotation invariant model (see also Fig. 4), whereas the rough sketch of an object is represented by a feature sequence. After the probability score $Pr(O|\lambda)$ has been calculated for every database element, those N images with the highest score are retrieved. Query sketches and corresponding retrieved images illustrating the feasibility of the approach are given in [6]. In order to further improve the retrieval procedure, we added color as a visual cue to the baseline system. The details of the integrated system using color and shape are given in the next section.

3   Integration of Shape and Color Features

By the use of streams (sets of features that are assumed to be statistically independent) within the HMM framework, it is possible to integrate inhomogeneous features derived from e.g. color and shape into a single statistical model (see also [2]). In this case, the probability density function (pdf) $b_j(o)$ of HMM state s_j is given by

$$b_j(o) = \prod_{s=1}^{S} b_{js}(o_s)^{\gamma_s} \tag{3}$$

where S denotes the number of streams, γ_s are the stream weights and the pdfs $b_{js}(o_s)$ are usually given by Gaussian mixtures. The stream weights provide the opportunity to adjust the influence of the different feature streams. Fig. 5 illustrates the generation of a shape and a color stream. Stream 1 of the sequence, which is derived from the shape of an object, is calculated by applying the steps depicted in the upper part of Fig. 5. Note that these preprocessing and feature extraction steps are identical to the steps described in Sec. 2 and in [6]. In order to calculate the color information (represented in an RGB color space), the binarization step is skipped and the remaining steps as illustrated in the lower part of Fig. 5 are carried out. The influence of the different cues shape and color can be controlled by stream weights (see Eq. 3), which thus become an integral part of the query. The techniques presented in this section have been evaluated on a color-image database consisting of 120 images of arbitrarily rotated objects. For every image of the database the feature extraction steps presented in Fig. 5 have been applied, followed by the training of an individual model utilizing the Baum-Welch algorithm. As discussed in Sec. 2 these models are concatenated with the modified filler HMMs and thus represent the image in a rotation invariant mode, thereby integrating shape and color features. Fig. 6 presents some results achieved with our system, where in every row the query sketch is shown first (light gray background), followed by those four images (dark gray background) with the highest probability scores. The numbers of features being aligned to the first and second filler models (f_1 and f_2, respectively) are given below the retrieved images together with an estimated rotation angle calculated from these values according to Eq. 2.

4   Improved Modeling of Deformed Objects

Heavily deformed shapes occur e.g. after applying segmentation steps to occluded objects in images. In order to handle the retrieval of deformed shapes, we propose an improved stochastic modeling, based on the use of (pseudo-)two-dimensional HMMs later in this chapter. However, even the stochastic modeling based on one-dimensional HMMs can be further improved, as will be explained in the following.

Taza and Suen [9] extended the shape matrix approach, as explained in Sec. 2, further by introducing weighting factors. These weighting factors are based on

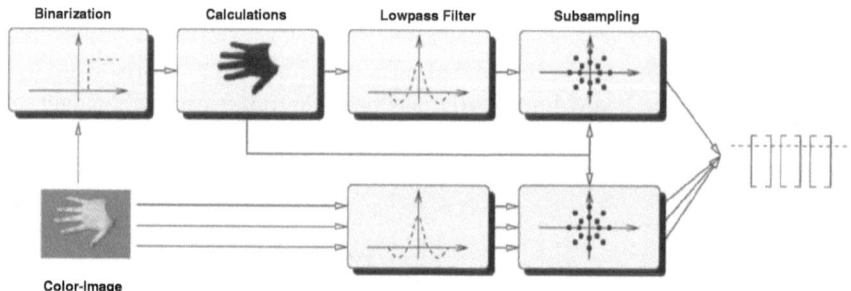

Fig. 5. Blockdiagram of the feature extraction steps

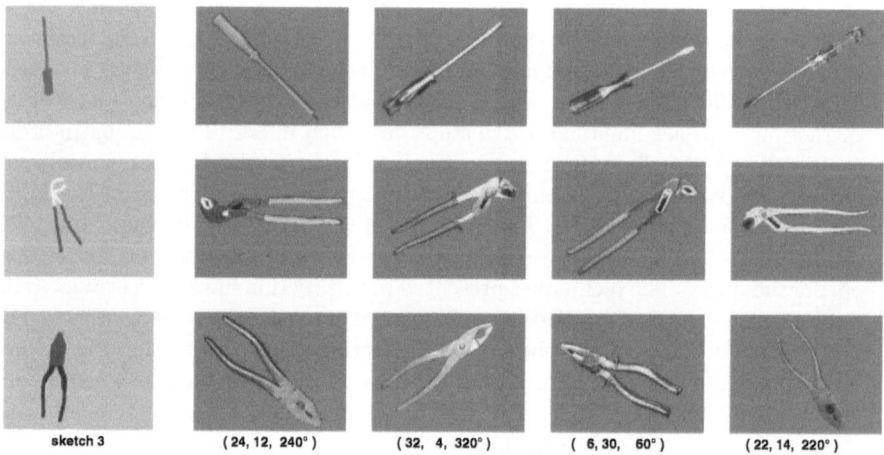

Fig. 6. Query sketches and retrieved images. Note that the colors match very well, the grips of the tong (sketch 2) are red and so are the grips of the first three retrieved tongs

the fact that the sampling density is not constant with the polar sampling raster, as can be seen in Fig. 3. Since the number of sampling points is constant for all the circles, and the circumference is larger on the outer circles, there is more information on the outer circles for the same number of sample points. In [9] it is shown that the weighting factor (defined as the inverse of the information redundancy) is direct proportional to the radius of the circle. These weighting factors can be elegantly integrated into the HMM framework, by separating the elements of each feature vector into streams and by setting the corresponding stream weights γ_s proportional to the radius. A more deformation tolerant matching might be achieved by applying the structure in Fig. 7 to the task of shape based retrieval. In this figure a similar structure to Fig. 4 is shown, namely concatenated HMMs with modified entry- and exit-transitions. Besides these obvious similarities, the individual HMMs shown in Fig. 7 are hierarchical HMMs,

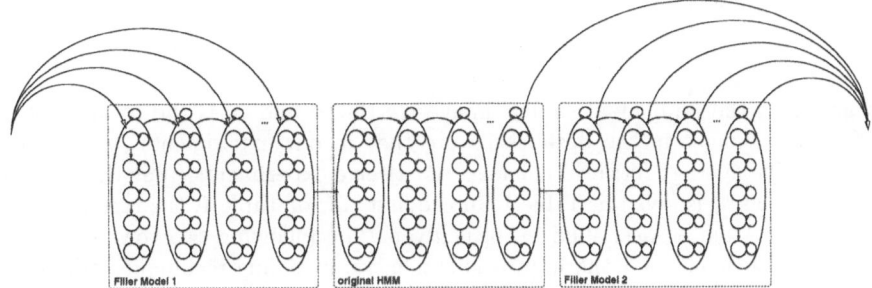

Fig. 7. Pseudo 2-D HMMs for the modeling of deformed objects

so-called pseudo 2-D HMMs (P2DHMMs) or planar HMMs, which consist of *superstates* (in horizontal direction) containing itself ordinary HMMs (in vertical direction). P2DHMMs have been introduced by Kuo and Agazzi in [4]. It is possible to use P2DHMMs for modeling polar sampled data (see also Fig. 3) in the following manner: Each set of samples taken at a constant angle, is aligned to one of the superstates of the P2DHMM, resulting in a circular warping of the pattern. Furthermore, within the superstate, the samples taken at a constant angle are aligned to one-dimensional HMM states, resulting in a radial warping of the shape.

In order to evaluate the proposed methods, experiments on a database consisting of artificially deformed objects have been carried out. Fig. 8 shows three examples of deformed shapes of scissors, where the artificial deformations closely

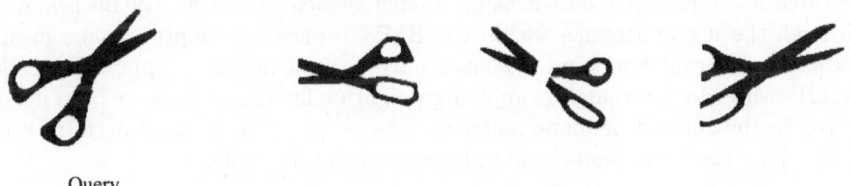

Query

Fig. 8. Artificially deformed shapes

resemble the effect of occlusion. The fourth shape in Fig. 8 represents an undeformed shape, which is used as a query image. The database consists of 12 classes of tools, each class contains four deformed objects and an undeformed query image. During the experiments the 12 undeformed shapes are presented to the system and those six images with the highest similarity score are examined. Table 1 presents the retrieval efficiencies η_T for the different approaches mentioned above. According to [5], the retrieval efficiency for a given shortlist of size T is given by

$$\eta_T = \begin{cases} \frac{n}{N} & if \quad N \leq T \\ \frac{n}{T} & if \quad N > T \end{cases} \tag{4}$$

where n is the number of similar images retrieved and N is the total number of similar images in the database. Note that in our experiments $N = 4$ and $T = 6$. The average retrieval efficiency for twelve experiments (one experiment for each class) is given in Table 1. In the first row of Table 1, the result for the retrieval system as described in [6] is given. The following two rows show the retrieval efficiencies for the improved stochastic modeling techniques described in this section.

Table 1. Retrieval efficiencies achieved in the experiments

method	retrieval efficiency η_T
1-D HMM	75.00%
1-D HMM + stream weights	83.33%
pseudo 2-D HMMs	79.17%

5   Summary

In this paper recent improvements in the stochastic modeling of shapes for content-based image database retrieval have been presented. Color has been added as a visual cue to our baseline system, which utilizes a polar sampling technique in combination with Hidden Markov Models. Shape and color derived features are integrated into a single model, which can elegantly be achieved through the use of streams within the HMM framework. Improvements in deformation tolerant matching of shapes have been achieved by applying pseudo 2-D HMMs or by alternatively applying weighting factors which have been introduced in the context of shape matrices. The proposed techniques perform very well, which has been demonstrated by experimental results.

References

[1] A. Goshtasby. Description and Discrimination of Planar Shapes Using Shape Matrices. *IEEE Trans. on PAMI*, 7(6):738–743, Nov. 1985. 257, 259

[2] V. N. Gupta, M. Lenning, and P. Mermelstein. Integration of Acoustic Information in a Large Vocabulary Word Recognizer. In *Proc. IEEE ICASSP*, pages 697–700, Dallas, 1997. 261

[3] A. K. Jain and A. Vailaya. Image Retrieval Using Color and Shape. *Pattern Recognition*, 29(8):1233–1244, 1996. 258

[4] S. Kuo and O. Agazzi. Keyword Spotting in Poorly Printed Documents Using Pseudo 2-D Hidden Markov Models. *IEEE Trans. on PAMI*, 13(11):1172–1184, Nov. 1991. 263

[5] B. M. Mehtre, M. S. Kankanhalli, and W. F. Lee. Shape Measures for Content Based Image Retrieval: A Comparison. *Pattern Recognition*, 33(3):319–337, 1997. 256, 263

[6] S. Müller, S. Eickeler, and G. Rigoll. Image Database Retrieval of Rotated Objects by User Sketch. In *Proc. IEEE Workshop on CBAIVL*, pages 40–44, Santa Barbara, 1998. 257, 258, 260, 261, 264

[7] L. R. Rabiner and B. H. Juang. An Introduction to Hidden Markov Models. *IEEE ASSP Magazine*, pages 4–16, 1986. 260

[8] R. Sabourin, J.-P. Drouhard, and E. S. Wah. Shape Matrices as a Mixed Shape Factor for Off-line Signature Verification. In *Proc. Intern. Conference on Document Analysis and Recognition (ICDAR)*, pages 661–665, Ulm (Germany), 1997. 257

[9] A. Taza and C. Y. Suen. Discrimination of Planar Shapes Using Shape Matrices. *IEEE Trans. on SMC*, 19(5):1281–1289, Sep/Oct 1989. 257, 258, 259, 261, 262

A Simple Approach to Recognise Geometric Shapes Interactively

Joaquim A. Jorge and Manuel J. Fonseca

Departamento de Engenharia Informática, IST/UTL
Av. Rovisco Pais, 1049-001 Lisboa, Portugal
jorgej@acm.org
mjf@ist.utl.pt

Abstract. This paper presents a simple method to recognise multi-stroke sketches of geometric shapes. It uses temporal adjacency and global geometric properties of figures to recognise a simple vocabulary of geometric shapes including solid and dashed line styles, selection and delete gestures. The geometric features used (convex hull, smallest-area regular polygons, perimeter and area scalar ratios) are invariant with rotation and scale of figures. We have found the method very usable with acceptable recognition rates although the multi-stroke approach poses problems in choosing appropriate values for time-outs.
Although we have privileged simplicity over robustness, the method has proved suitable for interactive applications.

1 Introduction

Recognition of hand-drawn geometric shapes has garnered new attention with the widespread adoption of Personal Digital Assistants (PDAs). While conventional off-line approaches to recognition of geometric figures have long focused on raw classification performance, on-line systems raise a different set of issues. First, geometric figures in CAD drawings are input precisely either by human draftspeople or through computer peripherals. Recognising these shapes deals mainly with noise introduced by sources outside the process, such as copy degradation or poor photographic reproduction. In online applications however, the noise is inherent to the process of information gathering and shapes are often sketched poorly due to media, operator and process limitations, yielding imperfect and ambiguous shapes that even humans find difficult to distinguish. One further difference from off-line algorithms is that input data are sequences of points rather than image bitmaps. Also, the online recogniser should cope with innumerable variations in hand sketches — it is not reasonable to require that all geometric shapes be drawn in a single stroke, especially if we want to recognise dashed lines.

We want to emphasise that our main concern is to be able to recognise positive samples, i.e. shapes the user intended to draw in the first place. As such, our motivation was not to develop a foolproof method, but rather to provide a

Atul K. Chhabra and D. Dori (Eds.): GREC'99, LNCS 1941, pp. 266–274, 2000.

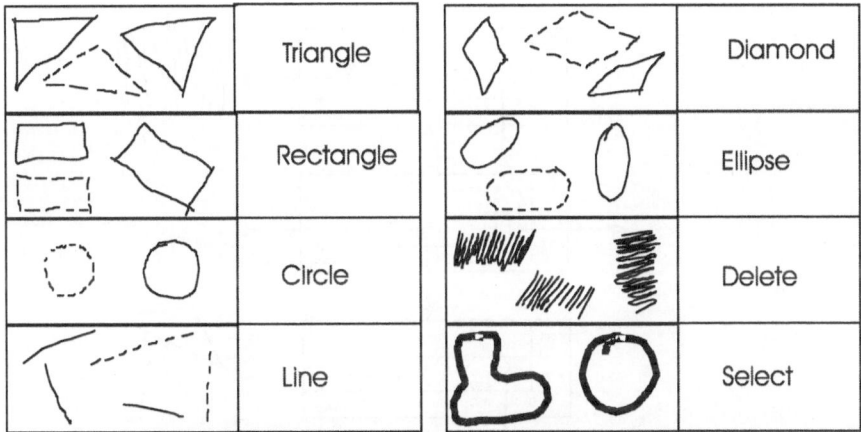

Fig. 1. Geometric shapes and commands recognised

tool to aid users in constructing diagrams and other structured drawings interactively. In the remainder of this paper we describe the feature extraction and classification processes, discuss experimental results and future work.

2   The Recognition Algorithm

The recognition algorithm is based on three main ideas. First, it uses entirely global geometric properties extracted from input shapes. Since we are solely interested in identifying geometric entities, the recogniser relies mainly on geometry information. Second, to enhance recognition performance, we use a decision tree to filter out unwanted shapes using distinctive criteria. Third, to overcome uncertainty and imprecision in shape sketches, we use fuzzy logic [3] to associate degrees of certainty to recognised shapes, thereby handling ambiguities naturally.

This algorithm recognises elementary geometric shapes, such as triangles, rectangles, diamonds, circles, ellipses and lines, and two gestures, delete and select, as depicted in Fig. 1. Shapes are recognised independently of changes in rotation, size or number of individual strokes. The recogniser works by looking up values of specific features in fuzzy sets at each decision tree node as illustrated by Fig. 2. This traversal process yields a list of plausible shapes ordered by degree of certainty.

This approach is largely based on a more restrictive method proposed by Kimura et. al.[2] which did not recognise non-rotated shapes, open/closed and dashed lines. Other authors have proposed more complex methods, involving neural networks [13] using a procedure that might prove more robust than ours, although such claims are not made explicit. Despite handwriting recognition being outside the scope of our work, we will shortly analyse the Graffiti [5] system.

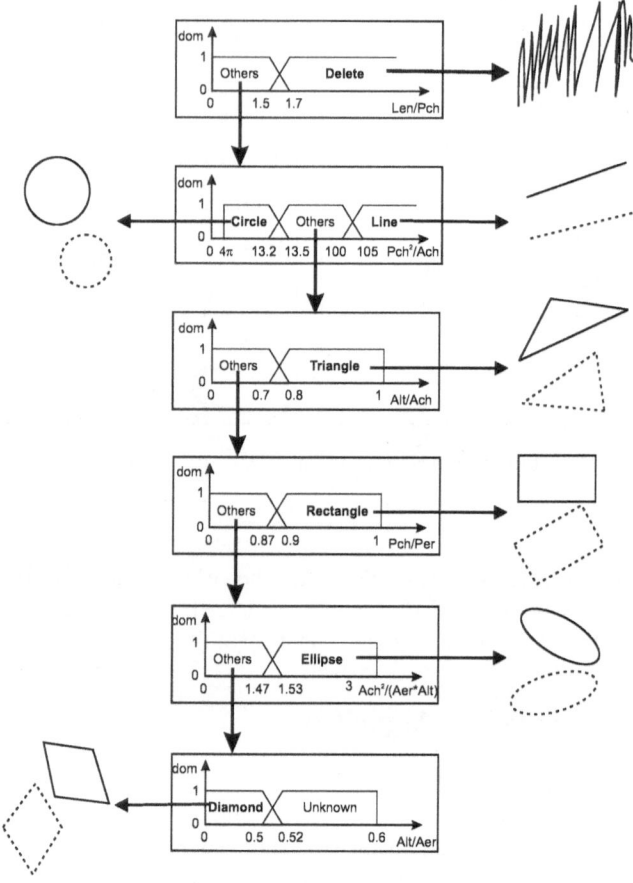

Fig. 2. Decision tree and fuzzy sets

This system recognises characters drawn using just one stroke. Using a single stroke makes the recognition process easier, but this approach requires users to learn new ways of drawing letters. The Graffiti system, as well as the majority of handwriting recognition systems, uses local features, such as drawing speed, while our method uses global geometric features. As a result, our recognition process uses simpler features, the strokes are analysed as a whole and the recognition result is relies less in the way individual strokes were drawn, than the shape overall geometric properties. Furthermore, most handwriting recognition systems rely on some form of constrained writing, while our approach allows shapes to be recognised regardless of orientation and size.

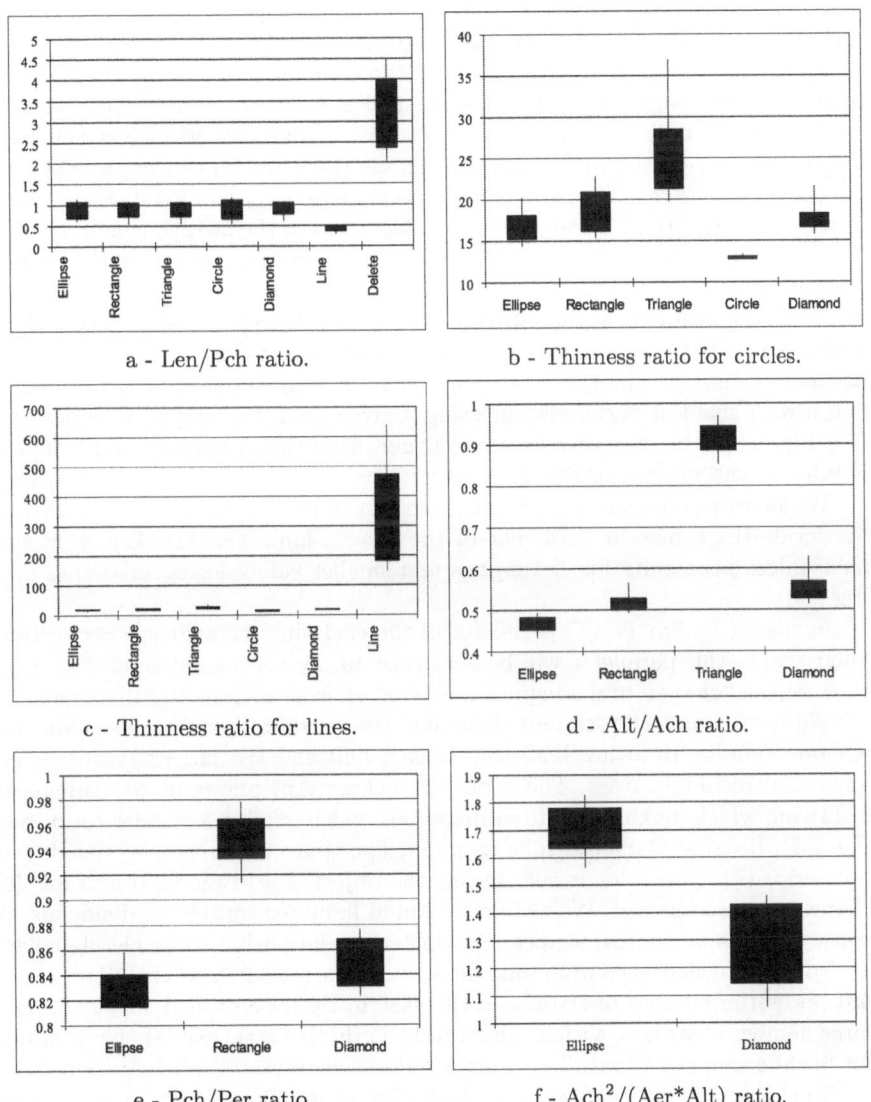

a - Len/Pch ratio.

b - Thinness ratio for circles.

c - Thinness ratio for lines.

d - Alt/Ach ratio.

e - Pch/Per ratio.

f - Ach^2/(Aer*Alt) ratio.

Fig. 3. Percentiles for area and perimeter ratios

2.1 Feature Extraction

We start the recognition process by collecting data points using a digitising tablet, from the first pen-down event until a set timeout value after the last pen-up. Next, we compute the convex hull of the set of input points thus collected [9]. We use the convex hull to compute two special polygons. Using a simple three-point algorithm we identify the largest-area triangle that fits inside the convex hull and the enclosing rectangle. Finally, we compute the area and perimeter of each polygon to estimate features and degrees of likelihood for each shape class.

Since this recogniser is intended for interactive use, we are interested in detecting gestures such as a set of zigzag strokes drawn in succession to signify erasing objects underneath. Using our geometry approach, we detect this pattern by comparing the total length of strokes (`Len`) drawn to the perimeter of the convex hull (`Pch`). The ratio `Len/Pch` is close to unity for closed shapes, such as rectangles or circles. Large values are associated to the `Delete` command (see Fig. 3.a). Open shapes, such as polygonal lines and arcs, have Len/Pch values approaching one-half (typical of straight lines).

To distinguish circles and straight lines from other shapes we use the *Thinness ratio* (`Pch`^{2}`/Ach`), where `Ach` is the area of the convex hull, and `Pch`^{2} is its perimeter squared. The thinness of a `Circle` is minimal, since it is the planar figure with smallest perimeter enclosing a given area, yielding a value near 4π (see Fig. 3.b). On the other extreme, `Lines` have thinness values approaching infinity, as can be seen in Fig. 3.c.

We identify triangles by comparing the area of the largest triangle (`Alt`) that fits inside the convex hull to that of the convex hull. The `Alt/Ach` ratio will have values near unity for `Triangles` and smaller values for other shapes (see Fig. 3.d).

Similarly, let `Per` be the perimeter of the enclosing rectangle[4]. For rectangular shapes this perimeter will be very close to the convex hull's (cf. Fig. 3.e), thus we use `Pch/Per` to distinguish `Rectangles` from ellipses and diamonds.

We have found ellipses and diamonds the hardest to distinguish. We use a more complex ratio involving the convex hull and the largest enclosed triangle and rectangle areas. The ratio `Ach`^{2}`/(Aer*Alt)` allows us to distinguish `Ellipses` which maximise it from diamonds which exhibit a smaller ratio (See Fig. 3.f). Because diamonds take up about two times the area of a triangle, an area ratio (`Alt/Aer`) under 50% means the object is a `Diamond`, otherwise the shape is not recognised. We should probably limit recognition of diamonds to constrained (*non-rotated*) shapes, for which the relationship above clearly holds.

To distinguish dashed from solid lines we use the ratio `Pch*NStrks/Len` where `NStrks` is the number of strokes in the sketch. Because dashed shapes have a large number of strokes, with a small total length, this ratio exhibits large values for `Dashed` shapes and smaller values for closed shapes.

To choose the "best" fuzzy sets describing shape filters in the decision tree we used a "training set" developed by three subjects who drew each shape ten times using solid lines and five times using dashed lines. We used these values as depicted in Figs. 3.a to 3.f to define the fuzzy sets used in the decision tree. Fig. 2 shows the different fuzzy sets for each filter, the shapes that each identifies and the order of application of the different filters. Fuzzy sets were derived from the extreme percentiles from experimental values, trading-off rejections for false identification and increase in classification category, e.g. increasing the maximum thinness value for circles will "confuse" some ellipses with circles, or a decrease

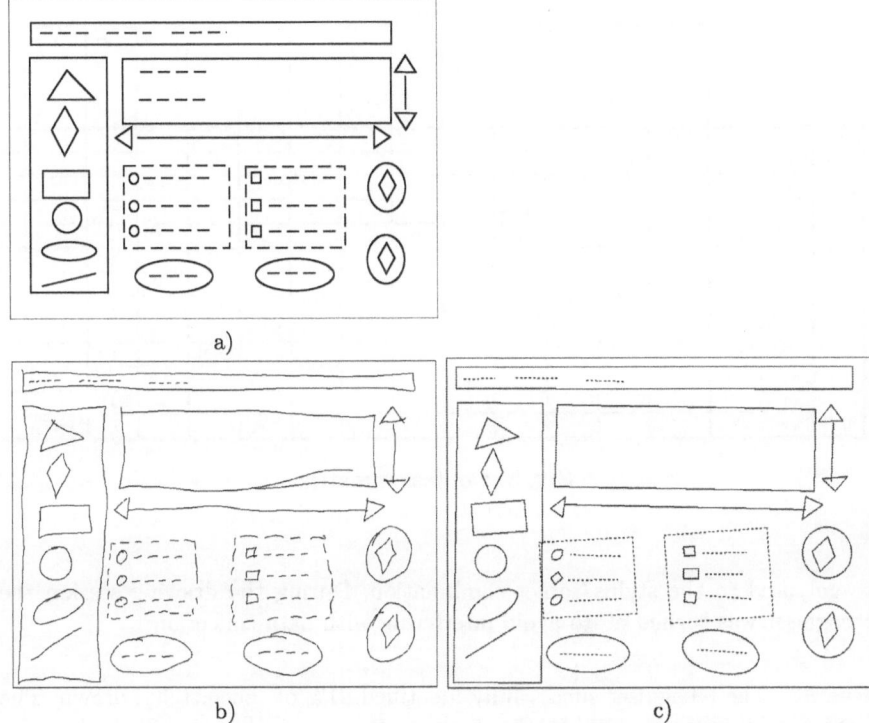

Fig. 4. a) Diagram. b) Sketch. c) Recognised shapes

in the line minimum thinness value will cause thin shapes (such as rectangles) to be identified as lines.

2.2 Experimental Setup

In order to evaluate the recognition algorithm, we asked seven subjects to draw each shape fifteen times each, ten times using solid lines and five times using dashed lines. Each subject also drew the diagram presented in Fig. 4.a, yielding a total of 934 shapes. Subjects were told that the experiment was meant to test recognition, so they didn't try to draw "unnatural" shapes. Fig. 4.b shows a sample diagram drawn by one of the subjects and Fig. 4.c shows the recognised shapes.

We used a Calcomp digitising tablet and a cordless stylus to draw the shapes. Three subjects were experts in using pen and tablet while four others had never used a digitising tablet. We gave a brief description of the recogniser to the users, including the set of recognisable shapes. We also told them about the multi-stroke shape recognition capabilities, the independence of changes in rotation or size and about the time-out. Novice subjects had a short practice session in order

		Recognised												
		Line S	Line D	Triangle S	Triangle D	Rectangle S	Rectangle D	Circle S	Circle D	Ellipse S	Ellipse D	Diamond S	Diamond D	Delete	Unknown
D	Line S	100%													
	Line D	3%	90%				5%								2%
	Triangle S			97%								2%			1%
r	Triangle D				91%								9%		
a	Rectangle S					96%				1%		3%			
w	Rectangle D						96%				2%		2%		
n	Circle S							73%		23%		3%			
	Circle D								83%		11%		6%		
	Ellipse S									85%		15%			
	Ellipse D										91%		9%		
	Diamond S					7%		1%		4%		88%			
	Diamond D						3%					9%	89%		
	Delete													100%	

Fig. 5. Confusion matrix

to get used to the stylus/tablet combination. During the drawing session the recogniser was turned off to avoid interfering with data collection.

Results The recogniser successfully identified 91% of the sketches drawn. The confusion matrix presented in Fig. 5 shows the recognition rate for each shape category and the shapes wrongly recognised. A cursory analysis of the confusion matrix shows that circles are easily recognised as ellipses, which is both an acceptable and *intuitive* behaviour. If we consider circles and "fat" ellipses in the same shape class the recognition rate increases to 93%. Second, ellipses are confused with diamonds, and have a low recognition rate. Third, diamonds also have a low recognition rate and are confused with rectangles and ellipses.

If we consider successful classification when the "correct" shape is one of the top three shapes identified, the recognition rate increases from 91% to 94%. This recognition rate increases to 97% if we further consider circles and "fat" ellipses as the same shape class.

3   Related Work

The idea of pen-centric interfaces is not new, even if we discount the fact that sketches and planar diagrams as a way of communication precede the invention of writing by more than 30 centuries [7]. In 1963, Sutherland presented Sketchpad [11] the first interactive system that used one light pen to draw diagrams directly over the screen surface. The main limitation of this system resided in the recognition capabilities, limited resources and high cost of the computer used.

Nevertheless, due in part to ergonomic problems with the light pen and the invention of the mouse in 1964, present–day graphical interfaces relegated pen–

based systems to specific CAD applications until the appearance of the first pen computers in 1991. Tappert [12], provides a comprehensive survey of the work developed in the area of non-interactive graphics recognition for the entering data and diagrams as vectorial information in CAD systems.

Mark Gross [6] describes a system fundamentally based in sketches that are partially interpreted for use in architecture drawings, using a recogniser substantially more simple and less robust than ours.

The Newton system [1], one of the first hand–held pen based computers, incorporates a hand written recogniser, a shape recogniser and a gesture recogniser. The shape recogniser only recognises solid shapes and requires the shapes to be drawn with just one stroke and aligned with the axes. The gesture recogniser is more suitable for text editing than for schematic drawing.

Even though significant progresses were made, most notably in the past decade, more work is required to make handwriting and sketch recognition systems truly usable in most settings. We believe that a combination of top–down techniques, using visual languages [8] and syntactic pattern recognition combined with improved bottom–up methods may provide a workable approach to this problem.

4 Discussion

We have described a simple and fast recogniser for elementary geometric shapes. Our intent was more to provide a means to support calligraphic interaction rather than a totally robust and "foolproof" approach to reject shapes outside the domain of interest. Our experience using this recogniser in interactive settings shows that the observed recognition rates make it usable for drawing input. The time-outs required to recognise shapes regardless of the number of strokes using temporal adjacency have proved to be the most unnatural constraint so far.

The high recognition rates and fast response characteristic of this recogniser make it very usable in interactive applications. We are currently looking at more natural input segmentation methods and improving the recognition rate and robustness of our approach through better computational geometry algorithms in order to make the recogniser publicly available.

References

1. http://www.paragraph.com. 273
2. Ajay Apte, Van Vo, and Takayuki Dan Kimura. Recognizing Multistroke Geometric Shapes: An Experimental Evaluation. In *Proceedings of the ACM (UIST'93)*, pages 121–128, Atlanta, GA, 1993. 267
3. James C. Bezdek and Sankar K. Pal. *Fuzzy Models for Pattern Recognition*. IEEE Press, 1992. 267
4. H. Freeman and R. Shapira. Determining the minimum-area encasing rectangle for an arbitrary closed curve. *Communications of the ACM*, 18(7):409–413, July 1975. 270

5. D. Golberg and C. Richardson. Touch-typing with a stylus. In *Proceedings of the ACM (InterCHI'93)*, pages 80–87, Amsterdam, 1993. 267

6. Mark D. Gross. The Electronic Cocktail Napkin - A computational environment for working with design diagrams. *Design Studies*, 17(1):53–69, 1996. 273

7. J. B. Harley and D. Woodward, editors. *The History of Cartography*, volume 1. University of Chicago Press, Chicago, IL, 1987. 272

8. Joaquim A. Jorge. *Parsing Adjacency Grammars for Calligraphic Interfaces*. PhD thesis, Rensselaer Polytechnic Institute, Troy, New York - USA, December 1994. 273

9. Joseph O'Rourke. *Computational geometry in C*. Cambridge University Press, 2nd edition, 1998. 269

10. L. Schomaker. From handwriting analysis to pen-computer applications. *Electronics & Communication Engineering Journal*, June 1998.

11. Ivan E. Sutherland. Sketchpad: A Man-Machine Graphical Communication System. In *Spring Joint Computer Conference*, pages 2–19. AFIPS Press, 1963. 272

12. Charles C. Tappert, Ching Y. Suen, and Toru Wakahara. The state of the art in on-line handwriting recognition. *IEEE Transactions on Pattern Analysis and Machine Intelligence*, 12(8):787–807, August 1990. 273

13. F. Ulgen, A. Flavell, and N. Akamatsu. Geometric shape recognition with fuzzy filtered input to a backpropagation neural network. *IEEE Trans. Inf. & Syst.*, E788-D(2):174–183, February 1995. 267

Part V

Engineering Drawings and Schematics

Syntactic and Semantic Graphics Recognition: The Role of the Object-Process Methodology

Dov Dori

Information Systems Engineering, Faculty of Industrial Engineering and Management
Technion, Israel Institute of Technology, Haifa 32000, Israel
dori@ie.technion.ac.il

Abstract. Recognition of graphics is made at two levels: syntactic and semantic. Machines are already functioning at the syntactic level quite satisfactorily, but at the semantic level they still lack the intelligence and cognition humans apply while interpreting graphic symbols. Understanding and communicating the structure and behavior of complex systems through a graphic representation is effective only if it constitutes a visual formalism that assigns a definite semantics to each symbol. Object-Process Methodology (OPM) is a graphics-based visual formalism that has been applied to analyze and design systems in a variety of domains. Through a set of Object-Process Diagrams (OPDs) we specify a generic graphics recognition subsystem that is integrated into a Document Analysis System. Beside the direct value of the OPD representation, this model serves as an instance of the way OPM can be used as a concise graphic representation that unifies the structure and behavior of complex systems in general and graphics recognition systems in particular.

1 The Value of Graphic Representation

Products and systems are becoming ever more complex. Many man-made, as well as natural systems feature complexity of their structure (how they are constructed), function (what they do) and behavior (how they change over time). Understanding these systems requires a well-founded, intuitive methodology that is capable of modeling their complexities in a coherent, straightforward manner. Artificial systems require development and support efforts throughout their entire lifetime. Systematic specifications, analysis, design and implementation of new systems and products is becoming more difficult and demanding, calling for a comprehensive, methodology to tackle these challenges. Document analysis systems in general, and automated graphics recognition systems in particular, are no exception. Modern systems of this type require prudent specifications, analysis, design and implementation.

Graphic representation of systems of any kind has been known to be effective for human comprehension and communication. In their book *Knowledge Elicitation*,

Atul K. Chhabra and D. Dori (Eds.): GREC'99, LNCS 1941, pp. 277-287, 2000.

discussing the question *"Does the knowledge require graphic representation?"* (p.31) Firlej and Hellens1 note that

> *The term 'graphic representation' ... means anything that can only be adequately represented by using drawings or sketches. Some domains do have a large component of graphic content. The expert may, in the process of explaining some idea or description of a behavior, suddenly reach for pad and draw sketches of what he/she does, and say "it has to look like this" or "I know just by looking at the chart if something is wrong".*
>
> *Sketching and drawing may ... provide a useful way of expressing idea on a paper that is difficult to express in words. ... These drawings may be indispensable for the user and a practical method for the representation of these drawings and plans may have to be found to achieve acceptable functioning."*

Indeed, diagrams are often invaluable for describing models of abstract things, especially complex systems. An accepted diagramming method has the potential of becoming a powerful modeling tool, provided that it really constitutes an unambiguous language, or a *visual formalism*[2,3,4]. A visual formalism is valuable if each symbol in the diagram has a defined semantics and the links among the symbols unambiguously convey some meaningful information or knowledge that is clearly understood by those who are familiar with the formalism. As Wand and Weber[5] note,

> *Without a set of common constructs, one cannot expect the appearance of a generally accepted paradigm of systems analysis and design that will enable the comparison and evaluation of methodologies. Also, without a theoretical paradigm, no generally accepted rules of design can be developed.*

2   Levels of Graphics Recognition

Graphics recognition can be considered at two levels: the syntactic level and the semantic level. At the syntactic level, the recognition involves locating the graphic symbols in the document and classifying them into the various classes by their shape and possibly their context. At the semantic level, the recognition requires assigning meaning to the syntactically recognized symbols. This meaning is domain-dependent, and it varies from one area of science and engineering to another. Most engineering areas have an established and accepted set of symbols. Systems engineering has just recently "joined the club" with the introduction of the Unified Modeling Language (UML), discussed below.

When we talk about graphics recognition, we implicitly allude to automated graphics recognition by computers. This recognition is, for the most part, at the syntactic level. The difference between human and automated graphics recognition is the level at which the interpretation is made: Humans have no problem recognizing graphic symbols at the syntactic level, i.e., identifying their shape or form. Young toddlers and kids are successfully trained at a very early age to recognize and point to shapes like rectangle, ellipse, star, rhombus, hexagon, etc., as one of their first cognitive missions, making their parents proud and happy. They accomplish this task even if the shapes are noisy, blurred, occluded and/or mixed with text. The ease of human syntactic graphics recognition is but one manifestation of the tremendous human visual capabilities, which machine vision has been trying to imitate, with only limited success in specific domains.

Graphic symbol recognition at the semantic level takes for granted the successful accomplishment of the earlier syntactic recognition phase. Semantic graphics recognition is aimed at high-level interpretation and understanding of the assembly of graphic symbols within the domain of discourse within which the recognition is being made. At the semantic level, graphic symbol recognition requires high-order cognitive skills, familiarity with the domain, its underlying concepts and rules, and the proper interpretation of the various graphic symbols within the appropriate context. This is a level of intelligence that is distinctly above the syntactic level. However, the semantic level itself is not single and uniform. Within a typical domain there is more than just one level of understanding. Taking the domain of mechanical engineering drawings, for example, we can talk of at least two distinct levels: two-dimensional understanding and three-dimensional understanding. The two-dimensional understanding pertains to such things as recognizing the dimension sets and verifying that they completely and unambiguously describe each 2-D view separately. The three-dimensional semantic level deals with reconstructing the 3-D structure of the object from its collection of 2-D views.

3   Ad-hoc Graphic System Representations

The fact that most people use some kind of diagramming technique to express their knowledge about systems in a plethora of domains is a testimony of the viability of graphic representation and the advantage it has over textual representations. Having acknowledged the merit of the graphic representation, we should, however, also recognize that a graphic representation of our knowledge about a system is indeed valuable if and only if it is backed by a comprehensive and consistent modeling methodology. Such methodology is essential if we are to be able to understand complex systems in any domain, communicate our understanding to others, and use the analysis results as a basis for designing solutions to existing problems, as well as modifying and elaborating current systems.

Reading through scientific and technical papers that describe artificial as well as natural systems of various kinds and domains, the lack of a common, acceptable formalism for describing systems is sorely apparent. In the better cases, diagrammatic system descriptions are done using a set of ad-hoc symbols that the authors make up spontaneously to be used in a specific diagram. In other cases the same symbol is overloaded with more than one possible interpretation or there is no systematic assignment of graphical symbols to logical entities in the diagram.

As Bubenko[6] (p. 295) wrote, no generally accepted, workable theory of information systems theory of information systems and their development has evolved. Although the requirement for standardizing system modeling is trivial, an accepted symbol set for general systems analysis, design and implementation is just beginning to emerge.

If we look at diagrams that people draw with the intention of expressing some system aspect, we often find ad-hoc, implicit, undocumented and arbitrary collection of symbols and links. In other cases we may even find that the same graphic symbol is overloaded with semantics or used in contradictory, perplexing ways.

Consider, for example, the graphic representation in **Figure 1** of "The KBS (knowledge-based system) modeling development process", as it appears in *Knowledge Elicitation* by Firlej and Hellens[1].

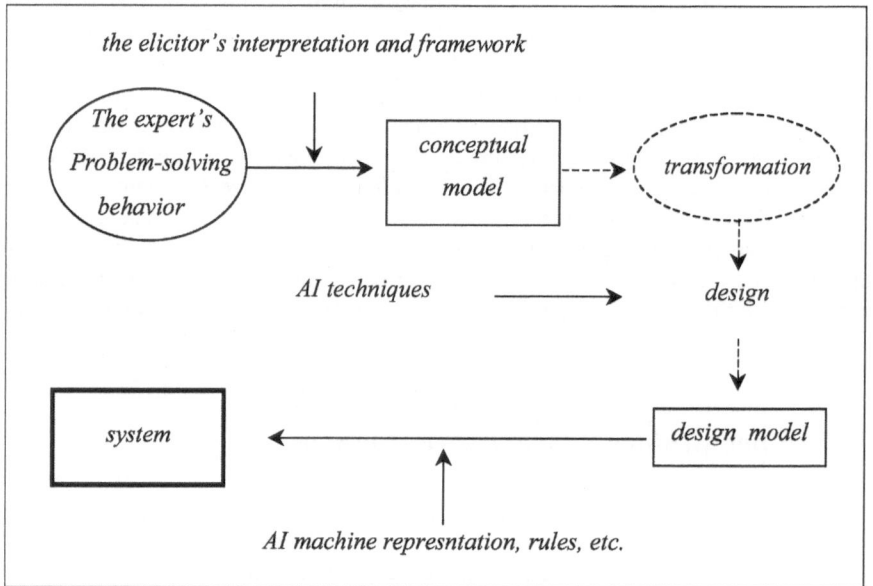

Figure 1. The KBS modeling development process

The automatic syntactic graphic recognition of this diagram does not pose special difficulties: the graphic symbols are simple, clear, and easy to recognize. Semantic recognition, however, is difficult not only to a machine, but to a human as well. While no legend is provided, one can try to infer the intentions of the symbols in the diagram. However, contemplating upon it for a while, many questions come to mind, regardless of the diagram content. For example, it is not possible to understand what is the difference (if any) between text surrounded by an ellipse, text surrounded by a rectangle, and non-surrounded text. Is it indeed the case that ellipses represent processes? Why, then, is "design" not surrounded also by an ellipse? Is it because there is a profound difference between transformation and design? Furthermore, why is one ellipse solid while the other is dashed? Why are some boxes drawn with a thin line while another with a thick one? Why are some arrows solid, while others are dashed? What is the meaning of an arrow anyway? What is the difference between an arrow connecting surrounded text and one that connects non-surrounded text with another arrow, or an arrow pointing at another arrow?

Surely the diagram designer must have had some intention in making distinctions through different graphic constructs to convey particular meanings, but how are we supposed to interpret it? Since we are supplied with neither legend in the diagram nor with explanation within the text, we are left puzzled with these questions. Is it our limited mental capability that prevents us from understanding this, or is it possible that there is no consistent intention behind the different symbols in the diagram?

Unfortunately, the example discussed in some length above is but one of numerous similar representations that abound in the best of textbooks and scientific journals as representations of systems or parts thereof. The scandalous state of affairs in graphic systems modeling is that this is the rule rather than the exception. Most graphic representations, at best, use ad-hoc symbols without explicit specifications, but many of these diagrams even contain inexplicable inconsistencies from one diagram to the next within the same article, or, even worse, within the same diagram.

It is not just the case that the richness of graphic symbology is not taken advantage of – the arbitrary use of graphic symbols potentially adds more confusion than it provides help. Hence, not only such diagrams are not always helpful, they may even hinder understanding of the textual description of a system or a process a system executes.

Recently, the Unified Modeling Language (UML) has been accepted as a standard. Rational University Web site7 defines UML as follows:

> *The Unified Modeling Language (UML) is the industry-standard language for specifying, visualizing, constructing, and documenting the artifacts of software systems. It simplifies the complex process of software design, making a "blueprint" for construction. The UML represents a collection of "best engineering practices" that have proven successful in the modeling of large and complex systems.*

4   Object-Process Methodology Highlights

The Object-Process Methodology (OPM) 8,9 is an integrated approach to the study and development of systems in general and information systems in particular. OPM unifies the system's structure and behavior throughout the analysis, design and implementation within one frame of reference using a single diagramming tool – the Object-Process Diagram (OPD) and a corresponding, English-like language – the Object-Process Language (OPL). OPM is not yet another object-oriented systems development method. It departs from the object-oriented paradigm by recognizing processes as stand-alone entities beside objects.

OPM caters to the natural train of thought humans normally apply while trying to understand and build complex systems. In such systems, it is usually the case that structure and behavior are intertwined so tightly, that any separation between them is bound to further complicate the already complex description. Founded on General Systems Theory, OPM is generic and therefore suitable for specifying systems of virtually any domain.

Current object-oriented methods evolved bottom-up from object-oriented programming languages. They therefore contain many ideas, such as the encapsulation of methods within objects that potentially yield good computer programs, but hinder faithful modeling of the system and its problem domain. OPM, on the other hand, has been designed top-down, with an eye toward modeling the real world. The basic premise of OPM is that objects and processes are two types of equally important classes of things, that together faithfully describe both the structure and the behavior of systems in a single model in virtually any domain. At any point in time, each object is at some state, and object states are transformed through the occurrence of a process.

OPM unifies structure, behavior and function within a single model. Processes in OPM are independent building blocks beside objects. They enable explicit dynamic modeling, intertwined with the object model. This unification paradigm of the static aspect with the dynamic aspect in a single model is unique to OPM. Using Object-Process Diagrams (OPDs) along with an Object-Process Language (OPL) provides OPM with a high expressive power. OPD is the graphic system representation, while OPL is its equivalent textual specification. The use of a single type of diagrams provides for a concise symbol system, thereby preventing the need for "mental translations" back and forth among the various models. By integrating the structural, functional and procedural system aspects and expressing them in analogous graphic and textual representations, OPM represents formally, yet intuitively, systems in various domains and at all levels of complexity.

The resulting specification explicitly states what the system is, what it does, and how it does it. It enables reasoning by telling us how processes transform (generate, consume and affect) objects.

5   Towards a Standardized Modeling Graphic Set

The lack of a common methodology for system specification is sorely hampering the development of integrated, well founded modeling solutions for complex systems.

OPM uses Object Process Diagrams (OPDs) for expressing the objects of a modeled system and the processes that affect them. Objects and processes in an OPD are denoted within rectangles and ellipses, respectively, while object states are marked as round-cornered rectangles.

OPM is useful for understanding system-related problems, communicating with application experts, preparing documentation, and designing solutions for the modeled system. OPM has been successfully applied in a variety of areas, including studyware design[10] Computer Integrated Manufacturing[11], R&D Management[12] and real-time systems[13]. In the specific area of graphics recognition, OPM was instrumental in works dealing with the Machine Drawing Understanding System (MDUS)[14,15], 3-D reconstruction from engineering drawings[16], document analysis systems and content-based image retrieval[17].

Based on the experience gathered in these, as well as other works, it is recommended that OPM be adopted by system designers as the method of choice for specifying and designing systems in general and document analysis systems in particular. The rest of the paper demonstrates the application of OPM for a graphics recognition subsystem.

6   An OPM Representation of a Graphics Recognition Subsystem

A document is a human-generated artifact that records a representation of some data, information or knowledge[17]. In the long term, interesting documents from the single enterprise are those that represent knowledge – a meaningful and useful digest of information and data. A document is the instrument that enables preservation of this knowledge, its transfer to other interested parties and its extraction through elaborate processing, such as OCR, graphics recognition and natural language understanding.

A Document Management System consists of three subsystems: The Generation Subsystem, the Exchange Subsystem and the Document Analysis Subsystem. The Document Generation Subsystem is the instrument used by the document author to generate the document. The Document Exchange Subsystem is the instrument that enables the communication of the document to its prospective audience.

Once acquired, the document must be properly processed and analyzed in order to make the knowledge recorded in it in a representational format that is readily available to humans. Documents can be recorded in two major different modalities: analog or digital. Documents with analog Modality are paper-based, while those with electronic Modality are electronic-based.

Figure 2 is an OPD that focuses on the Document Analysis Subsystem. It shows the parts of the Document Analysis process and the attributes of the paper document that are gradually exposed as a result of the various analysis processes. To be analyzed, a Paper Document must first be converted to an Electronic Document. The Analog-to-Digital Conversion process does this, usually by scanning or imaging. The Electronic Document is input to the Document Analysis process, which consists of three major parts: OCR & Layout Analysis, Graphics Recognition and Document Understanding.

OCR & Layout Analysis (and/or handwriting recognition) yield the textual content of the document information in ASCII form as well as information on the document's layout. Graphics Recognition yields the Document's Symbols & Graphic Objects. Text and Graphics Recognition constitutes the syntactic-level analysis. The most sophisticated sub-process – Document Understanding – is aimed at extracting the meaningful knowledge that the original paper document represents in a form that can be best digested by humans. Document Understanding makes use of the text and graphics recognition obtained at the syntactic level in order to achieve understanding at the semantic level.

This level makes use of all the information obtained by the previous Document Analysis parts and requires a substantial amount of what is known as "artificial intelligence." An example of a high level Document Understanding process is 3-D reconstruction of objects described in engineering drawings. Most contemporary document analysis systems are just beginning to show signs of semantic-level document understanding. Indeed, having solved the early analysis tasks, the challenge of current systems is to enhance their high-level understanding capabilities so that they exhibit a more intelligent behavior and hence be more useful to humans.

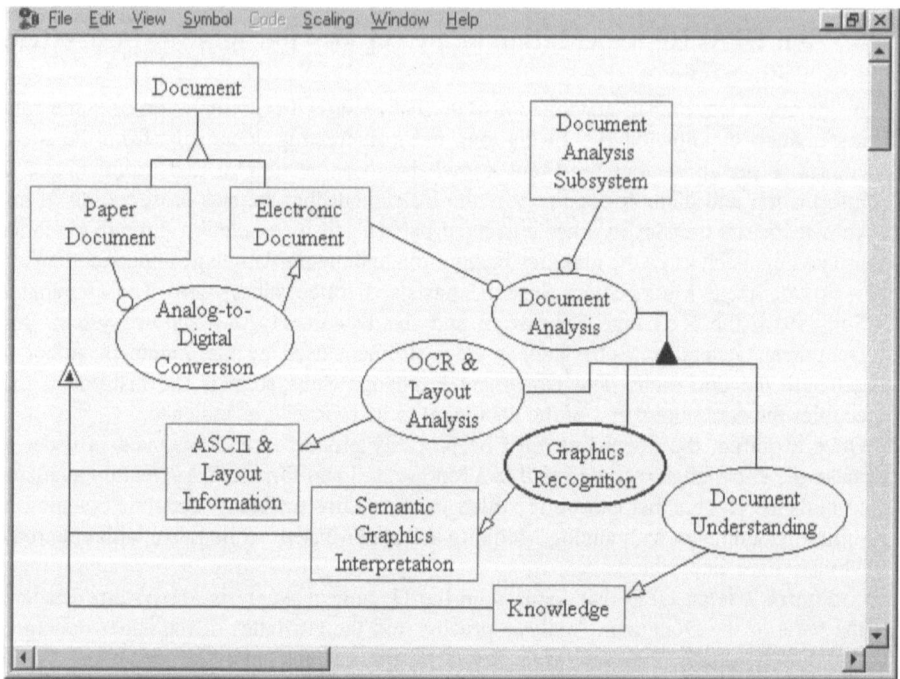

Figure 2. The Document Analysis Subsystem and the parts of the Document Analysis process

Figure 3 zooms into the Graphics Recognition process. The Electronic Document is input into the Syntactic Graphic Recognition. This process yields Symbols and Graphic Objects. This may be the end of the Graphics Recognition process. However, in the system we describe here this is followed by Semantic Graphics Recognition. This process is enabled by a Domain Graphics Rule-base and a Hypothesis. It yields Intermediate Graphics-related Semantics, which is input into Consistency & Completeness Checking. This checking yields the Boolean object "Semantics Consistent?" If so, the higher level process terminates and we end up with Semantic Graphics Interpretation. If not, then a new Hypothesis is generated and the Semantic Graphics Recognition is repeated in a loop.

This is a model for generic graphics recognition at both the syntactic and the semantic levels. Naturally, Domain Graphics Rule-base has to be adapted and specialized into the various domains insofar as the semantic part is concerned, while for the syntactic recognition a common graphic recognizer can be used.

In the Machine Drawing Understanding System18,19 we apply basically the same strategy: for the syntactic phase we have developed a generic graphics recognition algorithm20 that is basically domain-independent. A specialized, domain-specific module that exploits domain knowledge needs to be used for the semantic phase.

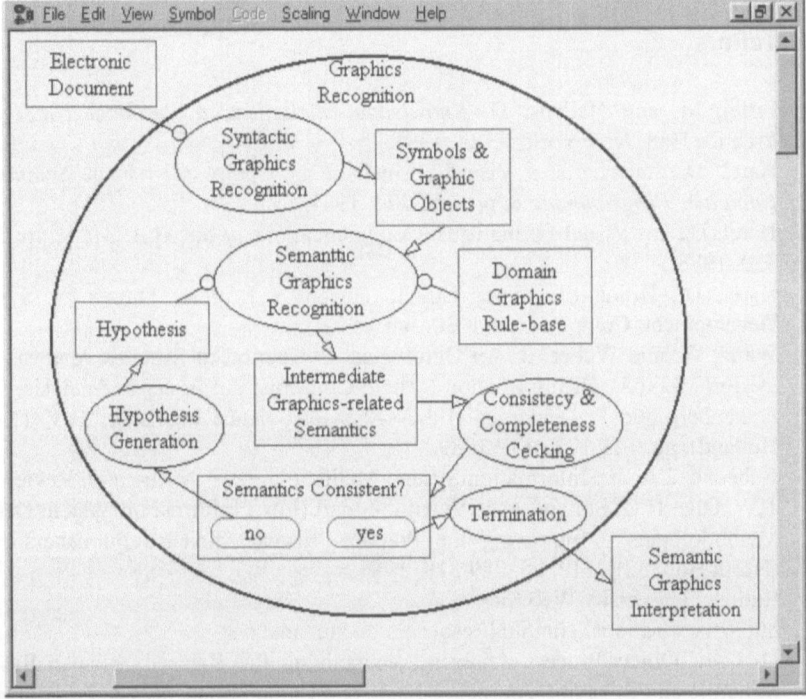

Figure 3. Zooming into the Graphic Recognition process

7 Summary

In this paper we argue that a distinction needs to be made between syntactic and semantic graphics recognition. While syntactic graphics recognition is already done by machines with considerable success, this is not the case with semantic graphics recognition. While the former is generic, as it deals with processing pixels and extracting the graphic symbols they represent, the latter is more complex as it requires a high level of cognition to correctly understand and interpret the meaning the symbols recognized at the syntactic level convey. It is often the case that a complete syntactic recognition is not achieved without devising hypotheses to resolve problems in consistency and completeness that are found out while trying to apply semantics to the recognized symbols.

Using the Object-Process Methodology (OPM) as a modeling tool, we have demonstrated how a generic system can be explicitly expressed with graphics means, making the point for the need to adopt a methodology that has a clear and concise visual formalism. Through scaling mechanisms built into OPM, the modeling can be done at any level of detail while maintaining a coherent view of the "big picture" with the single OPM model. Based on this application, as well as many others, it is recommended that OPM be used as the method of choice for modeling systems in general and graphics recognition systems in particular.

References

1   Firlej, M. and Hellens, D. *Knowledge Elicitation: a Practical Handbook.* Prentice Hall, New York, p.144, 1991.

2   Harel, D. Statecharts: a Visual Formalism for Complex Systems. *Science of Computer Programming* 8, pp. 231-274, 1987.

3   Harel, D., On Visual Formalisms. Communications *of the ACM* 31, 5, pp. 514-530, 1988.

4   Harel, D., Biting the Silver Bullet: Toward a Brighter Future for System Development. Computer, pp. 8-20, Jan. 1992.

5   Wand, W. and Weber, R. An Ontological Evaluation of Systems Analysis and Design Methods. In Information System Concepts: An in-depth Analysis. E.D. Falkenberg and P. Lindgreen (Eds.). Elsevier Science Publishers B.V. (North Holland), pp. 145-172, IFIP 1989.

6   Bubenko, J.A. Jr.. Information System Methodologies – A Research Review. In T.W. Olle, H.G. Sol and A.A. Verrijn –Stuart (Eds.) Information System Design Methodologies – Improving the Practice. Elsevier Science Publishers B.V. (North Holland), IFIP, pp. 289-318, 1986.

7   Rational University Web Site:
http://www.rational.com/uml/resources/documentation/

8   D. Dori, Object-Process Analysis: Maintaining the Balance between System Structure and Behavior. Journal of Logic and Computation. 5(2) 227-249, 1995.

9   D. Dori, Unifying System Structure and Behavior through Object-Process Analysis. Journal of Object-Oriented Programming, July-August, pp. 66-73, 1996.

10   D. Dori and Y.J. Dori, Object-Process Analysis of a Hypertext Organic Chemistry Studyware. Journal of Computers in Mathematics and Science Teaching, 15, 1/2, (1996),65-84.

11   D. Dori, Object-Process Analysis of Computer Integrated Manufacturing Documentation and Inspection Functions. International Journal of Computer Integrated Manufacturing, 9(5), 339-353, 1996.

12   D. Meyersdorf and D. Dori, The R&D Universe and Its Feedback Cycles: an Object-Process Analysis. R&D Management, 27 (4), 333-344, 1997.

13   M. Peleg and D. Dori, Extending the Object-Process Methodology to Handle Real-Time Systems. Journal of Object-Oriented Programming, 11, 8, pp. 53-58, 1999.

14   D. Dori, Representing Pattern Recognition Embedded Systems through Object-Process Diagrams: the Case of the Machine Drawing Understanding System. Pattern Recognition Letters, 16 (4), 377-384, 1995.

15   D. Dori, Arc Segmentation in the Machine Drawing Understanding Environment. IEEE Transactions of Pattern Analysis and Machine Intelligence (T-PAMI), 17 (1), 1057-1068, 1995.

16   D. Dori and M. Weiss, A Scheme for 3D Object Reconstruction from Dimensioned Orthographic Views. Engineering Applications in Artificial Intelligence, 9 (1), 53-64, 1996.

17   D. Dori and H. Hel-Or: Semantic Content-Based Image Retrieval Using Object-Process Diagrams. In A. Amin, D. Dori, P. Pudil and H. Freeman (Eds.) Advances in Pattern Recognition, Lecture Notes in Computer Science, Vol. 1451, 230-241, 1998.

18   Dov Dori and Liu Wenyin, Automated CAD Conversion with the Machine Drawing Understanding System: Concepts, Algorithms, and Performance. IEEE Transactions on Systems, Man, and Cybernetics, 29, 4, pp.411-416, 1999.

19   D. Dori and L. Wenyin, The Sparse Pixel Vectorization Algorithm and its Performance Evaluation. IEEE Transactions on Pattern Analysis and Machine Intelligence (T-PAMI), 21, 3 pp. 202-215, 1999.

20   L. Wenyin and D. Dori, A Generic Integrated Line Detection Algorithm and its Object-Process Specification. Computer Vision – Image Understanding (CVIU), 70, 3, pp. 420-437, 1998.

Efficient Categorization of 3D Edges from 2D Projections

Amitabha Mukerjee, Nilanjan Sasmal, and D.Sridhar Sastry

Center for Robotics, I.I.T. Kanpur, Kanpur, INDIA
amit@iitk.ac.in, {nilanjan.sasmal,dsastry}@mailcity.com

Abstract. In this paper w e re-consider the problem of converting a linear dra wing to a set of 3D edges and presen a more efficient solution based on a qualitatively complete classification of the possible states of 3-D edges and their projections. The projective constraints on possible 3D edges result in an one-pass generation of the 3D wire frame. Most existing algorithms (e.g. [6, 13]) consider either point-based constraints, or only a subset of the line constraints. The algorithm adopted here adopts the line-constraint approach and presents several improvements based on a qualitative analysis which results in considerably more efficient search. Since reconstruction of line segments is one of the most frequently performed tasks in the overall task of generating 3-D models from 2-D drawings, this improvement is of considerable interest to the CAD community.

1 Introduction

Automated methods are increasingly being used for manually-assisted solid model generation from legacy drawings, and more efficient methods for performing the simplest and oft-repeated tasks are an important necessit y One such core task is the matching of line data betw een multiple views, which often constitute the largest bulk of lines on most legacy drawings. In practice, many engineering drawings also contain flaws such as missing lines or details that humans can ignore but machines cannot. Thus the interpretation of line data must provide correct interpretation for data where available, and flag the missing lines for human intervention where needed. Even with multiple views, there may be many matches that are possible for each entity, whic h is wh engineering drawing has been called incomplete [9]. In general, the solid model generation must attempt to pro vide the most consisten input possible.

1.1 Point-Constraint

Algorithmically, the determination of 3-D entities in the rectilinear drawing domain considered here involv esa search to determine if a line or point in one projection is a line or a point in the other view. V oluminous w orkhas been done on various aspects of this problem and the reader is directed to [3] for a review of some of the w orkin this area. In brief, it may be said that one of

Atul K. Chhabra and D. Dori (Eds.): GREC'99, LNCS 1941, pp. 288-297, 2000.

the first attempts was through bottom-up search by matching 3-D points [4], with provisions for manual interaction. Wesley and Markowsky [7, 12] provide a very thorough analysis of both the wireframe generation and the wireframe to boundary representation (b-rep) problem. Although the wireframe generation algorithm itself uses a number of intermediate representations and is very complex, the elegant analysis and the number of special cases and examples provided in this work have provided test data in all subsequent attempts at the problem, including our work. Aldefeld [1] developed a system based on the identification of members in a set of primitives the combination of which constitute the model. He treated a complex object as a group of elementary volumes, and then recognized them from specific patterns in 2D representations. The limitation of this process is that it is valid only for extruded objects of uniform thickness. Bin [2] presents an interactive approach for inputing CSG representation directly from 2D drawing. The positions of key points for each primitive were "picked up" from an ordinary engineering drawing to define the primitives which later formed the CSG representations together with boolean symbols that are entered manually. More recently, several authors [6, 8, 11] have considered the problem of more general input such as arcs or elliptical sections, and also consider non-manifold geometry. Of these, Kuo discusses the efficiency characteristics in some detail, and we take their results to be indicative of the most efficient approach possible through 3D-point constraint propagation.

1.2   Line-Constraint

In contrast, Yan *et al* [13] model edge constraints, dealing directly with edges in a boundary representation. Using the basic properties of engineering drawing they design an efficient method for rectilinear objects. This work, though several years old now, remains one of the better known methods for line reconstruction, and has been used in further development as in [11] etc. This work essentially uses formalizes the line constraint idea by defining the qualitative partitioning of the search space.

Masuda [8] uses a cellular decomposition model between the wireframe model and final solid model which simplifies the latter stages of the conversion to 3D, but the wireframe generation method remains the same as that of the old Idesawa method. Shin and Shin [11] handle both rectilinear and curvilinear objects and combine the models from [12, 13, 10]. This algorithm takes longer processing time due to the combinatorial searches and complicated geometric operations, but some efficiency can be obtained by using the topology between pairs of geometric primitives.

Our approach is based on a qualitative analysis of the possible states of a 3-D line. This shows that the position of such a line with respect to the three coordinate axes can have only seven qualitative states. This is the basis for an algorithm that replaces most of the search-based methods of prior work with a constraint-based model, which together with a pre-processing step where the edges are pre-sorted, brings down the complexity of matching n line segments to $O(n \log n)$ and also makes for an easy to implement algorithm. The extra constraints provided by considering together the two end-points of a line provide for higher efficiency as compared to point-constraint methods [6] - whereas the best asymptotic time complexity with point constraints is $O(e^2 v)$ where e is the number of edges and v is the maximum number of vertices in a face loop, our results are $O(n \log n)$ in the total number of edges.

2   Edge-Based Reconstruction

Qualitative analysis

The key insight in our model is based on qualitative analysis of the possible states of an edge (or line segment) in 3-D. In qualitative analysis, one considers only the sign of a relation and not its actual magnitude [5]; thus x – y = 3 is the same as x – y = 30, and all are represented as x – y < 0. Thus relation between two scalars can be (< , = , or >). In our case, we can further simplify this, since for a line projection, the qualitative nature of the projection can be either a point (when the two endpoints of the line are equal) or a line (when they are not). Thus only two qualitative relations are of interest - $(\neq, =)$.

Let us now consider the relations possible between the two endpoints v1 and v2 of a 3-D edge. Consider the coordinates of these two vertices in the frame used for projecting the three views.

$$v1.x \begin{pmatrix} = \\ \neq \end{pmatrix} v2.x \quad , \quad v1.y \begin{pmatrix} = \\ \neq \end{pmatrix} v2.y \quad or \quad v1.z \begin{pmatrix} = \\ \neq \end{pmatrix} v2.z$$

There are 2×2×2 possible relations. Of these, the (= = =) relation is degenerate since it implies that both endpoints are equal in all coordinates - i.e. the line is a point. Thus there are seven possible relations with valid instantiations.

The mapping from the 3-D to space to the three projections Front View (F), Top View (T), and Side View (S) are obtained by discarding one of the coordinate axes. Thus, the 3D → mapping may be characterized by the 2×3 transform:

$$\begin{bmatrix} 100 \\ 001 \end{bmatrix}$$

which maps the x and z coordinates to create the F space. This is independent of whether it is first or third angle projection.

Where one coordinate is equal, it will result in parallel lines in the two views where that axis is present (three cases). Equal projections along two axes implies it is parallel to the third axis (three cases). Finally, in general position, all three coordinates are unequal and result in angled lines in all projections. All seven cases are shown in Figure 1; note that the the vertical axis represents the z- and y-axes (above and below) while the vertical axis represents the x- and y- axes (left and right). For example, the Front view, projecting onto xz, appears on top left.

Now, given a set of consistent views, one needs to determine, for a given line appearing in one view, the corresponding lines in the two other views, and

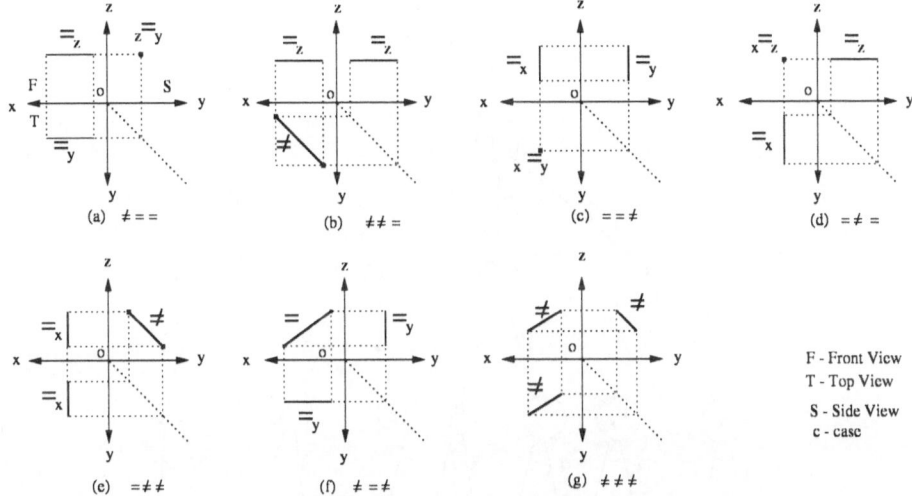

Fig. 1. Edge classification based on frontal view

also the case where one of the views it may be degenerate as a point. Instead of searching as in the early work, recent models such as [13] apply a set of constraints to determine the particular state. This results in a decision tree approach (Figure 2).

2.1 Reconstruction Algorithm

The Line drawings of each view are input as a set of lines with all vertices incident on it being listed; i.e. if there are k (colinear) vertices on a line then $\binom{k}{2}$ segments are input.

Algorithm

0. *Pre-Processing:* Pre-sort the edges e_t in increasing x e_s in increasing z. Edges are lexicographically sorted as ordered pairs of end-points.
1. For each edge e_f in the Front View, it can be parallel to the x-axis ($=_z$).
   - Identify any edge e_t in T matching the end-point constraints (min-x, max-x of e_f), Construct the 3-D edge(e_p) and push it on to a candidate edge stack. Note that e_t can be either parallel to x- again ($\neq==$), or at an angle ($\neq\neq=$).
   - For each e_p, test if any e_s exists at the exact projected points in S. If not discard e_p.
2. e_f is parallel to the z-axis ($=_z$).
   - Match as above. but first in S then in T (there may be an edge perpendicular to T but not to S). e_s can be either parallel to z ($==\neq$), or at an angle ($= \neq\neq$).

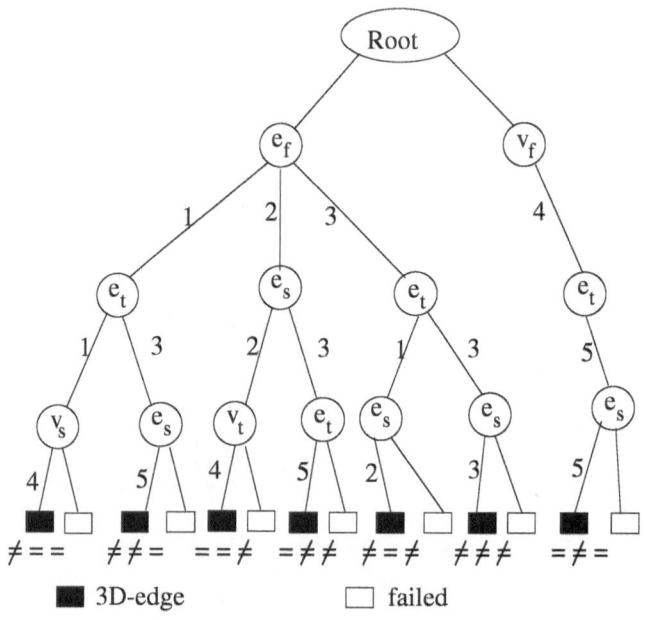

Fig. 2. Front view based decision tree of objects

3. e_f may be parallel to neither axis (case 3).
   - Match in T and in S using the end-point constraints. e_t and e_s may both
   be parallel to some axis ($\neq=\neq$), or they may both be skew ($\neq\neq\neq$).
4. An edge of the front face may still be an edge. For each v_f one can efficiently
   search for matching parallel-to-y edges in e_s and e_t at the z- and x- position
   of v_f. ($=\neq=$).

Figure 2 shows each case for different positions and orientations of an edge.

2.2   Correctness

We demonstrate the correctness of the algorithm by showing that a) all edges
generated by the algorithm are necessarily correct 3-D edges, and that b) all 3-D
edges present in the drawing are being sufficiently reconstructed.

For part (a), we see that any 3-D edge detected by the algorithm is the
result of a valid match of both endpoints in all three views, and is therefore
necessarily correct. For the part (b), we observe that a 3-D edge may lie in seven
qualitatively different states w.r.t. the three axes. These are covered in the steps
of our algorithm:

1. Cases ($\neq==$) and ($\neq\neq=$),
2. Cases ($==\neq$) and ($=\neq\neq$),
3. Cases ($\neq=\neq$) and ($\neq\neq\neq$),
4. Case ($=\neq=$).

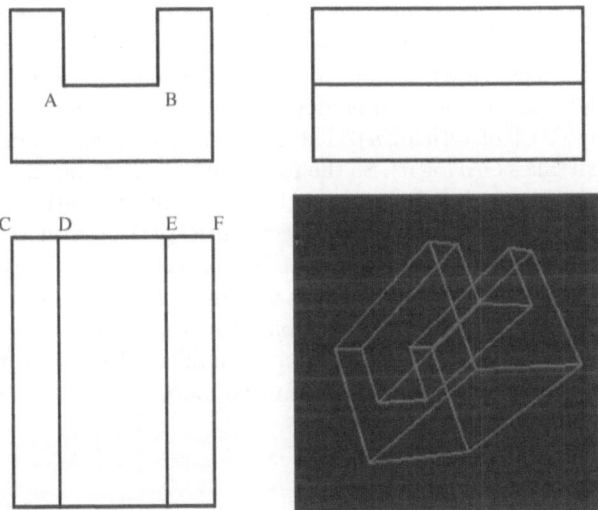

Fig. 3. Simple example. Earlier models were constraining only the orientation of an edge, e.g. AB could be matched to CD, CE, CF, DE, DF, EF, and all its parallel segments in the bottom line. A subsequent $O(n^2)$ effort was needed to remove these overlaps.

Since any 3-D edge present in the model must be in one or the other of these cases, the algorithm will have reconstructed it.

2.3 Computational Complexity and Comparative Analysis

The procedure outlined above is a significant improvement over Yan*et. al.* [13]. Although the latter is very similar in the decision tree aspects, their wireframe construction algorithm has a group of three distinct algorithms (i)Traverse a division tree (can be done in $O(\log n)$ time for pre-sorted input, although pre-processing is not mentioned in [13]. (ii) Resolve overlapping edges (up to $O(n^2)$ for computing possible intersections within $O(n)$ edges). (iii) Removal of redundant edges. $O(n \times k)$ for $O(n)$ edges with maximum of k edges incident at a vertex. In the algorithm outlined above however, the bounds checking does not generate the extra segments which are eventually removed by overlap checking. Also redundant edges are removed for the same reason - all edges satisfying all the bounds checks are actually valid candidates and not redundant.

This difference over the previous algorithm is illustrated in Figure 3. For the edge AB in front view all the edges in top view which are parallel to X-axis are CD, CE, CF, DE, DF, EF and another six segments from the bottom line will be the probable edges. But in our case for the edge AB the possible edge will be only DE and its opposite edge, because the other edges will not match the bounds checking. This pruning is possible by using the additional information already available at the prior step.

The computational costs may be estimated as follows. Let there be n edges in each view, or 3n edges overall. There is an $O(n \log n)$ cost in pre-processing (sorting edges in each view). In each step, for each of the n e_f in F, the edges or vertices in the bounded zone can be determined by binary search in 2log n time each for a total cost of $O(n \log n)$. The number of vertices is also $O(n)$ so the fourth step also takes $O(n \log n)$. So the total time taken in the algorithm remains $O(n \log n)$ in the worst case. In contrast the complexity for earlier line-constraint methods [13] is at least $O(n^2 \log n)$ due to an $O(n^2)$ step in the overlapping detection, and will be $O(n^3)$ without the pre-processing, and $O(n \times k)$ for the removal of duplicate edges where k is the maximum number of edges at a vertex. Similarly, the complexity for the point-based methods [6] is $O(e^2 v)$ where e is the number of edges and v is the maximum number of vertices in a face loop; thus the edge-based constraints are seen to be more efficient.

3 Results

The algorithm has been implemented under Linux and and OpenGL on a Pentium II/233 machine. We have tested this algorithm for a number of cases. Some results are shown in Figures 4 and 6. Figure 6 shows the partial reconstruction for a case where one edge was missing in the input; this is handled correctly.

So even for partially erroneous input, our algorithm handles the correct part of the input and can flag the incorrect aspects. In all our test cases (up to 50 edges), the algorithm ran under 0.02 seconds.

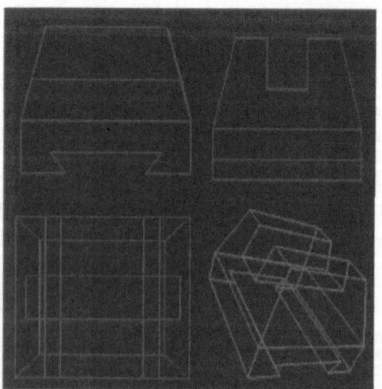
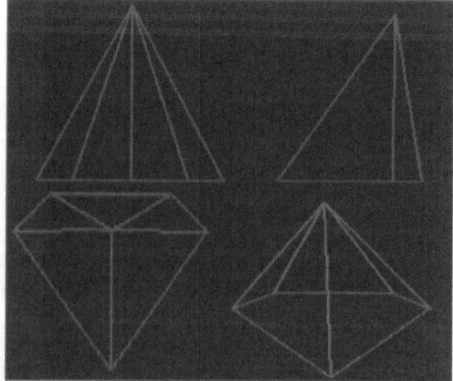

Fig. 4. Two simple machined parts where orthographic projections of a wedge with a slot and a pentagonal pyramid is completely reconstructed

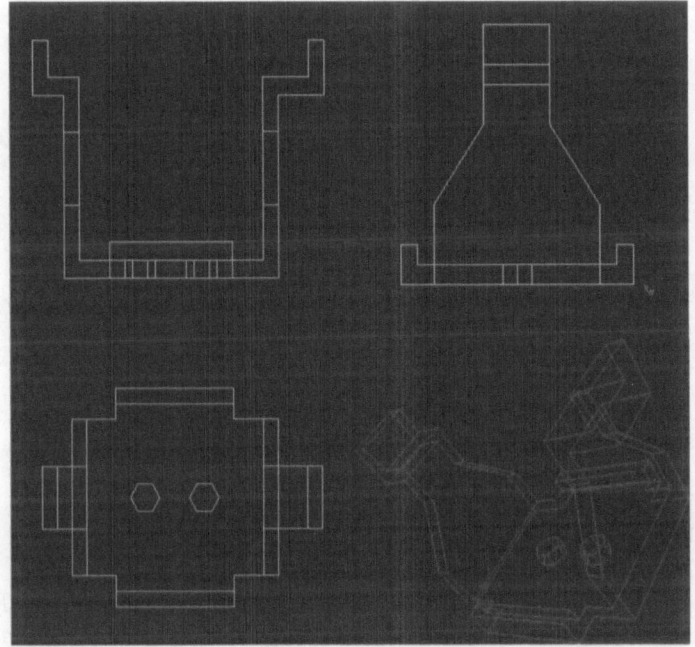

Fig. 5. An engineering object example (from [7])

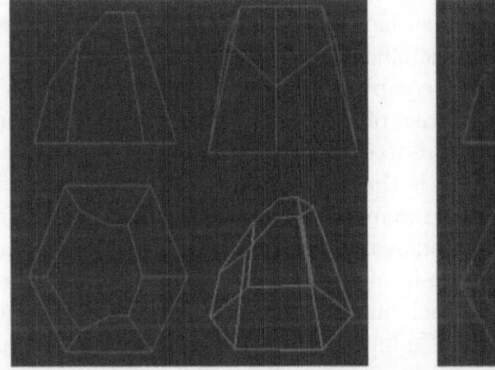 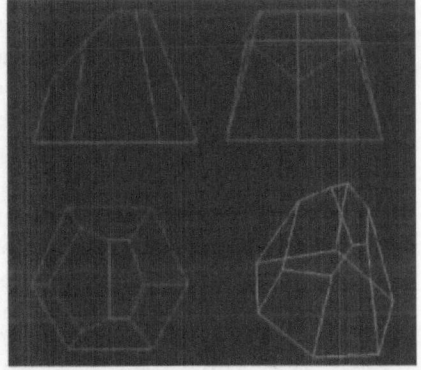

Fig. 6. *Inconsistent Input Data is flagged.* In this truncated hexagonal pyramid, the first figure (a) is missing an edge between the horizontal and slant truncation. This is identified and corrected in in (b) resulting in successful reconstruction.

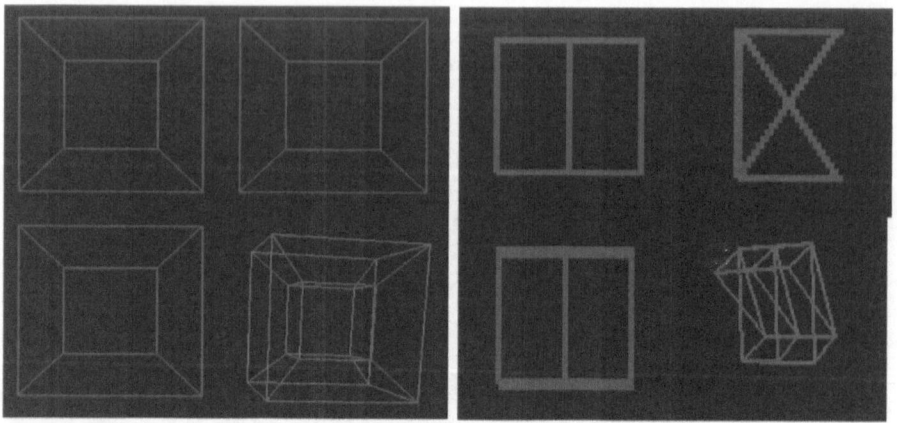

Fig. 7. These examples demonstrate the handling of ambiguous wireframe models. In such cases, all possible instances of the object are shown.

4   Conclusion

The algorithm proposed here addresses a very small part of the overall problem of 3D solid model generation from 2D drawings. However, this component of the task is a *core* component and is likely to be used more frequently than some of the more complex analysis. Also, the results of latter processes would depend on the constraints generated by reconstructing the 3-D line segments first. Improving the efficiency of this key step therefore is an important practical consideration. Unlike traditional models, the algorithm is based on 3D projections for input lines and not the input points. It is also a qualitatively complete segmentation and is guaranteed to cover all cases of 3D line projections. The efficiency increase over previous point-based methods is due to additional constraints imposed by considering a line together, while the efficiencies over previous edge projection methods is due to the qualitatively complete analysis. One of the issues worth exploring further is whether the process of b-rep generation from wireframe can also be integrated with this procedure to obtain even higher efficiencies.

Another aspect of the procedure is that it can flag inconsistent data at the bounds-checking stage; any edges not mapped by the process as a 3-D edge can automatically be flagged for correction by the human operator (Figure 6). As was originally pointed out in [7], no wire-frame generation model can resolve many of the possible ambiguous inputs including the famous square with diagonals drawn case that has 38,065 possible solutions. Another well-known example is shown in Figure 7(b), where our model generates all possible valid edges. In such cases (Figure 7) the procedure results in all the candidate edges being flagged and a human would need to provide additional inputs at an early stage to reduce the ambiguities. Here it is possible that additional heuristics may be generated by considerations of graph closure, as used in b-rep model generation. However, while the wireframe generation model above is applicable to any set of 3D edges, the graph closure algorithms are applicable only to closed surfaces so that the object must be a polyhedra or some other simple construct.

Acknowledgments We gratefully acknowledge the help provided by Dave Elliman of the University of Nottingham for sharing his perceptive review of the 3D reconstruction-from-drawings literature.

References

[1] B. Aldefeld. On the automatic recognition of 3d structures from 2d representations. *CAD, March 1983*, 15(2):59–64, 1983.

[2] Ho Bin. Inputting constructive solid geometry representations directly. from 2D orthographic engineering drawings, 1986.

[3] S.K. Ghosh, Y.B. Li, A.K. Munns, and X.C. Wang. Generating solid models from two dimensional representations,. *Journal of Material Processing Technology, 1995.*, 54:211–217, 1995.

[4] M. Idesawa. A system to generate a solid figure from three view. *Bull. Jap. Soc Mech. Engg.*, 16:216–225, February 1973.

[5] Benjamin Kuipers. *Qualitative Reasoning, Modeling and Simulation with incomplete knowledge.* MIT Press, Cambridge, MA, Artificial Intelligence Series, 1994,452 pp, 1994.

[6] M.H. Kuo. Reconstruction of quadric surface solids from three-view engineering drawings. *Computer Aided Design*, 30(7):517–527, 1998.

[7] George Markowsky and Michael A. Wesley. Fleshing out wire frames: reconstruction of objects, part i. *IBM J. Research and Dev, Sept 1980, reprinted in Advances in robotics, v.1, ed. Schwartz and Yap [87]*, 24(5):229–258, 1980.

[8] Hiroshi Masuda and Masayuki Numao. A cell based approch for generating solid models from orthographic projections. *Computer-Aided Design*, 29(3):177–187, 1997.

[9] A.A.G. Requicha. Representation for rigid solids: Theory, methods, and systems. *Computer Surveys, Dec. 1980*, 12(4), 1980.

[10] H. Sakurai and D.C. Gossard. Solid model input through orthographics views. *ACM Computer Graphics, 1983*, 17:243–252, 1983.

[11] Byeong-Senk Shin and Yeong Gil Shin. Fast 3d solid model reconstruction from orthographic views. *Computer Aided Design,vol 30,No 1,1998*, pages 63–76, 1998.

[12] Michael A. Wesley and George Markowsky. Fleshing out wire frames: reconstruction of objects, part ii. *IBM J. Research and Dev:582-597, November 1981, reprinted in Advances in robotics, v.1, ed. Schwartz and Yap [87]*, 25(6):259–295, 1981.

[13] Qing-Wen Yan, C.L. Philip Chen, and Zesheng Tang. Efficient algorithm for the reconstruction of 3d objects from orthographic projections. *Computer Aided Design, Vol 26(9) 1994.*, pages 669–699, 1994.

Automatic Interpretation of Construction Structure Drawings

Yang Cao, Ruoyu Yan, Jun Tan, and Shijie Cai

State Key Laboratory of Novel Software Technology
Nanjing University, Nanjing, China 210093
sjcai@netra.nju.edu.cn

Abstract. This paper does a lot of research and experiment on automatic interpretation of construction structure drawings. Based on the feature of Construction Structure drawings the syntax is summarized which support the interpretation of all kinds of construction elements and the relation between the elements. At the end the result of an automatic interpretation of CSD system is introduced. The use of the syntax summarized makes this system easily constructed and highly efficiently.

1 Introduction

The construction design has benefited a lot from CAD technique and has made big step towards the modernization. But the construction engineering is still in the backward condition of manual operation, Many work such as the quantity survey, which is time consuming and low quality, are still the bottleneck in construction development. Not only consultant company spend several main months in calculating the budget, but also the contract company has to spend time as much as the consultant company in verifying the quantity. When the two results are different from each other, both sides have to spend more time seeking for the correct answer together.

Graphics recognition techniques have been applied to many kinds of technical documents and drawings[1], [3], [4]. However few teams have been dealing with construction structure drawings. But lately, our team has started a project whose aim is to make out the budget of the architectural project by automatic interpretation of construction structure drawings (CSD). The backward condition of quantity survey has been innovated by using automatic interpretation system, it can offer a fast and accurate surveying tool that both the consultants company and the Contract Company would accept. And we can use the survey result in further construction project such as the steel matching.

This paper analyses the characteristic of CSD, and summarizes the syntax for element recognition and architecture structure recognition in CSD interpretation. A system for interpretation is also introduced. The top-level architecture of the system is shown in Fig.1.

Atul K. Chhabra and D. Dori (Eds.): GREC'99, LNCS 1941, pp. 298-304, 2000.

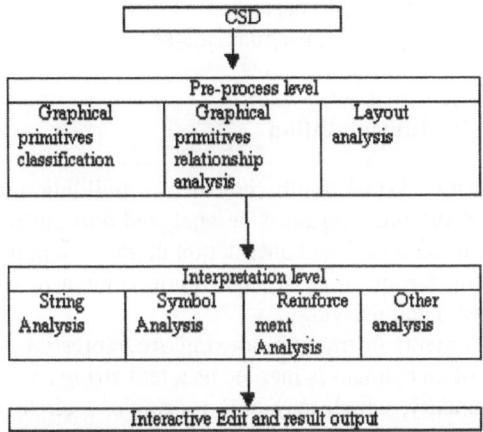

Fig. 1 Overview of the architecture of the system

2   Comparison between CSD and Mechanic Engineering Drawings

CSD can be divided into two classes: the framing drawing and the detail drawing. The framing drawings give the top view of each floor of a building while the detail drawings show the inside structure of each construction element such as beam, column, slab, wall, staircase and water tank. In many senses, construction structure drawings are similar to mechanic engineering drawings, as they typically represent orthogonal projections of the construction elements. But there are still many differences. The first difference is that some of the information is not explicitly shown on the drawings, but they can be interpreted according to the relative rules and engineer's experience. The engineers usually draw only one Polyline of steel reinforcement to represent a group of them having same attributes but different locations. Secondly, construction structure representations are very heterogeneous. For example, the drawing of a wall can be given by its top view, or its front view, its side view or by using only some texts to describe. Thirdly, some typical drawings are usually provided and to be refereed by many elements having the same structure but different sizes. Besides, there may be some errors existing in framing drawings and detail drawings; they can only be found and corrected by combining the framing data and detail data together.

3   Reinforcement Interpretation

3.1   Feature Definition

Reinforcement interpretation is base on feature. Tikerpuu and Ullman give the feature definition as any information group based on geometric shape that can be expressed by general parameters or characteristic and ratiocinated in application. Cunnigham and Dixon point that feature can be described as three Components: feature syntax, feature semantic, relationship between syntax and semantic.

3.2   Framing Drawing Interpretation

To calculate the quantity of steel reinforcement of a building, the framing drawings and detail drawings of the building must be analyzed and understood together. The topology structure information of the construction elements can be extracted from the framing drawings while the quantity of steel reinforcement of each element can be calculated from relative detail drawing.

The construction elements in framing drawing are expressed directly by graphical primitives. The name of an element is marked as a text string and the element shape is represented by its boundary, which may be a rectangle, a circle, or a close-chain of lines and arcs. They usually follow some kind of relationship rules but not always do. For example, marks or part of the lines could be omitted for some reason, and then the recognition of the framing drawing will be more difficult.

In order to recognize each element in a framing drawing, it is required to work out some kind of formal expressions about element's marks, shapes and their relationship. In this paper, the BNF is used[2]. For example, the condition of determining a column can be expressed in BNF as below:

<COLUMN>::={<ColumnMark> < ColumnMark-ColumnBoundary-Relativity>}
        <ColumnBoundary >
<ColumnMark>::=[<'A'|'B'|...|'Z'>][<'1'|'2'|...|'9'>]{<'a'|'b'|...|'z'>}
<ColumnMark-ColumnBoundary-Relativity >::=
                        <the distance between them is within a possible range>
<ColumnBoundary>::=<Proper-Position> <Proper-Boundary>
<Proper-Boundary>::=<Suitable-Size> <Boundary>
<Boundary>::=<Rectangle> | <Circle> | <Ellipse> | <Other-Shape>
<Other-Shape>::= <head-tail connected lines or arcs>
<Proper-Position>::=<Grid-Intersection> | <Special Position >
<Grid-Intersection>::=<intersection of Grid-Lines>
<Grid-Line>::=<line connecting to grid circle>
<Grid-Circle>::=<Coordinate-Mark><inside><circle>
<Coordinate-Mark>::=<'A'|'B'|...|'Z'> | <'1'|'2'|...|'9'>

According to the above grammar expression, the recognition of a column is started from the extraction of primitives, such as the rectangle, circle, ellipse and the 'other shape'. If some primitives match the relative grammar then they form a high level object in the BNF hierarchy, until that the column is recognized.

3.3   Architectural Symbol Recognition

There are three levels of symbol recognition: image level, graphical level, and syntactical level[6]. We only discuss symbol recognition of syntactical level in this paper. The most difference between architectural symbol and other symbols is that architectural symbol is multiform. That means one same symbol has several different forms. It brings some difficulty for recognition. Only one pictorial graphical approach can hardly satisfy all the recognition. While syntactic approach can solve this problem. Syntactic approach uses hierarchy to express the features of the symbols. We can extract the same features of the symbol and express them in one level. It makes the approach simple and high efficacious.

There are five main symbols in CSD: Section Symbol, Height Symbol, Truncation Symbol, Begin-End Symbol, and Middle Symbol. In this paper we use Section Symbol recognition as example. Fig.2 shows some typical Section Symbol in CSD.

Fig. 2 Section Symbol

The recognition model can be expressed in BNF as below.

<Section Symbol>::=<Cut Direction Line>{<Auxiliary Cut Direction Line >}
     {<View Direction Line>}{< Auxiliary View Direction Line>}
     <Section Text>

<Cut Direction Line>::=<The line whose length is less than twice text height and
     more than one text height, and the line is at the cut
     direction >

<Auxiliary Cut Direction Line >::=<The line which is parallel with the Cut
     Direction Line and its length is less one text
     height>

<View Direction Line>::=<The line whose function is to show the view direction.
     It is perpendicular with Cut Direction Line and it's
     length is no more than the length of Cut Direction Line>

< Auxiliary View Direction Line>::=<The function of < Auxiliary View Direction
     Line is to Auxiliary show the direction of
     the View Direction. Its length is less than
     the length of View Direction Line >

<Section Text>::=<'A'|'B'|…|'Z'>|<'1'|'2'|…|'9'>

3.4   Reinforcement Recognition

BNF is also used in interpreting the detail drawings. A group of steel reinforcement is usually expressed by three components: an annotation string indicating the steel type, diameter, amount of bars, serial number, and location attribute, a Polyline representing the shape of steel reinforcement, and the connection line connecting the two components (Fig.2). For example, the annotation string   "5Y10-200 T&B" represents five steel bars, which are located every 200-millimeter in both the top and bottom of the construction element. The annotation text string may also annotate a steel bar directly without a connection line (Fig.3). The following grammar expressions are used to express the above situations:

<Steel-Reinforcement>: :=<Line-Annotation-Steel-Bar> | <Direct-Annotation-Steel-Bar>

And the first one can be expressed by:

<Line-Annotation-Steel-Bar>: :=<Steel-Annotation-String> <Mark-Line-Relativity> <Annotation-Line> <Line-Bar-Relativity> <Steel-Bar>

Here the 'mark-line-relativity' is used to check the correspondence between an annotation string and an annotation line and the 'line-bar-relativity' is used to check the correspondence between an annotation line and a steel bar. The 'steel-annotation-string' has a basic rule to organize but actually different appearing. It can be recognized by the following grammars:

<Steel-Annotation-String>::={<ST-Amount>}   <Separator>   <ST-Type>   <ST-Diameter>   <Separator>   <ST-Number>   {<Separator>   <ST-Location-Attribute> <Other-Notation>}
<ST-Amount>::=<digital> | <digital><ST-Amount>
<Separator>::=<' '>|<'-'>|<','>|<'&'>
<ST-Type>::=<'T'>|<'Y'>|<'R'>|<'ET'>
<ST-Diameter>::=<10>|<16>|<20>|<25>|<32>|<40>

3.5   Shapes Standardization

The shape of the reinforcement has many different types. Architecture engineers give each type a shapecode. Different shapecode has different calculate formula. To correctly recognize the shapcode of reinforcement is one important work of reinforcement interpretation. The most difficulty of shape recognition is that engineers will bend or cut line for showing some detail. It leads that even some reinforcement will use one standard shapecode even it is not like the standard shape. To solve this problem we should standardize the reinforcement line. Fig 3 gives three main shape standardization examples.

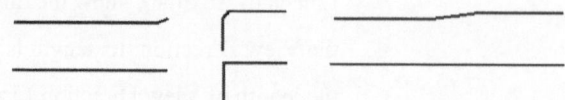

Fig. 3 Shape standardization examples

The above line shapes are the actual shapes in CSD. The below shapes are the standardized shapes.

4   Results

CSD interpretation system improves the efficiency and accuracy of architecture budget work highly. Table 1 and Table 2 give the comparison between CSD interpretation system and manual operation.

Table 1.

	Computer interpret time	Interactive edit	Manual process time
Beam	5_15seconds	1_10minutes	2_4hours
Slab	10_40seconds	5_30 minutes	7_8hours
Column	1_5seconds	5_20 minutes	2_4hours
Wall	5_15seconds	5_30 minutes	4_6hours
Staircase	5_10seconds	5_30 minutes	2_4hours

Table 2.

Project Name	Computer interpret time	Manual process time
Hongkong airport control tower	2_3days	4_6months
NGAU TAU KOK POLICE STATION	2_3days	2_3months
CHECK LAP KOK AIRPORT	1_2days	2_3months

5   References

1. K. Tombre. Analysis of engineering drawings: State of the art and challenges. In International Workshop on Graphics Recognition , pages 54-61, 1997.
2. Boris Pasternak, Gabriel Gabrielids, Rainer Sprengle. WIZ-Design and Development of a Prototype for knowledge-Based Interpretation of Technical Drawings
3. A. Okzaki, T.Knodo, Mori, S.Tsunekawa, and E. Kawamoto, "An Automatic Circuit Diagram Reader with loop-structure based symbol Recognition.: IEEE Trans. Pattern   Analysis and Machine Intelligence, vol. 10, no3, pp. 331-341, May 1988
4. S. Okazaki and Y. Tsuji, "Knowledge-based Approach for Adaptive Recognition of Drawings," Proc. Pattern Recognition : Fourth Int'l Conf., pp. 627-632, Mar.1988

5. BARTENSTEIN, O. & MADERLECHNER, G. 1984: Die Methode der diskriminierenden Graphen zur fehlertoleranten Mustererkennung, proc. DAGM/OEAGM, pp. 222-228.

6. BENJAMIN, D., FORGUE, P., GULKO, E., MASSICOTTE, J-B. & MEUBUS, C. 1988 The Use   of High- level Knowledge for Enhanced Entry of Engineering Drawings, Proc. 9th ICPR, pp. 119-124.

7. BERGENGR, LUHN, A., MADERLECHNER, G. & ERREITER, B. 1987: Dokumentanalyse mit Hilfe ATN's und unscharfen Relationen, Proc. 9. DAGM, pp. 78-81.BIEDER, H. & ZIMMER, H.G. 1988: Dokument-Segmentierung mit Bildpyramiden, Proc. 10th DAGM, pp.   305-311.

Automated Analysis of Scanned Ducting Diagrams

R. T. Ritchings[1], M. A. Berbar[1], D. E. Asumu[2]

[1] Department of Computation, UMIST
t.ritchings@umist.ac.uk,
m_berbar@hotmail.com
[2] BT Research Laboratories, Martlesham, UK

Abstract. The study is concerned with the automated analysis of scanned cable and associated diagrams for entry in the BT GIS system used by their Field Service Engineers. The analysis involves two distinct stages: the location of Joint Boxes in the diagrams using erosion/dilation techniques; followed by a novel line-following to identify the connections between the Joint Boxes and the duct end-points. The analysis has been successfully applied to scanned duct diagrams and cartographic maps.

1 Introduction

The study is concerned with the automated analysis of scanned cable and associated diagrams for entry in the BT GIS system used by their Field Service Engineers. The salient information in these diagrams is currently being extracted manually at great time and expense.

The information required from these diagrams, such as the one shown in Figure 1, is the ducting routes (lines) between their Joint Boxes (solid black squares) and the Distribution Points (circles) on their infrastructure network. Of key importance is the label within each Distribution Point. These labels are also present in the cartographic maps of the area and the ducting diagrams, and once detected, enables information held on the different diagrams to be linked together. The physical possibility of providing a new line to a property, for example, requires information to be derived from the cartographic map, and the associated ducting and cable diagrams.

The work described here is concerned with the identification of the ducting routes in the scanned ducting diagrams and cartographic maps. While there has been considerable research into automated analysis techniques for the analysis of telephone diagrams [1], digitised maps [2-3], line and engineering drawings [4-11], these have concentrated on specific individual problems associated with the analysis and interpretation of digitised documents. These methods are not directly applicable here because of the need for the fast interpretation and analysis of large poor quality documents where there are gaps in the lines and confusion caused by predominantly hand-written characters which touch both the lines and each other.

Atul K. Chhabra and D. Dori (Eds.): GREC'99, LNCS 1941, pp. 305-312, 2000.
© Springer-Verlag Berlin Heidelberg 2000

The results reported here builds on a preliminary comparative study of three line-following algorithms for these types of diagrams [12], and describes a fourth, more robust line-following algorithm for identifying the ducting routes, together with an approach for Distribution Point recognition.

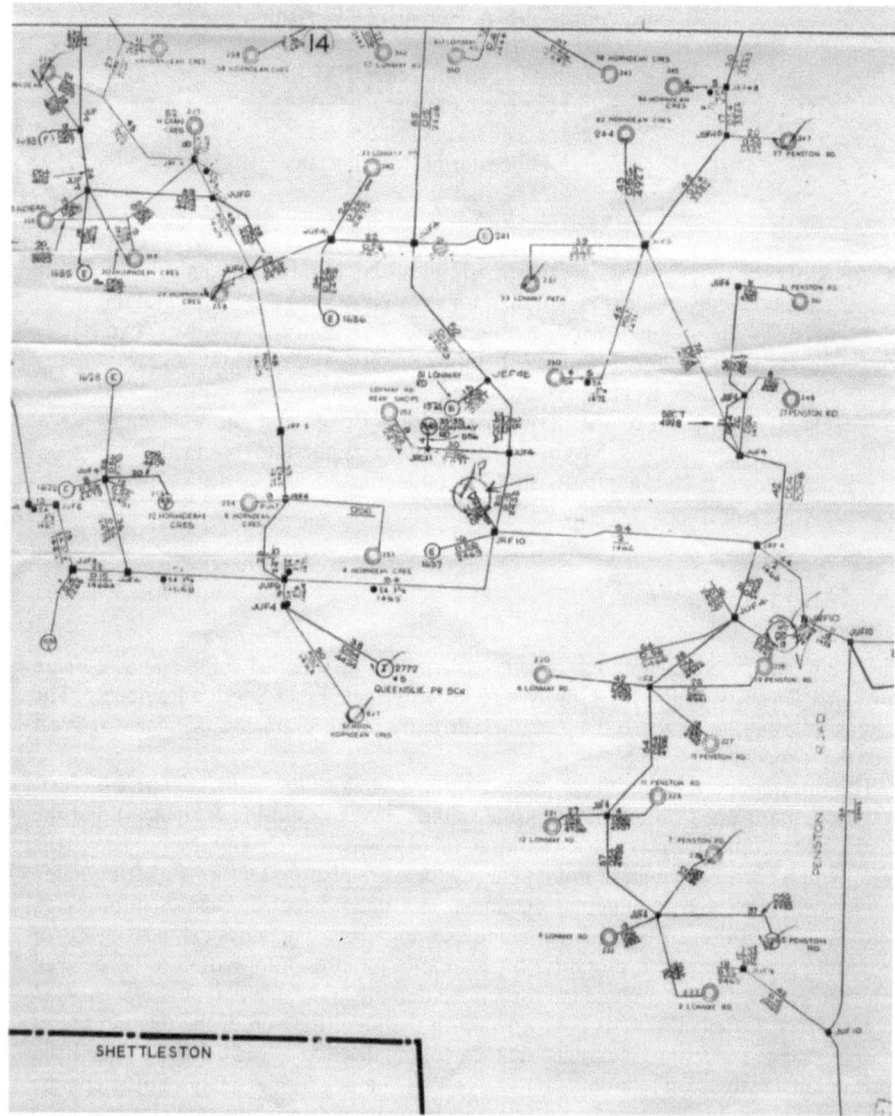

Figure 1 The scanned ducting diagram

2   Methodology

The ducting diagrams that have been used in this study were scanned at 200dpi DPI, and stored as greyscale images. Greyscale scanning was chosen in preference to the more usual binary because it was anticipated that the extra information would be useful when separating the touching text and lines, and bridging gaps along the lines. In order to avoid the computational problems encountered in the earlier approaches to line and curve following, which typically involve thinning and searching for all possible lines in a ducting diagram on a row-by-row basis, a model-driven approach was taken. With this approach the Joint Boxes were found first, and then used as the starting points for various line-following procedures. These attempted to follow the ducting routes, branching and bridging gaps as necessary, until either another Joint Box or became circular, which was indicative of a Distribution Point.

2.1   Locating the Joint Boxes

It may be seen for Figure 1 that the Joint Boxes are thicker than the lines, text and other features in the diagrams. Consequently, greyscale Erosion/Dilation [13] provided a simple and effective way of locating the Joint Boxes.

2.2   Line-Following Algorithms

A simple grey-level line-following algorithm was investigated first. In this algorithm, the grey-level values of the 8-neighbours surrounding the current pixel along a line are examined, and the pixel with the highest value is selected as the next pixel along the line, However, this was not successful as the width of the lines were compatible with the size of the neighborhood. However, it was found that basing the decision on the grey-level values of the 16 pixels surrounding these 8-neighbours gave much better results. This algorithm was, however, confused by text touching the lines and also stopped at any gap along a line. Consequently, it was necessary to extend this algorithm to handle these situations. The approach taken involve invoking an additional procedure whenever a branching line, which was indicative of a touching character, or gap was encountered, in an attempt to help the line-following continue along the genuine line or bridge a gap. Three procedures were evaluated in the earlier study [12]:

- The Maximum Repeated Direction for the previous 15 pixels was calculated and next pixel to be processed lies on the opposite end point is that one lies in this direction.
- The mean and Standard Deviation of the directions of the previous 15 pixels were calculated, and preference given, when choosing the next pixel, to those whose direction lies within one Standard Deviation of the mean direction of the current line.

- A straight line was fitted to the previous 15 pixels using the *least squares method* and pixels close to this line were given preference when choosing the next pixel.

In an attempt to improve on the reliability of the line-following procedure results, a new technique, based on the median direction of the pixels lying along a line, was also was implemented and evaluated on the set of scanned ducting diagrams:

- The median direction of the previous 15 pixels was calculated, and preference given to the pixel lying in this direction on the opposite side of a gap.

This procedure was applied to the same set of scanned ducting diagrams that was used in the earlier study, and found to be more robust and lead to a more accurate interpretation of the lines. The main failings of the new algorithm were large gaps along a line, and gaps in the region of sharp changes in the direction of a line

2.3   Locating the Distribution Points

The line-following terminates when the end of a line is reached, either because the line genuinely stops and there is too large gap, or because it starts to curve as it reaches Distribution Point. The location of the Distribution Points involves firstly recognizing that the latter situation has occurred and then fitting a circle to the 5 pixel coordinates lying on the center of the previous 5 segments.

3   Results

The result of applying the new line-following procedure to the ducting diagram of Figure 1 may be seen in Figure 2. This approach was found to be less susceptible to minor fluctuations in the positions of the pixels along the line due to noise effects, and so produced more robust line-following in the ducting diagrams the with the earlier techniques. The centers of the Distribution Point circles that were found are also indicated on the Figure 2. Although the centers may be slightly inaccurate because of the noise effects, they still permit the regions containing the labels to be extracted (one example is shown in the figure 2 and figure 4) and these can then be processed using standard OCR software.

This procedure has also been applied to a few cartographic maps containing ducting information (Figure 3). While these diagrams are clearly more complex than the pure ducting diagrams, the results are very encouraging as the approach successfully avoided lines associated with the geographical information, as may be seen in Figure 4.

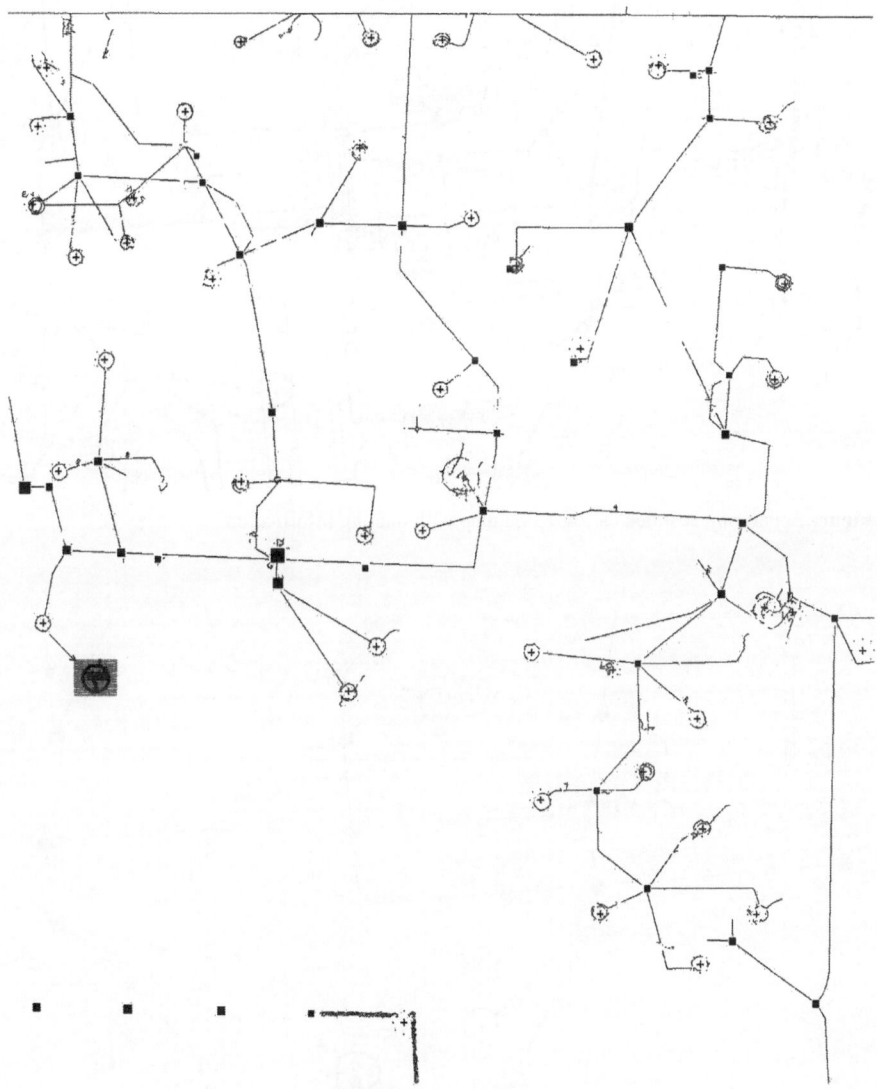

Figure 2. Processed diagram showing Joint Boxes (▪) and Distribution Points (+)

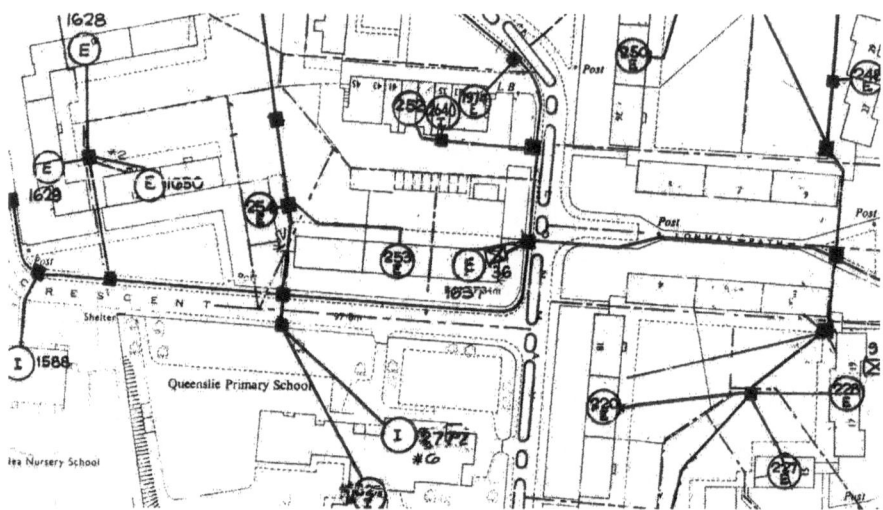

Figure 3. Part of a scanned cartographic map with ducting information

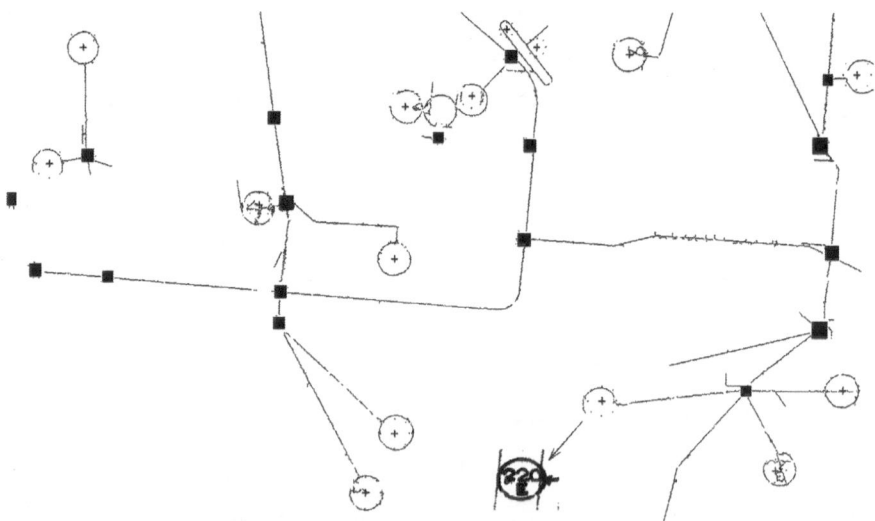

Figure 4. Ducting information derived from processed cartographic map

4   Conclusions

Four line-following algorithms have been evaluated on a small sample of scanned ducting diagrams. Joint Boxes are identified first and provide the starting points for a line-following algorithm. The algorithm that uses the median direction of the previous pixels along the line to locate the next pixel on the other side of a gap gives the best results. A simple circle fitting approach is locating approximately 90% of the Distribution Points. This enables the region containing the label to be extracted for OCR analysis. This basic approach has been applied to cartographic maps containing ducting information and the preliminary results are very encouraging.

Acknowledgements

M. Berbar would like to acknowledge funding by the Egyptian Government.

References

1. Arias J.F., Lai C.P., Surya S., Kasturi R., Chhabra A.: Interpretation of telephone system manhole drawing, Pattern Recognition letters, 16 (1995).355-369.
2. Kasturi R., Alemany J.:Information Extraction from Images of Paper-Based Maps. IEEE PAMI, Vol. 14 (1988).910-918.
3. Hartog J.E., Kate T.K., Gerbrands J.J.: Knowledge-Based Interpretation of Utility Maps. Computer Vision and Image Understanding, Vol. 63. (1996).105-117.
4. Kasturi R. , Bow S.T. , El-Masri W. , Shah J. , Gattiker J., and Mokate U.: A system for interpretation of line drawings. IEEE PAMI, Vol 12 (1990).978-992.
5. Kasturi R., Trivedi M.: Image Analysis Applications. Optical Engineering, Series Editor, Marcel Dekker, Inc., New York (1990).
6. Nagasamy V. and Langrana N. A.: Engineering drawing processing and vectorization system. CVGIP (49). (1990) 379-397.
7. Dori D., Liang Y., Dowell J., and Chai.: Sparse-pixel recognition of primitives in engineering drawings. Machine Vision Application. 6(2-3). (1993) 69-82.
8. Hori O., Tanigawa S.: Line fitting method for line drawing based on contours and skeletons. IEICE Trans. Inf. & Syst., Vol. E77-D. (1994).
9. Janssen R. D. T. and Vossepoel A. M.: Adaptive Vectorization of line Drawing Images. CVGIU, Vol. 65, No. 1. (1997). 38-56.
10. Wang L. and Pavlidis T.: Direct Gray Scale Extraction of Features for Character Recognition. IEEE Trans. on Pattern Analysis and Machine Intelligence, vol. 15 (Oct. 1993) 1053-1067.
11. Wang L. and Pavlidis T.: Detection of Curved and Straight Segments from GrayScale Topography. CVGIP: Image Understanding, vol. 58 (Nov. 1993) 352-365.

12. Ritchings R.T., Berbar M.A., Asumu D.: Model-based line-following in scanned cable diagrams, IEE Workshop on Document Image Processing and Multimedia, DIPM'99, London, UK (1999).
13. Haralick R. M., Sternberg S. R., Zhuang X.: Image Analysis Using Mathematical Morphology. IEEE PAMI 9(4) (1987), 532-550

Part VI

Performance Evaluation

Performance Evaluation of Document Image Algorithms

Robert M. Haralick

Department of Electrical Engineering, University of Washington
Seattle, WA 98195
haralick@ee.washington.edu

1 Introduction

Performance evaluation for document image processing has a different emphasis than performance evaluation in other areas of image processing. Other areas of image processing can tolerate some error. Because it is so easily done nearly perfectly by humans, document image processing must also be done nearly perfectly. So the first aspect of performance evaluation for document image processing is to determine the domain in which the performance is nearly perfect. Outside this domain, the algorithm makes errors. Such instances of errors need to be examined and classified and categorized so that the weaknesses of the algorithm can be characterized.

A parametric aspect of performance evaluation for document image processing is the determination of the performance as a function of increasing level of image perturbation. This perturbation is associated with the various kinds of noise that make a real document image page differ from the ideal. Since this aspect of performance evalution is associated with an explicit noise model, it is possible to do this evaluation by the generation of synthetic images which are perturbed by simulated noise in accordance with the noise perturbation model.

The last category of performance evaluation for document image processing is the category of overall performance in a specific document image population. This requires an experiment to be done with a significant sized population of document images suitably randomly selected to be representative of some real application domain.

Performance can be measured as a function of predefined categories of documents, as a function of noise perturbation parameters, or as a function of internal algorithm tuning parameters. To obtain a single number, the various different dimensions of performance must be weighted in an overall manner consistent with the application of interest.

Because performance is an empirical measurement, and because the set of images used in making this empirical measurement is in effect only a small fraction from a large population, a sample used in making the empirical measurement one time to another time will differ and induce differences in performance. These differences are due to sampling variations. The sampling variations induce variations in the estimated system parameters during training and induce

Atul K. Chhabra and D. Dori (Eds.): GREC'99, LNCS 1941, pp. 315–323, 2000.

variations in the performance values during testing. Therefore, another aspect of performance evaluation must include the measuring of the variation of estimated system tuning parameters due to the sampling variations in the document image training sample as well as the variation in estimated system performance dues to sampling variations in the document image testing sample.

Finally, there is the issue of testing the algorithm to determine if it meets its performance specifications. Being sure that an algorithm meets its specifications can require assessing its performance on a much larger sample than intuition might lead one to believe. And depending on what is meant by "meeting specifications" being sure that an algorithm meets its specification can require that its performance in an assessment be much better than intuition might lead one to believe.

2   The Method of Performance Evaluation

Performance evaluation uses the method of controlled experiment to measure the extent to which the algorithm segments recognizes, and locates the entities it is designed to handle. It must measure the sensitivity of performance ot changes in tuning parameter values, training set sampling variations and testing set sampling variations. It must have a protocol that permits the hypothesis to be tested that the system meets its requirement specifications.

The controlled experiment requires an experimental protocol having a measurement plan, a sampling design, and a statistical data analysis plan. The measurement plan states what quantities will be measured, how they will be measured and the accuracy with which they will be measured. The sampling design defines the population of document images and describes how a suitable random independent set of document images will be sampled from the population. The statistical data analysis plan describes how the raw data gathered from the experiment will be analyzed. The analysis itself consists of one part that estimates the performance statistic and another part that estimates the statistical deviation of the true value of the performance statistic from the estimated value. The data obtained by the analysis must be complete enough so that the hypothesis that the system meets its stated requirements can be tested. And it must be supported by a theoretically developed statistical analysis which shows that an experiment carried out according to the measurement plan and sampling design and analyzed according to the statistical data analysis plan will produce a statistical test itself having the required accuracy. This analysis, if it is standard, can refer to statistical texts for the test used.

3   Meeting Performance Requirements

The requirement statement for a recognition task is a statement of the form: the probability that the algorithm fails to recognize an entity of interest (depending on the kind of algorithm, entities of interest might be zones, lines, words, tables, figures etc.) in the given population is less that f_o. The experiment that is done to determine whether an algorithm meets its performance is called an acceptance test. In this section we give a short review of acceptance tests.

Any kind of acceptance test inevitably has two kinds of errors: the errors of omission and the errors of commission. A system may actually meet its requirements, but due to testing set sampling variations, there will be some probability that the hypothesis that the system meets the requirements will be rejected. This is an error of omission. As the sampling set size increases, this error will decrease.

On the other hand, a system may not actually meet its requirements, but due to testing set sampling variations, there will be some probability that the hypothesis that the hypothesis that the system meets its requirements will not be rejected. This is an error of commission. Again as the sampling set size increases, this error will decrease.

3.1   The Derivation

Consider the case for omission errors. The case for commission errors is obviously similar. Let N, the sampling size, be the total number of entities observed and let K be the number of times that the algorithm fails to properly recognize the entity out of the N entities observed.

The simplest intuitive way of making the comparison between f_o and K is to use K in the natural manner to estimate the true probability rate f. The maximum likelihood estimate $\hat{f}$ of f based on K is $\hat{f} = K/N$. If the estimate $\hat{f}$ of f is less than f_o, we judge that the algorithm passes the test. If the estimate $\hat{f}$ is greater than f_o, we judge that the algorithm fails the acceptance test. The issue with such a procedure is how sure are we if we apply such a procedure that the judgment we make about the algorithm's performance is a correct judgment. To answer this issue we must estimate the performance of our judgment. We start from the beginning.

To carry out the estimation, we suppose that, conditioned on the true error rate f, the algorithm's recognition failures are independent and identically distributed. Let X_n be a random variable taking the value 1 for an incorrect recognition and taking a value 0 otherwise, when the algorithm is judging the nth entity.[1] In the maximum likelihood technique of estimation, we compute the estimate $\hat{f}$ as the value of f which maximizes

$$Prob\ (\sum_{n=1}^{N} X_n = K \mid f) = \binom{N}{K} f^K (1-f)^{N-K}$$

Taking the partial derivative with respect to f and setting the derivative to zero results in $\hat{f} = K/N$, the natural estimate of f.

Suppose that we adopt the policy of accepting the algorithm if $\hat{f} \leq f_o$. To understand the consequences of this policy, consider the probability that the

---

[1] We assume the recognition incorrectness of the entities are statistically independent.

policy results in a correct acceptance decision. The probability that $f \leq f_o$ given that $\hat{f} \leq f_o$ needs to be computed.

$$Prob\ (f \leq f_o \mid \hat{f} \leq f_o) = \int_{f=0}^{f_o} Prob\ (f \mid \hat{f} \leq f_o)\ df$$

$$= \frac{\int_{f=0}^{f_o} Prob\ (\hat{f} \leq f_o \mid f)\ Prob\ (f)\ df}{Prob\ (\hat{f} \leq f_o)}$$

To make the mathematics simple, let f_o be constrained so that there is some integer K_o such that $f_o = K_o/N$. Then

$$Prob\ (f \leq f_o \mid \hat{f} \leq f_o) = \frac{\int_{f=0}^{f_o} Prob\ \left(\sum_{n=1}^{N} X_n \leq K_o \mid f\right) Prob\ (f)\ df}{\int_{f=0}^{1} Prob\ \left(\sum_{n=1}^{N} X_n \leq K_o \mid f\right) Prob(f)\ df}$$

The probability that the true value of f is less than or equal to f_o given that the observed value $\hat{f}$ is less than f_o will depend, in general, on the testor's prior probability function $Prob\ (f)$. So, depending on the acceptance testor's prior probability function $Prob\ (f)$, there will besome smallest number F, $0 \leq F \leq 1$, such that $Prob\ (f) = 0$ for all $f > F$. Here, the support for the prior probability function is the interval $[0, F]$.

For example, an acceptance testor who has had successful experience with previous algorithms from the same company might have a prior probability function whose support is the interval $[0, 2f_o]$. An acceptance testor who has had no previous experience with the company might have a prior distribution whose support is the interval $[0, 10f_o]$. An acceptance testor who has had an unsuccessful experience with a previous algorithm from the same company might have a prior distribution for f whose support is the interval $[0, .5]$.

In each of the above cases, we assume that neither we nor the testor know anything more about the prior probability function than the interval of support $[0, F]$, where we assume that $F \geq f_o$, since if not, there would be no point to perform an acceptance test to establish something we already know. In this case, we take $Prob\ (f)$ to be that probability function defined on the interval $[0, F]$ having highest entropy. Such a $Prob\ (f)$ is the uniform density on the interval $[0, F]$. Hence, we take $Prob\ (f) = \frac{1}{F}$, $0 \leq f \leq F$. Therefore

$$Prob\ (f \leq f_o \mid \hat{f} \leq f_o) = \frac{\int_{f=0}^{f_o} \sum_{k=0}^{K_o} \binom{N}{k} f^k (1-f)^{N-k} df/F}{\int_{f=0}^{F} \sum_{k=0}^{K_o} \binom{N}{k} f^k (1-f)^{N-k} df/F}$$

$$= \frac{\sum_{k=0}^{K_0} \binom{N}{k} B(k+1, N+1-k) I_{f_o}(k+1, N+1-k)}{\sum_{k=0}^{K_0} \binom{N}{k} B(k+1, N+1-k) I_F(k+1, N+1-k)}$$

$$= \frac{\sum_{k=0}^{K_0} I_{f_o}(k+1, N+1-k)/(N+1)}{\sum_{k=0}^{K_0} I_F(k+1, N+1-k)/(N+1)}$$

$$= \frac{\sum_{k=0}^{K_0} I_{f_o}(k+1, N+1-k)}{\sum_{k=0}^{K_0} I_F(k+1, N+1-k)}$$

where $I_{f_o}(k+1, N+1-k)$ is the incomplete Beta ratio function.

In each of the above cases, we assume that neither we nor the testor know anything more about the prior probability function than the interval of support $[0, F]$, where we assume that $F \geq f_o$, since if not, there would be no point to perform an acceptance test to establish something we already know. In this case, we take $Prob\ (f)$ to be that probability function defined on the interval $[0, F]$ having highest entropy. Such a $Prob\ (f)$ is the uniform density on the interval $[0, F]$. Hence, we take $Prob\ (f) = \frac{1}{F},\ 0 \leq f \leq F$. Therefore

$$Prob\ (f \leq f_o \mid \hat{f} \leq f_o) = \frac{\int_{f=0}^{f_o} \sum_{k=0}^{K_0} \binom{N}{k} f^k (1-f)^{N-k} df / F}{\int_{f=0}^{F} \sum_{k=0}^{K_0} \binom{N}{k} f^k (1-f)^{N-k} df / F}$$

$$= \frac{\sum_{k=0}^{K_0} \binom{N}{k} B(k+1, N+1-k) I_{f_o}(k+1, N+1-k)}{\sum_{k=0}^{K_0} \binom{N}{k} B(k+1, N+1-k) I_F(k+1, N+1-k)}$$

$$= \frac{\sum_{k=0}^{K_0} I_{f_o}(k+1, N+1-k)/(N+1)}{\sum_{k=0}^{K_0} I_F(k+1, N+1-k)/(N+1)}$$

$$= \frac{\sum_{k=0}^{K_0} I_{f_o}(k+1, N+1-k)}{\sum_{k=0}^{K_0} I_F(k+1, N+1-k)}$$

where $I_{f_o}(k+1, N+1-k)$ is the incomplete Beta ratio function.

If $f_o << 1$ and $k \le N f_o$, then $\frac{2 f_o (N+1-k)}{1-f_o} = 2 f_o N = 2 K_o$. Therefore

$$Prob \left(\mathcal{F}_{2(k+1),\ 2(N+1-k)} \le \frac{f_o(N+1-k)}{(1-f_o)(k+1)} \right) = Prob \left(\mathcal{X}^2_{2(k+1)} \le 2K_o \right).$$

Since

$$Prob \left(\mathcal{X}^2_{2(k+1)} \le 2K_o \right) = \sum_{i=k+1}^{\infty} e^{-K_o} (K_o)^i / i!$$

(Johnson and Kotz 1969, p. 114) we may use tables of the cumulative Poisson distribution (Pearson and Hartley 1958) and there results

$$Prob\ (f \le f_o \mid \hat{f} \le f_o) = \sum_{k=0}^{K_o} \left(\sum_{i=k+1}^{\infty} e^{-K_o} K_o^i / i! \right) \Big/ \sum_{k=0}^{K_o} \left(\sum_{i=k+1}^{\infty} e^{-K_1} K_1^i / i! \right)$$

where $K_1 = FN$. When $F >> \frac{k+1}{N+2}$, the value of $I_F(k+1,\ N+1-k) = 1$ since the variance of a Beta $(k+1, N+1-k)$ random variable will be smaller than $\frac{k+1}{(N+1-k)^2} << F$ for large N. In this case, the denominator is only a few percent smaller than K_o+1. ¿From the form of the Poisson approximation, it is apparent that $I_f(k,\ N+1-k)$ depends only on the product fN when $N >> 1$, $k \le f_o N$ and $f << 1$. This can also be seen directly from the formula.

Under the particular conditions we are interested in, $N >> 100$, $f << 0.1$, and $k << N$. Hence $I_f(k+1,\ N+1-k) \approx I_f(k+1,\ N)$. This can be observed from the recurrence relation

$$I_x(a,b) = x I_x(a-1,b) + (1-x) I_x(a,b-1).$$

Now when $a + b > 6$ and $x << 1$, $I_x(a,b) \approx \phi(y)$ where

$$y = \frac{3 \left\{ (bx)^{\frac{1}{3}}(1 - 1/9b) - [a(1-x)]^{\frac{1}{3}}(1 - 1/9a) \right\}}{\left[\frac{(bx)^{\frac{2}{3}}}{b} + \frac{[a(1-x)]^{\frac{2}{3}}}{a} \right]^{\frac{1}{2}}}$$

and ϕ is the cummulative normal $(0,1)$ distribution function (Abramovitz and Steger, 1972). From this approximation it follows that when $f_o N > 1$, $x << 1$, $f_o m k << 1$, $\frac{N}{m} >> 1$, and $m > 1$; then

$$I_{f_o}(k+1\ N+1-k) \approx I_{f_o}(k+1,\ N)$$

$$\approx I_{m f_o}(k+1,\ \frac{N}{m})$$

$$\approx I_{m f_o}(k+1,\ \frac{N}{m} + 1 - k).$$

This means that instead of having to parametrize by f_o and N independently, we can create tables parametrized by the product $f_o N$.

For example, if $f_o = 0.0001, F \ge 10 f_o$ and $N = 10^4$, then $K_o = 1$ and $Prob\ (f \le f_o \mid \hat{f} \le f_o) = \frac{1}{2}[0.6321 + 0.2642] = 0.4481$. If $f_o = .0001, F \ge 10 f_o$

and $N = 2 \times 10^4$, then $K_o = 2$ and $Prob$ $(f \leq f_o \mid \hat{f} \leq f_o) = \frac{1}{3}[0.8647 +$ $0.5940 + 0.3233] = 0.5940$. This means that with 2 or fewer observed incorrect recognitions out of 20,000 observations, the probability is only 0.5940 that the true false alarm rate is less than 0.0001.

It seems that such a policy does not provide very certain answers. Perhaps more observations would be helpful. If $N = 10^5$, then $K_o = 10$. In this case

$$Prob\ (f \leq f_o \mid \hat{f} \leq f_o) = \frac{1}{11}[10.0000 + 0.9995 + 0.9972 + 0.9897$$
$$+ 0.9707 + 0.9329 + 0.8699 + 0.7798 + 0.6672$$
$$+ 0.5461 + 0.4170]$$
$$= 0.8332$$

Thus, with 10 or fewer observed incorrect recognitions out of 100,000 observations, the probability is 0.8336 that the incorrect recognition rate is less than 0.0001. This is certainly better, but depending on our own requirement for certainty in our judgment it may not be sure enough.

Thus the acceptance test itself has a requirement: the probability with which we wish the acceptance test itself to yield correct judgement.

If we adopt a different policy, we can be more sure about our judgment of the true false alarm rate. Suppose we desire to perform an acceptance test which guarantees that the probability is α that the machine meets specifications. In this case, we adopt the policy that we accept the machine if $\hat{f} \leq f^*$ where f^* is chosen so that for the fixed probability $\alpha(f^*)$, $Prob\ (f \leq f_o \mid \hat{f} \leq f^*) = \alpha(f^*)$. This means to accept if $K \leq K^*$, where $K^* = Nf^*$. Proceeding as before to find K^*, we have

$$\alpha(K^*) = Prob\ (f \leq f_o \mid \hat{f} \leq f^*) = \frac{\displaystyle\int_{f=0}^{f_o} \sum_{k=0}^{K^*} \binom{N}{k} f^k (1-f)^{N-k} df}{\displaystyle\int_{f=0}^{F} \sum_{k=0}^{K^*} \binom{N}{k} f^k (1-f)^{N-k} df}$$

$$= \frac{\sum_{k=0}^{K^*} I_{f_o}(k+1, N+1-k)}{\displaystyle\sum_{k=0}^{K^*} I_F(k+1, N+1-k)}$$

$$= \frac{\sum_{k=0}^{K^*} \sum_{i=k+1}^{\infty} e^{-K_o} K_o^i / i!}{\displaystyle\sum_{k=0}^{K^*} \sum_{i=k+1}^{\infty} e^{-K_o} K_o^i / i!}.$$

Then if $f_o = .0001, F \geq 10 f_o, N = 10^5$, and $K^* = 8$, there results

$$\alpha\ (K^*) = \frac{1}{9}[1.000 + .9995 + .9972 + .9897 + .9707 + .9329 + .8699$$
$$= +.7798 + .6672]$$
$$= .9119$$

So if $\hat{f} \le 8/10^5$, the probability will be .9119 that the true incorrect recognition is less .0001.

In summary, we have obtained that $Prob$ $(f \le f_o$ and $K \le K^*) = \frac{1}{N+1} \sum_{k=0}^{K^*} I_{f_o}(k+1, N+1-k)$ and $Prob$ $(K \le K^*) = \frac{K^*+1}{N+1}$. Since $Prob$ (f) is uniform, $Prob$ $(f \le f_o) = f_o$. These three probabilities determine the missed acceptance rate $Prob$ $(f \le f_o \mid K > K^*)$, the false acceptance rate $Prob$ $(K \le K^* \mid f > f_o)$, the error rate $Prob$ $(f \le f_o$ and $K > K^*) + Prob$ $(f > f_o$ and $K \le K^*)$, the identification accuracy $Prob$ $(f \le f_o$ and $K \le K^*) + Prob$ $(f > f_o$ and $K > K^*)$, the acceptance capture rate $Prob$ $(K \le K^* \mid f \le f_o)$, and the capture certainty rate $P(f \le f_o \mid K \le K^*)$. Thus, the complete operating characteristics can be determined of the acceptance policy we have discussed.

4   Sampling Variations

Most recognition algorithms have their internal tuning parameters set to a value based on a training set. A training set consists of the images or subimages of the entities of interest along with their correct identifications. If the entire population of entities could be sampled and used for training, the value of the tuning parameter would be Θ. However, due to the finite sampling of the training set, the value obtained by training is $\hat{\Theta}$. By sampling the exact same size sample another time, the value obtained by training would differ from $\hat{\Theta}$. This issue of sampling variations is exactly put by asking how much variation will there be in the value $\hat{\Theta}$ due to the finite sample size, if we were to repeat the training process many independent times. For example, if we were to repeat the training process N times, and observe tuning parameter values $\hat{\Theta}_1, \ldots, \hat{\Theta}_N$, we could obtain a reasonable estimate of the covariance matrix Σ for $\hat{\Theta}$ by

$$\Sigma = \frac{1}{N} \sum_{n=1}^{N} (\hat{\Theta}_n - \Theta^*)'(\hat{\Theta}_n - \Theta^*)$$

where

$$\Theta^* = \frac{1}{N} \sum_{n=1}^{N} \hat{\Theta}_n$$

Then we could estimate the probability $P(\delta)$ that $\hat{\Theta}$ will lie within an hyperellipsoid of parameter δ

$$(\hat{\Theta}_n - \Theta^*)' \Sigma^{-1} (\hat{\Theta}_n - \Theta^*) \le \delta$$

by simply counting:

$$P(\delta) = \frac{1}{N} \#\{n \mid (\hat{\Theta}_n - \Theta^*)' \Sigma^{-1} (\hat{\Theta}_n - \Theta^*) \le \delta\}$$

For any interval Δ, we could then compute the fraction f of time that the training sample would yield a tuning parameter value in the hyperellipsoid annulus of width Δ around the point δ.

$$f(\delta; \Delta) = P(\delta + \Delta/2) - P(\delta - \Delta/2)$$

Associated with the subset

$$S = \{n \mid \delta - \Delta/2 \le (\hat{\Theta}_n - \Theta^*)' \Sigma^{-1} (\hat{\Theta}_n - \Theta^*) \le \delta + \Delta/2\}$$

is the corresponding set of tuning parameter values.

$$T = \{\Theta_n \mid n \in S\}$$

Now consider taking group of Q testing samples for which we test the algorithm when the tuning parameter values are set to a value in T. For each of the $Q\#T$ combinations, there will be an observed incorrect recognition rate. Thus for a given δ and Δ, there will be a distribution of observed incorrect recognition rates and an associated mean μ incorrect recognition rate and variance σ^2 of incorrrect recognition rate. As we change δ we can observe the dependency of μ on δ. From this dependency we can determine the variation in performance due to testing set sampling variation.

If in doing this kind of analysis we find that the variation in the system tuning parameters caused by training set sampling variations induces large changes in recognition accuracy, then it suggests that the algorithm is not robust and probably undertrained. Such a finding would lead us to more carefully inspect the reasons for the failures and we would take pains to redesign the algorithm as well as use larger sample size for training.

References

1. Abramovitz, M. and Stegum, I. (Eds.), *Handbook of Mathematical Functions,* Dover Publications Inc., New York, 1972.
2. Devijver, P. A. and Kittler, J., *Pattern Recognition: A Statistical Approach,* Prentice Hall International, London, 1982.
3. Fununaga, K., *Introduction to Statistical Pattern Recognition,* Academic Press, New York, 1972.
4. Jockel, K. H., "Finite Sample Properties and Asymptotic Efficency of Monte Carlo Tests," *The Annals of Statistics, Vol. 14,* 1986, pp. 336-347.
5. Johnson, N. and Kotz, S., *Discrete Distributions,* Hougton Mifflin Co., Boston, 1969.
6. Johnson, N. and Kotz, S., *Continuous Univariate Distribution-2,* Houghton Mifflin Co., Boston, 1970.
7. Marriott, F. H. C., "Barmarks Monte Carlo Tests: How many simulations?", *Applied Statistics, Vol. 28,* 1979, pp. 75-77.
8. Pearson, E. S. and Hartley, E. O., *Biometrical Tables for Statisticians, Vol. 1,* (2nd Edition) Cambridge University Press, London, 1958.
9. Pearson, K., (Ed.), *Tables of Incomplete Beta Function, 2nd Edition,* Cambridge University Press, London, 1968.

Edit Cost Index as a Measure of Performance of Graphics Recognition Systems

Atul K. Chhabra[1] and Ihsin T. Phillips[2]

[1] Verizon Communications
500 Westchester Avenue, White Plains, NY 10604, USA
atul.k.chhabra@verizon.com
[2] Department of Computer Science/Software Engineering
Seattle University, Seattle, Washington 98122, USA
yun@seattleu.edu

Abstract. In this paper, we propose *EditCost Index* as a goal driven metric to evaluate the performance of graphics recognition systems. We present the motivation for this metric and show how plots of *EditCost Index* can be used to compare systems.

We introduce a new metric for evaluating the performance of graphics recognition systems. This one metric takes into account the other metrics commonly used in pattern recognition such as the true positive rate, false alarm rate, and rate of missed detections, and the less often used metrics such as rates of partial matches.

While evaluating traditional classifiers, say in the context of OCR, for every image of a character, the isolated character recognizer produces one answer with a confidence level. If the confidence level of the answer is above the acceptance threshold, then the answer is either correct (true positive, or t) or wrong (false positive, or f). If the answer is below the acceptance threshold, it is rejected leading to a missed detection (or m). In this scenario, $t + m + f = 1$ (here t, m, and f are rates between 0 and 1). However, in graphics recognition, this does not hold.

Graphics recognition methods can generate many output entities corresponding to the image of one graphical entity. For example two crossing lines may be recognized as two lines, three lines, or four lines. Further, due to image noise, graphics recognition systems often fragment lines even where there are no crossing points or junctions among lines. For a given number of ground truth entities, a recognition system could produce any number of detected entities. Among the detected entities, those that have a match in the ground truth are true positives. The rest are false alarms. Then, looking at the ground truth data set, the entities that do not match with anything in the detected set are missed detections. Therefore, m is a fraction of the number of ground truth entities, whereas f is a fraction of the number of detected entities. For a given image, different systems produce vastly different number of detected entities. Another difference from OCR is that, in graphics recognition, when we raise the acceptance threshold,

Atul K. Chhabra and D. Dori (Eds.): GREC'99, LNCS 1941, pp. 324–328, 2000.

some entities drop out of the true positives. These entities than add to *both* the false alarms and the missed detections.

The development of the new metric, the *EditCost Index*, was motived by two key factors:

1. the desire to develop a goal directed performance metric that measures the cost of manual post processing required to correct the mistakes made by the recognition system, and
2. the difficulty in drawing an analogy between evaluation of OCR and graphics recognition.

From the goal directed view, missed detections and false alarms are equally costly. Therefore, this metric lumps them together into the cost measure. One minus this index gives a measure of the correctly recognized entities.

It is worth noting that the *EditCost Index* metric is useful in a goal directed way not only for graphics recognition systems, but for any recognition system where $t + m + f > 1$. For example, when OCR is applied to recognizing prose, the system could generate not only one-for-one false positives (substitutions) but also introduce additional false positives (insertions). At a word level, such systems could split words, merge words, and introduce additional words. All of these situations are similar to the problems in graphics recognition system. In order to evaluate such systems, one should look at more than the performance of the isolated character recognition system. The goal directed measure of goodness of such a system should account for the post editing effort required to clean up the recognition results.

We define the *EditCost Index* [1] as:

$$EditCostIndex = (false\_alarms + misses +$$
$$g\_one2many + g\_many2one +$$
$$d\_one2many + d\_many2one)/(N + M).$$

Here, N is the number of ground truth entities and M is the number of entities in the recognition results. $g\_one2many$ is the number of ground-truth entities that have one to many matches with detected entities. $g\_many2one$ is the number of ground-truth entities that have many to one matches with detected entities. $d\_one2many$ is the number of detected entities that have one to many matches with ground-truth entities. $d\_many2one$ is the number of detected entities that have many to one matches with ground-truth entities.

We can restate the above as:

$$EditCostIndex = 1 - \frac{2 \cdot one2one}{N + M}.$$

where *one2one* is the number of ground-truth entities that have one to one matches with detected entities.

Although we have not verified it empirically, we feel that the time for manual post processing (for graphics recognition) does not depend significantly on the

ds29.tif: 368 entities

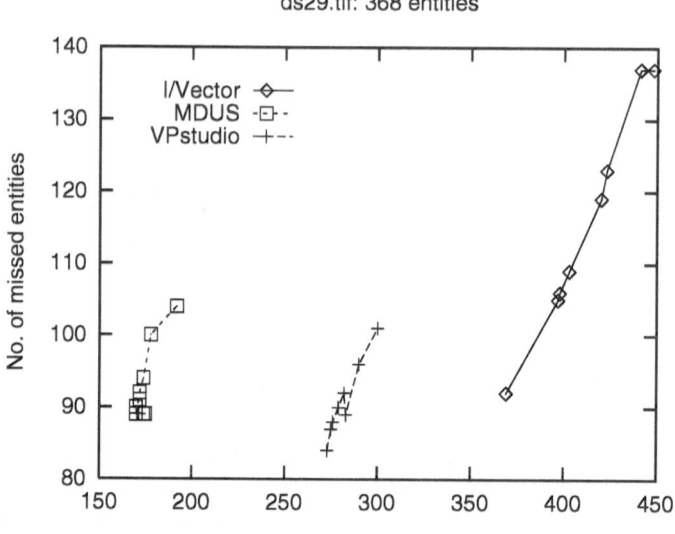

Fig. 1. Performance curves of the graphics recognition systems [2,3,4,5] for the image ds29.tif, image of a mechanical drawing (from [6])

length of a true positive, a missed entity, or a false positive. Time taken for adding or deleting a line in a CAD tool does not depend significantly on the length of the line. Many CAD tools have user interfaces that make it just as easy to place the end points of a long line as those of a short line. They accomplish this by automatically bringing up a pop-up window showing a zoomed in view of the surroundings of the cursor.

In OCR, every answer is accompanied by a confidence level. This is possible because the classifiers used are statistical or learning based. However, graphics recognition systems use deterministic techniques such as line tracking, rules to distinguish straight lines from arcs, grammar or syntax to correctly parse dimensioning notations, etc. As a result, none of the graphics recognition systems we studied provide a confidence level for each detected entity.

In our evaluation methodology of graphics recognition systems, we resort to reverse engineering. That is, not given a confidence in the detected results, we compute the goodness of match between every possible (and permissible) pair of detected and ground truth entities. We then use this goodness (or strength of match) measure to determine which matches are acceptable and which are not. We vary the *acceptance threshold* on this measure to obtain the performance curves.

It is natural to attempt to draw an analogy between Receiver Operating Characteristic (ROC) curves (often used in OCR) and the curves of the *EditCost Index* vs. the acceptance threshold. The ROC curve is obtained by plotting the rate of true positives vs. the rate of false alarms. The area under the curve is taken as a measure of the overall goodness of the classifier. We emphasize that

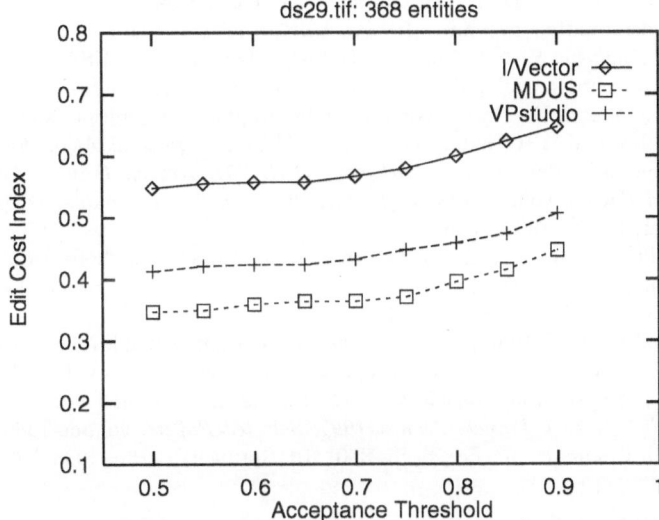

Fig. 2. *EditCost Index* curves of the graphics recognition systems for the image ds29.tif (from [1])

there is no similarity between ROC curves and the *EditCost Index* curves. ROC curves are meaningful only where there is one classifier output for a given input (in other words, when $t + m + f = 1$). This condition is not satisfied by graphics recognition systems.

While analyzing the results of the 1997 International Graphics Recognition Contest [6], we attempted to draw an analogy to the ROC curves by plotting the counts of false alarms vs. missed detections, while varying the acceptance threshold. An example of such a plot is shown in Figure 1. These curves were extremely difficult to comprehend and draw conclusions from. From these curves, plotted together for all recognition systems, once could not easily deduce the relative post processing effort required to correct the graphics recognition mistakes.

In contrast, the *EditCost Index* curves plotted in Figure 2 clearly show which system is better for recognizing the type of drawing under consideration. Better graphics recognition systems have flatter *EditCost Index* curves that are close to the horizontal axis.

References

1. I. Phillips and A. Chhabra. Empirical performance evaluation of graphics recognition systems. *IEEE Transactions on Pattern Analysis and Machine Intelligence*, 21(9):849–870, September 1999. 325, 327
2. I/Vector (Vectory) ver. 3.8 Raster to Vector Conversion Software. Graphikon, Berlin, Germany, and IDEAL Scanners & Systems, Rockville, MD, USA. http://www.graphikon.com and http://www.ideal.com. 326

3. L. Wenyin and D. Dori. Automated CAD conversion with the machine drawing understanding system. In *Proceedings of the IAPR Workshop on Document Analysis Systems*, pages 241–259, Malvern, PA, USA, October 1996. ftp://ftp.technion.ac.il/pub/supported/ie/dori/MDUS/sunmdus.gz. 326

4. L. Wenyin and D. Dori. Genericity in graphics recognition algorithsm. In K. Tombre and A. Chhabra, editors, *Graphics Recognition: Algorithms and Systems, Second International Workshop, GREC'97, Nancy, France, August 1997, Selected Papers*, volume 1389 of *Lecture Notes in Computer Science*, pages 9–20. Springer, Berlin, 1998. 326

5. VPstudio ver. 6 rev. 2 Raster to Vector Conversion Software. Softelec, Munich, Germany, and Austin, TX, USA. http://www.softelec.com and http://www.hybridcad.com. 326

6. A. Chhabra and I. Phillips. The second international graphics recognition contest – Raster to vector conversion: A report. In K. Tombre and A. Chhabra, editors, *Graphics Recognition: Algorithms and Systems, Second International Workshop, GREC'97, Nancy, France, August 1997, Selected Papers*, volume 1389 of *Lecture Notes in Computer Science*, pages 390–410. Springer, Berlin, 1998. 326, 327

Cost Evaluation of Interactively Correcting Recognized Engineering Drawings

Wenyin Liu[1], Liang Zhang[2], Long Tang[2], and Dov Dori[3]

[1] Microsoft Research, Sigma Center,
#49 Zhichun Road, Beijing 100080, PR China
wyliu@microsoft.com
[2] Department of Computer Science and Technology, Tsinghua University,
Beijing 100084, PR China
[3] Faculty of Industrial Engineering and Management,
Technion – Israel Institute of Technology, Haifa 32000, Israel
dori@ie.technion.ac.il

Abstract. We present a new scheme, which is based on the cost of interactively correcting detection errors, for performance evaluation of engineering drawings recognition algorithms. We correct an actual output graphic objects so that they to the expected output in a graphics editing tool using GUI, like Autocad. Through experiments, We define the time spent on the editing operations as the output element's editcost, which we use as a performance evaluation index.

1   Introduction

Performance evaluation of automatic engineering drawings vectorization has been proposed in several ways, including the number of matches (Kong et al. 1996, Hori and Doermann 1996, and Phillips et al. 1998), detection accuracy (Liu and Dori 1997, 1998), and edit cost (Phillips and Chhabra 1999). These proposed protocols provide indices for quantitative comparison among vectorization systems. However, the edit cost index (Phillips and Chhabra 1999) is more useful than others since the imperfect results of vectorization systems require manual corrections, so the parameter we wish to minimize is the edit cost. Edit cost is also based on the number of matches between the ground truths and detected entities.

Each class of graphic entities and each type of detection error may require a different amount of edit cost. For example, a short line, falling completely inside the editing window and a long one covering more than one window may require different amount of effort in the correcting action. Hence, the edit cost index based solely on the number of matches may not reflect the real edit cost required by the actual editing operations involved in correcting the detection error in terms of the time spent on the correction.

Atul K. Chhabra and D. Dori (Eds.): GREC'99, LNCS 1941, pp. 329–334, 2000.
© Springer-Verlag Berlin Heidelberg 2000

In this paper we propose an alternative definition of the edit cost index based on the actual cost of interactively/manually correcting the imperfect detection. The graphics-editing tool we used in the experiments is Autocad R14. We have measured the edit cost for the graphic classes of points, lines, arc, circles, and polylines. The proposed scheme can be extended to other classes of graphics.

The total editcost of the entire drawing of graphic object recognized by an algorithm is the sum of editcost of all recognized graphic objects. In order to give an normalized and uniform index of editcost performance of an algorithm, an index formed by the total editcost divided by the cost of redrawing all the graphic objects (actually redrawing all the ground truths) is used compare performance of the same algorithm on different drawings. In this case, the value of the uniform index is between 0 (which is best since no cost is needed) and 1 (which is the worst and means the cost is the same as totally redrawing the drawings). The smaller the edit cost index, the better the system. We have used the defined editcost indices to evaluate the MDUS system over the test images for the second IAPR graphics recognition contest (Chhabra and Phillips 1997) and the results are presented.

2   Basic Operations of Graphics Editing and Their Editcost

The editing operations (in typical graphics editing tools, e.g., Autocad) of all classes of graphic entities may consist of the following basic operations, the edit costs of which are also defined. We assume that the raster drawing is used as the background so that the locations of expected graphic objects (ground truth) are clear and can be used as guidance. The editing of other attributes (e.g., line style and color) of graphic objects are not considered in this paper.

1). Mouse click for picking an object (e.g., a point, a graphic object, etc., the picked object usually is distinguished from others) or click a window object (e.g., a button, scrollbar, etc.) with a cost of

$$C_{po} = a \qquad (1)$$

where, a is a constant that can be determined from experiments.

2). Locating a point (e.g., for redrawing an endpoint of a new line or for precisely drop a moving point when correcting a line) with a cost of

$$C_{lp} = b \qquad (2)$$

where, b is a constant that can be determined from experiments.

3). Drag and drop for moving a point or graphic object to a new position with a cost of a linear approximation:

$$C_d = k_1 * d_{sd} + c \qquad (3)$$

where d_{sd} is dragging distance from a start point to an end point, k_1 is a constant which is equivalent to the dragging speed, c is a constant. Actually, this operation includes two steps. The first step is dragging the object by a distance and the second step is precisely dropping it to a new location. The cost second step is exactly the same of Eq. (2). Therefore there should be a relationship be b and c: $c > b$.

4). Searching the next point for correction, C_{sp}. This operation is an important step during graphics editing. For instance, if the two endpoints of a line are not inside the same window, after editing the first endpoint, finding the second endpoint requires some time, which is denoted by C_{sp}. The definition of C_{sp} is complex for many situations. However, we can approximate it using the cost of scrolling the window from the current point located at (x_1, y_1) to the expected point located at (x_2, y_2):

$$C_{sp} = a((x_2-x_1)/w + (y_2-y_1)/h) \tag{4}$$

where w is the width (the default value is 640 pixels) and h is the height (the default value is 480) of the editing window.

We have used Autocad R14 as a test bed to evaluate the real editcost of some typical graphics objects. The user is a student familiar with PC and Windows though not an Autocad professional. His experience may be regarded as of typical users.

In the experiment the user tests picking up 10 points, 10 lines, 10 circles, and 10 arcs in the current screen are. The average of picking up an object is 1.19 seconds. Hence, the constant in Eq. (1) is

$a=1.19$

The experiments on locating (or dropping) a point yield a result of:

$b=3.03$

The reason that $b > a$ is that picking up an object do not need precise location while locating or dropping an object to a precise location need more deliberation.

The constants in Eq. (3) are also obtained by several dragging experiments. Their average values are:

$k_1=0.0083;$ $c=3.80$

3   Costs of Correcting and Redrawing Typical Graphic Objects

Having defined the editcost of those basic operations, the correcting cost or redrawing cost of a graphic object is defined as

$$Ec = \sum_{i=1}^{n} C_i \tag{5}$$

where C_i ($i=1..n$) is the editcost of the ith step operation involved in the correction or redrawing of the graphic entity. The typical classes of graphic objects may include the following basic operations.

1)   Point
The editing of a point consists of two steps: picking up the point and dragging and dropping it to the destination. Therefore the cost consist of Eqs. (1) and (2):

$$Ec = C_{po} + C_d \tag{6}$$

2)   Line
Usually we have two ways of correcting a line. One way is move the line such that one of its endpoints coincide with the expected one and then dragging the other endpoint to its correct location, as shown in **Figure 1**. Another way is correcting the two endpoints separately, as shown in **Figure 2**. The first method is cost effective if the line only translated from its expected location and other attributes are the same, in which case, only one step of moving (of the entire line) is enough. For other cases, the moving of both the two endpoints are required. Especially when the line is quite long

and the two endpoints are not shown simultaneously in the same screen area, the second way is recommended, whose cost includes moving of two endpoints (Eq. (5)) and the searching for the next point for correction (Eq. (3)):

$$Ec = \delta_1(C_{po} + C_{d1}) + \delta_2(C_{po} + C_{d2}) + C_{sp} \tag{7}$$

where δ_i ($i=1$ or 2) is 0 if the ith is at its expected location and needless to be corrected, and is 1 otherwise.

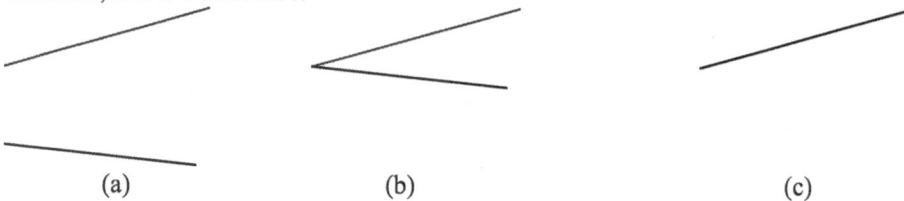

(a)   (b)   (c)

Figure 1. The first way of correcting a line. (a) original state, (b) move the line to coincide one endpoint, and (c) coincide another endpoint

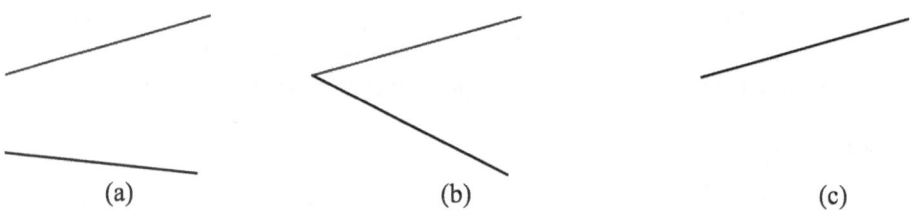

(a)   (b)   (c)

Figure 2. The second way of correcting a line. (a) original state, (b) coincide one endpoint, and (c) coincide another endpoint.

While redrawing a line consists of precisely locating the two endpoints and finding the second endpoint from the first endpoint. Therefore the cost of redrawing a line is

$$Rc = 2C_{lp} + C_{sp} \tag{8}$$

3)   Circle

We correct a circle by correcting the center and the radius of the circle (actually a point on the circle). The correcting cost and is equivalent to that of correcting a line in Eq. (5) and the redrawing cost is equivalent to that of redrawing a line.

4)   Arc

Similarly to a line, we correct an arc by correcting the three points (two endpoints and the center or another point on the arc). The correcting cost is

$$Ec = C_{po} + \delta_1 \cdot C_{d1} + C_{sp-1'2} + \delta_2 \cdot C_{d2} + C_{sp-2'3} + \delta_3 \cdot C_{d3} \tag{9}$$

The redrawing cost of an arc includes 3 times of locating points in Eq. (2) and twice finding the next point in Eq. (4).

5)   Polyline

We correct a polyline by correcting each point respectively. The correcting cost is

$$Ec = C_{po} + \sum_{i=1}^{n} \delta_i \cdot C_{di} + \sum_{j=1}^{n-1} C_{sp-j'j+1} \tag{10}$$

The redrawing of a polyline includes locating the points and finding the next points sequentially.

After defining the editcost and redraw cost of graphic objects, we observed that the calculated editcost may be greater than the redraw cost in some cases, e.g., a short recognized line matched with a long ground truth. Particularly in these cases we use the redraw cost as the final editcost of the object.

The editcost of the entire drawing is defined as

$$Ec_{total} = \sum_{j=1}^{m} Ec_j \tag{11}$$

where $j=1..m$ are the enumeration of the ground truths of the drawings. Note that some ground truth objects may not have a corresponding detection. The correction for this kind of error is simply redrawing the entire object, whose editcost is the redrawing cost.

Although the total edit cost of the drawing, defined in Equation (10), can be used as a performance evaluation index of the vectorization, it is not normalized and hence it cannot be used to compare among different drawings. In order to get a comparable edit cost index among all drawings, the edit cost index is normalized by dividing by the total redrawing cost for all the ground truths. In this case the normalized editcost falls in the range 0 to 1, it provides a comparable index not only among algorithms/systems but also among drawings and can serve as the unique index to indicate the relative performance evaluation of each vectorization system. The smaller the normalized editcost index, the better the system.

4   Cost Evaluation of MDUS

We have used the editcost definition to evaluate the Machine Drawing Understanding System (MDUS) (Liu and Dori 1996). Two test images (ds08.tif and ds33.tif) downloaded from the web page developed by Chhabra and Phillips (1997) for the second IAPR graphics recognition contest. We have only evaluated the editcost of lines and arcs and show the result in **Table 1**. Editcost of text is not evaluated since MDUS's ability on text segmentation is not so strong and OCR is not included.

The editcost is evaluated at different position tolerance level: 1, 3, and 5 pixels. The points within the allowed tolerance are not corrected and the corresponding editcost are saved. From **Table 1** we can see that the relative editcost of the two recognized drawings are very high. The editcost is still about two thirds of the cost of totally redrawing even though the tolerance is 5 pixels. Probably this is the reason why the users are unsatisfied with the current raster to vector conversion products.

Table 1. Editcost of lines and arcs recognized by MDUS on two test images

Image	Redraw Cost (seconds)	Edit Cost (seconds) at Different Tolerance (pixels)			Normalized Editcost Index at Difference Tolerance (pixels)		
		1	3	5	1	3	5
Ds33	2311	1945	1691	1562	0.84	0.73	0.67
Ds08	2096	1572	1315	1296	0.75	0.63	0.62

5   Summary

We have defined the editcost for some classes of graphics within the Autocad GUI environment and get the value of them only through limited experiments. However, the editcost within other editing tools, or by different people using different editor options and at different skill levels may have different evaluation of editcost. The purpose of this paper is provide a scheme of evaluating the editcost of graphic recognition results. More experiments should be done to obtain more objective evaluation of the editcost of graphic objects.

A conclusion may be drawn from the experiments that the relative editcost of recognized drawings is very high and this may be the reason why the current users are reluctant to use the raster to vector conversion products. We researchers may have to make some changes to the state of the art.

References

1. Chhabra A and Phillips I (1997) Web pages for the Second International Graphics Recognition Contest—Raster to Vector Conversion. http://graphics.basit.com/iapr-tc10/contest.html
2. Chhabra A and Phillips I (1998) The Second International Graphics Recognition Contest—Raster to Vecter Conversion: A Report. In: Tombre K, Chhabra A (eds). Graphics Recognition—Algorithms and Systems (Lecture Notes in Computer Science, Vol. 1389). Springer, 1998, pp390-410.
3. Hori O and Doermann DS (1996) Quantitative Measurement of the Performance of Raster-to-Vector Conversion Algorithms. In: Kasturi R, Tombre K (eds) Graphics Recognition -- Methods and Applications (Lecture Notes in Computer Science, vol. 1072). Springer, Berlin, pp 57-68
4. Kong B, Phillips IT, Haralick RM, Prasad A, Kasturi R (1996) A Benchmark: Performance Evaluation of Dashed-Line Detection Algorithms. In: Kasturi R, Tombre K (eds) Graphics Recognition -- Methods and Applications (Lecture Notes in Computer Science, vol. 1072). Springer, Berlin, pp 270-285
5. Liu W and Dori D (1996) Automated CAD Conversion with the Machine Drawing Understanding System. In: Proc. of 2nd IAPR Workshop on Document Analysis Systems, Malvern, PA, USA, October, 1996, pp 241-259
6. Liu W and Dori D (1997) A Protocol for Performance Evaluation of Line Detection Algorithms. Machine Vision Applications 9(5):240-250
7. Liu W and Dori D (1998) Performance Evaluation of Graphics/Text Separation. In: Tombre K, Chhabra A (eds). Graphics Recognition -- Algorithms and Systems (Lecture Notes in Computer Science, Vol. 1389). Springer, 1998, pp 359-371.
8. Phillips IT, Liang J, Chhabra A, and Haralick RM (1998) A Performance Evaluation Protocol for Graphics Recognition Systems. In: Tombre K, Chhabra A (eds). Graphics Recognition -- Algorithms and Systems (Lecture Notes in Computer Science, Vol. 1389). Springer, 1998, pp 372-389
9. Phillips I and Chhabra A (1999) Empirical Performance Evaluation of Graphics Recognition Systems. IEEE Trans. on PAMI, 21, 9, pp 849-870

Impact of Sparse Pixel Vectorization Algorithm Parameters on Line Segmentation Performance

Wenyin Liu[1,2], Xiaoyu Wang [2], Long Tang [2], and Dov Dori[3]

[1] Microsoft Research, Sigma Center,
#49 Zhichun Road, Beijing 100080, PR China
wyliu@microsoft.com
[2] Department of Computer Science and Technology, Tsinghua University,
Beijing 100084, PR China
[3] Faculty of Industrial Engineering and Management,
Technion – Israel Institute of Technology, Haifa 32000, Israel
dori@ie.technion.ac.il

Abstract. We present the impact of parameters in the Sparse Pixel Vectorization algorithm on the performance of the algorithm, which is evaluated using a pixel level performance evaluation protocol. Both theoretical and experimental analyses are presented, which show that the experimental results are well in accordance with the theoretical analyses. Both prove the robustness of the algorithm. Meanwhile the parameter values for the best performance of the algorithm are also found.

1   Introduction

Vectorization, also known as raster to vector conversion, is a process that extracts vectors—line segments—from raster images of line drawings. Vectorization is widely used in the area of Document Analysis and Recognition (DAR) as a preprocessing step for high-level object recognition, such as optical character recognition (OCR) and graphic objects recognition. Basic vectorization concerns grouping the pixels in the raster (binary) image into raw wires that are described by several attributes, such as characteristic points and line width. Advanced vectorization includes line fitting and extending, which yields fine wires. We refer to crude vectorization as the basic vectorization process that takes a raster image as input and yields coarse wire fragments, which may be bars (non-zero width line segments) or polylines (chains of bars linked end to end). Crude vectorization is a crucial preprocessing step in the interpretation process of line drawings in general and engineering drawings in particular, as the latter type of drawings requires maximal precision to avoid false alarms and misses in subsequent processing stages.

A typical vectorization algorithm requires the setting of a (sometimes significant) number of thresholds and other parameters. Examples include mesh size in the mesh pattern based algorithms (Lin et al. 1985) and scan line interval in the OZZ algorithm

Atul K. Chhabra and D. Dori (Eds.): GREC'99, LNCS 1941, pp. 335-344, 2000.

(Dori et al. 1993). As is the case with many other algorithms, setting the values of these parameters can have a profound effect on the algorithm performance.

Different drawings may have different parameter settings at which they exhibit peak performance. Based on theoretical analysis and supported by experiments, a subset of the parameters may be set to values that are near optimal for most drawings. To ensure algorithm robustness, the parameter settings should not affect the performance in a range near the default values to a significant extent.

For best performance, a trial-and-error process, which is part of the algorithm development, determines these parameters to some default values. In most cases, the performance is judged by the developers using human vision perception. Quantitative evaluation is seldom reported. Consequently, the values set for the parameter do not guarantee peak performance in terms of objective criteria.

The Sparse Pixel Vectorization (SPV) algorithm (Dori and Liu 1999) is a basic (crude) vectorization method that is fast due to accessing the pixels sparsely while preserves the original shape information to a large extent. Like most other algorithms, SPV features a number of parameters whose value settings may affect its performance. In this paper we examine the effect of these parameter values on SPV's performance, using the performance evaluation protocol we developed (Liu and Dori 1997).

We carry out a theoretical analysis for the parameter values for the best performance. We then determine a combination of these parameter values for which SPV operates at its best performance. The experimental results we present are in good accord with the theoretical analysis, and both prove the robustness of the SPV algorithm.

2   The Sparse Pixel Vectorization Algorithm

To familiarize the reader with SPV in the context of this research, we present the algorithm briefly with emphasis on its parameters and their settings. The SPV algorithm scans the entire image every several pixels. The *scan line interval* is the first parameter in the algorithm. When a scan line encounters a foreground pixel (e.g., on the boundary of a line area), a process starts aiming at finding the first reliable medial point (e.g., P_0 in **Figure 1**), which is the midpoint of both the horizontal and the vertical runs of the foreground area passing through it.

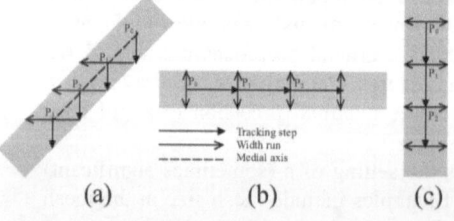

Figure 1. Illustration of the SPV general tracking process. (a) Slant segment. (b) Horizontal segment. (c) Vertical segment

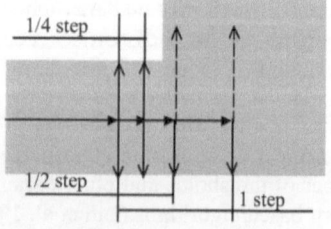

Figure 2. Illustration of the Junction Recovery Process

The longer of the two (horizontal and vertical) runs at that point is determined as the *tracking direction* or the *length direction* (the line's inclination, either horizontal or vertical) of the line area. The width direction is defined to be orthogonal to the length direction. Once the length (tracking) direction is determined, the *General Sparse Pixel Tracking* process starts from the reliable medial point along the length direction. The process takes a *tracking step* in the tracking direction. A tracking step is the distance from the current medial axis point to a *stop pixel* – a foreground pixel within the current line area. The tracking step should be less than a predefined *maximal tracking step*. This implies that the stop pixel, where the current tracking step stops, can be one of the following: (1) a pixel on the edge of the line area (the previous pixel of the encountered background pixel), as shown in **Figure 1**(a), (2) inside the line area, when the distance exceeds the maximal tracking step, as shown in **Figure 1**(b) and (c).

This *maximal tracking step* is the second SPV parameter that requiring setting. At each tracking step, we calculate the width run (which is the cross section of the line area parallel to the width direction at the stop pixel). We then take the width run midpoint at a new medial axis point for the next iteration of tracking if the following set of "next iteration conditions" is met. (1) Width continuity: The largest difference among line widths, represented by the width runs at the medial axis points found during tracking, along a neighborhood of some small number of adjacent medial axis points, is below a predefined threshold. We define this number as the *maximal width difference*, which is the third parameter in the SPV algorithm. (2) Sole occupancy:The medial point should not be occupied by another, already detected vector. (3) Direction preservation: The length direction at the stop pixel should be the same as the length direction at the last medial axis point during one tracking procedure. (4) Tracking length: The tracking step is non-zero.

If one or more of the conditions (1)-(3) of the next iteration conditions set is not met, an iterative Junction Recovery process, illustrated in **Figure 2**. Backtracking to the last medial axis point and going ahead with half of the normal tracking step, we may find that the violated conditions are met at the new stop pixel. If so, the tracking procedure continues from the new medial axis point with the normal tracking step. If the conditions are still not met, we backtrack again to the last medial axis point and cut the tracking step by half again. We iterate this "backtrack and cut by half" process until either we find a stop pixel that meets the conditions or the tracking step is reduced to zero. If the tracking step becomes zero, the tracking procedure for the current part of the line area stops and another tracking starts with a new foreground pixel found by the scan line.

The result of the line tracking procedure is a chain of point, called *polyline*, that lies on the approximate medial axis of the black area. Although the polyline can be considered as a vector representation of the corresponding black area, some of its detected intermediate medial axis points are redundant because they are (approximately) on the straight line segments formed by their neighbor points. To obtain the minimal description vector representation of this black area, these points should be removed from the polyline's point chain. This point removal process, called *Polygonalization*, should result in a polyline with the smallest number of edges (or vertices) that approximate the original line's black area shape.

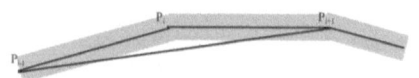

(a)   (b)

Figure 3. Illustration of the polygonalization approximation

Figure 4. Illustration of the effect of the scan line interval parameter: (a) Larger one: line not detected. (b) Smaller one: line detected

The SPV Polygonalization process, shown in **Figure 3**, ultilizes the polygonalization algorithm developed by Sklansky and Gonzalez (1980). It tests the criticality of the points in the chain and removes non-critical points from the chain. The criticality of a point in a point chain is determined by its distance to the line joining the two neighboring critical points on both sides of the tested point. for three consecutive points. If the distance of the middle point to the segment formed by its two immediate neighbor is not greater than a predefined threshold ε, the middle point is non-critical and should be removed from the chain. This procedure is repeated until no more points can be removed from the chain. The predefined threshold ε is the fourth parameter in SPV and is referred to as the *maximal polygonalization error*.

3   Theoretical SPV Parameters Analysis

We have defined four parameters that may affect the vectorization performance: the *scan line interval*, the *maximal tracking step*, the *maximal width difference*, and the *maximal polygonalization error*. In order to see the impacts of the SPV parameter values on its performance, we define a set of quantitative objective performance indices.

3.1   The Performance Evaluation Protocol

We use the performance evaluation protocol for general line detection algorithms (Liu and Dori 1997). Since SPV is a vectorization algorithm, we require that it preserves the original image shape as much as possible. The pixel level performance indices (Liu and Dori 1997), explained below, are therefore used. The total Pixel Detection Rate for the entire image, D_p, is defined as the ratio of those foreground pixels covered by the detected vectors from the image to the total foreground pixels in the image. D_p represents the detection ability of the algorithm. The bigger D_p, the better the vectorization algorithm. The total Pixel False Alarm Rate for the entire image, F_p, is defined as the ratio of those background pixels covered by the detected vectors from the image to the total area covered by these detected vectors. It represents the error of the vectorization. The smaller F_p, the better the vectorization algorithm. A good vectorization algorithm requires a large D_p and a small F_p. Therefore the Pixel Recovery Index (PRI) is defined as PRI = $(D_p + 1 - F_p)/2$. PRI is a single index that represents the performance of the algorithm. The bigger the PRI, the better the vectorization algorithm.

3.2   The Scan Line Interval

The scan line interval is the distance in pixels between two adjacent scan lines. As **Figure 4** shows, the raster image is scanned line by line. Only when the scan line encounters a black pixel can a sparse pixel tracking procedure start. If no scan line encounters a pixel of a line black area, the whole line may not be detected. Therefore, as the scan line interval increases, more lines can be missed.

As the scan line width increases, D_p is expected to decrease. However, F_p is not directly affected, since no more false lines are detected. Overall, PRI decreases accordingly. This phenomenon, shown in **Figure 4**, often occurs when the method is applied on images with many thin, nearly horizontal lines. Theoretically, if the value of the scan line width is set to 1 pixel, all lines will be encountered by the scan lines and the PRI is therefore the biggest for all images. Nevertheless, there spare-pixel effect will be much smaller and the speed of the algorithm will be the slowest.

3.3   The Maximal Tracking Step and the Maximal Width Difference

As we can see from **Figure 5**, the maximal tracking step and the maximal width difference can jointly affect the performance of detecting some special areas.

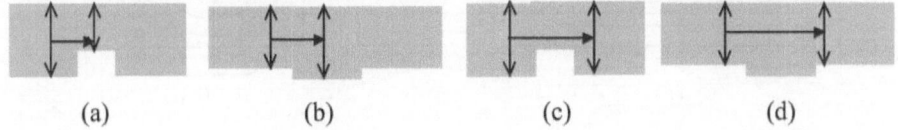

| (a) | (b) | (c) | (d) |

Figure 5. Illustration of the impacts of the maximal width difference and the maximal tracking step

There is a cavity in the line area in **Figure 5**(a) and a protrusion in **Figure 5**(b). Both may violate the condition of width continuity constrained by the parameter of the maximal width difference during the sparse pixel tracking process. When the condition is violated, the general tracking process pauses and a junction recovery process begins. As shown in Figure 5(a) and (b), if the maximal tracking step is smaller than the length of the cavity/protrusion area and the maximal width difference is smaller than the depth of the cavity/protrusion area, the whole area is detected as three distinct line segments. The middle of these is the cavity/protrusion area. On the other hand, if the maximal tracking step is bigger than the length of the cavity/protrusion area or the maximal width difference is bigger than the depth of the cavity/protrusion area, the area is detected as a single line. This is shown in **Figure 5**(c) and **Figure 5**(d).

D_p in **Figure 5**(c) is the same as that in **Figure 5**(a) while F_p in **Figure 5**(c) is higher than it is in **Figure 5**(a). D_p in **Figure 5**(d) is lower than that in **Figure 5**(b) and F_p in **Figure 5**(d) is the same as that in **Figure 5**(b). Therefore, in general, PRI will be lower if the junction is passed through. However, since these cavity and protrusion areas are much smaller than the whole line areas, their impact on the performance is small. Therefore the effect of the maximal width difference and the maximal tracking step on SPV performance is negligible. Therefore, this parameter can be set to some value. We set 20 pixels for the maximal tracking step and 2 pixels for the maximal width difference.

3.4   The Maximal Polygonalization Error

The polygonal approximation result is affected by the parameter of the maximal polygonalization error. As the value increases, more points are removed from the polyline. As we can see from **Figure 3**, assuming that the polyline is exactly the same as it is in raster, after more points are removed, D_p is lower than it is originally, while F_p is higher. Therefore, the PRI decreses as the maximal polygonalization error increases. The impact of this parameter is remarkable especially when there are many circular arcs in the image. To preserve the original shape to the most extent, this parameter should be set to a value between 0.5 and 1.0 pixel.

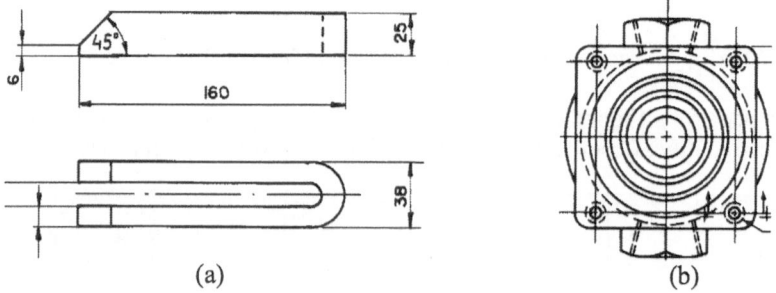

Figure 6. Real life drawing images used in the experiments. (a) horseshoe.tif. (b) ansidash.tif

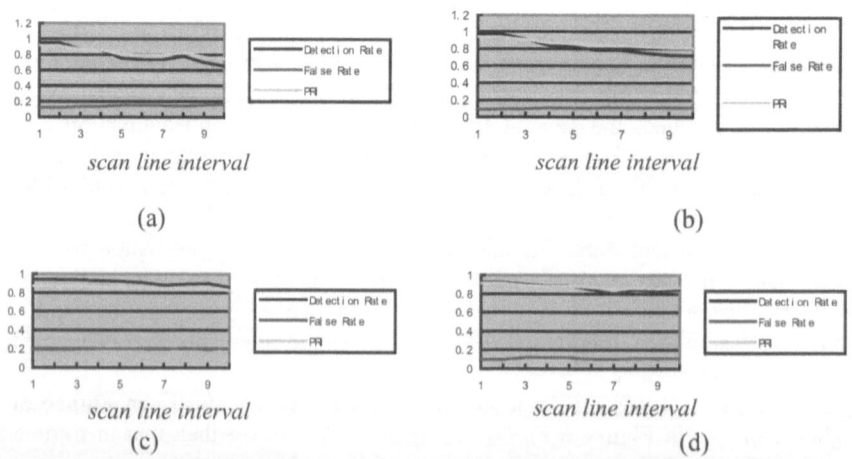

Figure 7. The changes of the pixel performance indices of SPV on four test images as the scan line interval changes from 1 to 10 pixels. (a) ds34.tif (b) ds33.tif (c) ansidash.tif (d) horseshoe.tif

4   Experiments and Discussion

We have evaluated the performance of SPV with different parameter settings using many different kinds of drawings. The experiments on four images are presented below, including two test images (ds34.tif and ds33.tif, which are referred to as contest test images thereafter) downloaded from the web page developed by Chhabra and Phillips (1997). The other two images displayed in **Figure 6** are real life drawing images.

4.1   The Experiments on the Scan Line Interval

We change the value of the scan line interval from 1 to 10 pixels and follow the changes in SPV performance, which are shown in **Figure 7**. The settings of other parameters are as follows. The maximal tracking step is 20, the maximal width difference is 2, and the maximal polygonalization error is 0.7. The performance index values on the four test images are presented in Tables 1-4 and the graphical illustration of the changes of these index values are shown in **Figure 7** (a-d). As we can see from **Figure 7**, the results are in accord with our theoretical analysis of the impact of the scan line interval to the SPV performance presented in Section 3.2. The detection rate and the PRI drop significantly as the value of the scan line interval parameter increases. The false alarm rate fluctuates slightly (the changes of the pixel false rate are less than 0.04 for the two contest images and less than 0.01 for the two real life drawing images). Therefore the scan line interval for best performance is 1. We can see from Table1~4 that the run time decreases dramatically when the scan line interval increases. This empiracally proves the analysis on the impact of the scan line interval to the vectorization speed in Section 3.2.

4.2   Maximal Tracking Step and Maximal Width Difference

We changed the value of the maximal tracking step from 8 to 25 pixels and show the changes of the SPV performance on the two real life drawing images in **Figure 8** and **Figure 9**. The values set for the other parameters are as follows. The scan line interval is set to 1 pixel, the maximal width difference is 2 pixels, and the maximal polygonalization error is 0.7. As we can see from **Figure 8** and **Figure 9**, the performance index values do not change almost at all (the change in **Figure 8** is less than 0.01), in accord with the theoretical analysis in Section 3.3. Experiments on other images also show that the changes of the performance index values are almost non-existent as the maximal tracking step varies, especially when the maximal tracking step is bigger than 20. Therefore the default value of the maximal tracking step in SPV is set to 20 pixels. Next, we change the value of the maximal width difference from 1.0 to 3.5 pixels and present the changes of the SPV performance on the two real life drawing images in **Figure 10** and **Figure 11**. The settings of other parameters are as follows. The scan line interval is set to 1 pixel, the maximal tracking step is 20 pixels, and the maximal polygonalization error is 0.7. As we can see from **Figure 10** and **Figure 11**, the performance index values remain almost constant as the maximal width difference varies. This is also in accord with the theoretical analysis in Section 3.3. Experiments on other images also show the same conclusion: the impact of changing the maximal width difference on the SPV performance is almost unnoticeable. The default value of the maximal tracking step in SPV is set to 2.0 pixels.

4.3   Maximal Polygonalization Error

We change the value of the maximal polygonalization error from 0.1 to 3.5 pixels and present the changes of the SPV performance on the two real life drawing images in **Figure 12** and **Figure 13**. The settings of other parameters are as follows. The scan line interval is set to 1 pixel, the maximal width difference is 2 pixels, and the maximal width difference is 2.0.

Table 1. Performance indices of SPV on the image of ds34.tif

Scan Line Interval	1	2	3	4	5	6	7	8	9	10
Detection Rate	0.954	0.950	0.863	0.862	0.753	0.737	0.737	0.779	0.699	0.654
False Rate	0.122	0.124	0.136	0.139	0.153	0.153	0.151	0.142	0.155	0.162
PRI	0.916	0.913	0.864	0.861	0.800	0.792	0.793	0.818	0.772	0.746
Run Time (secs)	87.77	31.37	20	15.66	10.1	11.1	8.62	9.66		

Table 2. Performance indices of SPV on the image of ds33.tif

Scan Line Interval	1	2	3	4	5	6	7	8	9	10
Detection Rate	0.972	0.971	0.913	0.836	0.820	0.784	0.784	0.749	0.729	0.721
False Rate	0.091	0.092	0.097	0.107	0.105	0.107	0.112	0.107	0.109	0.110
PRI	0.941	0.939	0.908	0.865	0.857	0.838	0.836	0.821	0.810	0.805
Run Time (secs)	21.03	13.62	9.45	12.74	9.73	8.13	7.58	8.46		

Table 3. Performance indices of SPV on the image of ansidash.tif

Scan Line Interval	1	2	3	4	5	6	7	8	9	10
Detection Rate	0.945	0.942	0.939	0.932	0.926	0.911	0.884	0.894	0.902	0.862
False Rate	0.196	0.194	0.199	0.203	0.203	0.201	0.198	0.207	0.195	0.207
PRI	0.874	0.874	0.870	0.865	0.861	0.855	0.843	0.844	0.854	0.827
Run Time (secs)	1.78	0.99	0.72	0.6	0.49	0.44	0.38	0.33		

Table 4. Performance indices of SPV on the image of horseshoe.tif

Scan Line Interval	1	2	3	4	5	6	7	8	9	10
Detection Rate	0.926	0.925	0.903	0.888	0.891	0.848	0.806	0.842	0.826	0.846
False Rate	0.101	0.098	0.118	0.121	0.119	0.107	0.101	0.113	0.109	0.109
PRI	0.913	0.914	0.893	0.883	0.886	0.871	0.852	0.865	0.858	0.868
Run Time (secs)	1.15	0.61	0.49	0.39	0.33	0.28	0.22	0.27		

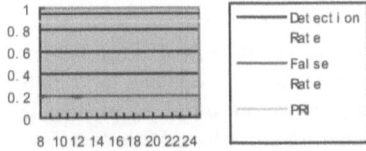

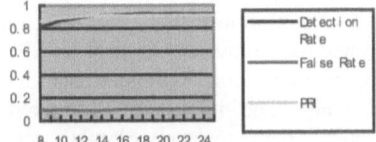

Figure 8. Variations in the pixel performance indices of SPV on ansidash.tif as the maximal tracking step varies from 8 to 25 pixels

Figure 9. Variations in the pixel performance indices of SPV on horseshoe.tif as the maximal tracking step varies from 8 to 25 pixels.

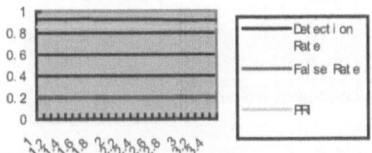

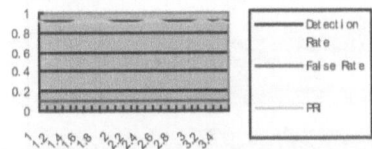

Figure 10. The changes of the pixel performance indices of SPV on ansidash.tif as the maximal width difference varies from 1.0 to 3.5 pixels

Figure 11. The changes of the pixel performance indices of SPV on horseshoe.tif as the maximal width difference varies from 1.0 to 3.5 pixels

As we can see, the performance index values decrease monotonically as the maximal polygonalization error increases. However, the speed of decreasing in **Figure 12** is bigger than that in **Figure 13**. This is because there are more circular arcs in **Figure 12** than in **Figure 13**, which can be seen from **Figure 6**. This result is also the same as the theoretical analysis in Section 3.4. From **Figure 12** and **Figure 13** we can also see that the changes of the performance index values remain almost unchanged when the maximal polygonalization error is less than 0.7. This is because these values of the parameter are precise enough and cannot affect the SPV performance. Therefore the default value of the maximal polygonalization error in SPV is set to 0.7 to obtain maximum speed of SPV while maintaining its accuracy.

5   Summary

We have presented a theoretical analysis and experimental results of the impact of the SPV algorithm parameters on its performance. Four parameters may affect SPV performance: scan line interval, maximal tracking step, maximal width difference, and maximal polygonalization error. Our experiments confirm the theoretical analysis, and both support the following findings. As the scan line interval increases, the detection rate and PRI drops while the false alarm rate is not affected since some horizontal thin lines may be missed and no more false line can be detected. Therefore the scan line interval for the best performance is 1 pixel. It should be born in mind that this has a price in terms of processing speed, so if time is a major factor, one may wish to compromise this. The maximal tracking step and the maximal width difference have only little impact on SPV performance. The default settings of these two parameters, found by experience of trial and error, are 20 pixels and 2.0 pixels, respectively. The impact of the maximal polygonalization error is noticeable, especially if there are many circular arcs in the image. As the value of this parameter increases, the SPV performance becomes deteriorates. The default, optimal value for the maximal polygonalization error was found to be 0.7. This value obtains both best vectorization accuracy and processing speed. Our findings support the claim that SPV is a robust algorithm, since these parameter settings are suitable for almost all drawing images. SPV can therefore be used for vectorization of any class of line drawings, including drawings that contain a large amount of text.

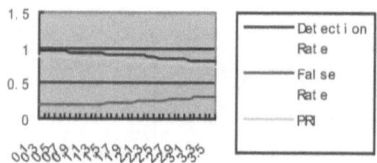

Figure 12. The changes of the pixel performance indices of SPV on ansidash.tif as the maximal polygonalization error varies 0.1-3.5 pixels

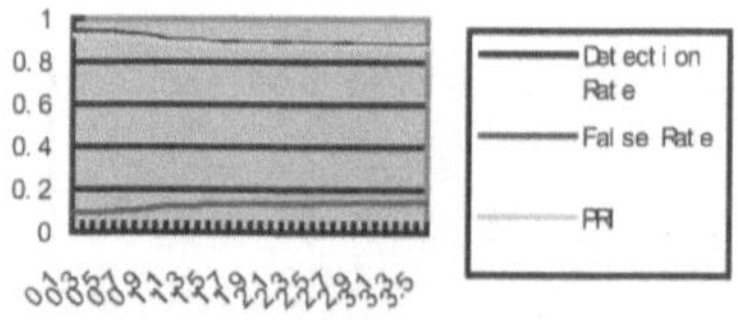

Figure 13. The changes of the pixel performance indices of SPV on horseshoe.tif as the maximal polygonalization error varies 0.1-3.5 pixels

References

1. Chhabra A and Phillips I (1997) Web pages for the Second International Graphics Recognition Contest. http://graphics.basit.com/iapr-tc10/contest.html
2. Dori D, Liang Y, Dowell J, Chai I (1993) Spare Pixel Recognition of Primitives in Engineering Drawings. Machine Vision and Applications, 6:79-82
3. Dori D and Liu W (1999) Sparse Pixel Vectorization: An Algorithm and Its Performance Evaluation. IEEE PAMI. 21(3):202-215.
4. Lin X et al. (1985) Efficient Diagram Understanding with Characteristic Pattern Detection. Computer Vision, Graphics and Image Processing 30:84-106
5. Liu W and Dori D (1997) A Protocol for Performance Evaluation of Line Detection Algorithms. Machine Vision Applications. 9:240-250.

Author Index

Lecture Notes in Computer Science

For information about Vols. 1–1875
please contact your bookseller or Springer-Verlag

Vol. 1911: D.G. Feitelson, L. Rudolph (Eds.), Job Scheduling Strategies for Parallel Processing. VII, 209 pages. 2000.

Vol. 1912: Y. Gurevich, P.W. Kutter, M. Odersky, L. Thiele (Eds.), Abstract State Machines. Proceedings, 2000. X, 381 pages. 2000.

Vol. 1913: K. Jansen, S. Khuller (Eds.), Approximation Algorithms for Combinatorial Optimization. Proceedings, 2000. IX, 275 pages. 2000.

Vol. 1914: M. Herlihy (Ed.), Distributed Computing. Proceedings, 2000. VIII, 389 pages. 2000.

Vol. 1915: S. Dwarkadas (Ed.), Languages, Compilers, and Run-Time Systems for Scalable Computers. Proceedings, 2000. VIII, 301 pages. 2000.

Vol. 1916: F. Dignum, M. Greaves (Eds.), Issues in Agent Communication. X, 351 pages. 2000. (Subseries LNAI).

Vol. 1917: M. Schoenauer, K. Deb, G. Rudolph, X. Yao, E. Lutton, J.J. Merelo, H.-P. Schwefel (Eds.), Parallel Problem Solving from Nature – PPSN VI. Proceedings, 2000. XXI, 914 pages. 2000.

Vol. 1918: D. Soudris, P. Pirsch, E. Barke (Eds.), Integrated Circuit Design. Proceedings, 2000. XII, 338 pages. 2000.

Vol. 1919: M. Ojeda-Aciego, I.P. de Guzman, G. Brewka, L. Moniz Pereira (Eds.), Logics in Artificial Intelligence. Proceedings, 2000. XI, 407 pages. 2000. (Subseries LNAI).

Vol. 1920: A.H.F. Laender, S.W. Liddle, V.C. Storey (Eds.), Conceptual Modeling – ER 2000. Proceedings, 2000. XV, 588 pages. 2000.

Vol. 1921: S.W. Liddle, H.C. Mayr, B. Thalheim (Eds.), Conceptual Modeling for E-Business and the Web. Proceedings, 2000. X, 179 pages. 2000.

Vol. 1922: J. Crowcroft, J. Roberts, M.I. Smirnov (Eds.), Quality of Future Internet Services. Proceedings, 2000. XI, 368 pages. 2000.

Vol. 1923: J. Borbinha, T. Baker (Eds.), Research and Advanced Technology for Digital Libraries. Proceedings, 2000. XVII, 513 pages. 2000.

Vol. 1924: W. Taha (Ed.), Semantics, Applications, and Implementation of Program Generation. Proceedings, 2000. VIII, 231 pages. 2000.

Vol. 1925: J. Cussens, S. Džeroski (Eds.), Learning Language in Logic. X, 301 pages 2000. (Subseries LNAI).

Vol. 1926: M. Joseph (Ed.), Formal Techniques in Real-Time and Fault-Tolerant Systems. Proceedings, 2000. X, 305 pages. 2000.

Vol. 1927: P. Thomas, H.W. Gellersen, (Eds.), Handheld and Ubiquitous Computing. Proceedings, 2000. X, 249 pages. 2000.

Vol. 1928: U. Brandes, D. Wagner (Eds.), Graph-Theoretic Concepts in Computer Science. Proceedings, 2000. X, 315 pages. 2000.

Vol. 1929: R. Laurini (Ed.), Advances in Visual Information Systems. Proceedings, 2000. XII, 542 pages. 2000.

Vol. 1931: E. Horlait (Ed.), Mobile Agents for Telecommunication Applications. Proceedings, 2000. IX, 271 pages. 2000.

Vol. 1658: J. Baumann, Mobile Agents: Control Algorithms. XIX, 161 pages. 2000.

Vol. 1766: M. Jazayeri, R.G.K. Loos, D.R. Musser (Eds.), Generic Programming. Proceedings, 1998. X, 269 pages. 2000.

Vol. 1791: D. Fensel, Problem-Solving Methods. XII, 153 pages. 2000. (Subseries LNAI).

Vol. 1799: K. Czarnecki, U.W. Eisenecker, Generative and Component-Based Software Engineering. Proceedings, 1999. VIII, 225 pages. 2000.

Vol. 1812: J. Wyatt, J. Demiris (Eds.), Advances in Robot Learning. Proceedings, 1999. VII, 165 pages. 2000. (Subseries LNAI).

Vol. 1932: Z.W. Raś, S. Ohsuga (Eds.), Foundations of Intelligent Systems. Proceedings, 2000. XII, 646 pages. (Subseries LNAI).

Vol. 1933: R.W. Brause, E. Hanisch (Eds.), Medical Data Analysis. Proceedings, 2000. XI, 316 pages. 2000.

Vol. 1934: J.S. White (Ed.), Envisioning Machine Translation in the Information Future. Proceedings, 2000. XV, 254 pages. 2000. (Subseries LNAI).

Vol. 1935: S.L. Delp, A.M. DiGioia, B. Jaramaz (Eds.), Medical Image Computing and Computer-Assisted Intervention – MICCAI 2000. Proceedings, 2000. XXV, 1250 pages. 2000.

Vol. 1937: R. Dieng, O. Corby (Eds.), Knowledge Engineering and Knowledge Management. Proceedings, 2000. XIII, 457 pages. 2000. (Subseries LNAI).

Vol. 1938: S. Rao, K.I. Sletta (Eds.), Next Generation Networks. Proceedings, 2000. XI, 392 pages. 2000.

Vol. 1939: A. Evans, S. Kent, B. Selic (Eds.), «UML» – The Unified Modeling Language. Proceedings, 2000. XIV, 572 pages. 2000.

Vol. 1940: M. Valero, K. Joe, M. Kitsuregawa, H. Tanaka (Eds.), High Performance Computing. Proceedings, 2000. XV, 595 pages. 2000.

Vol. 1941: A.K. Chhabra, D. Dori (Eds.), Graphics Recognition. Proceedings, 1999. XI, 346 pages. 2000.

Vol. 1942: H. Yasuda (Ed.), Active Networks. Proceedings, 2000. XI, 424 pages. 2000.

Vol. 1943: F. Koornneef, M. van der Meulen (Eds.), Computer Safety, Reliability and Security. Proceedings, 2000. X, 432 pages. 2000.

Vol. 1945: W. Grieskamp, T. Santen, B. Stoddart (Eds.), Integrated Formal Methods. Proceedings, 2000. X, 441 pages. 2000.

Vol. 1948: T. Tan, Y. Shi, W. Gao (Eds.), Advances in Multimodal Interfaces – ICMI 2000. Proceedings, 2000. XVI, 678 pages. 2000.

Vol. 1952: M.C. Monard, J. Simão Sichman (Eds.), Advances in Artificial Intelligence. Proceedings, 2000. XV, 498 pages. 2000. (Subseries LNAI).

Vol. 1954: W.A. Hunt, Jr., S.D. Johnson (Eds.), Formal Methods in Computer-Aided Design. Proceedings, 2000. XI, 539 pages. 2000.

Vol. 1968: H. Arimura, S. Jain, A. Sharma (Eds.), Algorithmic Learning Theory. Proceedings, 2000. XI, 335 pages. 2000. (Subseries LNAI).

Vol. 1969: D.T. Lee, S.-H. Teng (Eds.), Algorithms and Computation. Proceedings, 2000. XIV, 578 pages. 2000.